FREDERICK THE GREAT

The Ruler, the Writer, the Man

Frederick the Great

The Ruler, the Writer, the Man

BY

G. P. GOOCH, C.H., D.Litt., F.B.A.

DORSET PRESS
New York

This edition of Frederick the Great,
First Edition is published by Dorset Press,
a division of Marboro Books Corporation,
by arrangement with
Longman Group UK Limited, London.
1990 Dorset Press

ISBN 0-88029-481-7

Printed in the United States of America
M 9 8 7 6 5 4 3 2 1

PREFACE

Frederick the Great ranks with Cromwell and Peter the Great, Washington and Napoleon, Cavour and Bismarck, Lenin, Masaryk, and Mustapha Kemal, Mussolini and Hitler among the men of action who have been denounced as arch-destroyers by some and applauded as master-builders by others. Since all of them were house-breakers as well as architects, it depends on our nationality and ideology which aspect we stress. What is not in dispute is the significance of their work, the depth of the furrows as they plowed their way towards their goal, their influence not only in the land of their birth but in neighboring countries and sometimes in more than one continent. No agreed verdict can be pronounced on any one of them, for their judges wear spectacles of various tints.

None of these makers of history has been the object of more conflicting valuations than the man who by almost superhuman efforts hoisted Prussia into the rank of the great powers and unwittingly paved the way for a united Germany under the ægis of Berlin. No foreign historian except Carlyle has found much to admire in the character of the ruler who inaugurated his reign by the rape of Silesia and thereby doomed Europe to a generation of bloody strife. Joseph de Maistre hailed him as a great Prussian but denied him the title of a great man. The part played by Germany in the staging and waging of two World Wars in our own time has increased the general distaste for the father of Prussian militarism. Yet to the majority of his countrymen Old Fritz has been an object of veneration and gratitude, not only during the sunshine of the Hohenzollern Empire, but in the chill gloom of the Weimar Republic and amid the feverish excitements of the Third Reich. Everyone knows the passage in *Dichtung und Wahrheit* in which Goethe describes his victories in the Seven Years' War as the first real inspiration of German poets, and declares that he and his young contemporaries were all "Frederick-minded." Frederick and Bismarck stand side by side in the national Valhalla, the laurels of victory on their brow, incomparable in resolution and resource; but since 1914 inaugurated a second Thirty Years' War, the sorely tried ruler has meant even more to his countrymen than the Iron Chancellor who knew only success. His grim and dynamic figure has stamped itself on the Prussian character too deeply to be ignored in any interpretation of modern Germany. Without him there might have been no Bismarck, who required a preponderant Prussia for his far-reaching aims, and without the Iron Chancellor there could hardly have been a Hitler and a Third Reich.

This book, portions of which have appeared in the *Contemporary Review* and are reproduced by permission, is not another biography, for nothing of the sort is required; the advanced student will turn to the monumental work of Koser, the general reader to William Reddaway, Norwood Young, Georg Winter, and Pierre Gaxotte. The immense political and military achievements of the patron saint of Germany, as Lord Rosebery described him, have tended to divert attention from the man and overshadowed his activities as writer, thinker, and correspondent. The object of these studies is to portray a unique and many-sided personality, at once fascinating and repulsive, from various angles, though no attempt has been made to cover the whole field. Students of his poetry, his military treatises, and his musical compositions must look elsewhere. The three opening chapters summarize his share in the making of Prussia, but the larger portion of the volume is devoted to the analysis of his character, his friendships, and his ideology. Most of the evidence is supplied by himself in solid political treatises, voluminous histories, and the sixty volumes of his correspondence. We can check this testimony by the numerous witnesses, German and non-German, who have described their contacts with the most celebrated figure of his age. How much he has meant to his countrymen, how deeply he has left his mark on the national character and the national tradition, is outlined in the closing chapter, for what nations think of their heroes may well concern the inhabitants of other states. The mind and face of Europe today would be very different had he not made Prussia a great power and popularized aggression by his spectacular success.

G. P. G.

CONTENTS

FREDERICK THE GREAT

The Ruler, the Writer, the Man

Chapter I

THE MAKING OF PRUSSIA

FROM the moment that Frederick ascended the throne in May 1740, we are able to reconstruct his foreign policy, often from day to day, from the *Politische Correspondenz*. Though he had received no training during his father's reign, he took to diplomacy like a duck to water. He had accumulated an extensive fund of knowledge of the courts of Europe and knew exactly what he wanted to do, though he realized that plans must wait on opportunity. He resolved to be his own Foreign Minister, which involved that certain secrets must be locked in his own bosom. "If I thought that my shirt or my skin knew anything of my intentions," he declared, "I would tear them off." The Prussian officials soon discovered that their new master was very different from the old. Podewils, whom he continued as Foreign Minister and who was informed of most things, freely expressed his opinions, and there was very little that the faithful Eichel, his Political Secretary, whom the Corps Diplomatique rarely saw, did not know; yet the decisions were always his own and he shared the contempt of the soldier for the layman in military affairs. "When the ministers discuss negotiations," he reminded the Foreign Office shortly after his accession, "they know their business, but when they talk about war it is like an Iroquois discoursing on astronomy."

Frederick had long been resolved that his kingdom should not remain a mere patchwork stitched together by the army, the bureaucracy, and the crown. He was the first of his house to pursue an independent policy, for the Great Elector, Frederick I, and Frederick William I had advanced by services rendered to the Emperor or the King of France. His eyes turned to Jülich and Berg in the Rhineland and to West Prussia in the East, but he was interested above all in the claims of his house in Silesia. That the Emperor, a man of fifty-five, would die in the same year he could not foresee; yet he was prepared for any emergency, and when the news of his death on October 20 arrived, not a moment was lost. All was foreseen, he wrote to Algarotti,

3

all had been thought out. "So it is only a question of executing designs I have long had in mind." No one was informed of the project except Podewils and Schwerin, the most trusted of his generals. An elaborate joint Memorandum of October 29, drafted by the former, discussed the best way of carrying out the decision to seize Silesia.[1] The wisest course, they argued, would be to approach the court of Vienna with a plan. In return for Silesia the King should undertake to use his influence to secure the election of the Grand Duke of Tuscany, husband of Maria Theresa, as Emperor; to guarantee the possessions of the house of Austria in Germany and the Low Countries against all comers; and to cede to the house of Austria his rights to the succession of Jülich and Berg. A final argument, only to be employed in case of need, would be the offer of money, of which the court of Vienna stood in dire need. In that way alone could the dismemberment of the house of Austria be averted and its historic connection with the Imperial dignity be preserved. If this offer were declined he should arrange a partition with Saxony and Bavaria, taking Silesia as the price of his support of their claims. France's guarantee of his possession of the latter could be gained by the prospect of assistance against Austria and the maritime powers, by the cession of Prussian rights in Jülich and Berg, and by the election as Emperor of the Elector of Bavaria. Possible opposition by Russia should be neutralized by arranging with Turkey to keep her occupied in the south in case of need. Since neither the experienced Podewils nor his young master expected the proudest dynasty in Europe to cede its richest province in return for a paper promise from one robber to defend it against other covetous neighbors, the latter part of the Memorandum was the more important.

Frederick explained his more radical ideas in a remarkable Memorandum. "Silesia is the portion of the Imperial heritage to which we have the strongest claim and which is most suitable for the house of Brandenburg. It is consonant with justice to maintain one's rights and to seize the opportunity of the Emperor's death to take possession. The superiority of our troops, the promptitude with which we can set them in motion, in a word the clear advantage we have over our neighbors, gives us in

[1] The materials relating to the claim on Silesia are collected in *Preussische Staatsschriften aus der Regierungszeit König Friedrichs II*, I, 41–271.

this unexpected emergency an infinite superiority over all other powers of Europe. If we wait till Saxony and Bavaria start hostilities, we could not prevent the aggrandizement of the former which is wholly contrary to our interests. If we act at once, we keep her in subjection and by cutting off the supply of horses prevent her from moving. England and France are foes. If France meddles in the affairs of the Empire England could not allow it, so I can always make a good alliance with one or the other. England could not be jealous of my getting Silesia, which would do her no harm, and she needs allies. Holland will not care, all the more since the loans of the Amsterdam business world secured on Silesia will be guaranteed. If we cannot arrange with England and Holland we can certainly make a deal with France, who cannot frustrate our designs and will welcome the abasement of the Imperial house. Russia alone might cause us trouble. Next spring we shall find no one barring our path; thus if Russia wishes to attack us she may be sure she will have the Swedes on her hands and find herself between the hammer and the anvil. If the Empress lives, the Duke of Kurland, who has rich possessions in Silesia, will want me to preserve them, and we can bribe the leading counselors. If she dies, the Russians will be so occupied with their domestic problems that they will have no time for foreign affairs. In any case an ass laden with gold for St. Petersburg is a possibility. All this leads to the conclusion that we must occupy Silesia before the winter and then negotiate. When we are in possession we can negotiate with success. We should never get anything by mere negotiations except very onerous conditions in return for a few trifles." Aggressors always reckon on a lightning stroke. Though the Hapsburg Empire was vastly superior in size and resources, Frederick trusted to its notorious unreadiness for war, to the probability that France and other states would join in the scramble, but above all to his large disciplined army and his plentiful supply of cash.

In his first memorandum of October 29 Podewils had said nothing about the validity of Prussian claims, but in commenting on his master's arguments he ventured to pour a little water into the wine. "On the question of right I must point out with profound respect that, whatever well-founded pretensions the house of Brandenburg once possessed to the duchies of Liegnitz, Brieg

5

and Wohlau, to Ratibor and Oppeln, to the principality of Jägerndorf and the circle of Schwiebus, there are solemn treaties to which the house of Austria will appeal and by which the house of Brandenburg was induced, though by fraudulent means, to renounce claims in return for trifles. However, we can always manage to revive these ancient rights." To these scruples Frederick's reply, which has found its way into all the biographies, was short and sharp. "The matter of right is the business of the ministers, it's yours; it is time to work at it, for orders have been given to the troops." Other warnings, such as that Austria could buy off France or Bavaria, or that Poland might invade his territories, were brushed aside. "Since nothing will stop me, I have today dispatched orders to the regiments. Please God, my troops will march at the beginning of December, and I hope everything will go according to program." Two days later he wrote joyfully to Podewils: "The Empress of Russia is at death's door, God favors us, and destiny is on our side." He gave false orders to the Berlin regiments to march to Halberstadt with the object of confusing the chancelleries. "We must use every means to lead them astray. Unless heaven frowns on us we shall have the finest game in the world. I intend to strike my blow on December 8 and to launch the boldest and biggest enterprise that any prince of my house has ever undertaken. Adieu, my heart promises me good luck and my troops victory."

If anything was more repulsive than the decision to steal a portion of his neighbor's vineyard it was the attempt to dress up the crime as a service to the prospective victim. "The house of Austria," explained Frederick to his uncle George II, "exposed to all its enemies since the loss of its head and the total disintegration of its affairs, is on the point of succumbing under the efforts of those who openly advance claims to the succession and secretly plan to seize a part. And as owing to the situation of my territories I have the chief interest in averting the consequences and above all in preventing those who may have formed the design to seize Silesia, the bulwark of my possessions, I have been compelled to send my troops into the duchy in order to prevent others seizing it, to my great disadvantage and to the prejudice of the just claims which my house has always had to the larger part of that country. I have no other purpose than the preservation and the real benefit of the house of Austria." Before giving

6

the signal that for a generation was to drench Europe with blood, the aggressor dispatched his terms to Vienna to be presented directly the Silesian frontier was crossed. He had recognized the succession of Maria Theresa and written her friendly letters. Now he would guarantee all possessions of the house of Austria in Germany, form a close alliance with the court of Vienna, Russia, and the maritime powers, use all his influence to procure the election of her husband the Duke of Lorraine as Emperor, and supply two or even three million florins. Such valuable services and the risks they entailed would require a proportionate reward—namely, the cession of the whole of Silesia. It was in vain that the friendly British Government advised Vienna's acceptance of these terms. Though he pretended to be surprised and shocked by Maria Theresa's indignant reaction to the attempted blackmail, Frederick would have despised her had she submitted, and she alone of the crowned heads of Europe won his abiding respect.

For over two hundred years since the Emperor Sigismund sent Frederick, Burgrave of Nuremberg, to northern Germany in 1412, the Electorate of Brandenburg counted for less within the loosely knit framework of the Holy Roman Empire than Bavaria and Saxony. It was not till the seventeenth century that it began to spread its wings. Cleves, Mark, and Ravensberg in the distant Rhineland were added by inheritance in 1609. The equally remote province of East Prussia, the old domain of the Teutonic Knights, which had been secularized by Albert of Hohenzollern, the last of the Grand Masters, in 1525, came under the rule of Berlin in 1618. On the accession of the Great Elector in 1640, Europe was compelled to reckon with a new political force. Prussia, in Acton's phrase, was not a giant but an athlete, and the sufferings of the Thirty Years' War taught her the need to develop her muscles. The Treaty of Westphalia in 1648 brought her eastern Pomerania, the secularized bishoprics of Halberstadt and Minden, and the reversion of the Archbishopric of Magdeburg. In 1660 the suzerainty of Poland over East Prussia came to an end. The forty-eight years of this strenuous reign witnessed no less important changes in domestic affairs. The Great Elector broke the power of the feudal Estates, created a small but highly trained standing army, substituted an excise for the occasional subsidies granted by the Estates, welcomed industrious Huguenot exiles from France, and set the example of Enlightened Autocracy, which his descendants endeavored to follow. At his death in 1688 Brandenburg-Prussia was the most powerful of North German states.

His son Frederick, an unconvincing imitation of *Le Roi Soleil*, the builder of stately palaces in Charlottenburg and Berlin, and the founder of the University of Halle and the Prussian Academy, procured from the Emperor the title of King a century before the rulers of Saxony, Bavaria, and Württemberg obtained similar promotion at the hands of Napoleon. Leopold believed that the satisfaction of the Elector's darling wish would bind the Hohenzollerns to the interests of his house in the approaching struggle with France, and Prussia rendered the promised help in the War of the Spanish Succession. Prince Eugene, on the other hand, looking further ahead, declared that the ministers who advised the concession deserved to be hanged. His censure, so far as they were concerned, was misdirected, for they had warned their master that Prussia might sooner or later deprive his family of the Empire. The coveted title embodied and stimulated the ambitions of the dynasty. The new monarchy automatically assumed the position of the head of the Protestant interest in Germany, which the Electors of Saxony had held since the Reformation and had recently forfeited when Augustus the Strong turned Catholic in order to qualify for election to the Polish throne. Here was a triple potential menace to Hapsburg hegemony—a kingdom, a North German power, and a Protestant champion. The full implications of his act were beyond the range of Frederick I, but the possibilities were grasped by his grandson a generation after his death.

His son, Frederick William I, made a less spectacular but far more solid addition to the power of his house. The true founder of the bureaucratic-military state forged the sword that his successor was to wield. He created the most formidable fighting force in Europe, introduced a modified form of conscription by assigning the recruitment for each regiment to a particular province, centralized the administrative machinery of the army, finance, and royal domains in the *General Directorium,* founded village schools, and extracted the last ounce of energy from a virile and obedient people. He economized in everything except

8

the giant grenadiers who were his passion and his pride, and transformed the private estates of his family into crown domains, on which he freed the serfs. He proudly declared that he had established his sovereignty like a rock of bronze, and the hardest worker in the kingdom saw with his own eyes that his orders were carried out. He described himself as the Finance Minister and the Field-Marshal of the King of Prussia. He bequeathed to his successor an overflowing treasury, a standing army of 80,000, an efficient bureaucracy, a tradition of discipline that, under a ruler of outstanding ability, might change the face of central Europe. Well might Schön describe him as the greatest of Prussia's kings in the field of domestic policy. To his predecessors, above all to the Great Elector and his own irascible father, Frederick the Great pays unstinted homage in his *Histoire de la Maison de Brandebourg*. No one knew so well as he that without their exertions he could never have shown his mettle nor achieved his burning desire for fame.

Frederick William I loved his soldiers as a miser loves his gold; they were too precious to be exposed to the hazards of war. They aroused no alarm, for it was generally assumed that he would never fight for his own hand. In domestic affairs he knew what he wanted and got his way, but beyond the frontier he felt himself an amateur whose wisest course was to avoid major risks. He was proud to have fought at Malplaquet, but he had no passion for war, and no sovereign of his time was less aggressive in thought or deed. Besides adding a portion of Swedish Pomerania, including Stettin, and the larger part of Gelderland to his dominions, he longed for the duchies of Jülich and Berg on the lower Rhine when the childless ruler, a member of a junior branch of the Palatine Wittelsbachs, should die; yet he never dreamed of fighting for the prize. Nothing could be done without the goodwill of the Emperor, who promised support for his claims but persuaded him to limit his ambitions. By the Treaty of Wusterhausen with Austria in 1726 he withdrew his demand for Jülich, and two years later Düsseldorf, the capital of Berg, was excluded from the scope of the Emperor's promise. Soon even this limited obligation was canceled by a declaration of his right to decide on the succession. The King felt that he had been tricked, but he had no choice except to submit. He had only a little over two million subjects, and the revenue of the

9

state at the time of his death was only about a million pounds a year.

The exclusion of Crown Prince Frederick from any share in the direction of affairs left the young man ample time to study the European situation and to plan his course. The spectacle of his country with a well-filled treasury and armed to the teeth, yet reckoned as a mere pawn on the chessboard of Europe, filled him with anger. The fundamental principle of great monarchies, Frederick wrote in his *Antimachiavel,* had been ceaseless aggrandizement; aggressive wars, however detestable when waged for inadequate reasons, were justifiable if required by the coolly calculated interests of the state. As he bent over the map in his library at Rheinsberg, he discovered possibilities both in the east and in the west. In 1703 the Emperor Leopold I decided that in the absence of male heirs females might succeed to the Hapsburg dominions, adding that the daughters of his elder son, Joseph, should take precedence of those of his younger son, Charles; but on succeeding his brother Joseph I as Emperor in 1711, Charles VI made a secret family law in 1713 known as the Pragmatic Sanction to ensure the undivided succession of his scattered territories to his own daughter in the absence of male heirs.

The need for such planning was emphasized by the death of his only son in infancy. Renunciation of their claims under the decree of 1703 was obtained from the daughters of Joseph, who found Saxon and Bavarian husbands. This, however, was not enough for the Emperor, who proceeded to secure recognition of the Pragmatic Sanction from the Estates of his scattered dominions, including Hungary and the Austrian Netherlands. It was a good start, but it was far more essential to win the consent of foreign potentates. The process proved easier than was expected, Spain leading the way in 1725, Russia, Prussia, England, Denmark, and some minor German states following suit. The Imperial Diet at Regensburg approved it in 1732, France in 1735, Sardinia and Naples in 1739. By 1740 all the powers except Bavaria and the Palatinate had accepted the prospective succession of his daughter Maria Theresa, though in certain cases not without concessions or promises in return. But would the promises be kept? Engagements might be interpreted in different ways, the plan violated the old principle of male succession, and no signatory could bind his heirs. Charles realized the danger, and he would have been still more alarmed had he guessed that the Political Testament of the Great Elector, composed in 1672, discovered in 1731, and published by Ranke a century later, envisaged the invasion of Silesia. Moreover, he had ignored the warning attributed to Prince Eugene that a strong army and a full treasury would be the best guarantee of his scheme. His dominions were racked by provincialism, his soldiers wearied by the latest Turkish campaigns. Never had a proud and mighty state been less prepared, both materially and spiritually, to fight for its life. The Pragmatic Sanction was a scrap of paper and nothing more.

The house of Brandenburg possessed certain claims of varying validity, not to the whole, but to portions of Silesia. A jurist of the University of Halle named Ludwig, who had often been employed to draft official memoranda, forwarded a voluminous dossier to Berlin and was commissioned to draw up a short memorandum. Though he honestly believed that part of Silesia had been fraudulently withheld from his house, Frederick was more interested in prospects than in parchments. Here are the outlines of the Prussian case. Brandenburg claimed three of the nine duchies of Lower Silesia—Liegnitz, Brieg, and Wohlau—under an arrangement with their ruler in 1537. The claim was declared invalid by Vienna in 1546, but the right of the Hapsburgs to a veto was never accepted at Berlin. Secondly, Brandenburg claimed the return of the Duchy of Jägerndorf in Upper Silesia, which had been forfeited when its Duke, a son of the Elector Joachim Friedrich, took the losing side in the Battle of the White Mountain in 1620. In 1686 the Great Elector surrendered his claim to the four duchies in return for the district of Schwiebus, the promise of an annual subsidy, and the payment of his debts. This surrender would have remained valid had not the Emperor Leopold at the same time secretly compelled Frederick, later the first Prussian King, to promise to restore the latter as the condition of support in a family affair. Portions of Prussia were left by the Great Elector to his sons by a second marriage, and it was to cancel this arrangement that the Crown Prince was willing to pay a substantial price. Thirdly, the Pragmatic Sanction had been recognized by Prussia in return for an Austrian promise to help in securing the reversion of Jülich and Berg. This understanding was broken when the Emperor secretly transferred his support to the Palatine house of Sulzbach in 1739. Neither Frederick nor Podewils nor the jurists, however, suggested that Prussia had a legal right to the whole of Silesia: the claim was only to the four duchies of Liegnitz, Brieg, Wohlau, and Jägerndorf. Carlyle's characterization of the rape as "a rushing out to seize your own stolen horse" is grotesque, but Vienna had had plenty of warnings that the claims of the house of Brandenburg would one day be revived.

These arguments were mainly for the chancelleries, the public, and posterity. The King would probably have seized the coveted province had there been no claims at all, as he almost admitted in the celebrated letter to Jordan of March 3, 1741. "My youth, the fire of passions, the desire for glory, yes, to be frank, even curiosity, finally a secret instinct, has torn me away from the delights of tranquillity. The satisfaction of seeing my name in the papers and later in history has seduced me." Yet this damaging confession must not be taken as a complete explanation of the step that opened a new chapter of European history as surely as the cannonade at Valmy half a century later. The deeper cause was the resolve to secure for Prussia the status of a great power, to grasp the rich prize to which he thought her entitled by her vital needs and growing strength. In his own striking phrase, she was a hermaphrodite, more electorate than kingdom. His dominions were scattered across northern Europe from the Rhineland to the Russian frontier, the central core being separated from the outlying possessions by blocks of foreign territory. Cleve, Mark, and Ravensberg could not be defended against France, nor East Prussia against Russia, and the frontier of Saxony was only thirty miles from Berlin. His most plausible argument was found in the map of his heritage, a thing of shreds and patches unique in Germany. Such sprawling possessions clamored for a change, and Silesia was the first and most important item in the program of consolidation. A further consideration was the extreme poverty of his inheritance, much of it consisting of sand and forest. Even his father's energy could never extract from the little state the resources needed to secure and maintain a place in the sun. More taxpayers, more soldiers, more food, more industries were urgently required. The patriotic purpose was assumed to justify the means. "Frederick the Great stole Silesia," remarked Bismarck to the elder Bülow, "yet he is one of the greatest men of all time."

When every allowance has been made for ancient claims and for the fact that moral considerations meant little to any eighteenth-century ruler except Maria Theresa, the rape of Silesia ranks with the partition of Poland among the sensational crimes of modern history. Austria was taken completely by surprise. Though Macaulay's essay on Frederick the Great is among his weakest performances, his rhetoric contains a good deal of truth. The Pragmatic Sanction, he declares, was placed under the protection of the public faith of the whole civilized world. "Even if no positive stipulations had existed, the arrangement was one which no good man would have been willing to disturb. It was an arrangement acceptable to the great population whose happiness was chiefly concerned. It was an arrangement which made no change in the distribution of power among the states of Christendom. It was an arrangement which could be set aside only by means of a general war. The sovereigns of Europe were therefore bound by every obligation which those who are entrusted with power over their fellow-creatures ought to hold most sacred to respect and defend the rights of the Archduchess. Her situation and her personal qualities were such as might be expected to move the mind of any generous man to pity, admiration and chivalrous tenderness. But the selfish rapacity of the King of Prussia gave the signal to his neighbours. The whole world sprang to arms. On the head of Frederick is all the blood which was shed in every quarter of the globe. The evils produced by his wickedness were felt in lands where the name of Prussia was unknown, and in order that he might rob a neighbour whom he had promised to defend, black men fought on the coast of Coromandel and red men scalped each other by the Great Lakes of North America."

That the aggressor had promised to defend Maria Theresa is untrue: his father had accepted the Pragmatic Sanction, but he never undertook to fight for it. Here is Frederick's reply to this particular charge, extracted from the Memorandum drafted in his own hand and, after revision by Podewils, circulated to his representatives at foreign courts. "It would be wrong to accuse the King of infringing the Pragmatic Sanction. His Majesty does not contest the succession in Austria but is merely maintaining his own rights, of which the late Emperor could not dispose since they were not his property and which for that reason he could not transmit to his daughter. Moreover, the house of Austria could not demand the fulfillment of the guarantee promised by the late King of Prussia in a treaty between that prince and the Emperor Charles VI, since that monarch, far from carrying out its obligations, made another contract diametrically opposed to it in a manner that reflects little honor on the good faith of the court of Vienna." If the young King had contented himself with the four duchies to which alone he laid claim, his reasoning would have been more impressive; but since even such a limited demand would undoubtedly have been refused, he threw legality to the winds and gambled for the larger prize.

Though Frederick William I did not dream of competing with Austria in power or prestige, he believed in Prussia's destiny and attributed to the Hapsburgs the settled design of placing obstacles in his path. On one occasion, pointing to his son, he exclaimed: "There stands one who will avenge me." Frederick was the first of his house to whom the Empire was merely the consecration of anarchy, a pretentious sham, which had long ceased to be either Holy or Roman or an Empire, its machinery rotten and crumbling, an empty shell that served as cover for the dynastic ambitions of a rival family. Thus, in launching his challenge he was free from the inferiority complex that had paralyzed his father's arm. As Elector of Brandenburg, it is true, he was Hereditary Arch-Chamberlain; but the feeling of solidarity, never strong in Germany, had long been overlaid by the growth of particularism as the Electorates increased in size and power. Brandenburg-Prussia, he felt, had come of age, and she was not the first member of the Empire—that queer and antiquated institution, as he called it—to pursue an independent course. The Elector Palatine had unleashed the Thirty Years' War by accepting the offer of a crown from the Bohemian Protestants. The Treaty of Westphalia, which not only ended the Wars of Religion by leaving the north to the Protestants and the south to the Catholics, but authorized the princes to make treaties and possess their own troops, devitalized the Empire. The War of the Austrian Succession proved that opposition to the leading Catholic power was not confined to Protestant rulers, for the rulers of Bavaria and Saxony, who had married daughters of Joseph I, joined the ranks of its enemies. The eighteenth century was an epoch of dynastic wars, and every German prince played unashamedly for his own hand. The King of Prussia was merely the strongest and the most audacious, the gambler who achieved the most striking success.

In deciding to seize Silesia Frederick thought of his own little state and of nothing else. The vision of a united Germany was beyond the range of his contemporaries, for German nationalism was the child of the French Revolution. That his subjects were exclusively German while those of Maria Theresa were a racial mosaic was true but irrelevant; for he was as ready to attack Saxony as Austria or Poland. The endeavor of Droysen, the most whole-hearted of his academic champions, to exhibit him as the standard-bearer of Germanism failed to convince even his own countrymen: before the French Revolution, declared Bismarck, a national German party was not to be found in Prussia. Frederick and Bismarck were aggressors; but their territorial aims, though extensive, were not unlimited. Both wished Prussia to be strong enough to stand up to Austria in matters of vital interest, but the former had no wish to set the Imperial crown on his head. So far as the Hapsburgs were concerned he was satisfied with the conquest of Silesia.

"Farewell, gentlemen," cried the King to his officers; "to the rendezvous of fame, whither I shall follow you without delay." The seizure of Silesia without a declaration of war proved easier than he expected. It had only cost him twenty men and two officers, he declared, though Austrian garrisons held out in Glogau, Neisse, and Brieg. That northern Silesia was mainly Protestant and that the whole province had a Protestant majority was a great help. "The whole land rejoices at our arrival," he wrote to his brother, "and is only afraid that we shall leave." Its retention proved more difficult. Again and again in the course of the three wars that followed he was so near the abyss as to have broken the nerve of almost anyone else; yet he never regretted his decision and was prepared to die rather than to surrender the smallest portion of the loot. His iron resolution extorted a certain admiration from his sharpest critics, but in Maria Theresa he met a will as tenacious as his own. The most radiant figure in the portrait gallery of the eighteenth century had inherited none of the limitations of her commonplace father, and her instinctive courage was fortified not only by dynastic pride but by the well-founded conviction that in the Silesian struggle right was on her side. While her feeble husband, Francis of Lorraine, whom she loved more than he deserved and made co-Regent, was ready for a deal with the aggressor, she rejected all approaches with scorn. She would rather cede a whole province to Bavaria, she cried indignantly, than a single village to Prussia.

Throughout the eighteenth century winter was a close time, but the spring of 1741 brought an Austrian army into the field. Frederick had never seen a battle and was still only in nominal command, for the immediate responsibility rested with the veteran Schwerin; but he had no fear of the collision that was to decide the fate of Silesia and he was prepared for all personal risks. "There are no laurels for the lazy," he wrote to Podewils on March 7; "they go to those who work hardest and are most intrepid. By the way, I have had two escapes from Austrian hussars. If by bad luck I am ever captured I command you— and you will answer for it with your head—that in my absence you will disregard my orders, that you will advise my brother, and that the state will stoop to no unworthy act to achieve my liberation. On the contrary, in such an event I order that even greater energy shall be displayed. I am King only when I am free. If I am killed I wish my body to be burned in the Roman way, the ashes to be placed in an urn at Rheinsberg, and Knobelsdorff to erect a monument to me, like that of Horace at Tusculum." The famous sentence "I am King only when I am free" was to find its way into all the school-books and is part of the legacy of the greatest of Prussia's kings.

The news that the stubbornly contested struggle at Mollwitz, fought in the snow on April 10, was a resounding Prussian victory was brought to the King after he had been advised to leave the broken front for fear of capture; the cavalry in which he had fought was routed before the incomparable infantry saved the day. Though no lack of courage need be imputed to him, he never referred to this undignified episode. It was the first big battle in the history of Prussia, and Europe suddenly realized that a new military power had emerged: the work of Frederick William had borne fruit. Other birds of prey, encouraged by his evil example, swooped down on what they believed to be the soft shell of the Hapsburg state. "He's a fool, that man is mad," exclaimed Louis XV when he heard the news of the invasion of Silesia, but Mollwitz converted him. Explaining that she had accepted the Pragmatic Sanction subject to the recognition of third-party rights, France promised in the Treaty of Nymphenburg, in May 1741, to champion Bavarian claims both to the Austrian succession and to the Imperial crown. The death of the Emperor provided an excuse to the Bourbons to renew the struggle with the Hapsburgs, which had lasted for two centuries, and they feared that if the husband of Maria Theresa were elected to the highest post he might try to recover his old Duchy of Lorraine, which had been given to Stanislas, ex-King of Poland and father-in-law of Louis XV. Marshal Belle-Isle was dispatched to Frederick's camp, and in June a treaty pledged France and Prussia to co-operation in the field and the support of the candidature of the Elector of Bavaria for the Imperial crown. Saxony also joined in, and the war which began as a duel between Prussia and Austria broadened into a European conflagration. England granted Austria a subsidy, not because she was an enemy of Prussia but because she was the traditional enemy of France. The decision was unimportant, for a few months later George II, in his capacity as Elector of Hanover, agreed to remain neutral in the war.

Austria was too weak to risk another pitched battle for Silesia during the campaigning season of 1741, and on October 9 a secret convention with Prussia was signed at Kleinschnellendorf which seemed to indicate the approach of peace. The fortress of Neisse, then under siege, was to be surrendered to Frederick, after which he would take no further offensive action; he would content himself with Lower Silesia and Neisse and would try to conclude a definite treaty at the end of the year. Austria, desiring to use her Silesian forces elsewhere, in return undertook not to attack. England alone was informed, and a few movements by both sides were to be made *pro forma*. During the winter, unless a general peace had been made, a new agreement should be negotiated. That the convention was merely a breathing-space between the rounds both signatories were well aware; Frederick regarded Lower Silesia as an installment, and Maria Theresa hoped to recover the whole province. For the moment the tide of battle rolled towards the west. In November the French stormed Prague, the Elector of Bavaria was crowned King of Bohemia in December, and on January 24, 1742 he was elected Emperor as Charles VII. On the other hand Austrian troops entered his capital at Munich on the same day, and the Hungarian nobles pledged themselves to the military support of their hard-pressed Queen.

Frederick's limited resources demanded a short war, and now that Maria Theresa had France, Bavaria, and Saxony on her hands, there seemed to be little danger in slipping out of the fight. At the opening of 1742 he hinted to Vienna that it was not his aim unduly to depress the house of Austria in Germany or to deprive it of any territories beyond Silesia, Bohemia, and Moravia. On the contrary he desired it to remain in a position to balance the Wittelsbachs of Bavaria, and would do his best for it in any negotiations for peace. In March he set forth the conditions on which he was prepared for peace. He should receive Lower Silesia and the County of Glatz; the Queen of Hungary should promise reasonable satisfaction for his allies and he should remain in occupation of Upper Silesia, except the principality of Teschen, till the general peace, though the latter stipulation might be waived if Austria was not very anxious to conclude hostilities. To clarify his thoughts he drew up two memoranda, the first setting forth the reasons for continuing hostilities, the second for ending them. It was bad to break one's word without reason, he began, and so far he had no reason to complain of France or his allies: that was the way to earn the reputation of unreliability. "If this campaign ends happily, the Prussian arms will have all the honor; perhaps a victory will discourage the Dutch and English and bring us peace. If so, the Prussians will be the arbiters of peace and their interests will not suffer; the Empire will attach itself to the King of Prussia, who will enjoy the authority of the Emperor while the Elector carries the burden." There could be no secure peace with the Queen of Hungary, and without the separation of Bohemia and Moravia it would only be a truce. The second Memorandum contained still more cogent arguments for concluding peace. The French would probably lose a battle, for distance impeded the flow of supplies; his treaty with the allies did not stipulate the number of his troops; the aggrandizement of Saxony would be

18

contrary to Prussian interests; the war was expensive, and the Emperor and the French had asked for a large loan; Maria Theresa was about to obtain substantial aid from Hungary; a reverse might deprive him of all he had gained, and the war might reach his own territories. The balance-sheet left little doubt what the decision would be: he would retire from the fray as soon as possible.

Before the goal was reached Frederick made a brief re-entry into the campaign, for his cavalry had been thoroughly reorganized since Mollwitz. Maria Theresa's revelation of the Convention of Kleinschnellendorf in order to compromise him with his allies provided an excuse, and there was a growing fear that Austria might become too strong for his liking and in consequence refuse to cede any part of Silesia. On May 17, 1742 he routed the Austrians at Chotusitz, his second battle and the first in which he was in effective command; this time his cavalry proved worthy of the infantry. Now was the moment to conclude peace, for Austria would doubtless be eager to buy him off, all the more since he still only asked for Lower Silesia. Upper Silesia, he wrote to Podewils on June 8, was a ruined country, incapable of defense, whose inhabitants would never be loyal. Negotiations began, in which Carteret played the part of mediator, and the preliminaries of peace were signed on June 11, 1742. "Perhaps with time we might have had a more advantageous treaty," he wrote to Podewils, "but it might equally have been worse. When we meet I will tell you all my reasons, and you will agree that as a statesman and in the interest of my people I could have done nothing else. It is a great and happy event, which brings my house one of the most flourishing provinces of Germany after a most glorious war. One must be able to stop in time. To force good fortune is to forfeit it, and always to be wanting more is never to he happy." The Treaty of Breslau, ceding almost the whole of Silesia to Prussia, was confirmed in Berlin in July.

"Peace at last!" wrote Frederick to Jordan on June 15. "I know what people will say, but I expect satirical reflections and commonplaces, which fools and ignoramuses—in a word, those who do not think—repeat from mouth to mouth. But the senseless gabble of the public does not trouble me. I ask all the doctors of jurisprudence and political ethics whether, after doing my utmost to fulfill my engagements, I am obliged to stick to them when I see on the one hand an ally who does nothing and on the other an ally who does the wrong thing, and when, in addition, I am in danger at the first mishap of being abandoned by the most powerful of my allies in a patched-up peace. I ask if, when I foresee the ruin of my army, the exhaustion of my finances, the loss of my conquests, the depopulation of the state, the unhappiness of my people—in a word, all the evil involved in the hazard of war and the duplicity of statesmen; I ask if, in such a case, a sovereign is not right to guard himself by a wise retreat from certain shipwreck or evident peril."

In breaking the news to his allies the King attempted to justify his withdrawal from the strife. "It is with bitter feelings," he wrote to the Emperor, "that I have to inform Your Imperial Majesty of the collapse of your cause. You will admit that my zeal for your interests has never flagged and that I have done everything imaginable to help you to occupy your domain. I have labored for eighteen months almost without a pause, sustained by the hope that my allies would share my anxieties and dangers." Owing to the errors of the French and Saxons, the situation of the allies was worse than in the previous autumn. To reduce the court of Vienna would demand three more victories. How much luck and how much time would be needed! It could not be done in a single campaign. "If we suffer a defeat and other powers intervene, I foresee fatal consequences for the allies. The French and the Cardinal are tired of the war, the King of Poland is in touch with the court of Vienna, and wherever I turn, the whole burden of this war rests on my shoulders." English guineas were affecting policy in Russia and arming Hungary. In view of the inaction of the Saxons and the feebleness of the French it was clear that any efforts to recover what had been lost by the fault of some and the malice of others would be useless. "Seeing myself thus reduced to a situation in which my sword can no longer help, I assure you that my pen will always be at your service; my heart will always be yours; if I cannot do all I wish you will always find me the same, yielding only to necessity, but firm in my engagements, incapable of vacillation in my promise to you concerning the Palatinate succession, vowing my arms and even ready to shed my blood for you on condition that it would be of use, full of compassion and deeply grieved not to be able to rescue you from your present situation and to see you enjoying a fate worthy of your great qualities and your character, which I shall always respect. These are the sentiments, my brother and cousin, of your good brother and faithful ally Frederick."

To Cardinal Fleury he wrote in the same self-righteous strain. "You are aware that since our agreement I have done everything possible to support the designs of the King your master with inviolable fidelity. I detached Saxony from the Austrian party, I gave my vote to the Elector of Bavaria, I accelerated his coronation, I helped you to contain the King of England, I decided the policy of the King of Denmark. In a word, by negotiation, by arms, by rigid fidelity in the discharge of my obligations, I rendered all the services I could. I yield to necessity alone. No one is condemned for not having done the impossible. Within the sphere of possibilities you will find in me unchanged fidelity. The course of this war forms, so to speak, a tissue of marks of my goodwill to my allies. I am sure you will agree in deploring the caprice of fortune that has frustrated designs so salutary for Europe and ourselves." Writing to Marshal Belle-Isle, the French commander, he compared the struggle to a voyage undertaken by several persons bound for the same destination in the course of which shipwreck confers on every passenger the right to think of his own safety, to swim away, and to reach land wherever he can.

For the moment Frederick seemed to have scored, for he had won the larger part of Silesia at the modest cost of two battles. The reasons for withdrawing were strong, but there were risks in coming out as well as in staying in. Koser, the greatest of Frederician experts, who finds excuses for the rape of Silesia, condemns the *volte-face* on the ground that the desertion of France damaged such reputation as he still possessed, lost a promising chance of smashing Austria with the aid of powerful allies, and allowed her a welcome interval to prepare for another round. It is true that the arguments were almost evenly balanced, but the desirability of a short war on financial grounds turned the scale. "As for the future security of our new possessions," he wrote to Podewils, "I base it on a good and large army, a well-filled treasury, stout fortresses, and the show of alliances, which impress people. The worst that could happen to us would be an alliance between France and the Queen of Hungary, but in such a case we should have England, Holland, Russia, and many others on our side. The task of the moment is to accustom the chancelleries to our new situation, and I think that studied moderation and consideration towards all our neighbors may effect our purpose."

The elaborate instructions of October 18, 1742 to the Prussian Minister at Vienna reflect Frederick's hopes and fears. In addition to doing his best to restore good relations his chief task would be to penetrate the secrets of Austrian policy. "He must study the real disposition of the Queen of Hungary towards the King, whether she is sincerely resolved to observe the peace treaty, or whether they are only trying to gain time and have their hands free in order some day to recover the lost provinces, whether the court of Vienna is still in secret touch with Silesia, whether people in the ceded provinces are in communication with or report to the court of Vienna, what arrangements are being made in the Queen's provinces adjoining the ceded territory, whether they are planning to construct fortresses, establish magazines, and increase the forces." The Minister was instructed to collect and forward the smallest details so that the King might be informed in good time. That Maria Theresa would accept the loss of Silesia a day longer than she was compelled to do so by superior military force he never imagined. Relieved of her most formidable adversary and further assisted by Saxony's withdrawal from the fray, her prospects improved so materially that in the autumn of 1743 he began to realize that his position in Silesia was by no means assured.

A pregnant Memorandum dated September 27, 1742 admitted the change in the situation and drew the obvious conclusion. "It is absolutely necessary that the general peace should not be made without Prussia's participation—in other words, that she should shape the settlement: firstly, in order to consolidate the acquisition of Silesia by the guarantee of the powers of Europe; secondly, to attach the German princes to the Emperor; thirdly, to snatch this palm from the hands of the King of England, whom Prussia must always regards as being on principle the enemy of the aggrandizement and prosperity of such a formidable neighbor; finally, for all the advantages that the conclusion of peace can bring Prussia for her claims, for a hundred little arrangements; above all, for the considerable influence that this mediation will give us in regard to the election and policy of some future emperor. The crux of the matter is the longing of the court of Vienna to despoil the Emperor of Bavaria, which involves his forced surrender of the Imperial dignity. If Prussia submits to this abdication she may as well deliver herself bound hand and feet into the power of her most irreconcilable enemies. What, then, are the best means of reaching this goal (a general peace) so salutary for Europe, so glorious and profitable for Prussia? Negotiation has failed so far, and negotiations without arms produce as little impression as musical scores without instruments. So we must give weight to any proposals of mediation by putting an army in the field in support of the Empire. The great difficulty lies in uniting all these different rulers and making people realize the danger of independent action. It would be very difficult to persuade certain princes to furnish their contingent if they are not supplied with funds. This would be the task of the Emperor, or rather of France. Thus the Emperor's ministers must draw up a plan and send it to Versailles so that subsidies may be provided in the Emperor's name to the Palatinate, Hesse, etc. If this is done without delay I might find myself in July 1744 at the head of the largest forces of the Empire and thus compel the King of England and the Queen of Hungary to accept our terms of peace. The Dutch will join the Empire, and Prussia will be for a time the arbiter of the European situation."

While Frederick was busy with diplomatic and military preparations to re-enter the arena, the death of the childless ruler of Ostfriesland on May 25, 1744 enabled him to make a small but welcome addition to his dominions. His claim rested on an arrangement between his grandfather and the Emperor Leopold, who granted the reversion to the house of Brandenburg in compensation for the damage wrought by the Swedish invasion, which ended at Fehrbellin. Since other rulers coveted the little principality, there was no time to be lost. Letters written from the baths at Pyrmont three days later ordered a small body to join the little Prussian garrison stationed at Emden. No opposition was expected and force was only to be used if they were attacked. The troops and officials of the late ruler would enter the service of Prussia. Yet the iron hand peeped out of the velvet glove. "If anyone, contrary to my expectations, proves troublesome, I shall be reluctantly compelled to adopt unpleasant measures, so that they understand that I shall without fail maintain my possession of this principality and in case of need employ all the power given me by God." Traditional rights and privileges, he promised, would be respected. The change of ruler and dynasty took place without friction. Neither George II, as Elector of Hanover, nor Holland, the western neighbor of East Frisia, made trouble, and the little state became a contented Prussian outpost in the west. Like his other Baltic ports, Königsberg, Elbing, and Stettin, Emden had to wait till the nineteenth century for its commercial importance to be realized.

Frederick's withdrawal from the fray in 1742 gave Maria Theresa a new lease of life, and her position was further alleviated by England's entry into the war against France in 1743. At the opening of 1744 he analyzed Prussian interests in relation to the European situation in an elaborate Memorandum. Drawing a line down the middle of the paper, he set forth on one side the arguments for a fresh plunge under the title "Articles that cause just apprehensions in regard to the pernicious designs of the Queen of Hungary and the King of England," on the other the reasons for caution. Among the latter considerations was the possibility that France might be bought off by tempting offers from Vienna; moreover, all action was a gamble. "One should never risk the certain for the uncertain. We hold Silesia. If we fight again we reopen the question. The chapter of accidents is long, the fortunes of war are unpredictable." Yet the writer was never afraid to take risks, and the upshot of his meditations was clear enough. "I admit the principle *qui sta bene non se muove*,[1] but we must distinguish momentary from real security. I have shown that my situation is one of suspense, that projects are formed against me and the batteries trained, and that they are only awaiting a favorable moment to attack. That is the moment we have to anticipate. The war I must wage is necessary to avert the unconcealed designs of my enemies. If my situation is not wholly favorable for attack, the longer I wait the worse it will become. Thus I must make a virtue of necessity and underpin the Silesian enterprise." The first task was to renew the alliance with France, which was no difficult matter,

[1] In a good position one does not move.

since despite the desertion in 1742 any partner in the exhausting struggle against Austria was welcome, and now she had England on her hands. After the signature of the treaty on June 5, which bound the two states for twelve years, Frederick wrote to Louis XV that it should unite their interests forever. The reigning mistress, Mme de Châteauroux, also received a letter from "your very affectionate friend Frederic," expressing esteem and gratitude for her share in renewing the co-operation of the two states. His international position was further improved by two royal marriages, that of his sister Luise Ulrike to the Crown Prince of Sweden and that of his candidate, a Princess of Anhalt-Zerbst, to the Russian heir.

On taking the field in August 1744, Frederick drew up an *exposé des motifs*. "The King feels obliged to inform Europe of the plan that the present situation compels him to adopt for the welfare and tranquillity of Europe. His Majesty being no longer able to witness with indifference the troubles that are desolating Germany, and after fruitlessly attempting every means of conciliation, finds himself driven to employ the forces that God has put at his disposal in order to bring back peace and order, to restore law, and to maintain the head of the Empire in his authority. Since the success of the Hungarian troops in Bavaria the Queen of Hungary, far from using her victories with equity and moderation, has treated the hereditary possessions of the Emperor with infinite rigor and cruelty. This princess and her allies have formed ambitious plans with the pernicious intention of enslaving forever Germanic liberty, for the past century the principal object of the dangerous policy of the house of Austria. We have only to examine the events of the last two years to realize the malignity of the intentions of the court of Vienna and to perceive in all its doings that it has acted entirely contrary to the laws and constitutions of the Empire." After a long list of complaints the memorandum concludes with a burst of self-glorification. "His Majesty believes that the noblest and worthiest use he can make of the forces that God has entrusted to him is to employ them for the support of his country, which the Queen of Hungary desires to enslave, to avenge the honor and the rights of all the Electors of which this princess wishes to deprive them, to give powerful succor to the Emperor in order to sustain him in all his rights, and to keep him on the throne from which the Queen of Hungary desires his removal. In a word, the King asks nothing, and his personal interests are not in question. His Majesty takes up arms only to restore liberty to the Empire, dignity to the Emperor, and tranquillity to Europe."

It was true enough that the conqueror of Austria's richest province coveted no further portion of the Hapsburg dominions, but his posturing as the selfless champion of the rights of other rulers was a sorry farce. He had always acted and believed it his duty to act with a sole view to the interests of Prussia as he conceived them. No ruler of modern times was less of the good European. While his nominal purpose was to save the puppet Emperor from catastrophic defeat, his real motive was to avert danger ahead. For if France were to weary of the unprofitable struggle and, following his own example in 1742, to make peace with Vienna, he might find it difficult if not impossible to retain his prize.

The Second Silesian War opened auspiciously in August 1744 with the invasion of Bohemia and the capture of Prague; but Saxony now changed sides, Frederick had to withdraw from Bohemia, and the French were far away. No pitched battle was fought, but by the close of the campaign of 1744 he had nothing to show for his pains except heavy losses during a disastrous retreat to Silesia. While he was planning the next round an event occurred which profoundly modified the European situation. On January 20, 1745, Charles VII died, and though his son succeeded as Elector of Bavaria, the highest post in the Empire was vacant for the second time in five years. The experiment of choosing an Emperor outside the Hapsburg dynasty, which had held it for three centuries, had completely failed. *"Et Cæsar et nihil,"* sneered the satirists as they contemplated the Wittelsbach puppet of Prussia and France.[1] His resources were so meager that he could only maintain himself with the aid of French and Prussian bayonets, and the Bavarian *intermezzo* proved that the holder of the highest post needed to be buttressed by the resources of a major state if it was to be more than a shadow on the wall. Frederick's letters to his ambassadors and allies are filled with lamentations and alarm. "Here is the Emperor dead," he wrote to Louis XV, "and the Queen of Hungary,

[1] At once Emperor and nobody.

26

through her majority in the Electoral College, already perceives the Imperial crown on her husband's head. I beg Your Majesty to tell me your views in this terrible crisis. The Emperor could not have died at a more unfortunate moment for all our interests and it upsets all our plans. Only Your Majesty can provide a remedy." Despite these flattering phrases the writer knew that, to quote his own famous aphorism, his best allies were his own troops. Bavaria bought peace with Austria by promising to support the candidature of Francis for the Imperial crown, and France, in deadly grapple with England, had proved a broken reed. Would it be possible to hold Silesia in the coming campaign?

The timid Podewils was so upset by the death of Charles VII that his master bade him pull himself together. "If all my resources, all my negotiations—in a word, all conjunctures—declare against me, I prefer honorable death to forfeiting my glory and my reputation. I have made it a point of honor to have contributed more than anyone else to the aggrandizement of my house, and I have played a distinguished part among the crowned heads of Europe. If I were Podewils I should share your feelings; but I have crossed the Rubicon, and I will either maintain my power or die with the very name of Prussia buried in my grave. Be calm and learn patience. If the enemy attacks we shall surely beat him; if not, we will all die fighting for the safety of the fatherland and the glory of my house. My mind is made up. What captain is such a coward that, when surrounded by the enemy and seeing no chance of succor or escape, he does not blow up his ship? Remember how the Queen of Hungary never despaired when her enemies stood before Vienna and her most flourishing provinces were invaded. And you lack the courage of this woman when we have not yet lost a battle or sustained a check and when a happy stroke can carry us higher than ever! Adieu, my dear Podewils. Fortify your courage, pass it on to others, and if misfortune comes, meet it with a stout heart. That is all that Cato and I have to say to you."

A few days later, on May 8, Frederick explained his attitude at greater length. "I believe you are surprised to see me so tranquil in the most violent crisis of my life. I reply that it has cost me a struggle to attain this self-control. The only way to keep the mental elasticity essential in such circumstances is to face all eventualities. Thank heaven I can deal calmly with all the great arrangements I have to make. That has not meant less suffering, but vigorous action is my only resource. I am not the master of events, but I will use all my wits, and if it comes to a fight, I shall spare myself as little as the meanest soldier. I admit that I am playing for high stakes and that if every conceivable misfortune breaks over my head I am lost. But there is no other course, and a battle is the emetic that in a few hours will decide the fate of the sick man." He was right: there was no way back. The seizure of Silesia had condemned him to a life of conflict with the house of Austria and any allies it could secure.

Sunshine broke through the dark clouds at last when Frederick routed the Austrians and Saxons at Hohenfriedberg in Silesia on June 4. "Passing triumphs do not puff me up," he reported to Podewils; "you need not fear I shall do anything rash. I gain time to develop my negotiations for an advantageous settlement. In a word, I only wage war to arrive at peace, and you may be sure I am too much of a philosopher to indulge my passions in matters of such importance involving the safety of the state. You have no idea of war, otherwise you could imagine the terror felt by our enemies. No one could believe it unless he saw it; we drive them before us everywhere. I think that we have softened the hard heart of Pharaoh and that he will now be in a more tractable mood." A second resounding victory was scored on September 30 at Soor in Bohemia, described by Frederick as the fiercest of the four battles he had fought. A third victory at Hennersdorf over Austrians and Saxons on November 24 was followed by the Old Dessauer's triumph over the Saxons at Kesselsdorf near Dresden on December 15. The year, which had opened in tears, had closed in joy. In the Second Silesian War, as in the first, the aggressor never knew defeat. His financial resources, on the other hand, were again exhausted, and he was no less anxious for the end than Maria Theresa. The second round of the Austro-Prussian boxing-match ended with the Treaty of Dresden, signed on Christmas Day 1745. For the second time Maria Theresa, with bitterness in her heart, consented to the loss of Silesia, and Frederick recognized her husband as Emperor Francis I after his election in September 1745. Once again, following the example of the new Elector of Bavaria, he left France in the lurch.

Prussia had gained the substance, Austria the shadow. The Silesian Wars created German dualism, but they also pointed the way to a distant escape. In Germany the younger state had passed its senior in the race, though the latter remained formidable elsewhere. Henceforth Prussia had no rival in the north, while Austria could find compensation for Silesia in no German land save Bavaria, which could be won only at the price of war. Both parties were aware that it was merely another truce. The light-hearted mood of 1740 was gone forever. "Henceforth," confessed Frederick, "I would not attack a cat except to defend myself. We have drawn upon ourselves the envy of Europe by the acquisition of Silesia, and it has put all our neighbors on the alert; there is not one who does not distrust us." One man could start a war, but one man, he discovered, could not keep the peace. The elaborate instructions for his new Minister to Vienna, drafted in May 1746, reveal his fears. "Since the sacrifice of Silesia must leave a lively resentment, Count Podewils (nephew of the Foreign Minister) must be on his guard and distrust, without showing it, all assurances to the contrary, merely replying that I sincerely desire good relations." His chief task would be to discover and report on trends of policy, the army, and the finances. These inquiries were all the more necessary since information had reached him from more than one quarter that the courts of Vienna and St. Petersburg were planning to despoil him of Silesia by an Austrian irruption from Bohemia and Moravia and a Russian attack on East Prussia. Knowing that Maria Theresa was impervious to either threats or blandishments, the envoy was charged to gain the confidence of the new Emperor. Frederick was not yet seriously alarmed, for Austria and France were still at war and were steadily exhausting their resources. Though in 1746 Austria and Russia signed a defensive treaty, and in 1747 England concluded a subsidy treaty with Russia, these potential threats came to nothing. If the Queen of Hungary, as he always called Maria Theresa, were to attack him she would quickly discover her mistake. When the long War of the Austrian Succession ended with the Treaty of Aix-la-Chapelle in 1748, Prussia's possession of Silesia was recognized by all the signatories: she alone of the many combatants, indeed, had profited substantially. Recognition, however, was a satisfaction to his pride rather than an addition to his security, and he realized that to keep the new province his kingdom must continue to be an armed camp. "In my state," he declared, "a lieutenant stands higher than a chamberlain." His watchword was *toujours en vedette.*[1]

Frederick had had his fill of battles. "I am happily cured of this passion; the intoxication is over." His First Political Testament, written for his brother and heir in 1752, indicated his conviction of Prussia's need for further aggrandizement in West Prussia, Swedish Pomerania, and Saxony; but such prizes, he hoped, might be secured without an appeal to arms. Meanwhile his hands were full at home. Julius Cæsar, declares Mommsen at the close of his superb panegyric, worked as no man had ever worked before. Frederick, we may add, surpassed every ruler of his century, perhaps of the modern world, by his many-sided activities. He admired the saying of Vespasian recorded by Suetonius, one of his favorite authors, that an Emperor should die standing. He felt he had no time to lose, for war might break out again and he did not expect to live longer than his father and grandfather, who had passed away in middle age. Now was the time to prove that his ideal of the ruler as the first servant of the state was no empty phrase.

The first task was to nurse Silesia back to life, to develop the resources of what had been and would be again the richest and most populous of his provinces. The Protestants had prayed for his victory. The resentment of the Catholics was partially assuaged by the recognition of equality of status between the Churches, not only there but in Berlin, where the building of the Hedwigskirche earned the thanks of Benedict XIV. Special attention was paid to the crown domains, which covered about a third of the whole country. While agriculture necessarily remained the main pillar of the state, the King realized the necessity of industry. The textile and silk enterprises of Silesia were encouraged, and a Royal Porcelain Factory was established in the capital on the model of Meissen. An orthodox mercantilist, like his contemporaries, he subordinated private interests to what he regarded as the needs of the community, and aimed at the maximum of economic self-sufficiency in view of the chronic danger of war. A state bank was founded. None of his activities attracted so much attention throughout Europe as the reform of justice

[1] Always on guard.

undertaken by Cocceji at his command. The task of codification in the Corpus Fredericianum, a blend of Roman and Germanic law, the first German code, was interrupted by the jurist's death in 1755, and much of the work had to be done over again in the evening of the reign by Carmer and Suarez. The most striking reforms were the raising of the standard of the judges, the acceleration of procedure, and the abolition of torture, though brutal punishments deemed necessary to maintain discipline in the army were retained. Extensive swamps on the middle Oder were drained and colonized by non-Prussian immigrants attracted by temporary exemption from taxation and military service.

Though diplomacy, the army, and finance were his primary concern, every department of the administration was controlled by the monarch.[1] He traveled all over his dominions, hearing complaints, making suggestions, measuring the progress achieved from year to year. The arts were not neglected. Sans Souci and the stately Opera House in Berlin were among the best of his many buildings. The Academy, founded by his grandfather under the auspices of Leibnitz and utterly neglected by his boorish father, was revived in a French setting with Maupertuis as president. Frederick, who found time for everything, wrote verses and dramas, histories and treatises, composed marches and played the flute. His happiest hours were spent in conversation with French intellectuals. In the words of Voltaire, it was Sparta in the morning, Athens in the afternoon. The Thirty Years' War had thrown back German culture by a century, and at this stage of his reign he can hardly be blamed for seeking to fill the void with the brightest spirits of France. The Augustan age of German literature was not yet in sight.

[1] How the most trifling personal matters, which in other countries were left to subordinates, came before him and were settled in a few pregnant sentences may be seen in a volume of selections from his autograph *Randbemerkungen*, edited by Georg Borchart.

BIBLIOGRAPHICAL NOTE

The fullest bibliography is in Dahlmann-Waitz: *Quellenkunde zur deutschen Geschichte*, ed. 1931. The latest short lists are in Gaxotte: *Frederick the Great*, and Berney: *Friedrich der Grosse*, Vol. I. The only up-to-date large-scale work covering the whole period is in Koser's monumental *Friedrich der Grosse*, 4 vols., one of the half-dozen masterpieces of recent German historical scholarship.

Carlyle's famous book is still worth reading as the testimony of a brilliant amateur. The most satisfactory short biographies are by W. F. Reddaway (1904), Georg Winter (1907), Norwood Young (1919), and Pierre Gaxotte (1936). Gerhard Ritter: *Friedrich der Grosse: Ein historisches Profil*, based on university lectures at Freiburg (1936), is a suggestive commentary. Of Berney: *Friedrich der Grosse* (1934), the most-ambitious biography since that of Koser, only the first volume, coming down to 1756, has appeared. Ranke's *Zwölf Bücher preussischer Geschichte*, which should be read in the edition of the Berlin Academy, and Droysen: *Geschichte der preussischen Politik*, are essential for foreign policy, but they stop in 1756. The best brief summary of Prussian history is in Sidney B. Fay: *The Rise of Brandenburg-Prussia to 1786* (1937). The best survey of the later years of the reign is in Reimann: *Neuere Geschichte des preussischen Staates*. The campaigns should be studied in *Die Kriege Friedrich des Grossen*, compiled by the Great General Staff; Bernhardi: *Friedrich der Grosse als Feldherr;* and Delbrück: *Geschichte der Kriegskunst*, Vol. IV. The *Œuvres de Frédéric le Grand* in thirty volumes were edited by Preuss, 1846–57. The *Politische Correspondenz*, which starts in 1740, is almost wholly concerned with foreign affairs; the forty-sixth volume reaches 1782. The three volumes of *Preussische Staatsschriften aus der Regierungszeit Friedrichs des Grossen*, edited by Koser and Krauske, covering 1740–56, contain valuable declarations and memoranda. Arneth: *Maria Theresa*, 10 vols., must be consulted for Austrian policy, which is excellently summarized by J. F. Bright in his biographies of Maria Theresa and Joseph II in the *Foreign Statesmen* series. French policy during the middle years of the reign of Louis XV may be studied in Bourgeois: *Manuel historique de politique étrangère*, Vol. I; Waddington: *Louis XV et le renversement des alliances;* Vandal: *Louis XV et Elisabeth de Russie;* and, above all, in the numerous monographs of the Duc de Broglie. The *Cambridge History of British Foreign Policy*, Vol. I; Basil Williams: *The Whig Supremacy 1714–60, Newcastle and Carteret*, and *Life of Chatham;* Sir Richard Lodge: *Studies in Eighteenth Century Diplomacy 1740–8*, and *Great Britain and Prussia in the Eighteenth Century;* Lord Ilchester and Mrs. Langford Brooke: *The Life of Sir Charles Hanbury-Williams*, and D. B. Horn: *Sir Charles Hanbury-Williams and European Diplomacy, 1747–58*, are indispensable for British policy. Kurd von Schlözer: *Friedrich der Grosse und Katharina die Zweite*, and Bain: *A Daughter of Peter the Great*, are useful for Russia. Albert Sorel's masterpiece, the first volume of *L'Europe et la Révolution Française*, is illuminating for many aspects of eighteenth-century politics.

Chapter II

THE SEVEN YEARS' WAR

FREDERICK's domestic labors during the decade of peace were combined with a watchful eye on the European situation. "A prince's neighbors are usually his enemies," he declared in *The General Principles of War,* written in 1748; "as such we must regard the Russians, the Saxons, and particularly the Austrians." That Maria Theresa would move heaven and earth to recover Silesia if she saw her chance he was well aware; he admired her character and courage and would have acted in the same way had the parts been reversed. In March 1749 he wrote to his sister the Crown Princess of Sweden that he expected the outbreak of war that year. "I shall probably be attacked at the same time as Sweden, judging by the preparations of the Russians and Austrians." The danger blew over, but the anxiety remained. "I do not say that the attack is near," he wrote to his brother and heir in 1753, "but I am certain it will come. If we have as many allies as enemies we shall be all right, thanks to our discipline and mobility."

In the middle fifties both Austria and Prussia were looking round for friends. The appointment in 1753 of Kaunitz, fresh from the Austrian Embassy in Paris, where he had cultivated the acquaintance of Mme de Pompadour, placed at the side of the Empress the cleverest diplomatist in Europe—perhaps the greatest diplomatist of the eighteenth century—who was destined to pilot the ship of state through stormy waters for forty years. As early as 1749, only a year after the end of the War of the Austrian Succession, he had warmly recommended a complete change of policy and he converted Maria Theresa to his views. The loss of Silesia, he argued, could not be forgotten, and Frederick was by far the most dangerous of her foes. Prussia must be cast down if the house of Hapsburg was to hold its own, and a powerful ally was needed for the task. France alone could render effective aid and must therefore if possible be transformed from an enemy into a friend. Since she required help against England, why should the historic feud last forever?

33

In his First Political Testament, composed in 1752, Frederick still assumed the permanent antagonism of Bourbons and Hapsburgs, but this was merely wishful thinking. The anti-Austrian party was no longer in unchallenged command at Versailles, where Mme de Pompadour, Choiseul, and the Abbé de Bernis were gaining the ear of Louis XV. The Franco-Prussian treaty of 1744 was due to expire in March 1756, and no ties of sentiment bound France to Frederick, who had twice left his ally in the lurch. If she were able to join forces with Austria, the whole political landscape would be transformed: Austria might then be able to defeat Prussia and France could stand up to England. Frederick had some idea of what was brewing, for, like other rulers, he had spies and agents everywhere. He had received information from a secretary of the Austrian Embassy at Berlin since 1747 and from a clerk in the Saxon Foreign Office at Dresden since 1753. Through the latter he obtained copies of the dispatches from Vienna and St. Petersburg and of Count Brühl's replies. Like Bismarck a century later, his sleep was troubled by "the nightmare of coalitions," for he was the possessor of stolen goods. The early admiration of the Tsarina Elizabeth for him had turned to hatred; and her defensive alliance with Austria, concluded in 1746, might easily develop into a fighting pact, for a secret article, of which Frederick learned in 1753, envisaged the recovery of Silesia.

The opening months of 1756 witnessed the regrouping of the powers—commonly known as *le renversement des alliances*—who had taken part in the War of the Austrian Succession.[1] In the Convention of Westminster, signed on January 16, Frederick secured the partnership of England by the promise to defend Hanover against a prospective French attack, a promise implicit in the formula of joint resistance to the entry of any foreign troops into Germany. To his great delight he had been approached in the previous autumn by George II, who, in view of the approaching struggle with France in India and Canada, was eager to safe-

[1] The *Politische Correspondenz* for 1756 must be supplemented by *Preussische Staatsschriften*, Vol. III. Frederick's decision to take the offensive is discussed by Max Lehmann: *Der Ursprung des siebenjährigen Krieges*, and in the rejoinders to which it gave rise. The fullest discussions of the whole complicated problem are in Waddington: *Louis XV et le renversement des alliances*, and in Ranke: *"Der Ursprung des siebenjährigen Krieges,"* in *Zur Geschichte von Österreich und Preussen 1748–1763*.

guard his beloved Electorate from possible enemies and to limit his military commitments on the Continent. He had concluded a treaty with Russia in September 1755, pledging her in return for subsidies to defend Hanover with 55,000 men against France or Prussia, the ally of France. But that was not enough to set his mind at rest: only a second insurance could remove his fears. Frederick was aware that this virtual declaration of independence would not be to the liking of the court of Versailles, but he advanced some plausible reasons for his new course. His convention with England, he wrote to his Ambassador in Paris, was in the general interest, for it was merely designed to keep Germany neutral in the event of hostilities elsewhere: France, though not consulted before nor during the negotiations, was fully informed. "I see no harm in what I have done," he wrote on February 3, 1756, "nor is there any good reason why I should have asked her consent. Now that my treaty with her is about to expire I must look round for allies. Though England was anxious for an alliance with me, my inclination is to France and I should like to renew my alliance with her, provided she treats me with consideration and avoids unjustifiable threats. Moreover, my convention with England is only a passing and precarious affair. Surely France will understand that I am thereby relieving her of 60,000 Russians and 60,000 Austrians. The time for an expedition against Hanover was last August. Today, even if there was no convention between myself and England, it is certain that an attack on Hanover would fail, owing to the King of England's vigorous measures in concert with his allies, and it would inevitably involve France in a general war. You will explain that I have in no way tied the hands of France as regards making war on land when it suits her, since, save for the stipulated neutrality of Germany, she can always fight in the Low Countries, which I have expressly excepted and where she can operate with most success. Finally, you must do your best to penetrate her real disposition and to discover whether the ministers conceal leaven in their heart even if they wear a friendly look."

Frederick's explanations failed to diminish what his Ambassador described as the consternation of the French Government, and his offer to renew the treaty of 1744 was ignored. He had seriously underestimated the resentment of France. Yet he was not alarmed, for his old conviction that Bourbons and Hapsburgs

35

could not co-operate remained unchanged, and he hoped that England's friendship would hold Russian hostility in check. "It is an axiom," he wrote on February 21, "that it will never be a French interest to foster the aggrandizement of the new house of Austria. We know the great efforts of Richelieu to diminish the power of the old house of Austria and what it cost France to succeed. Can one ever believe that a French minister would wish to commit such a glaring error against the most essential interests of his country? Weary as I am of all these disputes and reproaches about the most innocent affair, I leave it to them to choose their course; if it conflicts with my interests I shall not break my heart and I shall know how to parry their hostility." When the Ambassador recommended an autograph letter to Mme de Pompadour he replied that such a step could only be considered in the last resort. Moreover, the favorite was now working for a rapprochement with Austria, of which the indications from Vienna as well as from Paris were becoming too precise to be ignored. Frederick's convention with England was the chief but not the sole cause of the new orientation, which might have occurred in any case; but the lack of consideration he had displayed for the feelings of his old ally reinforced the influences at Versailles already working in that direction. England, it was increasingly realized, was now the most formidable rival, not Austria. In the middle of February Louis XV declared himself ready for some form of co-operation with Austria, and on May 1 the Treaty of Versailles, with its Secret Articles, created a defensive partnership. If France or Austria were attacked by any other power in the course of the Anglo-French conflict, help was to be afforded to the aggressed party. Austria had as little wish for a war with England as France for a war against Prussia, but circumstances might override such desires. The treaty was a triumph for Vienna, which had taken the initiative, since the resourceful Kaunitz could be trusted to provoke Frederick to action that would raise the *casus fœderis,* and in practice it is only a step from a defensive to an offensive alliance.

Another powerful ally for Austria was also in sight, for the personal hostility of the Empress Elizabeth, the daughter of Peter the Great, to the King of Prussia was unconcealed, and Russia was not less covetous than her neighbors. She had taken no part in the War of the Austrian Succession, but now it would make all the difference if she threw her sword into the scales. In reviewing Prussia's relations to her neighbors as he lay on his death-bed, Frederick William had warned his son that more was to be lost than gained from a war with Russia, a sentiment with which the Crown Prince fully agreed. But the Tsarina watched the emergence of Prussia as a great power with unfriendly eyes, and in 1746 she concluded a treaty with Austria for mutual defense. Frederick, indeed, was more alarmed by her preparations than by the Austro-French treaty, believing that only if she joined his foes would there be real danger of war; and his hope that her subsidy treaty with England would keep her out of the fray was waxing faint. Kaunitz had invited her in March to co-operate in an attack on Prussia and had received her ungrudging assent. He now urged her to wait till 1757, by which time he hoped to transform the French defensive partnership into full alliance; everything, he explained, depended on keeping the secret as long as possible. When big issues were at stake the Austrian statesman was never in a hurry to act.

Though Frederick never believed that France desired to attack him—for since England's declaration of war in May 1756, she had a world-wide colonial struggle on her hands—she had given herself to Austria and he rightly feared that she would be dragged along in her train. "Austria's plan, I know for certain," he wrote to his Ambassador in Paris on June 19, "is as follows. First to detach Russia from England and then to launch her against me. Next, the court of Vienna is making great preparations for attack. The plan, I believe, is to march a considerable army from Bohemia through Saxony, who may perhaps join up and invade my territories. Another corps would enter Upper Silesia, where a Russian army corps, now near Smolensk on the frontiers of Poland, would link up for an invasion of Silesia, while Russian troops stationed in Livonia and Kurland would invade [East] Prussia. I know too from various princes of the Empire that the court of Vienna only seeks a pretext to start hostilities and, failing to find one, will fall back on a war of religion against one or more Protestant princes."

A striking Memorandum in the King's hand, dated June 28 and composed for the British Government, surveyed the new European situation. The change, he explained, followed the Anglo-Prussian neutrality treaty. "They thought in France that

37

orders from Versailles would be blindly followed, and Prussia was blamed for not carrying fire and sword into the Electorate of Hanover. The late Franco-Prussian treaty was never an offensive alliance, and the neutrality convention to which France so strongly objects was an instrument for preserving Europe from a war in which only French and English were concerned for their colonial possessions. In their first fury the Versailles ministers resented my pretended disobedience to their orders; then they softened their tone, but they had already gone too far. The court of Vienna knew something of my negotiations and was angry to see its hopes disappointed. It had counted on Prussia attacking Hanover and on utilizing the opportunity with the aid of Russia to recover Silesia. That court has three objectives: to establish its despotism in the Empire, to ruin the Protestant party, and to recover Silesia. It regards the King of Prussia as the obstacle to its vast designs, believing that if it can be eliminated the rest will be easy. Accepting the highest bid, Russia will doubtless follow the counsels of the court of Vienna, and France will doubtless pay Russia the subsidies hitherto received from England. Such is the present European situation. The equilibrium is destroyed, both as regards the great powers and within the Empire. The evil is great but not without remedy." Turkey, Denmark, Holland, and several of the German princes, he believed, might be won over to the Anglo-Prussian side. "Germany is threatened with great calamities. Prussia is faced with war, but all these difficulties do not dismay her. Three things can restore the balance of Europe: the intimate union of two courts, new alliances, and courage."

That an attack on Austria would automatically bring France into the arena seemed to Frederick on the whole a lesser evil than to allow the Grand Alliance, which included Sweden, to complete its preparations for a simultaneous onslaught from north, south, east, and west in the spring of 1757. "The whole iniquitous plot stood clearly revealed," he wrote to Wilhelmina on July 22, and on July 23 he decided to get his blow in first. He had begun to mobilize in June. He had one foot in the stirrup, he confided to his sister, and the other would soon follow. "If we wait till all the princelets do us the justice to realize that we are not aggressors, it will be too late and we are lost." Pointing to a picture of Maria Theresa in his study, he remarked to the

38

British Ambassador: "That lady wants war and she shall soon have it." On July 26 he informed his Ambassador in Paris that it was inescapable. Since his subjects only numbered four millions in 1756, he had no itch for a struggle against three great powers, each of them with territory, population, and resources vastly superior to his own; but he was convinced that delay would make his prospects worse, and if he chanced to win he might hope to add Saxony and West Prussia to his dominions. Russia coveted East Prussia, Austria Silesia, the Swedes Prussian Pomerania, the Saxons Magdeburg and Halle, the French Wesel and Cleves. His allies were England, Brunswick, and Hesse-Cassel. When Podewils, the old Foreign Minister, again urged caution on the ground that a concerted attack was not an absolute certainty and that a Prussian offensive would be playing Vienna's game, his master sarcastically observed: *"Adieu! Monsieur de la timide politique"* ("Good-by, Mr. Timid Policy!") He had gambled successfully in 1740 and was ready to gamble again. The generals, with the exception of Winterfeldt, his favorite military adviser, were equally opposed to playing for such high stakes; and his brothers, deeply alarmed, were roughly informed that if they were afraid they could stay at home. Even the faithful Eichel confessed to Podewils, though not to his master, that he was worried.

The King, who had never lost a battle, was almost childishly confident. "If our enemies compel us to fight," he wrote to the Prince of Prussia on August 12, "we must ask not how many but where they are. We have nothing to fear. They run more risks, and according to the law of probabilities we shall escape from the trap with flying colors. Let the women at Berlin talk of treaties of partition; Prussian officers who have been through our wars know that neither numbers nor difficulties could rob us of victory. They are the same troops as in the last war, and the whole army has more experience of maneuver. If grave mistakes are avoided, it is morally impossible that we should fail. There, my dear brother, is a tonic which I hope will disperse the fogs that the politicians and the political women have spread in the capital." To the veteran Schwerin he wrote that they would have to meet many foes, but that he had no fears. He divided his army of 150,000 into four groups, one in Pomerania to watch the Swedes, the second on the Russian frontier, the third under Schwerin in Silesia, the fourth and largest under his direct command standing ready to enter Saxony. Even had he felt less sure of himself he could hardly have chosen a different course. The apprehensions of his critics were better founded than he was willing to confess, yet none of them explained how the danger could be averted by allowing the coalition to complete its preparations and choose the moment for attack. Before the Treaty of Westminster, France might conceivably have stood aloof, but after the Treaty of Versailles there was little chance of her drawing back.

Before unsheathing his sword Frederick requested Maria Theresa to explain the object of her military preparations. "For my security and that of my allies," was her reply to the Prussian Ambassador on July 26; "they are not aimed at anyone." Regarding this evasive formula as decisive, he proceeded to mobilize, but for the sake of appearances he knocked once again at the door. This time he was even more precise. He had learned new details of the Austro-Russian negotiations and understood that the opening of hostilities was postponed till the spring of 1757; would Austria promise not to attack him during 1756 and 1757? "We must know if we are at peace or at war. It is for the Empress to decide. If the reply is ambiguous, I call heaven to witness that I am innocent of all the misery that ensues." Her response, which reached Potsdam on August 25, ignored the question but denied the existence of an Austro-Russian offensive alliance. The statement was verbally correct, for the treaty, though agreed in principle, was not actually signed till January 1757. Now there was nothing to wait for. The answer, wrote Frederick to the Prince of Prussia on the following day, was impertinent and contemptuous. "Not a word about the assurances I asked for. So the sword alone can cut the Gordian knot. I am innocent of this war. I did what I could to prevent it, but however great one's love of peace, one must not sacrifice safety and honor." On September 2 a second attempt was made by the Prussian Ambassador to extract an answer to the question whether Maria Theresa would disavow any intention to attack in 1756 or 1757. On September 7 she replied that the invasion of Saxony had already taken place and that in view of such a palpable aggression she had nothing more to say. The conspiracy was formed, declares Frederick in his *History of the*

Seven Years' War, and his enemies were about to strike. What else could he do? There seemed no satisfactory answer to this question in 1756, for the ring was closing round him. Yet, whatever we may think of his decision to get his blow in first, his ultimate responsibility was beyond challenge. The Seven Years' War, like that of the Austrian Succession, was the direct outcome of the seizure of Silesia. The chickens of 1740 had come home to roost.

Before the armies clashed, Frederick issued a shrill indictment of Austria entitled *Exposé des motifs qui ont obligé sa Majesté le Roi de Prusse à prévenir les dessins de la Cour de Vienne,* which was circulated to his representatives abroad, was studied in many countries, and was welcomed with enthusiasm in an English translation.[1] Since the peace of Dresden in 1745, it began, the court of Vienna had sought every means of breaking it. "To impose servitude on the German princes, to establish despotism in the Empire, to abolish the Protestant religion, the laws, the government, and the immunities enjoyed by that republic of princes and sovereigns, the court of Vienna, after the Treaty of Aix-la-Chapelle, found in its path France, the guarantor of the Treaty of Westphalia, Prussia, who had every reason to resist such undertakings, and the Grand Turk, whose diversions in Hungary could wreck the best-laid plans. These were so many dikes which had to be successively sapped. It decided to begin with Prussia, believing that under the pretext of claiming a province ceded to the King by treaty, it would divert attention from more secret designs. For this purpose it concluded the Treaty of St. Petersburg. Not content with a defensive alliance, to which nobody would have objected, it schemed to embroil the courts of Berlin and St. Petersburg and to make a treaty with the Empress of Russia against the Ottoman Porte." These aims were attained, and the Treaty of Versailles was made with France. "In such a critical situation, when the court of Vienna was stirring up Europe from end to end in order to mobilize the enemies of the King, to calumniate his actions, to place evil interpretations on the most innocent matters, was striving to dazzle, seduce, or lull the powers for its own designs, when munitions and supplies were being collected in Moravia and Bohemia, when camps of 80,000 men were being formed, when peace resembled war though

[1] *Preussische Staatsschriften,* III, 172-81.

41

Prussian troops had not stirred, the King thought it time to break silence."

Frederick proceeded to recapitulate his two approaches to Maria Theresa and her replies. "We see by this proud and contemptuous rejoinder that the court of Vienna, far from desiring peace, breathes only war, and plans by chicanery and pride to goad the King to attack in order to have a pretext of claiming the assistance of its allies. But surely these allies cannot have promised aid in order to authorize unjust proceedings and to prevent the King from anticipating designs that are only too clear since, in refusing the assurances for which he asked, it proved its resolve to disturb the tranquillity hitherto enjoyed by Germany." A third approach had proved equally fruitless. "His Majesty flatters himself that, having tried everything that could be expected from his moderation, all Europe will do him justice and will be convinced that it is not the King but the court of Vienna that has willed the war."

The lengthy argument concluded with a defense of the invasion of Saxony. "It is true that the King begins hostilities; but since this term is often confused with aggression, and since the court of Vienna is always seeking to incriminate Prussia, the meaning must be explained. By aggression one understands any action opposed to the meaning of a treaty of peace. A league for offensive purposes, incitement to war against a third power, the plan of invading the territories of another prince, a sudden invasion: all these things are aggressions. Whoever anticipates them may commit hostilities, but he is not the aggressor. . . . Since the court of Vienna resolves to infringe treaties guaranteed by all the powers of Europe; since its ambition bursts the most sacred barriers against human cupidity; since it aims at tyrannizing over the German Empire; since its vast designs involve the overthrow of this republic of princes that it is the duty of the emperors to maintain, the King has decided to oppose the enemies of his country and to frustrate this odious project. His Majesty declares that the liberties of the Germanic body will only be buried in the same grave as Prussia. He calls heaven to witness that, having vainly tried to preserve his own country and all Germany from the scourge of war, he is forced to take up arms in order to destroy a conspiracy against his possessions and his crown. He only abandons his habitual moderation because it ceases to be a virtue when it is a question of defending his honor, his independence, his country, and his crown."

The bloodiest drama of the eighteenth century opened on August 28 with the invasion of Saxony, which, though nominally neutral, was in touch with the coalition and had the misfortune to form the gateway to Bohemia. When the King Elector expressed his painful surprise, Frederick replied that he had vainly attempted to extract a promise from Vienna not to attack him that year or next. "It is not cupidity nor ambition that dictates my course, but the protection I owe to my peoples and the necessity of averting plots that would become more dangerous from day to day if the sword did not cut the Gordian knot while there is still time." There was virtually no resistance from the little army which fell back towards the Bohemian frontier. Dresden was captured, and after a defeat of the Austrians at Lobositz, in northern Bohemia, on October 1, the Saxon troops capitulated in their entrenched camp at Pirna and were forced into the Prussian service. "I have not the slightest apprehension," wrote the victor on October 31. The winter was spent in Dresden, and in January 1757 he paid a short visit to Berlin for the first and last time during the Seven Years' War.

The advantage derived from the strategic initiative was quickly exhausted, and henceforth Frederick was fighting for his life. On January 10 he drew up the secret instruction that has thrilled his countrymen ever since. "If I am killed affairs must continue without the slightest alteration and without anyone noticing that they are in other hands. If I have the bad luck to be captured I forbid the smallest consideration for my person or the slightest attention to anything I may write in captivity." The sky was darkening, for the Convention of St. Petersburg, signed on January 22, 1757, bound Russia and Austria to provide 80,000 troops each and to fight till Prussia was destroyed and Silesia secured for Austria. "It being impossible for the peace of Europe to be assured," declared the Empresses, "unless the King of Prussia is deprived of the means of troubling it, Their Imperial Majesties will make every effort to do this service to humanity." In March French troops crossed the German frontier.

A costly Prussian victory in May outside Prague, in which the veteran Schwerin was killed, was followed in June by Daun's triumph at Kolin, which flung the King back into Saxony. Few observers, whether friends or foes, believed that he could hold out for any length of time after such a smashing defeat. France had now burned her boats, and the Second Treaty of Versailles, signed on May 1, 1757, promised 115,000 troops and large subsidies for the recovery of Silesia. With her eyes on East Prussia, Russia had abandoned neutrality; Sweden, despite her Hohenzollern Queen, was tempted by the promise of Prussian Pomerania; Austria's army and administration had become much more efficient; the Diet at Regensburg decided to form an army to deal with the disturber of the peace of the Empire; England's struggle with France in India and the New World diverted the larger part of her strength from the Continent, and she could not spare ships to defend the Prussian coast against Sweden and Russia. "With God's help," declared Kaunitz, the haughty architect of the Grand Alliance, "we will bring so many enemies against the insolent King of Prussia that he must succumb." Though his highly trained troops fought as valiantly as ever, in the words of Napoleon it was not the army that defended Prussia for seven years, it was Frederick the Great. The world watched the swaying struggle with bated breath, and the capital was occupied by both Russian and Austrian troops. The Swedes never fought a battle, but they needed watching in the north. Frederick's varying moods are vividly reflected in his voluminous correspondence with his Foreign Ministers, Prince Henry, d'Argens, and Lord Marshal Keith, in the reports of Sir Andrew Mitchell, and in the conversations with de Catt.

The disaster at Kolin, due to gross miscalculation on his part, shook Frederick to the depths. "Fortune has turned her back on me," he wrote to Keith. "I ought to have been prepared for it: she is a woman and I am not a gallant. Success often creates a dangerous confidence; we shall do better another time. The Great Elector would be much surprised to see his great-grandson at grips with the Russians, the Austrians, nearly the whole of Germany, and a hundred thousand auxiliaries. I am not sure whether it will be a disgrace for me to succumb, but I do know that there will be little glory in vanquishing me." To d'Argens he wrote more fully in the same strain. "My dear Marquis, you must regard me as a wall broken down by ill fortune for the last two years. I am assaulted from every side. Domestic trials, secret afflictions, public misfortunes, approaching calamities—

such is my daily bread. But do not imagine I am weakening. If everything collapses I should calmly bury myself beneath the ruins. In these disastrous times one must fortify oneself with iron resolutions and a heart of brass. It is a time for stoicism: the disciples of Epicurus would find nothing to say. Next month will be terrible and decisive for my poor country. I expect to save it or share its doom, and I have adjusted my mind to the situation. We can only compare it to the time of Marius, Sulla, the Trium-virate, and the fiercest scenes of civil war. You are too far away to visualize the crisis and the horrors that surround me. Think, I beg you, of the loss of my dear ones [his mother], and of the misfortunes bearing down on me. What remains to distinguish my plight from that of poor Job? My health, weak though it is, holds out, I know not how, against all these assaults, and I am astonished to keep going in circumstances I could not have con-templated three years ago without a shudder. Philosophy, my dear friend, is good to soften past or future evils, but it is not equal to the trials of the present."

A few months later the indomitable ruler snatched victory from the jaws of defeat. Despite the stricken field of Kolin, 1757 was the most glorious year in Prussian history between the Great Elector's triumph over the Swedes at Fehrbellin and the crown-ing mercy of Leipzig in 1813. The Duke of Cumberland had failed to hold Hanover and help was urgently needed in the west. The French and the army of the Empire, who were threatening Magdeburg, though superior in numbers, were routed at Ross-bach, to the west of Leipzig, on November 5, and gave Frederick little more trouble for the rest of the war; for a born soldier, Prince Ferdinand of Brunswick, brother of the Queen, who suc-ceeded the Duke of Cumberland in command of the Hanoverian army, kept them at bay. The discomfiture of the French made Frederick a popular hero—"the Protestant hero"—in England, where sign-boards entitled *The King of Prussia* adorned many a public-house. Here at any rate there was something to show for Pitt's subsidies. That George II continued to hate his famous nephew was of no importance. None of his victories was pur-chased at so trifling a cost and none was so welcome in Germany, but he was well aware how little it meant except in terms of prestige. "This year, my dear Marquis," he wrote to d'Argens on November 15, "has been terrible for me. I attempt the impossible to save the state, but in fact I need more than ever secondary causes for success. The affair of November 5 was very favorable. We captured eight French generals, 260 officers, and 6,000 men. We lost one Colonel, two other officers, and 67 soldiers; 223 were wounded. Never could I have hoped for such a result. For the moment our good Berliners need not fear a visit from the Austrians or Swedes, and my victory enables me to confront my other enemies. These terrible times and this war will surely mark an epoch in history." Before Rossbach he had written to the Duchess of Gotha: "Heaven grant that it will be for the deliverance and safety of Germany!" But this was a mere phrase, for half Germany was in arms against him. Prussia, not Germany, was graven on his heart.

A month after Rossbach, Frederick, racing back from the west, routed the Austrians on December 5 at Leuthen near Breslau, which they had captured, and drove them out of Silesia, which they had held for a few weeks. This double triumph, which made him the greatest celebrity in Europe, procured a breathing-space but nothing more, for the Russian hosts were slowly gathering in their might. For a brief moment even Maria Theresa had wavered, but Kaunitz stood firm. The victor, indeed, was well aware that the worst was still to come. "My divine Marquis," he wrote on December 13, "could you make up your mind to pass the winter with me in Silesia when things settle down? It would be an act of charity. I have no society and no help. We will banish all draughts and wrap you in cotton wool. Bring Mme d'Argens if you like. I await your answer as a criminal awaits sentence or pardon." The valetudinarian French man, whose sympathies in the war were with Frederick, overcame his dread of physical discomforts and accompanied his acceptance of the invitation with words of praise. If anything could puff him up, replied the King, it would be such letters. "But, my dear fellow, in my own mind I discount three fourths of the eulogy. All that you so eloquently exalt is only a little steadfastness and a good dose of luck. You will find me unchanged, and you must believe that these things which make such a splash at a distance are often quite petty at close quarters. There seems a good prospect of a general peace and no one desires it more than I. Meanwhile I shall devote my leisure to study in your company; that is unquestionably the best use of one's time. You will see a deluge of verses that have overflowed my campaign. Some are for you, and there are epigrams for all my enemies."

D'Argens arrived in January 1758, stayed till April, and found his host in tolerable spirits. "I am in for big adventures," wrote Frederick to Keith on February 7; "the kings, the emperors, and the journalists are all on my track, but I hope to defeat the whole lot. I await the event philosophically, knowing that anxiety is useless and that destiny or fortune decides." As the campaigning season approached, his tone becomes more somber. France quickly lost stomach for the fight, but the Empresses were implacable. "If everyone looked at things as philosophically as you and I," he wrote on March 20, "peace would have come long ago. But we are dealing with people cursed by God, for they are devoured by ambition. That is why I send them to all the devils." The payment of the British subsidy for 1758 was accompanied by the Declaration of London, making military and naval aid dependent on British needs in America, for even Pitt at the height of his influence had to consider public opinion. On the eve of his first encounter with the Russians, who had entered East Prussia in January and marched slowly west during the early summer, he made no attempt to conceal his anxiety. "Mine is a dog's job," he confided to Keith on July 28. "If the slightest thing goes wrong, I am lost. Have Masses said for the soul of your friend, who is in purgatory."

The Battle of Zorndorf, near Küstrin, in August 1758, was the fiercest he had ever fought, and it might well have been even worse than Kolin. "We were on the very brink of destruction," reported Sir Andrew Mitchell, who accompanied Frederick on his campaigns. "The Russians fought like devils. The King's firmness of mind saved all. Would to God I was out of this scene of horror and bloodshed!" Though reckoned as a Prussian victory, for the Russians withdrew from the battlefield, it was in reality a drawn game, for Frederick was too exhausted to pursue. The Russians, unlike the Prussians, had plenty of reserves, but, as he thankfully observed, they lacked a general. Throughout the Seven Years' War, in fact, he owed his survival more to the lack of co-ordination among his enemies than to his own daring

47

leadership and the valor of his troops. He was an object of hate to all Europe, he confessed to Keith, and he needed the patience of Job to bear up.

Frederick's anxieties were increased by an Austrian victory at Hochkirch in western Saxony in October, on the same day that his beloved Wilhelmina died. "Our campaign is finished," he added on November 23. "There is nothing to show on either side beyond the loss of many good fellows, the misfortune of many poor soldiers permanently maimed, the ruin of provinces, the pillaging and burning of flourishing towns. Such, my dear Lord, are the exploits that make humanity shudder, the sad results of the wickedness and ambition of certain powerful men who immolate everything to their uncontrolled passions." The light-hearted aggressor of 1740 was now suffering from persecution mania, but there was never a thought of compromise. "Beg for peace," he wrote on December 9, "and bend before enemies who have persecuted me in such a cruel and atrocious manner— that I will never do." He had some reason to complain of the Russians, for he had done them no harm, but Austria was merely paying off old scores. Happily for Frederick, France had never set her heart on the destruction of Prussia, and at this stage of the struggle she reduced her subsidy to Austria. Indeed, it required all the skill and authority of Kaunitz to counteract her growing desire for peace.

1759 opened under a frowning sky. "I have only my sword and my just cause," wrote the King on January 2. That was not strictly true, for Pitt and the Duke of Brunswick were doing their best; but they could render no direct help against the formidable Austrian and Russian hosts in the south and east, and the quality of his troops was deteriorating for lack of training. He lamented that he had lost all his most intimate friends. This, too, was an exaggeration. His affectionate letters to Keith and d'Argens reveal how much they meant to him, though no one could make up for Jordan, Keyserling, and Wilhelmina. "The campaign will start early this year," he wrote to d'Argens on March 1. "What my fate will be I cannot say. I shall do everything in my power to keep up and the enemy will have to pay dear if I succumb. The death of the King of Spain may make a difference of thirty to forty thousand men, but that is not enough to put me at my ease. Just think, I shall have three hundred thousand men on my hands, and only half that number to resist them. This war is frightful, it grows more barbarous and inhuman every day. This polished century is still very ferocious, or, to be more correct, man is an untamable animal when he gives rein to his passions. I spent the winter like a Carthusian monk. I dine alone, I pass my life in reading and writing, and I have no supper. In days of sadness it is too much of an effort always to conceal one's troubles, and it is better to suffer in solitude than to worry other people. My only comfort is my work, which dispels sinister thoughts while it lasts, but when it is done they reappear. Maupertuis was right; I am convinced that the sum of evils outweighs the blessings. Yet it is all the same to me, for I have little more to lose and my short remaining span of life no longer causes me much concern. Write to me more frequently. I recommend you to your bed, to your apothecary, to the protection of fortune, which decides everything in our sublunary sphere and which mocks at you and me, at politicians and generals, at sages and madmen alike." The next letter to d'Argens, of March 27, is in the same doleful strain. "Hundreds of thousands of men take no room on paper. But when one has to fight them, when they press upon you from every side, when there are ten equally dangerous projects that one must counter without possessing the means, rushing armies from one side of the world to the other, employing every conceivable stratagem to maintain oneself, one feels the full weight of the burden, and I confess that without some lucky accident there is no way out."

The long-expected blow fell on August 12, when a superior Russian and Austrian force routed the largest of the Prussian armies at Kunersdorf, near Frankfurt an der Oder. Two horses were shot under the King and a bullet flattened a snuffbox in his pocket. Half his army of 45,000 was left on the ground. "Save the royal family," he wrote to Finckenstein; "I have no more resources and, to tell the truth, I think all is lost. I shall not survive the ruin of my country. Adieu forever." As usual, he poured out his heart to d'Argens. "We have been unfortunate, my dear Marquis, but it is not my fault. Victory was ours, indeed it would have been complete, when our infantry lost courage and retired at the wrong moment. The Russian infantry is almost entirely destroyed. All the fragments I can collect amount to 32,000 men. I shall stand in their path and either

49

perish or save the capital. I am not a prophet. If I had more than one life I should be done with it, and I feel I may be allowed to think of myself. There are limits to everything. I fear misfortune without losing my courage. But I am quite determined, if it fails, to be no longer the sport of fortune." A week later the cry of distress is even shriller. "The torments of Tantalus, the pains of Prometheus, the punishment of Sisyphus are nothing to my sufferings of the last ten days. Death is sweet in comparison with such a life. Go to Tangermünde [on the Elbe], where you will be safe enough, and await events. I am hiding a lot of unpleasant things as I do not wish to worry you or anyone else. I could not advise you to leave these unfortunate countries if I had any hope." Never before or after was he in such a despairing mood, and the thought of his poison pills was often in his mind.

The worst was soon over. By what he called "the miracle of the house of Brandenburg," the Russians failed to follow up their victory by marching on Berlin, and Daun's caution at such a moment was less a virtue than a vice. The Russian and Austrian commanders had no love for each other and little notion of team-work. On September 4 the King wrote to d'Argens that he could now safely return to Berlin. "The crisis is past, but there will be plenty of bad moments before the close of the campaign. My martyrdom will last another two months, when snow and frost will bring it to an end." To the naïve suggestion that he should play for time and stick to defensive war, he replied that it was easier said than done. "I have so many enemies that I have no choice but to attack. I am here [Cottbus] in a triangle, with the Russians on the left, Daun on the right, the Swedes on my flank. I have only kept going by attacking whenever I can and by scoring little advantages, which add up. In this war I have been making my novitiate in stoicism; if it continues I believe I shall become more indifferent, more impassive, than Empedocles or Zeno himself." In his scanty leisure he compiled a careful study of the Swedish hero Charles XII, who had also known dark days. At last the longed-for winter arrived, and the hunted monarch began to breathe again. "Patience to the end of this infernal campaign!" he wrote to d'Argens on November 28. "This year I summon up all my philosophy; not a day passes that I am not obliged to have recourse to the impassivity of Zeno.

I confess it is a hard task if it goes on. Epicurus is the philosopher of humanity, Zeno of the gods, and I am a man. For four years I have been in purgatory; if there is another life, the Eternal Father ought to take account of what I have suffered here." The black year of Kunersdorf, relieved only by Ferdinand of Brunswick's rout of the French at Minden, ended in deepest gloom, for a considerable Prussian force was compelled to surrender without a fight to the Austrians at Maxen. "I am more than ever tired and disgusted with life. Accuse me of hypochondria and anything else you like; I admit it. But past evils, present evils, and, above all, the prospect are enough to disgust sufferers like myself of life. I groan in silence—that is all I can do." He knew that his generalship was sharply criticized, but he had too much pride as well as too much self-control to let either his subjects or his enemies know the agony of his heart.

1760 opened as inauspiciously as 1759. "Our situation is hard and cruel," he wrote on January 3. "I resist the torrent of misfortune as best I can, but despite philosophy I suffer no less. When I bid defiance to my personal misfortunes, those of the fatherland crowd upon me and shatter my constancy. So, dear Marquis, I have nothing cheerful to tell you. When I am oppressed by grief, I write verses to distract my thoughts and snatch a brief moment of security." The next letter, on January 15, continued in the minor key. "You are too kind to the verses I sent you. How could they be good? My soul is too unquiet, too oppressed, for my mind to produce anything worth while. This film of sadness is spread over all I write and do. Peace is only a possibility, a hope, a dream, nothing more. All I can do is to strive unceasingly against adversity, yet I can neither recapture fortune nor reduce the number of my enemies. Thus my situation is unchanged. One more reverse would be the *coup de grâce*. Truly life becomes quite insupportable when one has to drag along in grief and mortal anxiety; it ceases to be a blessing of heaven and becomes an object of horror resembling the most cruel vengeance of tyrants."

The campaign of 1760 opened later than usual. The danger from Russia seemed to recede, though her troops remained on the Oder: this year it was Austria's turn to call the tune. "We are on the march to Silesia," wrote Frederick to d'Argens on August 1. "If we are lucky, I will let you know; if not, I take my leave of you and everybody in advance. We shall probably fight between the 7th and the 10th." The Battle of Liegnitz was fought on the 15th, a victory, indeed, but, like all his previous triumphs in the Seven Years' War, deciding nothing. "This is not the end of the story," he reported; "we shall have to climb higher if we are to reach the top of the escarpment, which we must do to crown our work. I had my clothes damaged and my horses wounded. Hitherto I am invulnerable. Never have we confronted graver perils or suffered more enormous hardships. What will be the end of our labors? Have pity, my dear Marquis, on a poor philosopher who has strayed far from his sphere."

In reply to d'Argens's exuberant congratulations Frederick pointed out how comparatively little had been achieved. "At other times, my dear Marquis, the affair of August 15 would have decided the campaign; today this action is only a skirmish. To decide our fate a great battle is needed. We seem likely to get it soon and then will be the time to rejoice if we win. All the same, I am grateful for your congratulations. Many stratagems and much skill were needed to bring things so far. Don't talk to me about dangers. The last action only cost me a coat and a horse—a small price for victory. Never have I been in a tighter place than in this campaign. Believe me, miracles will be needed to overcome all the difficulties I foresee. Assuredly I shall do my part, but remember that I am not the master of fortune, and that I must allow for the chapter of accidents. I have to complete the labors of Hercules at an age when my strength is ebbing and infirmities are increasing, and, to be frank, when even hope, the sole consolation of the unfortunate, begins to fail. You know too little to judge of all the dangers that threaten the state. I know them, I hide them, I keep all my fears to myself, I tell the public only of my hopes and the little good news there is. If the stroke I am planning succeeds, it will be time to rejoice. Till then let us not flatter ourselves lest a new disappointment strike us down. My life is that of a military Carthusian. I have plenty of work; my leisure is devoted to letters, which are my consolation. I know not if I shall survive this war. If I do I am resolved to pass the rest of my days in retreat in the bosom of philosophy and friendship."

September found him in the same gloomy strain. The victory at Liegnitz, he explained, had left things as they were. "The crisis changes in form, but there is no decision, no indication of the end. I burn on a low fire. I am like a body in process of mutilation which loses a limb every day. Heaven help us! We need it sorely. You are always speaking of my person. You should know that it is not necessary that I should live, but only that I should do my duty and fight to save my country if it can be done. I have had plenty of small successes, and I am inclined to take as my device *Maximus in minimis et minimus in maximis.* You can't imagine our hardships. This campaign is the worst of all. Sometimes I do not know to which saint to appeal. But I bore you with this story of my anxieties. My gaiety and good humor are buried with those I loved. The end of my life is painful and sad. Do not, my dear Marquis, forget your old friend."

In October he was on the move and forecast the result of the remainder of the campaign. "We shall recover Leipzig, Wittenberg, Torgau, Meissen; but the enemy will keep Dresden and the mountains of Silesia, which will enable him to knock me out next year. Fortune, dear Marquis, sports with us frail mortals. Weary of her favors and her caprice, I am contemplating a situation when I shall have nothing to fear from men or the gods. I look on death with a stoic's eyes. I shall never see the moment that will compel me to make a disadvantageous peace; no persuasion, no eloquence, can drive me to dishonor. Either I shall be buried under the ruins of my country or, if that seems to the destiny that persecutes me too sweet a consolation, I shall know how to end my misfortunes when they become unbearable. After sacrificing my youth to my father, and my mature years to my country, I think I have the right to dispose of my old age. I repeat that never will I sign a humiliating peace. Brandenburg existed before I was born and will continue to exist when I am dead. At fifty there are so many reasons for despising life. The prospect before me is an old age of infirmity and sorrow, worries and regrets, ignominy and outrage. I have lost all my friends and dearest relatives, I have nothing to hope for. I see my enemies treating me with derision, and in their pride they are preparing to trample me underfoot."

The long-expected clash with the Austrians took place on November 3, 1760, at Torgau on the middle Elbe. The last major encounter of the whole war, in which three horses were shot under the King and a bullet knocked him down, is described in the finest of Carlyle's battle-pieces. He knew well enough that to be saved from annihilation once again did not mean winning the war. "We have just beaten the Austrians," he reported to d'Argens two days later; "both sides suffered prodigious losses. This victory will perhaps give us some rest during the winter, but that is all. Next year it will all start again. I had a contusion on the chest, a little pain but no danger, and I can pursue my usual course. I shall finish this campaign as well as I can; no more can be asked of me." A longer letter five days later from Meissen was equally somber. "I have pressed the Austrians back to the gates of Dresden, to their camp of last year, but I cannot dislodge them. If they stay there, I shall have to pass this winter like the last in narrow cantonments, and all the troops will be employed as a cordon to maintain our footing in Saxony. That is a sad prospect, little worthy of our immense efforts in this campaign. My only support is my philosophy. So you see, my dear Marquis, that I am not puffed up by my successes. My enemies crowd upon me—that is the real cause of so many reverses and misfortunes. We saved our reputation on November 3, but do not imagine that our enemies are sufficiently reduced to be compelled to make peace. In fact, the outlook is as black as if I were at the bottom of a tomb. Adieu, dear Marquis. Write to me sometimes, and do not forget a poor devil who curses his existence ten times a day and would like to be in a place whence no one returns with news." Comforting letters always provoked the reply that things looked better at a distance than on the spot. The King of Prussia, in a word, was as miserable as his enemies felt he deserved to be. Peace soundings in St. Petersburg before and after the campaign of 1760 had proved fruitless.

1761 was the least eventful phase of the Seven Years' War. During the usual winter pause Frederick read omnivorously in history and literature, constantly returning to his old Latin and French favorites. Neither the Austrians nor the Russians seemed in a hurry to try their luck again, but he could hardly believe that the summer would pass without terrible and perhaps fatal collisions. "This profound calm," he wrote to d'Argens on June 7, "may be the prelude to a violent tempest, probably at the end of the month. I am ready for everything, for good or evil fortune; sing a little hymn to this Fortune whose protection we need. The Queen of Hungary is set on war. It is hard to be always suffering, and I feel that vengeance can be a divine pleasure, as the Italians say; it is only a question of seizing the right moment. My philosophy receives such shocks that it sometimes gives way. A man would be canonized who, after suffering outrages such as mine, would have sufficient self-mastery to pardon his enemies without reservation. I confess that my feeble virtue cannot attain to this perfection, and that I shall die content if I can partially revenge myself for what I have suffered. It will be as my good angel, luck, or fortune decides. While awaiting the decree of fate I am tranquil and solitary; I think about the future; I read and occupy myself in silence."

The letters of 1761 are a trifle less gloomy, but he knew that only some lucky accident could save him. Meanwhile Europe was sinking ever deeper into the mire of war. "It is time for peace," he wrote to de Catt, "else famine and plague will avenge humanity for the plagues and tyrants, and will carry off aggressors and defenders, friends and enemies alike. God preserve us from such things, and have mercy on your soul and mine if we have a soul." Contrary to precedent and expectations, the campaigning season of 1761 passed without a pitched battle. He had survived, indeed, but there was not the slightest prospect of peace. He was hopelessly outnumbered and he could no longer be sure of England's subsidies. "The more I reflect on events," he confessed to Prince Henry on December 29, "the more I conclude how right were the Romans to consecrate a golden statue to Fortune and the emperors to place it on the altars of their domestic gods."

1762 opened with such dark clouds in the sky that the hunted King felt it necessary to be prepared for the worst, and a letter to Finckenstein of January 6, written in his own hand, contemplated the possibility of having to ask his enemies for terms. "I have explained to you the reasons that render all our military enterprises useless unless the situation changes and the Turks promise help. Since our miserable position no longer allows us to expect a recovery or even to hold out in the coming campaign, we must think of preserving for my nephew by negotiations whatever we can extort from my greedy enemies. So you should consider whether in such case you should approach England or whether you may have to address yourself to France, Vienna, or St. Petersburg. I suggest negotiation so that you do not deliver yourself bound hand and foot to the discretion of the enemy. All this needs careful reflection, for which you will have time before I hear from Constantinople. You may be sure that I should not write in this way if I saw any prospect of restoring the state on its old foundations. But physical and moral causes show me that this is impossible, and the only service I can now render to the state in my position of isolation without the Turks is to suggest this course." His intention was clear enough: if surrender was unavoidable it would have to be faced by his successor.

The lucky accident for which he had almost ceased to hope occurred on January 5, 1762, when his inveterate enemy the Empress Elizabeth passed away. Her health had been undermined by drink and immorality, and her death had been one of the possibilities of escape from the iron ring that he had always had in mind; but the chance of relief from that quarter coming in time seemed remote, for she was only in middle age. The news reached him at Breslau a fortnight later, and he parted from her with a vicious kick:

> *O passant; ci-gît Messaline,*
> *Du Russe et du Cosaque elle fut concubine,*
> *Et les épuisant tous elle quitte ces bords*
> *Pour chercher des amants dans l'empire des morts.*[1]

Her nephew and successor, Peter, the unloved and unloving husband of Catherine the Great, regarded him as his hero, promptly liberated all Prussian prisoners, and recalled his troops from Prussian territory. Frederick was aware of the sentiments of the new ruler, but he wondered whether other influences might not gain control. For the moment he confined himself to congratulations, and his letters breathe a note of cautious hope rather than exaltation. Not till January 31 did he let himself go. "I send you the good news," he wrote to Prince Henry, "that Tchernischev and his Russians are leaving for Poland. This time we have nothing more to fear from these folk. Thank heaven our flank is clear. Our troops watching Berlin are now at your disposal if required. This great event means that the Austrians

---

[1] *Ye passer-by: here Messalina lies,*
The concubine of Russian and Cossack.
She quits these climes now she has worn them out,
And seeks new lovers in the realm of death.

will look entirely to the French. The Swedes will inevitably follow the Russian lead. So all our troops in Pomerania and Mecklenburg will now be available. Thank heaven for this event, which promises even better results."

Frederick's letters to d'Argens and Keith pass straight from the minor to the major key. "You know that the Emperor of Russia is as favorable to our interests as the best citizen of Berlin," he wrote on February 11, "that we are about to make peace at once and perhaps an alliance, which relieves us of this infamous and devastating horde of savages and consequently of the Swedes. The Austrians, the circles, and your compatriots remain on our hands. That is more than enough, and you will understand that we need the good news of a diversion to free us from this accumulation of dangerous enemies. I shall know about this at the end of the month. If that happens, though I am neither an astrologer nor a prophet, I anticipate peace at the opening of next year. That is the object of my wishes; but I desire this peace to be honorable and conformable to the dignity of the state and to our efforts. You can now write off the Russians and the Swedes." Five days later he supplied a little more information. "We have just learned that the Messalina of the North is dead and that her successor is well disposed towards us. We know nothing more. It looks as if this will lead to a separate peace between us and Russia, but not to a general peace. The Austrians will fight till they have spent their last halfpenny. I have not asked Vienna for peace. Our situation is improved, but we have not got so far as you imagine. The war continues and we still have two formidable powers on our hands. Yet, as two are less than three and four, our situation becomes fifty per cent more tolerable."

Autograph letters to the new ruler overflowed with gratitude. "Conduct so noble and so uncommon in our century may be expected to receive admiration, as is happening to Your Majesty. The first measures of his reign win him the benedictions of all his subjects and of the soundest part of Europe. May it be long and fortunate." An armistice was concluded in March and the Tsar invited the King to draft a project of peace. Frederick's reply was brief but to the point. "As the Emperor has declared in his declaration of February 12 that he renounced his conquests in the war and was resolved to restore my ancient possessions,

57

I have nothing to add to this generous proposition except to ally myself as closely as possible with a prince who thinks so nobly and magnanimously." Never before had Frederick written such grovelling letters to any human being. "Your Majesty surpasses my expectation and comes to my aid when the whole universe abandons me. He asks for a project of peace and I comply. But I confide myself to a friend. Let him decide as he will. I sign everything. His interests are mine and I know no others. Nature has given me a feeling and grateful heart, and I am touched by all Your Majesty has done for me. Let him regard me as his ally. I cannot help telling Your Majesty that he gives an example of virtue to all sovereigns which should win him the heart of all honest men. Let him tell me how I can please him and he may rest assured that I will meet him in every possible way." When peace was signed on May 5, Frederick ordered *Te Deums* and fetes in his army. He had every reason to rejoice, for the Tsar promised him the assistance of a token force of 18,000 men against the Austrians. "The King of Prussia," reported the Saxon Minister in St. Petersburg regretfully, "is the Emperor of Russia."

"If I were a pagan," wrote Frederick ecstatically to his bene-factor on May 21, the day after receiving the news, "I should have erected a temple and altars to Your Imperial Majesty as to a divine being who gives to the world examples of virtue from which all rulers should learn. I thanked heaven on the arrival of your letter and the treaty of peace, the symbol of your virtues and disinterestedness, the nobility of your sentiments, and many other admirable qualities that make you an object of adoration to all who have the happiness to know you. You have a multitude of subjects who are or ought to be attached to you, but I venture to say none so sincerely and inviolably as myself. You may reckon my heart among your first conquests, and there is noth-ing finer for sovereigns than to acquire an empire through their virtue alone. Today we shall all celebrate that happy day. My officers all say Long live our dear Emperor!"

The conclusion of peace with Sweden on May 22 raised the King's spirits still higher. "So our tribulations are ceasing," he wrote to d'Argens, "and the fickle goddess who grants and with-holds her favors according to her caprice seems to be making it up with us. All these things lead me to count on peace at the

58

end of the year and after that on Sans Souci with the dear Marquis. A gentle calm is reborn in my soul, and feelings of hope unknown for six years console me for past trials. Compare my situation next month with that of last December. Then the state was on its death-bed; we were awaiting extreme unction before drawing the last breath. Now I am freed from two enemies, and my army will be encased between twenty thousand Russians on my right and two hundred thousand Turks on my left, of whom twenty-six thousand Tartars are at my disposition. That makes two Emperors as my acolytes, with whose aid I shall say a Mass in the presence of the Queen of Hungary and shall make her sing the *De profundis.* That is only joking, for in my heart of hearts I say with the sage: Vanity of vanities, all is vanity! Political follies, follies of ambition, follies of interest—such things ought not to afflict creatures so transient as ourselves. But prejudices and illusions govern the world, and though we all know that our life is a brief pilgrimage, a core of ambition remains in our soul that makes us susceptible to glory. Naturally the news and the prospect of prosperity give me pleasure. I am not surprised that our good Berliners are delighted; they are not less interested in peace than myself."

On June 19 Frederick wrote hopefully to d'Argens of the coming campaign: "The Russians will join us on the 30th, and their arrival will end our inaction. Then I shall embark on big adventures and take my chance. Now for the seventh act of this tragedy! The piece is too long; the Emperor of Russia starts the game and I must try to finish it as best I can. I have a multitude of arrangements to make; everything must be planned and foreseen as far as possible. Add the lively negotiations and you will visualize the cares, embarrassments, and labor it involves and the weight of the burden on my poor shoulders. So, my dear Marquis, we are on the eve of events that will decide this campaign and the issue of the war. We must await them patiently since only the smallest part of what happens depends on ourselves." D'Argens had written that all speculations on the future were mere frivolity. "Who knows that better than I," replied the King, "who have been buffeted for six years by all the political tempests of Europe, always on the verge of shipwreck, hitherto preserved as if by miracle, yet always confronted by fresh dangers? What happened in Russia could not be foreseen by Count Kaunitz; what happened in England, the worst feature of which you do not know, did not enter into my calcula-- tions. All this shows that to govern states in troubled times is to play a dupe's part. That is what above all disgusts me with this thankless and unfruitful task, and brings me back more than ever to the love of letters, which one can cultivate in silence and in the bosom of peace. A man of letters works on a firm foundation while a politician has scarcely anything to go on." The *volte-face* in Russia was all the more welcome because in England there was a new King, a new Minister, and a new policy. With the retirement of Pitt, the British subsidy was likely to be cut off, for Bute was bent on peace with France. Though the approaching defection of England was of far less military significance than the transformation of the Russian foe into a friend, Frederick never forgave what he regarded as the desertion of his ally.

The dethronement of the Tsar Peter on July 9, 1762, quickly followed by his assassination, changed the situation once again. The news of the downfall of his best friend reached Frederick on July 19. "You can imagine my cruel embarrassment," he wrote to Prince Henry. Catherine was now in command and he hastened to salute the rising sun. Without a moment's delay he wrote to wish her prosperity, to thank her for her prompt assurance that she would confirm the peace made by her husband, and to ask for the continuation of her friendship. It was comforting to learn that Russia would not re-enter the fray, but a change of temperature at St. Petersburg was indicated by the withdrawal of the troops recently sent to his assistance. The palace revolution confirmed his profound conviction that chance ruled the affairs of men. Fortune, as he knew from long experience, could smile one moment and frown the next. "Our affairs, my dear Marquis," he wrote on July 21, "were beginning to go nicely when suddenly I am confronted by one of those political events which one can neither foresee nor prevent. The peace I made with Russia will continue, but the alliance is gone. All the troops are returning to Russia and I am left alone. However, we have knocked out two detachments of Austrians. We must see if that will lead up to something solid. I doubt it, and now I am again in an uncomfortable, difficult, and delicate situation. I am fortune's spinning-top and she mocks me. Today we took a thousand men and fourteen cannons. That decides nothing, and anything short of a decision merely increases my embarrassment. I imagine plenty of things are going wrong in Berlin and elsewhere. But what would you like me to tell you? Destiny, which directs everything, is stronger than I, and I have to obey. I am worried and greatly embarrassed, but what can I do? Patience! If I wrote you a foolish letter today, put it down to politics. I am so sick of it that, if I can once get out of this unfortunate war, I think I shall renounce the world." He had expected the revolution in Russia, he added, and had warned the Emperor, who resented the advice to take precautions. His misfortune arose from the attempt to take some of the property of the clergy; the priests engineered the plot. "This prince, possessing all the qualities of heart one could desire, had too little prudence, of which much is needed to govern that nation."

With Russia and Sweden out of the war and France having little stomach for the fight, Austria alone remained to be seriously considered. The summer passed without any major clashes, but the goal seemed as distant as ever. "You talk of peace between the English and the French," wrote Frederick to d'Argens on August 23. "I do not believe it has got as far as the journalists suggest, and I think their doings may be regarded by you and our good Berliners with comparative indifference. A general peace is greatly to be desired, but it must also be good, advantageous, and solid. I can only say that all Europe desires it, but when one has to deal with female devils one finds more caprice, illusions, and animosity than reason. Meanwhile I am growing gray and I begin to believe I shall be dead before peace is made." The capture in October of the fortress of Schweidnitz after a long siege broke Austria's hold on Silesia, and at the close of the same month Prince Henry routed the combined Austrian and Empire army at Freiberg in Saxony, the last battle of the war. The military operations, wrote the King on November 7, had gone well, but he could not say the same of politics. "These two crutches, which ought to help me to walk, never match, and make me lame on one side or the other."

A letter of November 7 to Princess Amelia is half serious, half gay: "I know your interest in our happy successes and my brother's victory. It came just at the right time when we must try to force our enemies to an honorable and reasonable peace. You who have access to heaven (as Abbess of Quedlinburg) may know how your stepfather favors or chastises us. I, poor mortal who does not know even a dog in paradise, am in complete ignorance, accepting good fortune with pleasure and bad with resignation. But allow a poor outsider to indicate some difficulties at the core of your sublime doctrine. The pagans represented Fortune as blind because as a rule she is unjust. She was reputed capricious and inconstant because that is what she is. So, if you substitute Providence for Fortune, you must also charge it with the petty insults launched by the pagans, which, as I see it, is blasphemy. So I, who have a very deep respect for the divine essence, refrain from attributing to it conduct that would be thought unjust, fickle, and blameworthy in the least of mortals. For this reason, my dear sister, I prefer not to believe that a good and omnipotent Being intervenes in the petty affairs of mankind. I attribute all that happens to created beings to the necessary results of secondary causes, and I bow in silence before this adorable Being, confessing my ignorance of his ways which it has not pleased his divine wisdom to reveal to me. Adieu, dear spouse of Jesus Christ. Even should you not find me orthodox, at any rate do not send me to the stake."

Frederick's letters to the Duchess of Gotha, aunt of George III, during December are filled with wrathful complaints of the conduct of Bute. "The English have betrayed me. Poor Mr. Mitchell has had a stroke. It is a terrible affair. The treaty stipulated that neither peace nor truce should be made without consent of the allies and contained a solemn reciprocal guarantee of all our possessions. I am the only one of England's allies whose interests she sacrifices. Bute is even negotiating on all sides to stir up enemies against me and to drive me to a humiliating peace. You could not tell such unpleasant truths to the Princess of Wales without hurting her, so you had better not mention them, all the more because the interests of Germany and the Protestant religion are arguments that mean nothing to the accursed Bute. He has even enunciated the principle that England should always sacrifice her allies to national interests. After that, madam, what more is to be said except that, in renouncing the sentiments of honor and good faith, a traitor can commit perfidies without a blush? I shall wait patiently till the English Ministry comes to itself and realizes the full shame of its conduct, which ought to happen when the first hectic desire for peace wears off. Perhaps we may have peace this winter. The circles [of the Empire] wish to withdraw their troops—the Bishop of Bamberg, the Elector of Bavaria, the Elector of Mainz—and the others will doubtless follow suit. The brands must be snatched from the conflagration and then perhaps the fire will go out. The Austrians will remain the last champions in the arena, as has been the case in all the wars: perhaps it will result in their getting a worse peace. Well, madam, we must hope that, like everything else, this accursed war will have an end."

At the close of 1762 the sky at last began to clear. If Austria could not destroy, "the wicked man" with the aid of France and Russia, how could she expect to conquer when she stood alone? Even Maria Theresa had no answer to give. Discussions began at Hubertusburg, a hunting lodge of the Elector of Saxony close to the Prussian frontier and within easy reach of Leipzig, where Frederick was spending the winter. Here is the summary of his instructions as noted down on December 28, 1762 by Hertzberg, the last and greatest of his foreign ministers, who was in charge of the negotiations.

"I. I must give the strongest assurances of the pacific intentions of the King.

"II. I must listen to the Austrian Minister's proposals and take them *ad referendum*. If he finds it difficult to make a start, I may declare that the King merely asks for the restoration of the *status quo ante*.

"III. I must utterly reject any proposal for cessions, especially Glatz, pointing out that the King has more right to compensation than his enemies, though he makes no such claim.

"IV. In emphasizing the King's losses I must not speak of the Russians, but of his enemies in general.

"V. The King is not disinclined to favor the views of the court of Vienna in regard to the election of the Archduke as King of the Romans, and those of Saxony in regard to the vacant bishoprics, but these suggestions I must hold in reserve.

"VI. I must not hurry the negotiations, so that the King need not evacuate Saxony before the end of February."

Since both sides accepted the return to the frontiers of 1756, there was little to discuss beyond details. "We are on the point of making peace," wrote Frederick to Keith from Leipzig on January 28, 1763. "Negotiations are proceeding vigorously. I have no wish to be either dupe or rascal, and I hope to make the best peace possible under the circumstances. There are plenty of worries, but that is better than the opening of a new campaign. I am only too happy, after seven acts, to reach the end of a bad piece in which I have been an unwilling actor. Here is a denouement which no one could have anticipated a year ago. I think that we shall sign peace next month and that this great affair will end happily. Imagine a man at sea who has long been buffeted by the tempest and at last sights land. This is precisely my case. I rejoice so much at this happy prospect that sometimes I doubt its reality, but thank heaven there is nothing to fear. I hope to be home in April, and may destiny never make me leave it again for a similar reason. So, my dear Mylord, the great danger is averted, and repose, which everyone so greatly needs, is on the point of being restored all over Europe. I know you will share my joy."

The Seven Years' War was terminated, so far as Prussia was concerned, by the treaty signed at Hubertusburg on February 15, 1763, five days after England, France, and Spain had concluded the Peace of Paris. Though the main burden of the discussions was borne by Hertzberg, the King was saluted by the British Ambassador as the greatest negotiator who ever lived. The compliment was excessive, for the terms merely reflected the military stalemate. He withdrew from Saxony, which he had hoped to retain in whole or in part, and after three costly struggles Austria made no further armed attempt to recover Silesia. Though in a military sense it was a drawn war, Frederick emerged as the victor since he retained the fair province that had been the cause of the struggle. Despite the widespread devastation and loss of life, Prussia counted for more in the eyes of Europe in February 1763 than on the summer day in 1756 when he struck the first daring blow at the coalition that had vowed his destruction.

When congratulated on the peace—"the happiest day of your life"—the King acidly replied that the happiest day in his life was the last. Gray, bent, and prematurely aged at fifty-one, with a permanently damaged digestion, he remarked that his proper place was in a home for elderly invalids. Though he felt deep satisfaction that he and his country had emerged from the valley of the shadow of death, he had suffered too much to rejoice like the rest. "We have had letters from Vienna," he wrote to d'Argens on February 20, "saying that the Empress thought of embracing the messenger. The ratifications will arrive tomorrow or the day after. What really matters in all this, my dear Marquis, is not myself, but the peace. It is quite right that the good citizens and the public should rejoice. For myself, poor old fellow, I return to a city where I shall know only the walls, where I shall find none of my acquaintances, where an immense task awaits me, where I shall before long leave my bones in a place of refuge troubled by neither war, nor calamities, nor the villainy of man." A month later he was back in Berlin, a sadder if not a wiser man. "I am a stranger here," he confided to his sister, the Queen of Sweden. "These seven years of war have changed the whole city. I know few people and, except for the buildings, I should feel as strange here as in London."

Chapter III

CATHERINE THE GREAT AND
JOSEPH II

Twenty-three years of the reign were over and an equal number lay ahead.[1] The King quickly recovered his resilience, and his passion for work was undimmed. He had had an alarming stroke at the age of thirty-five, but the trouble never recurred. He had emerged as the man of the century and was now often spoken of as Frederick the Great. In Goethe's striking phrase, he was the pole-star round which Prussia, Germany, and all the world seemed to revolve. Though there was no sunshine in his heart, for he compared the devastation of his country to that of the Thirty Years' War, he dedicated his later years to healing the wounds that his youthful ambition had caused. When his doctor ordered the old man of sixty-nine to cancel a journey of inspection, he received the reply: "You have your duties and I have mine, and I will carry them out to the last breath." The erection of the sumptuous Neues Palais near Potsdam was undertaken, primarily, to provide work for artists and artisans, but also as a demonstration that the Prussian tree was still full of sap: in his own phrase it was a piece of bravado. There was no court in the ordinary sense of the term, and his household expenses were small and strictly controlled. His only extravagance was his collection of jeweled snuffboxes.

The work of reconstruction, unspectacular as it was in comparison with the drums and trumpets of the first two decades of the reign, ranks high among the qualifications for the title of Frederick the Great. The army was maintained in full numbers and efficiency; the finances were quickly established, for there were no loans to be repaid; the debased currency was called in; population and revenue steadily increased; seed corn was supplied where needed, and cavalry horses were transferred to the farms. The journeys of inspection were resumed, and every village could bring forward suggestions and complaints. The ruler

[1] The fullest account of the years 1763–86 is in Reimann: *Neuere Geschichte des preussischen Staates*, 2 vols. Preuss: *Graf von Hertzberg*, is also useful.

proudly described himself as *le roi des gueux* and *l'avocat du pauvre*.[1] The Prussian bureaucracy was the most efficient in Europe. Educational standards in schools were raised with the aid of Zedlitz, an official after his own heart.[2] The idea of hiding anything from the ruler rarely occurred to servants of the state, for Frederick, like his father, was a stern master and had his eye on them all. On the other hand, his measures, though always well intentioned, were not invariably wise, and his narrow mercantilism strangled business initiative. The French system of farming out the indirect taxes, inaugurated in 1766, led to a great deal of smuggling, failed to produce the expected yield, and aroused such hatred that the *Régie* and the French excisemen, who could search houses at any time for untaxed coffee and tobacco, disappeared directly he was in the grave. His political ideology was unaffected by the long struggle in arms, and the system of social stratification was rigidly preserved. The bourgeois soldiers promoted *faute de mieux* in the Seven Years' War were soon weeded out. It was the task of the nobility to supply officers; of the peasantry to grow food and provide soldiers; of the bourgeoisie to engage in industry, commerce, and the civil service. That the people might desire and deserve a share in the responsibilities of government, local or national, was beyond his vision. Regarding his high office as a trust, he felt able to fulfill its duties without their aid. To use a modern phrase, it was a one-man show, and his subjects, lacking political training, were content to have it so. He was at once the absolute master and the first servant of the state. No one spoke or dreamed of self-determination till the tocsin rang out from Paris in 1789. In Prussia, to use Sorel's language, the King could count on the *noblesse* instead of having to reckon with it; and the other classes did not count at all.

The cornerstone of Frederick's foreign policy in the second half of the reign was co-operation with Russia, designed to avert the deadly peril of another three-power coalition.[3] He had no alternative, for France and Austria were hostile and he stood alone. "The English deserted us," he explained to Prince Henry

---

[1] King of the beggars and poor man's lawyer.
[2] See *"Friedrich der Grosse und die preussischen Universitäten,"* in Koser: *Zur preussischen und deutschen Geschichte.*
[3] Kurd von Schlözer: *Friedrich der Grosse und Katharina die Zweite,* provides a useful summary of Prusso-Russian relations, 1740–72.

in 1770, "and after Hubertusburg we needed several years of solid peace to restore the ruined provinces. The Russian alliance provided this advantage." Peter, whose change of front had saved him in 1762, was gone, and Catherine had never shared his enthusiasm for Prussia and her warrior King. There was no longer anything German about her except her blood: Russia was her home, Russia the instrument of her boundless ambitions. Yet to her people she was at this stage still the foreigner, surrounded and supported by the murderers of her husband, and the dispatches of the resident diplomatists emphasized the insecurity of her position. In four to six years, wrote the Prussian Ambassador, her son the Grand Duke Paul would assume control. Her best chance of keeping her power lay, it seemed, in resuming the expansionist policy of Peter the Great and winning military triumphs abroad. For this purpose careful preparation of the ground was needed.

The Prussian alliance concluded by the Tsar in June 1762 was not ratified by his widow, but she was quite ready to negotiate a new treaty on more favorable terms, for there was clearly more to be gained from the friendship than from the enmity of Frederick. Prussia, unlike Austria, had no ambitions in Turkey, at whose expense Catherine hoped to enlarge her dominions. Moreover, Prussia might be useful in furthering her schemes in Poland, which she was eager to bring within her sphere of influence, and it was therefore essential to veto a third Saxon king. Augustus III, an indolent mediocrity, was an elderly man and it was time to think of a successor. A letter from Frederick, written on the very day of the signing of the Treaty of Hubertusburg and forwarding a copy of the document, inaugurated the exchange of ideas which was to lead to an alliance in the following year. "The King of Poland is ill and I hear from Warsaw that he is not expected to live long. If he dies unexpectedly there is a danger that the intrigues of the different courts may rekindle the fires of war so recently extinguished. I am ready, madame, to consider any steps you may propose, and to save time I will explain my own attitude. Of all the pretenders to the Polish throne it is only princes of the house of Austria whom sound policy compels me to veto, and I imagine that the interests of Russia point in the same direction. I may add that a Piast [Polish nobleman] would suit both of us best. Profound secrecy will be

68

necessary to prevent intrigues among those to whom such a solution would be unwelcome."

Catherine's rejoinder was encouraging. "In the event of a vacancy I would gladly consent to the exclusion of any Austrian prince provided that Your Majesty will reject any candidate sponsored by France. I quite agree in preferring a Piast, but not someone on the brink of the tomb or in the pay of any power. If you approve this arrangement, please prevent Saxon troops from entering Poland." Frederick hailed the young Empress as the arbiter of the Continent. "I am delighted at the interest of Your Majesty in the recent treaty of peace. No one is more anxious that it should endure than myself. My age, the well-being of the state, the good of my family, demand it, and I am convinced that it depends on you alone to sustain it. You are in a position, by consenting to a treaty, to remove all the seeds of discord which might become new germs of war and trouble. I agree with all your ideas about Poland. I will not support the candidate of France and I will bar the entry of Saxon troops." On receiving word from Catherine that she would be glad to know his suggestions for a treaty, he proposed a defensive alliance, containing a mutual guarantee of territories and stipulating the number of troops to be supplied in case either party should be attacked. She might not care to furnish them if his dominions in the Rhineland were menaced, and in that case there would be no obligation for him to supply troops against Persians and Tartars: in such emergencies help should be rendered in the form of subsidies. A clause relating to commerce would also be advantageous to both parties. Secrets were difficult to keep, and on September 8 Frederick informed the Empress that anxiety about her Polish plans was felt in Vienna, Saxony, and Poland itself. Here was a fresh argument against delay. "You will make a king without war, madame. But the alliances that these people might conclude should be counterworked in order to prevent measures that would impede the execution of your designs."

Little progress had been made in the discussions when the death of Augustus III, on October 5, 1763, gave Frederick his chance. Neither ruler wanted a third Saxon king, which would virtually turn Poland not only into a hereditary monarchy but into a permanent Saxon dependency. If Catherine were to send troops into Poland and to notify the new Elector of Saxony that he must not aspire to the Polish crown, Europe would doubtless be spared a new war. Her candidate, Stanislas Augustus Poniatowski, a member of the great Czartoryski clan and one of her earliest discarded lovers, was warmly approved by the King, and the opportunity was seized to remind his correspondent of his desire for an alliance. "I could not avoid the last war, for a conspiracy against me had long been planned: policy, reason, and good sense pointed to preventive action in order to avert destruction in the following year. My country suffered most in the war, and I need time and tranquillity to restore it. Moreover, my years warn me that I have not long to live and I shall not employ the end of my career in vast projects. Those times are over, and I desire to go to the tomb without anxieties or hostilities so as to bequeath to my successors a happy country and an assured situation. For this purpose I desire alliances. There, madame, is the whole of my policy, and you will see that my sentiments coincide with yours. I feel sure that your choice will meet with little or no opposition in Poland, and that the court of Saxony, knowing your intentions, will not try for the throne. In any case, the Saxon army of 12,000 men is too weak to act, and if necessary I would refuse it passage through Silesia. I hope, madame, to convince you by my actions of the sincerity of my intentions. I leave it to you to fix the time for the alliance, and shall wait patiently for the moment that suits you best to finish this affair."

Going cap in hand to Catherine, begging for an alliance, supporting the candidature of her old lover, and assuring her that he would make no trouble in the world was a new role for the King of Prussia, and his subservience is the measure of his need. The bitter memories of the Seven Years' War were ever with him. Austria, he knew, was irreconcilable and France was her ally, but if Catherine were a friend no great harm could come to Prussia. A Russian alliance, on the other hand, would not be an unmixed blessing, for an Austro-Russian quarrel would automatically drag him into the fray. After 1763 no ruler needed or desired peace more than Frederick, and his main preoccupation was to prevent Catherine and Joseph flying at each other's throats. Though his task was facilitated by the substitution of the Prussophil Panin for the Austrophil Bestuschev as Russian Foreign Minister, the Tsarina seemed in no hurry to proceed with the negotiations for an alliance. Not till January 1764 did the Prussian Minister receive the Russian counter-project to the Prussian proposals of the spring of 1763. The alliance, it was suggested, should be for eight years, and in the event of war each was to supply 12,000 men or an equivalent in subsidies. Secret articles envisaged mutual support for the election of Stanislas Poniatowski to the Polish throne. Frederick made no difficulties, and on April 11, 1764 the longed-for Russo-Prussian treaty embodying a guarantee of each other's territories and a defensive alliance for eight years was signed. Three months later the two powers agreed to protect the Evangelical and Greek Orthodox Christians in Poland against oppression by the Catholic majority. In 1767 the partnership was strengthened by a secret treaty binding the King to declare war against Austria if Austrian troops entered Poland.

The fulfillment of his hopes inspired Frederick to one of his most exuberant tributes to the ruler whom he had described as eaten up with vanity. "Madame, my sister, I have received with infinite satisfaction the treaty that Your Imperial Majesty has been pleased to ratify. I regard this happy epoch as the foundation of the close union which, please God, will always exist between the two nations. For myself, madame, I shall cultivate this happy union with all the care of which I am capable while endeavoring to anticipate your desires in every possible way. Though I have never received the celestial inspiration so often claimed in past times, I shall be no less accurate a prophet when it is a matter of announcing your successes. I base myself on your wise measures, on their vigorous execution, on the insight with which you grasp and direct affairs. While your enemies will fear you, madame, permit me to admire you." Silesia, he felt, was secure at last, and with the goodwill of Catherine further alluring projects seemed to come within range. He resented the notion of Poland and her ruler being completely dominated by Russia, but as the friendship of Catherine was unobtainable on cheaper terms, he was ready to pay her price.

The election of a Polish nobleman to the throne on September 7, 1764, which at a distance looked like a concession to national sentiment, was a smoke-screen to cover Russian designs, and indeed Russian rubles had played their part in the game. Though far too weak and divided to stand up to a big bully, the Poles detested dictation from St. Petersburg. Stanislas himself was too patriotic to be content with the role of a puppet, but he had neither the personality, the popularity, nor the means required for a national leader. During the opening years of his reign the country split into factions which quarreled over the reform of the antiquated Constitution and the status of the Protestant and Greek Orthodox minorities, the Greek Orthodox looking to Russia, the Protestants to Prussia, to defend them. Catherine was always ready to pay her puppet's debts, and Russian gold worked wonders among the impoverished grandees. The Diet gave little trouble, and a treaty between Russia and Poland, signed on February 24, 1768, placed Poland, her antiquated Constitution, and the privileges of the minorities under Russian guarantee. This abject surrender led the smaller nobility to form the Confederation of Bar and to launch a revolt that, though never formidable in numbers or equipment, dragged on for four years. Though the idea of a Russian stranglehold was odious to Prussia and Austria alike, they were too suspicious of each other and too full of bitter memories to co-operate. Since no one knew better than the Tsarina that Maria Theresa had had her fill of war, and that Frederick required her friendship as a makeweight against the Austro-French partnership, she held the winning cards. The more closely the situation was studied in Vienna and Berlin, the clearer it became that the loosening of her grip on Poland was impracticable, and that the task of realistic statesmen was to arrange a deal. Should it prove impossible to prevent the aggrandizement of Russia, there would have to be a share out all round on the familiar principle of the balance of power.

In the middle of the eighteenth century Poland was the largest state in Europe except Russia, but she was also one of the poorest, the most backward, the most socially divided.[1] Nowhere else were there such anomalies as the elective monarchy and the *liberum veto;* nowhere was the gulf between a corrupt nobility and a brutish peasantry so deep; nowhere else were religious antagonisms fiercer. Her notorious weakness, combined with her

[1] The best recent account of the First Partition is in the *Cambridge History of Poland.* Albert Sorel: *La Question d'orient au dix-huitième siècle,* connects it with the wider issues of the time. Duncker's long essay: *"Die Besitzergreifung von West Preussen,"* in his book *Aus der Zeit Friedrichs des Grossen und Friedrich Wilhelms III,* is indispensable. Horn: *British Opinion on the First Partition of Poland,* shows how little Englishmen were interested in her fate. The *Politische Correspondenz,* Vols. XXIX–XXXII, is essential.

lack of natural frontiers, had long stimulated the greedy appetites of her neighbors. In his classical work *The Eastern Question in the Eighteenth Century,* Sorel describes a number of projects from the sixteenth century onwards, and in the early years of the reign of Stanislas the idea of partition was in the air. Russia was in the strongest strategic position to assert her claims, and alternative methods of procedure were carefully considered by Catherine and her advisers. The ideal solution would be the bloodless appropriation of the whole country, which was already within her sphere of influence, but that was too much to hope for. The prospective victim could offer no effective resistance, but neither Austria nor Prussia would watch with indifference such a disturbance of the balance of power, and if they acted together they could block the road. The alternative was to purchase their consent by the simple expedient of collective spoliation. In Catherine's opinion the matter was not urgent, for Poland seemed to be growing weaker year by year. She hoped to choose her own time for giving the signal, knowing that no major change could happen without her consent. On the other hand, the outbreak of war with Turkey in 1768 played into the hands of her Prussian ally, now her only friend among European rulers, and early in 1769 she granted his request for a prolongation of the alliance until 1780.

The first serious suggestion of partition appears in the form of a kite flown in February 1769, for a vague hint of such a possibility by Panin at the end of 1763 was not followed up. "Count Lynar has come to Berlin to marry his daughter," wrote Frederick to Count Solms, his Minister at St. Petersburg. "He has had the somewhat singular idea of combining the interests of the princes in favor of Russia and changing the face of Europe. He would like Russia to offer to the court of Vienna, in return for its assistance against the Turks, the town and surrounding district of Leopol and Zips, and to give us Prussian Poland with Varmia and the protection of Danzig, while Russia would compensate herself for the expenses of war by taking whatever she likes. Then, with the cessation of their jealousy, Austria and Prussia would help Russia against the Turks. This plan is striking and seductive, and I feel I must inform you of it. You who know Count Panin's ideas can suppress or utilize it as you think best, though in my view it is more brilliant than solid." The

73

father of this *ballon d'essai*,[1] of course, was not Count Lynar but the King himself. The Prussian Minister replied that he thought the plan would not appeal to the Foreign Minister. Russia had too little confidence in Austria for such bargaining, and she desired to keep an integral dependent Poland, who might be useful to her in a war against Turkey and to Prussia in a war against Austria. He would, however, mention the plan without indicating its source.

On March 3, 1769 Count Solms reported that he had discussed the project with Panin; Zips, declared the Foreign Minister, would be a very suitable acquisition for Austria but the town of Leopol (Lemberg) was too far away from her frontier. Secondly, it would not be worth while for three great powers to combine merely to thrust the Turks beyond the Dniester; they should drive them out of Europe and a large part of Asia. A sincere alliance between the three powers would be the best method of assuring the peace of Europe, and he proceeded to explain his own scheme. Since the jealousy and rivalry between the Prussian and Austrian courts was a principal obstacle to co-operation, it was necessary to remove the germ of the trouble. Austria should renounce all claims on the house of Brandenburg and should compensate herself with portions of Turkey, which the three powers would obtain by arms, after which she could forget Silesia. Prussia could take Prussian Poland and the Bishopric of Varmia. Then the three powers could easily liquidate the Turkish Empire in Europe, which had only lasted so long owing to the jealousy of the Christian states, and Constantinople would become the capital of a republic. When the Prussian Minister remarked that there was no mention of gains for Russia, Panin rejoined that she would not share in this partition since she already possessed far more territory than she could govern; except for some frontier strongholds, she could not think of acquiring provinces. Panin's plan, concluded the report, was easier to conceive than to carry out. Frederick agreed, adding that Austria would be the chief difficulty. For the time she was busy with the restoration of her finances, but in a few years this phase would be over.

At the end of 1768 Kaunitz argued in a lengthy Memorandum that Silesia might perhaps be recovered if Frederick were to

[1] Diplomatic kite.

74

receive Kurland from Russia and West Prussia from Poland. The outbreak of the Russo-Turkish War in that year opened up possibilities of action which the court of Vienna decided to utilize. In the spring of 1769 a military cordon was drawn on the Polish and Turkish frontiers, and posts bearing the Austrian eagle were erected to prevent a violation of Hapsburg territory. Not content with this defensive measure, however, the Austrians included thirteen towns of the County of Zips, a district in the Tatra Mountains south of Cracow, which Hungary had mortgaged to Poland as far back as the fifteenth century and had definitely renounced in 1589. This step, which marks the beginning of a new period of Austrian expansion, proved that the Emperor and Kaunitz, if not Maria Theresa, were as ready as Russia and Prussia to carve up Poland if they saw their chance.

A new and arresting figure now advanced towards the center of the European stage. Elected Emperor at the age of twenty-four on the death of his father in 1765 and appointed co-Regent by his affectionate mother, Joseph's influence in foreign affairs steadily increased. He never shared her loathing of Frederick, with whom he was quite prepared to do business. Indeed, he desired to meet him when he visited Saxony in 1765, but he was overruled by his mother and Kaunitz. Their attitude changed when the Russo-Turkish War broke out in 1768; Russia was now felt to be the chief rival, and it might be useful to learn something of her plans from her Prussian ally. With this object in view the Austrian Minister in Berlin informed the King in October 1768 that Austria had renounced Silesia forever and proposed a meeting between the sovereigns. The initiative came from Joseph, but Frederick was no less eager to form an impression of the young Emperor. It was finally arranged to meet at the old fortress town of Neisse in Silesia in August 1769. The King prepared himself for the historic occasion by asking his Minister in Vienna what topics the Emperor liked to discuss. Knowing that Austria and Russia were on unfriendly terms, and expecting an attempt to drive a wedge between Berlin and St. Petersburg, he was on his guard. The rulers spent three days together (August 25–28), though Joseph, traveling as Count Falkenstein, insisted on staying at a modest hotel. There was an element of anxiety at Vienna, and Kaunitz furnished his young master with elaborate notes for his guidance. A full account of the occasion is provided in

75

Joseph's journal written for his mother's eye and in his annotations to the Kaunitz Memorandum. Here is an abridged version: "I arrived at the King's headquarters, where there were a number of officers. He stepped forward to meet me. I embraced him, Prince Henry, and the Prince of Prussia (the heir). Directly we were alone he expressed his desire for a sincere friendship and a complete reconciliation." When Joseph suggested that that required more mature reflection, his host replied: No, let us start today. "I told him that I regarded Silesia as an absolute necessity for him like Alsace and Lorraine for France. We had entirely forgotten it. The mutual advantages we could obtain without striking a blow were more considerable than Silesia would be for us or part of Bohemia for him. He agreed, though without conviction. He said that it would be impossible to be my enemy and showered me with compliments. He knew it was difficult at first to have confidence in a reconciled enemy, but with time the patriotic German system, as he called it, could take shape. I explained how much even the name of a liaison would achieve. It would cut Europe in half and draw a cordon from the Adriatic to the Baltic to preserve tranquillity. Then we could reduce our armies and succor our peoples. No, he replied, that I cannot advise, for one can never answer for events. Then we dealt with the points mentioned in my instructions." At the visitor's request the host talked at length and very modestly of the battles of the Seven Years' War. "We spoke much of our common intentions for peace, and I told him in strict confidence of our arrangements for mobilization, adding that we were ready at any moment. This made little impression on him. He assured me that as a young man he had been ambitious and had acted wrongly, but that these times were over and that his present ideas were much more stable. You think I am full of bad faith. I know it and in some degree I have deserved it. Circumstances demanded it, but that is all changed."

Passing from declarations of goodwill, the monarchs proceeded to discuss particular topics. Frederick strove to arouse fear of Russian designs in Turkey and spoke contemptuously of the conduct of the opposition in England, adding that, petty prince though he was, he would not exchange with the King of England. The two rulers agreed in desiring the end of the troubles in Poland, but no reference to partition was made.

Joseph's proposal of a promise of neutrality in all succeeding wars prompted Frederick to reply that it would infringe his alliance with Russia. Yet he spoke of his ally with unconcealed distrust. All Europe, he declared, would have to combine if Russia were to be kept within bounds. Joseph was on his guard, for at this point the ice was thin. "The more he tried to alarm me about the Russians, the more tranquil I became." Joseph extricated himself from a difficult position by an adroit compliment to the Prussian army. "Sire, in the event of a general conflagration you are the advance guard, so we can sleep quietly in the knowledge that you can do with the Russians what you will." Frederick demurred, confessing that he feared them; that the alliance was necessary but very uncomfortable; that he paid half a million crowns a year in lieu of his stipulated contingent of men. He had the luck and the skill to get out of the latter by telling the Russians that if he sent a corps, Austria would attack and that he would have to defend himself, in which case they would get neither troops nor money.

At the end of the visit an exchange of letters took place at the desire of the host. "After the inestimable happiness of receiving Your Imperial Majesty nothing could be more precious than the letter you have been good enough to write to me. I find in it the most certain proof of your friendship and above all what I most desire, the perfect reconciliation between two houses unhappily so long estranged. Yes, Sire, I repeat in writing that it is impossible for my heart to be the enemy of a great man. Heaven grant that this first step may lead to others that will unite us still more closely. I promise, by the faith of a King and on the word of a man of honor, that, even if war is renewed between England and the Bourbon houses, I will faithfully preserve the peace happily restored between us; also, if some other unpredictable conflict breaks out, that I will observe the most scrupulous neutrality for your present possessions, as you will do for mine." The Emperor's letter, to which that of Frederick was supposed to be a reply, was in reality written a day after its receipt and echoed its substance, though with more reserve. "I see nothing, now we are so sincerely reconciled, which could reasonably prevent the establishment and maintenance between us of as much confidence and friendship as hitherto there was mistrust. These odious sentiments, I hope, will now disappear

77

forever." Joseph proceeded to repeat the formula of neutrality contained in Frederick's letter.

Frederick was impressed by the charm and culture, the ability and ambition of his guest. "He would be attractive as a private citizen," he reported to d'Alembert. "He will equal if not surpass Charles V by his craving for self-instruction, his ardor to fit himself for his career. No one could be more considerate or polite. He showed me the most cordial friendship. He is gay, natural, hard on himself, tender for others. In a word, he is a prince from whom only great things are to be expected and who will set people talking of him in Europe when he is his own master." The report to his Foreign Minister reveals the darker apprehensions that he carried away from the momentous meeting. "I feel he is a man devoured by ambition who is brooding over some great plan, who is temporarily held in leash by his mother, but is fretting to throw off the yoke, and who when his arms are free will start off with a big coup. I could not discover whether his eyes are turned towards the Republic of Venice, Bavaria, Silesia, or Lorraine, but there is no doubt that there will be a flare-up in Europe when he is in control." To his Minister in Vienna the King reported in a striking phrase: *"Il est tout feu"* ("He is all fire"). A few days later Frederick summed up his final impression in a further letter to Finckenstein: "The Emperor is frank and candid, and I am almost sure that he wishes me no ill—on the contrary. Yet politics often draw princes into engagements and measures that compel them to act against their inclination, so that I cannot guarantee the future."

If the host had hoped to win the confidence of his visitor he had entirely failed. "The King was throughout excessively polite and full of assurances of his friendship," wrote Joseph in his journal; "but one can be fairly certain that the old mistrust lingers in his soul and still more in his character. It was very interesting to see him once, but God preserve me from a second experience. He threatens to come to Kolin once again." With the blemished record of the older man and the fiery temperament of the younger there was indeed little prospect of ensuring peace in central Europe. If the Neisse meeting cannot be dismissed as a total failure, it was certainly not a solid success. Yet it was not without advantage to Frederick, for Catherine, slightly alarmed by the secret conversations of her neighbors, renewed her treaty with Prussia on October 12, 1769, prolonging it till 1780 and guaranteeing the reversion of the little Brandenburg duchies of Bayreuth and Anspach.

A year later the King returned the visit and the monarchs spent four days together at Neustadt in Moravia. (September 3–7, 1770). This time Joseph was accompanied by Kaunitz who relieved his master of political discussions. Kaunitz, reported Frederick to Prince Henry, treated the Emperor as his son, and the Emperor treated him like his father. The Russo-Turkish War and the desirability of ending it was again on the agenda, but the conversations ranged over the whole European situation. The Austrian Chancellor asked leave to begin by explaining the system of which he was so proud. "As I wished our talk to be of some practical use," he reported to Maria Theresa in a volu-minous dispatch, "I begged him to listen without interrupting, so that he should understand our general policy and in particular our attitude towards himself, knowing as I did that he was too great to make improper use of what he learned."

The King's alliance with Russia, began Kaunitz, like Austria's alliance with France, was purely defensive. It was not to the interest of either Austria or Prussia to attack each other, for if their respective allies joined in the fight, they would demand compensations, which neither of them desired. The two alli-ances, in fact, were in the best interest not only of the four powers concerned but of Europe as a whole. Austria had no intention of drawing closer to Russia, and Prussia would doubtless make no approach to France. Between Austria and Prussia no treaty was necessary, but he had set forth the principles which in his opinion guided both powers in a *Catéchisme Politique* which he pro-ceeded to read to the King. Frederick entirely approved, but his request for a copy to study at leisure was refused on the ground that it was not intended to be an object of negotiation. When the Chancellor had finished his lecture Frederick jumped up and embraced him, expressing his delight that these views were much the same as his own. Passing to specific problems he suggested Austrian mediation to end "this accursed Turkish war," adding that the Tsarina required very careful handling. It was equally desirable, interjected Kaunitz, that she should make her peace with the Poles. Once again it was agreed that the Russo-Turkish War should not disturb their good relations. The main anxiety

79

of Kaunitz, it was clear from the conversations, was in regard to the strength and ambitions of Russia. Austria, he explained, could not let her take Moldavia and Wallachia, for so mighty a neighbor would be a threat to Hungary; nor could she admit that Russia should dominate Poland. No reference was made to a partition.

In their final interview Frederick expressed his pleasure at the similarity of views on the existing situation. "But the shape of things may change, as you know better than I. So I think it would be well to meet once a year or, at any rate, when something occurs on which it would be good for us to reach agreement. Would that not be possible, or, at any rate, could you not in such a case send me someone enjoying your entire confidence?" "It would be useful and indeed necessary," replied Kaunitz, "to concert measures on every occasion; but, given perfect confidence, it should not be difficult to reach agreement through the ordinary channels even if such frequent personal meetings could not be arranged." The good of humanity, no less than the interest of the two states, he added, was the sole object of all his talks. The King and the Chancellor parted with the usual expressions of confidence and goodwill.

Frederick had listened with interest to the dissertations, but was less impressed than Austria's political schoolmaster believed. "Prince Kaunitz," he reported to his Minister at Vienna, "has given me a lengthy lecture, and I think I have read his character. I take him for a very clever man. His judgment is sound and clear, but he is so full of himself that he thinks himself an oracle in politics and other people pupils whom he has to teach. I believe he takes me for a soldier without any idea of politics, and I confess that he rather amused me. Yet I have been very glad to make his acquaintance, and no one would deny him a fine brain and wide knowledge of affairs." Frederick had guessed right. Kaunitz was not in the least overawed by the old warrior's fame and returned from Neustadt with the conviction of his intellectual superiority over all his contemporaries stronger than ever. The King, he reported, had no system and did not know how to negotiate. The Chancellor's high opinion of his own performance was shared by the Emperor. The King, declared Joseph, thought himself the cleverest of men, but Kaunitz had shown himself his superior. The second and last meeting of the two rulers ended like the first, for surface cordiality failed to conceal the ineradicable distrust on both sides. All that the meetings of 1769 and 1770 had achieved, reported Frederick to Prince Henry, was to remove the animosity.

If Kaunitz and his master had hoped to loosen the ties between Berlin and St. Petersburg they were disappointed, for the Russian alliance was the sheet-anchor of Frederick's policy. Yet Catherine was worried by the meeting of the rulers of Prussia and Austria, and, hearing that Prince Henry was to visit his sister the Queen of Sweden, she urged Frederick in a letter of July 30, 1770 to let him extend his journey. The invitation was so pressing, explained the King to his brother, that it could hardly be declined, adding: "We must humor this woman." Henry, who was instructed not to stint his flatteries, reached St. Petersburg on October 12, 1770. The principal object of the journey, explained Frederick to his Minister in the Russian capital, was to draw the ties between the courts so close as to be indissoluble: that was the only advantage he sought. Count Solms was not told the whole truth, for Henry was determined to discuss the future of Poland if he saw his chance.

Shortly before the Prince left Berlin in August 1770, Frederick had drawn a military cordon round the Polish territories on the pretext of isolating cattle disease. During the first weeks of his brother's sojourn in St. Petersburg the talks were concerned with two burning questions of the day—the termination of the Russo-Turkish War, for which Frederick had grudgingly to furnish subsidies, and the pacification of Poland. But at the end of the year Austria's occupation of the remainder of the County of Zips, accompanied by the announcement that it was now definitely incorporated in the Austrian state, opened the door to the discussion of a far more important matter. Though the notion of a major assault on the integrity of Poland was hatched by the greedy rulers of Prussia and Russia, it was Austria who gave the signal to close in on the victim; for, not content with recovering lost property, she occupied territory that Hungary had never possessed. In taking this important step without consultation she forgot that the spoliation of a defenseless country was a game at which more than one ruler could play. "These people set the example," commented Frederick, "so Russia and I are entitled to follow suit."

On January 8, 1771 Henry reported that he expected to leave the Russian capital at the end of the month, but a postscript was added the same evening. "Since writing this letter I have visited the Empress, who said to me jokingly that the Austrians had seized two starosties in Poland and set up the Imperial arms: why should not everyone follow suit? I replied that, although you had drawn a cordon in Poland, you had not occupied any starosties. But why doesn't he? rejoined Catherine with a smile. At this moment Count Czernichev came up and remarked: Why not take the Bishopric of Varmia? After all, everybody must get something. Though it was said in joking fashion, there was obviously something in it and I have no doubt that you will be able to profit by the occasion." It was fortunate for Frederick that the seizure of Zips synchronized with his brother's visit, for Henry was *persona gratissima* at the Russian court.

Three days later, on January 11, the Prince reported a conversation with Panin, who spoke with disapproval of Austria's action and made no reference to a Prussian occupation of the Bishopric of Varmia. There were two parties in the capital, he explained, "The champions of aggrandizement wish everyone to take something in order that Russia may profit at the same time, whereas Count Panin leans to tranquillity and peace. I shall find out more about this affair, and I feel that you run no risk in taking this bishopric on some plausible pretext if it is true that the Austrians have definitely taken two starosties to which they advance claims on documents in the Hungarian archives." Frederick commented without enthusiasm on the reported conversations. "I realize, my dear brother, that there are differences in the Council at St. Petersburg, but I can say positively that Count Panin's ideas about Austria are impracticable. The secret hatred felt in that country for the Russians passes all imagination, and, if I may say so, I am the only person who tries to prevent an explosion. If the Russians instructed their Minister in Vienna to take soundings they would see that I have understated things. As for the acquisition of the Duchy of Varmia, I have abstained: such a trifle would not be worth the outcry it would arouse. Polish Prussia, on the other hand, is a prize, even without Danzig, for we should have the Vistula and free communication with East Prussia. That is worth paying for, even a large sum. Snatching at trifles suggests a character of insatiable greed worse than that which I already bear in Europe." Playing at partition made no appeal to Frederick. If anything were done, let it be in the grand style, and let the balance of power be preserved, but at the moment he was disinclined to take risks.

On his return in February Henry spent a week at Potsdam in eager talks about his eventful mission. He brought a letter from the Tsarina thanking the King for permitting the visit, and Frederick replied in the fulsome style he adopted to her alone. "He has returned, madam, overwhelmed by your kindness, more charmed with the happiness of meeting you than with all the astonishing things he has seen. His talk transports me in imagination to Russia. He tells us of the great things Your Imperial Majesty has accomplished in that vast empire, of your maternal care for your people, of your immense establishments, of your infinite concern for the morals and culture of a young race, of your legislation. Then he dilates on the details of your personal life, telling me that no ordinary person, however sensible, allows more freedom and liveliness than a great Empress when she deigns to leave the throne for a few minutes to seek diversion among her subjects from the burdens of government."

After digesting the oral report Frederick accepted Henry's opinion that the time to act had come and that no serious risk was involved. Austria's occupation of Polish territory, he wrote to Solms, was intended to be permanent. "Thus there is no longer any question of preserving Poland intact; but the question remains of preventing this dismemberment from affecting the balance of power between the house of Austria and my house, which is so important for me and so closely concerns the court of Russia. I see no other means of preserving it than by imitating the example set by the court of Vienna, of vindicating, as it has done, ancient rights based on my archives, and of taking some small province of Poland, to restore it if the Austrians draw back, of keeping it if they do not." This was the beginning of formal negotiations which could have only one end since Catherine favored partition and Panin ceased to oppose. "I hope our mutual interests will be combined and assured by a treaty," he wrote to Henry. "If so I can laugh at the Austrians, who, deriving no support from their allies [the French], will have to accept our wishes. Moreover, peace overtures have been made, and Russia's terms [to Turkey] are so moderate that the Austrians cannot object. Though a good deal of ink-spilling remains, I begin to see daylight." A fortnight later detailed propositions arrived from Russia. "My share will be in Pomerelia as far as Netze, Culm, Marienburg, and Elbing. That is very handsome, and worth the subsidies and other expenses which this war against the Turks has caused me." Kaunitz, he added, was in bad humor, and his reply to Russia about the settlement with Turkey would doubtless estrange the two courts more than ever.

It was easier to agree on the principle than on the details of partition, and negotiations between Berlin and St. Petersburg dragged on for months. Austria was too powerful and too interested to be ignored, but her attitude was unpredictable, for Vienna and St. Petersburg, so recently allies, were now rivals. From the meridian of Berlin this new antagonism possessed both advantages and disadvantages. The greater the Austrian menace to Russia, the more valuable was the Russian alliance, since Austria, Turkey, and the Polish malcontents represented a very formidable hypothetical combination; but equally, the keener the Austro-Russian rivalry, the graver the danger of a war in which Prussia would inevitably be involved. Frederick could do little except keep his powder dry. By the late summer of 1771 he had come to take a pessimistic view of the prospects of peace. "I much fear that you and I will not enjoy sweet repose in our solitude next year," wrote the hermit of Potsdam to the hermit of Rheinsberg. "The Russians want everything, the Austrians refuse all concessions. As I am beginning to believe that war is inevitable, I am arranging that nothing is lacking so that we can stand up to all the enemies we have to meet. By December or January we should be able to grasp the plans of the Austrians, and then we must get ready to enter on the campaign about the end of August next year. Do not be surprised if I keep worrying you with my politics and all my annoyances. My present situation is critical and alarming till the hour of decision arrives. The more I hear and the more I reflect on the designs of the great powers, the more certain I grow that war is inevitable; and you will see, my dear brother, that this accursed Wallachia and Moldavia [claimed by Russia from the Turks] will be the cause. In vain do I appeal to them not to insist, though, on the other hand, I cannot guarantee that the Austrians would not be encouraged by such moderation to ask for more. So it is certain that when they draw the sword I shall have to take part. Supposing the Russians are beaten, I lose an ally and place myself at the discretion of reconciled enemies in whom I could never feel confidence. Supposing the Austrians are defeated, the Russians, prouder and more arrogant than ever, will resent my peaceful disposition, and indeed I might be sacrificed to a rapprochement between those two powers after their fight is over."

At the end of September 1771 the King wrote in more cheerful mood. "I see, my dear brother, that you are astonished at the strange situation in Europe, to which I can remember no parallel. Since my last letter things have become infinitely more favorable to our interests. The Russians, annoyed by the stiff and imperious reply of the Austrians, have resolved to send fifty thousand men to Poland in January. All their animosity is directed against the Austrians. They wish to cede Moldavia and Wallachia to the Turks, and even to persuade Turkey to declare war against Austria. Now is the moment to sign our convention with them. We shall get better terms, and this new army stationed between Sandomir and Cracow will prevent the Austrians from taking action; thus we shall gain our acquisitions without drawing the sword. You ask about Saxony's relations with Austria. I reply: neither good nor bad. The Elector has reduced his army and will reduce it still further to no more than twelve thousand men, which would not be much help to Austria. Whatever the good Elector does, if the conflagration starts he will be drawn in. The Austrians will meet a thousand difficulties in France; how far they will succeed in the Empire we shall learn in a few months. I entirely agree with you, my dear brother, that if war comes we must spare no expense to win. I am attending to this, but as we must not waste money, I await the decision of this crisis to take action and to start negotiations in all the directions you so wisely indicate."

A few days later Frederick reported that he was striving for the inclusion of Danzig in Prussia's share. "If we do not get it now we never shall. Now is the moment to conclude our treaties with Russia since Austrian armaments are exercising their minds. The arrival of fifty thousand Russians in Poland will probably make the Austrians more circumspect and therefore diminish Russia's apprehensions. I have added to the draft convention that each party should occupy his sphere directly the treaty is signed in order that, having our bird in the hand, we run no risks, possession being as a rule the deciding factor in such acquisitions. Czernichev may come here to arrange a plan of campaign in case the Austrians move, though I cannot imagine they will risk a break with Russia. The honor of coming events will be equally due to you, my dear brother. It is you who laid the foundation stone of this edifice, and without you I should not have formed such projects, being unaware before your journey to St. Petersburg of the attitude of that court towards me. So far things have gone well, and if that continues till the conclusion of peace our desires will be entirely fulfilled."

Since Frederick needed Catherine more than she needed him, he had to go her leisurely pace; for she desired to postpone final decisions on the details of partition and the date of occupation till she knew what Austria was likely to do, a riddle that the silence of the Hofburg made it difficult to guess. "I see from your report," he wrote in exasperation to Solms on November 13, "that nothing has been decided at St. Petersburg. They wish for acquisitions but lack the nerve to occupy them; they desire my aid but refuse what I ask. This uncertainty will ruin Russia's affairs and all our plans. The Austrians have acted with much more resolution in seizing what they wanted without a word to anyone. You Russian gentlemen wish me to join in your quarrels, you want my troops, and thus I risk being involved in a general war. Very good, but West Prussia and Danzig are my price. So, my dear Russians, be good enough to make up your mind whether you need me or not. Just as grain is dearer after a poor harvest, so in the absence of other allies pay my price for the goods you require."

Two days later the King drafted a Memorandum for his Minister on the best time to take possession. "Assuming that Russia is resolved to compensate herself in Poland for her immense outlay in the Turkish war, it remains to examine the most suitable moment to apply the plan. I think we must reject all notion of an arrangement with the court of Vienna. Why? Because it is ill-disposed to the Russian court, and because Prince Kaunitz, the proudest of men, regarding himself with some justification as the arbiter of the north and the east, likes to humiliate those who make such proposals and to decide their fate. I have too much self-respect to submit to his judgment, and I do not suppose that anyone in Russia will advise the Empress to subordinate her actions to his whims, as if we could not occupy the territories we need without his approbation and investiture. On the contrary, I think we should imitate the conduct of the court of Vienna, which, without prior consultation or permission, occupied certain districts." There was no need to await the conclusion of the Turkish war; Austria would be obliged to consent, and if she were not satisfied with her share she could compensate herself with Belgrade or something else. "As for the Poles, when we occupy our respective portions they will doubtless raise shrill cries, as this vain and insolent nation always does; but this [Russian] army on the Vistula will soon silence them and, when peace with Turkey is concluded, will proceed to pacify Poland."

Though Frederick resented the claim of Kaunitz to conduct the orchestra, his arrogance served Prussian interests. "The conduct of the Austrians," he wrote to Henry, "is more useful to me at St. Petersburg than all my negotiations. His imperious tone offends them, and the Austrian armaments cause them anxiety. Moreover, the Turks reject the peace proposals of the Empress. So at this moment Russia needs help and without my assistance she cannot get out of the rut." The Russian army and navy, he heard, were unready for war, so he believed everything would be arranged to his satisfaction. At the opening of 1772 the sluggish wheels of diplomacy began to revolve more rapidly. In view of Catherine's unbending opposition Frederick ceased to press for Danzig. So important a negotiation, he explained, should not be wrecked for an advantage that was only postponed, and Danzig fell to Prussia in the Second Partition only six years after his death. On January 15 he and Catherine agreed to partition Poland; it only remained to bring Austria into the scheme, for otherwise, as he pointed out, the Poles would look to her as their champion and trouble might ensue. After a futile attempt to recover Silesia in return for the transfer of her prospective share of the spoils, Austria succumbed to temptation and accepted the principle of partition. *"Elle pleure mais elle prend"* ("She weeps and yet she takes her share"), sneered Frederick as he witnessed the surrender of Maria Theresa. "The Empress Catherine and I," he remarked, "are two brigands; but that pious Queen-Empress, how has she settled it with her conscience?"

Frederick reminded his ally of the necessity of equalizing the shares of the three partitioning powers. Now that the booty was at last in sight, there was talk in St. Petersburg and Berlin of the Polish agreement leading to a Triple Alliance. "As for more intimate relations with the court of Vienna," wrote Frederick, "I shall never oppose them; indeed, I should welcome them if Russia takes the same steps. Union between our three courts will be a happy time for the tranquillity of Russia." That was mere wishful thinking, for the necessary confidence was lacking.

The King's unflattering opinion of his prospective victim is enshrined in a letter to d'Alembert in January 1772. "We who are the neighbors of this rustic nation, we who know the individuals and the party chiefs, believe they deserve nothing but contempt. This Confederation [of Bar] was created by fanaticism; all the leaders are divided; they act with imprudence, fight with cowardice, and are capable only of the sort of crimes that cowards commit. You have seen by the plot against their King what they are like. The cause of their hatred against this prince is that he is not rich enough to give them the pensions they covet; they would prefer a foreigner who could feed their extravagance out of his own pocket. I pity philosophers who interest themselves in this people, so contemptible in every way. Their only excuse is their ignorance. Poland has neither laws nor liberty; the government has degenerated into license and anarchy; the nobility exercise the most cruel tyranny over their slaves. In a word, it is the worst government in Europe except that of the Turks."

On February 17, 1772 a treaty was signed at St. Petersburg between Russia and Prussia, and two days later Maria Theresa and Joseph signed a provisional act in Vienna accepting the plan of partition on condition that the three powers should receive equal treatment. "The larger portion of our work is achieved," wrote Frederick to Henry on April 9, 1772. "We are only waiting for the Austrian proposals, for they have shuffled so much that it is impossible to guess where they will finally take their stand. I believe, however, that in order not entirely to alienate their allies they will be content to take their bit of Poland. That, my dear brother, will reunite the three religions—Greek, Catholic, and Calvinist. For we shall partake of the same eucharist,

Poland; and if it does not benefit our souls it will surely bring great profit to our state."

While the final negotiations at St. Petersburg relating to the accession of Austria were still in progress, Frederick visited his prospective possession in June 1772. "I have seen this Prussia [West Prussia] which in a way I receive from your hands," he wrote to Henry. "It is an excellent and most advantageous acquisition both politically and financially, but, to incur less envy, I tell people I saw nothing but sand, fir trees, heath, and Jews. True, it will mean a lot of work, for I imagine Canada is as well policed as this Pomerelia. No order; no system; the towns are in a deplorable condition. For instance, Culm should have 800 houses; only 100 are standing, and their inmates are Jews or monks. We come off best from the commercial point of view. We become the masters of all Poland's products and imports, which are considerable. The greatest score is that our control of the wheat trade will always save us from famine. There is a population of 620,000—soon it will be 700,000—and all the Dissenters in Poland will find refuge there." The tripartite treaty of partition was signed on August 5, 1772, and the King took formal possession of his new province. Among the letters of congratulation was one from the heir to the throne, now in his thirtieth year, and the King seized the opportunity of reading him a lesson. "I labor for you, but one must think of keeping what I make, and if you are idle and indolent, what I have accumulated with so much trouble will melt away in your hands." This brief autograph postscript to a dictated letter of thanks reveals his greatest worry in his sixtieth year.

By the First Partition Poland lost a quarter of her territory and four million subjects, a fifth of her population. Prussia secured West Prussia, the bridge between Pomerania and East Prussia, with an area of 20,000 square miles and 600,000 inhabitants, which Frederick had coveted for forty years. Austria's portion was Galicia without Cracow, while the Tsarina seized White Russia, the lion's share of the spoils. "The most impudent association of robbers that ever existed," exclaimed Horace Walpole, but no one outside Poland really cared. The amputation was carried through without a hitch, and four years later the three powers guaranteed each other's new Polish frontiers; yet none of them was entirely satisfied. Catherine would have preferred to gobble up the whole country; Frederick regretted that his portion did not include the busy port of Danzig and the fortress of Thorn; Kaunitz had vainly suggested that Silesia should be returned to Austria, and that the aggressor of 1740 should compensate himself at the expense of some other neighbor. Yet there was much to be thankful for. All three had enlarged and strengthened their states without drawing the sword, and had discovered that in agreement they could do what they liked in Poland.

The occupation of West Prussia by Frederick's troops and officials was unresisted. He compared the neglected and illiterate inhabitants of his new province to aborigines. "I have been given a bit of anarchy to reform," he remarked, and he set to work with his usual energy. Only with time and education, he declared, could he civilize these Iroquois. There was little national feeling to overcome. The nobility was hostile, for their day was over; the peasantry was apathetic, and the Catholic opposition, as in Silesia, was partially disarmed by considerate treatment. Since there were few towns and scarcely any bourgeoisie, it was necessary to build from the foundations. Schools were introduced, roads were made, stock was improved, a canal was constructed from the Vistula to the Oder. In the material sphere the difference between the Polish and the Prussian regime was salutary and profound.

Having added Silesia, East Frisia and West Prussia to his dominions, Frederick had no wish to fight for further territory. Though the whole or part of Saxony he hoped would some day be secured, he had no expectation of it in his lifetime. He had had his fill of adventure and had narrowly escaped from the jaws of death. Henceforth, like Bismarck after 1871, he played the part of the good boy, the resolute champion of the *status quo;* the headstrong Joseph II was now the firebrand. Though he had no military talents and no craving for military glory, he regarded war as an instrument of national policy and shrank from its risks as little as any of his contemporaries. Vergennes, the French Foreign Minister, after meeting him during his visit to France in 1777, pronounced him ambitious and despotic.

Though Frederick believed that it would be for his successor to deal with the Bavarian problem on the death of the childless

Elector, he, like other rulers and statesmen, was continually turning it over in his mind.[1] "You say, my dear brother, that the Austrians will seize Bavaria. I agree that no one can stop them, for they are neighbors and will subjugate it in less than a fortnight. Moreover, you realize that if we, the Russians, and the English wish to go for Austria we must attack her elsewhere than in Bavaria, where France alone could operate effectively. To form a league against the Emperor it would be necessary for Russia to be disgruntled against Austria, for the German princes to fear her despotism, for France or England to feel the need of opposing the overweening ambition of a young monarch ready to gobble up everything. These powers might possibly be united for a moment, but they would soon cool off and fall apart, and the court of Vienna might even induce some of them to become its allies. Here is my plan. The Elector Palatine (the childless heir) and the Zweibrücken family (his heirs) would have to complain of the pernicious designs of the court of Vienna and to persuade all the powers to unite in their just defense. Then we could come in as auxiliaries, then some others, and such an alliance would make the court of Vienna desist from its projects." His policy, he added, was to keep close to Russia, to watch every movement of Vienna, and to be on the best possible terms with all other powers so that if Prussia ever needed allies she could negotiate with them.

Frederick had encouraged Austria to take Galicia from Poland as the best way of preventing an Austro-Russian conflict into which he would have been drawn, but the ambition of Joseph filled him with alarm. Glancing at his bust he remarked: "I keep my eyes on him; he is a young man whom I must not forget. He has brains and could go far. A pity that he always takes the second step before the first." Bukovina was squeezed out of Turkey in 1777, though Austria had taken no part in the Russo-Turkish War. A rumor had reached Berlin that Vienna was considering the exchange of Tuscany for Württemberg and had plans in Bavaria when the Elector should die. Frederick even believed that Austrian troops had begun to move when the news reached the Hofburg that he was dangerously ill. "I have

[1] The War of the Bavarian Succession must be studied in the *Politische Correspondenz*, Vols. XXXIX–XLII. Temperley: *Frederick the Great and Kaiser Joseph*, utilizes British dispatches.

certain knowledge," he wrote to Henry in April 1777, "that Prince Kaunitz has said: 'The Imperial court will never put up with Prussian power; that we may rule it must be destroyed.'" That ominous sentence, he declared, should be engraved on every Prussian heart. Under these circumstances the news of the death of the Elector of Bavaria on December 30, 1777 found him fully prepared.

The Bavarian line of the Wittelsbachs was at an end, and the heir, Karl Theodor, the Elector Palatine, was an idle weakling. Fearing the prospective increase of Bavaria's power by the addition of the Palatinate after centuries of separation, and thirsting for territorial aggrandizement, Joseph decided to carry out plans that had been long under consideration and to seize an opportunity "such as only occurs once in centuries. The circumstances of Europe appear favorable. The attention of all the world is occupied elsewhere and I flatter myself that this stroke will succeed without a war." The occasion, the excuse, and the wishful thinking are ominously reminiscent of 1740, for in both cases the antiquarian arguments were merely a smoke-screen for aggression. His ambitions were encouraged by the fact that the new Elector had no legitimate children and cared nothing for his nephew and heir, Karl of Zweibrücken. He feebly consented to a treaty signed on January 3, 1778, recognizing Austria's claims to Lower Bavaria, the territory bordering on the Hapsburg dominions, about a third of the whole Electorate, in return for money and titles for his bastards. So far it was plain sailing, but Joseph had reckoned without the King of Prussia, who was vitally interested in the balance of power in central Europe. "This morning," wrote Frederick on January 4 to his Ambassador in St. Petersburg, "I received the news that the Elector of Bavaria has died of smallpox. His death will upset the court of Vienna and perhaps divert its aggressive intentions from the Hungarian side. You know how the Bavarian succession has always inflamed its appetite and what projects of annexations it has formed. Now it will be difficult to decide which of these two conquests shall have priority. All this causes me anxiety, and the court will certainly push its conquests too far if it meets no obstacles in its path. France, though an ally, will be embarrassed, and I know she will never approve Austria's appropriation of a large part of Bavaria. Moreover, she is on the eve of hostilities with England. So the European situation may become very stormy this year. In a few weeks we shall see more clearly."

When Austrian troops crossed the Bavarian frontier the King looked around for allies. The outlook, he reported to Henry, was promising. France would do nothing for her ally, Russia offered help to Prussia, the King of Sardinia was ready to act against Austria in Italy. "So, my dear brother, the court of Vienna may repent of its unjust, tryannical, and precipitate conduct. The whole Empire cries out against it. Everything suggests that the Elector Palatine will recant and come back to us. Saxony puts herself in our hands, and I have asked the Elector to beg the protection of Russia. I shall write to the Empress and dilate on the range of her influence, her power, and her glory. Never has so much ink been spilled in my house: couriers are pouring in from all quarters and preparations are being made. There is a good prospect of winning over the Elector Palatine, or at any rate setting in motion the Prince of Zweibrücken. Never have I had so many wills, conventions, treaties, Imperial constitutions passing through my hands. I am perfectly tranquil about the future, resolved to do my duty as letter-writer or soldier. This is not a case of aggrandizement but of frustrating Austria's ambition and preventing her bossing the Empire, which could be very bad for us. So whatever acquisitions they may offer me I shall reject them, being resolved only to sheathe the sword when they have surrendered all their usurpations." The case against Austria was fully and forcefully stated by Hertzberg in a widely read brochure.

Prussia was not the only state menaced by Joseph's designs, but Frederick alone possessed the drive and resources to check them. "I am entirely of your opinion about the conduct of the court of Vienna," he wrote to Henry on March 3; "I see in it nothing but pride, arrogance, and violence. The gentlemen in Saxony are keeping me busy. These princes of the Empire are all broken reeds, without energy or honor. The Prince of Zweibrücken has been pushed along; left to himself, he would have accepted the infamy like his uncle the Elector Palatine. It is the disgrace of our century and I blush for Germany. I realize all the difficulties ahead. That is why I have to go slow and not tread before I know by soundings if the ground is firm. I know what a poor lot these princes of the Empire are, so it is not my intention to become their Don Quixote. But to let Austria usurp despotic authority in Germany is to furnish her with arms against ourselves and to make her far more formidable than she is today, which no one in my position should tolerate. The balance of the respective forces is the second reason that compels me to intervene, so as not to connive at her becoming so superior to us that some day we could not resist her. I regard war as inescapable; the Emperor wishes it and the armies are gathering."

Henry replied in his usual cautious vein. Since the news of the invasion of Bavaria he had expected Frederick to fight. "In my view a war undertaken with several allies would compel Austria to renounce Bavaria, whereas a war between equal forces would have no effect. All my hopes are fixed on your happy escape from this labyrinth. If I had not hopes of France I should be much afraid, not exactly of misfortune for the state, but of a most unhappy conflict from which you would emerge without the least advantage, leaving Austria in possession of Bavaria." Knowing his brother's shrinking from risks, Frederick was not ruffled. "I confess we have not got all the help we should like, but we shall not be found wanting in case of need." Henry was invited to discuss the coming campaign and received command of the army in Saxony, but he disclaimed all political responsibility. "Though we have not reached the point where all reasoning ceases, I see that all the most precious possessions of the state will soon be at stake—property, life, reputation, glory, the safety of society. I confess I had formed wishes that neither you, my very dear brother, nor your state should again be exposed to extreme danger; but since things have gone too far to change, I wish your preservation and prosperity, and I desire to be as useful to you as my feeble talents allow."

Frederick expressed surprise at these somber reflections at a time when he saw no reason for alarm. "Man is made for action, and how can we ever act more usefully than in breaking the tyrannical yoke that the Austrians desire to impose on Germany? On such an occasion we must forget ourselves, think only of the fatherland, and not cherish impossibilities such as peace." "You speak of somber reflections," replied Henry; "somber they would be if I only looked at the dark side, which is not my way. They would be light if I only counted on good fortune and illusions. I think there is a middle way which is the best and which

94

I try to follow, though it is the most difficult to find." His chronic pessimism, increased by anxieties about his delicate health, continued to provoke remonstrances from the King. "I am grieved that you see everything in such dark colors," he wrote on January 17, "and that you forecast a gloomy future, whereas I see only the uncertainties that precede all great events. There is no glory but in overcoming difficulties, and things that cost no trouble are not deemed worth having. All will go well. Courage and self-confidence! Then I guarantee that Joseph, Cæsar though he be, will learn to mix water with his wine." For the moment he was content to wait. Austria's occupation of all or part of Bavaria would upset the balance of power and endanger the liberty and Constitution of the Empire, and he would oppose it with all his strength. She should not be allowed to take a village, even at the cost of a war that might entail her ruin or his own. If ever a prince had a right to protest, he declared, it was the Duke of Zweibrücken.

Since Russia was his ally and would naturally disapprove the aggrandizement of her Austrian rival, even if she did not supply troops, Frederick's first task was to discover the attitude of France, for only with her active support could Joseph reach his goal. "Is it possible to imagine," he wrote to his Ambassador in Paris on February 2, "that an action so unjust, violent, and tyrannical as that of the Austrians against the Elector Palatine has not caused the least sensation in the French Minister and that he talks of peaceful sentiments when he ought to be shocked? I know Maurepas is nearly eighty and that French finances are unsatisfactory, and above all I know that the Minister fears the ascendancy of the young Queen, who is a sister of the Emperor. But what becomes of the solemn guarantee of the Treaty of Westphalia by France and Sweden, the Capitulations and Constitutions of the Empire overthrown, the security of successions dependent on the caprice of the court of Vienna, the liberty of the German princes oppressed? Do not imagine that the court of Vienna will stop at the first move; its views on Bavaria are not confined to these acquisitions. It will wait till the death of the Elector Palatine to put forward its remaining claims, including Bavaria and the Upper Palatinate, making the latter duchy once more an Electorate in favor of Archduke Maximilian. The task is to restrain the ambition of the house of Austria, to save the Empire from oppression, to keep the authority of the Emperor within its rightful bounds. If France can suggest some easy way of reaching this goal I shall be the first to follow it. If all good arguments fail, as in view of the arrogance and pride of the court of Vienna I anticipate, please find out if France, renouncing her guarantee of the Treaty of Westphalia, will at any rate adopt a policy of neutrality in this matter and give me sufficient assurances. The whole Empire, Catholic and Protestant, is horrified by this conduct. If we can combine our interests with those of France, that could lead to an alliance that Russia might join and that, in terminating this incident, might contribute to the stabilization of Europe." Allies would be forthcoming, and the Elector of Saxony had already invited his assistance.

It was a new experience for the robber of Silesia to find himself the champion of hereditary right, and he played the card of legitimacy for all it was worth. The poacher had turned gamekeeper. France was again reminded on February 9 that as a guarantor of the Treaty of Westphalia she was pledged to maintain the rights of the Elector Palatine to Bavaria and the Germanic Constitutions. In consenting to Austria's demands the childless Elector Palatine had broken the Treaty of Westphalia and had failed to secure the assent of the other branches of the Palatinate Wittelsbachs, the Dukes of Zweibrücken and Birkenfeld. Moreover, Austria had seized territory claimed by Saxony and Mecklenburg. "Both demand my aid. No prince of the Empire, myself least of all, will ever acquiesce in the despotic and tyrannous manner in which the court of Vienna tries to dispose of the succession of an Elector. Though I am as attached to peace as the French Government, I should always prefer war to peace in defense of these rights if Austria persists in her violent usurpations."

Since the Elector Palatine had sold his hereditary right for a mess of pottage, Frederick's hopes centered on his heir, the Duke of Zweibrücken. "He requests your protection," the Prussian Minister at his court reported on February 8, "and promises that he will never accede to the treaty with the Elector." "Your letter," replied Frederick, "is a great satisfaction. Your consent would injure Bavaria irretrievably. You have everything to lose by it and nothing to gain." His only fear was that Austrian threats might weaken the Duke's resolve. Anxious though he was, he felt that Austria's action had provoked a volume of opposition too strong to overcome. "I am convinced," he wrote on February 17, "that she realizes that this affair is too important and her own action too violent not to mean war. Perhaps, however, seeing France occupied with England, and Russia with Turkey, she imagines she need not trouble about me. But cool and experienced observers know that it would be sheer cowardice to let her trample on all law and the Constitutions of the Empire. I shall continue my negotiations with the court of Vienna. When I see that it is deaf to the voice of justice and equity, I shall have no choice but to urge Saxony, the Duke of Zweibrücken, and all the other interested parties to demand, in the name of the Empire, the guarantee of France and Sweden, and ultimately to draw the sword in order to obtain the justice that this court so obstinately refuses to all oral and written representations." He was not bluffing, for he felt himself on firm ground: in opposing Austria's designs on Bavaria he was safeguarding Silesia as well as upholding the rights of the Empire and stiffening the back of the Duke of Zweibrücken. Since he never believed that Joseph would retreat except under compulsion, war seemed to him inevitable.

Early in March 1778 the Russian Minister at Vienna reported that Austrian troops were moving to the frontiers; that Maria Theresa groaned at the prospect; that Joseph seemed eager for war, believing that France would not drop the Austrian alliance; that Russia was fully occupied with the Turkish war, and that Prussia was Austria's only antagonist. "He is burning with impatience and activity, goes in person to the Ministry of War, and hurries up military preparations. He is already sleeping in his camp bed and talks only of the coming fight. He says he runs no risk, since, if he is killed, he would always be the hero of the century, and that, if successful, it would be his glory to have beaten Your Majesty. I see no prospect of stopping him by negotiations." On receiving this news Frederick proceeded to prepare for a struggle. Henry refused to believe that Austria would challenge the whole of Europe, but the King was the better prophet.

After three months of fruitless discussion through the ordinary diplomatic channels, the Emperor forwarded a draft agreement to Frederick in an autograph letter dated April 13. The King of

Prussia was to recognize the validity of the treaty of January 3 between Austria and the Elector Palatine and the ensuing occupation of Bavarian territory, while Austria would accept the incorporation of Anspach and Bayreuth in Prussia on the death of their ruler. Frederick's rejoinder was a courteous but uncompromising refusal. "No one is more anxious than myself to preserve peace and harmony among the powers of Europe, but there are limits to everything and certain matters are too thorny for goodwill alone to suffice. Allow me to explain the present situation. The question is whether the Emperor can dispose of the fiefs of the Empire according to his will, in which case they are only held for life. But that is contrary to the laws and customs of the Empire. No prince will accept it. Every one will appeal to feudal law, which assures the transfer of his territories to his descendants, and none of them will consent to buttress the power of a despot, who sooner or later will despoil him and his children of their immemorial possessions. That is why the whole Empire cries aloud at the invasion of Bavaria. As a member of the Empire I am directly concerned in maintaining its liberties and rights and the Imperial Capitulations which limit the power of the Emperor in order to prevent abuses. That, Sire, is how things stand. I have no personal interest in the matter, but I am sure you would regard me as a coward and unworthy of your esteem if I basely sacrificed the rights, immunities, and privileges that the Electors and I have inherited. I speak freely. I love and honor your person. It will assuredly be hard to fight against a prince endowed with excellent qualities and whom I esteem." After reminding Joseph that the interests of Zweibrücken, Saxony, and Mecklenburg must be considered, he concluded by dismissing the offer in the draft convention. "The Anspach succession has nothing to do with it, for our rights are so clear that dispute is impossible."

A second letter from the Emperor, dated April 16, rebutted the charge that he had abused his power. The King, he declared, had misunderstood the position. "In all that has occurred in Bavaria it is not the Emperor who has acted but the Elector of Bohemia and the Archduke of Austria, who has vindicated his rights and reached a friendly agreement with his neighbor the Elector Palatine, now the sole heir of Bavaria. The right to reach an understanding with a neighbor without consulting third parties has always been regarded as an indispensable prerogative of an independent power, and all the princes of the Empire have exercised it." The claims of Saxony and Mecklenburg, he continued, could be discussed with the Elector Palatine, and the Duke of Zweibrücken had no rights so long as his uncle lived. "For these reasons I think Your Majesty will be convinced that the word 'despotism,' which I abhor as much as he, is inappropriate." This apologia made no impression on Frederick. "I beg Your Majesty not to believe that, seduced by a crazy ambition, I am mad enough to wish to play the part of arbiter among sovereigns. The lively passions are not in season at my age, and my reason prescribes limits to my activity. If I concern myself with recent events in Bavaria, it is because they involve the interests of the princes of the Empire, of whom I am one. I have examined the laws, Germanic Constitutions, and the article of the Treaty of Westphalia relating to Bavaria. I have compared them all to see if they can be reconciled with this occupation, and I have found only contradictions." Though two more brief letters expressed the hope that hostilities might be avoided by further negotiations, he was convinced that Joseph had gone too far to draw back, that his desire for a campaign was stronger than his desire for peace, and that he was merely playing for time, since his army was not quite ready for war. Frederick was prepared for the transfer of a small portion of southwest Bavaria in return for a small equivalent to the Elector elsewhere, but more he could not approve.

At the end of June, Kaunitz confessed that further negotiations would be fruitless, and on July 5 Frederick invaded Bohemia. Henry drew up a plan of campaign, which evoked the highest praise: a god, declared the King, must have inspired it, and he would found his plans upon it. No pitched battle was fought, but Henry's maneuvers won fresh eulogies. "What do I not owe you? Be assured that I shall never forget and that my gratitude will take tangible form." The War of the Bavarian Succession, popularly known as the Potato War because the soldiers did more stealing than fighting, is the only armed conflict on record that ended without anything worse than an occasional skirmish. Frederick had lost his dynamic energy, and his troops suffered grievously from illness and the desertion of many non-Prussian units.

The attempt to limit Joseph's ambitions found support in an unexpected quarter when hostilities began. "The recall of the Prussian Ambassador and the entry of Your Majesty's troops into Bohemia," wrote Maria Theresa on July 12, in the first letter she had ever addressed to her hated neighbor, "fill me with concern at the outbreak of a new war. My age and my desire for the preservation of peace are known to all, and I could not give a more striking proof than by taking this step. My mother's heart is justly alarmed to see two of my sons and a cherished son-in-law with the army. I am acting without informing the Emperor, and I beg that it remain a secret whether or not it succeeds. I desire to renew and conclude the negotiations hitherto directed by him and, to my great regret, broken off. Baron Thugut has full powers from myself." A postscript on the following day added that she was about to tell the Emperor of the mission, though without entering into details, in order to avert hasty action. Frederick replied on July 17, the day of Thugut's arrival, that the mission was being kept a profound secret. "It was worthy of Your Majesty to give signs of magnanimity and moderation in this controversial issue after having sustained your heritage with heroic firmness. Your Majesty's tender attachment for the Emperor and the princes deserves the approval of all sensitive souls and increases, if that is possible, my high respect." He added a few articles to the draft agreement brought by Thugut, which appeared to him too vague. "Pending your reply I will do nothing to cause you alarm for your family and for an Emperor whom I like and respect despite our different principles in regard to Germany."

Thugut's lengthy report to Kaunitz from Frederick's camp describes his obvious pleasure at the propositions of the Empress, which envisaged the evacuation of a portion of the Bavarian territories recently occupied. "Why were these sentiments not expressed a month ago?" he exclaimed. The ice was broken, but Frederick, mindful that Joseph was unaware of his mother's action, was on his guard. "These people wish to restore part of Bavaria and reach an understanding," he reported to Finckenstein and Hertzberg. "I do not know if they are in earnest, but the Empress has made the approach." Five days later he was less hopeful. "I must tell you that, though I am ready to reopen negotiations, I cannot feel any confidence in the sincerity of these new demonstrations. I believe they are only playing with us and that, having had plenty of time to make acceptable propositions, if such was their intention, their object is only to drag things out and make us lose the moment for action. The best plan will be to come to the point and to break off at once if they procrastinate or make difficulties about our proposals." To clear up the situation he forwarded new and detailed suggestions, which allotted a slice of Bavaria to Austria. Thugut quickly returned with a new offer from Maria Theresa to restore the occupied portion of Bavaria and to cancel the treaty with the Elector Palatine on condition that Frederick would undertake for himself and his successors not to unite the Margraviates of Bayreuth and Anspach with Prussia. This offer, surprising both by what it conceded and what it asked, was promptly declined by the King, who explained that the Margraviates were not a matter for discussion. He confided to his ministers that he distrusted Kaunitz even more than the Emperor: the duplicity that marked all his actions would prevent any agreement, and further negotiations would be a waste of time. It should be explained to France and Russia why they had failed and that he had done everything possible, so that Russia should be willing to render prompt military aid since the Austrians were simply trying to throw dust in the eyes of the public.

A letter to Finckenstein of September 10 reflects the King's mood after the failure of the Thugut mission. Russia was friendly, but her action was always very slow. "As for France, I am sure she greatly dislikes this war, partly because she feels she is not discharging her duties as a guarantor of the Treaty of Westphalia and because her failure to render assistance to Austria has virtually destroyed the alliance. As for the court of Vienna I will tell you exactly what I think. I have known the Empress-Queen since 1740, Prince Kaunitz since 1756, and my experience of their duplicity makes me distrust one as much as the other. In making acquisitions in Poland this princess is said to have shed tears over the occupation of provinces to which she had no right. Yet this consideration did not prevent her from extending her acquisitions considerably beyond the agreed limits and only returning the smaller part. So I do not take very seriously the supposed differences between mother and son in regard to German affairs. Aided by Kaunitz, she has all the power in her hands and can do what she likes. The finances and the army are at her disposition. The pretext of inability to secure the Emperor's consent is in my opinion a subterfuge to keep Bavaria or secure even greater advantages. Only the following considerations, I believe, would lead the court of Vienna to peace: (I) the lack of money; (II) the representations of France; (III) vigorous declarations by Russia; (IV) if Russia takes action in my favor, as I feel almost sure she will, that alone will incline the court of Vienna to peace. If these factors do not operate, it will be difficult to dislodge the Austrians from their present position and to carry the war into Moravia, where alone we could strike real blows and thus secure peace. Our greatest embarrassment in this conflict is that our enemy is everywhere in fortified posts where it would be very risky to attack him. But a Russian diversion would compel Austria to detach at least 30,000 men and thus enable my brother and'myself to act." Frederick was in no buoyant mood. "This campaign has not been brilliant," he wrote to the Dowager Queen of Sweden; "we must hope for better chances in the next. I do not know, my dear sister, when or whether I shall see Sans Souci again. The task I have undertaken is difficult and requires the vigor of youth." At the age of sixty-six the old campaigner had become as cautious as Henry.

At the end of November the first peace feeler was made by Vienna through Frederick's nephew and the most distinguished of his generals after Prince Henry, the hereditary Prince of Brunswick. "Prince Lichnowsky," he reported from Troppau, "has arrived here with passports from the Empress-Queen. He asks to wait on Your Majesty at Breslau in order to explain her sentiments and her ardent desire to see the end of this war before she dies if only the honor of the Emperor is saved. If the court of Vienna can retain a very small part of Bavaria it would be content, would indemnify Saxony, would drop the idea about the Margraviates, and would perhaps cede some mountain districts in the Neisse region. He tells me the Emperor will be in Vienna tomorrow, and that he is inclined to peace provided it is not entirely dishonorable." Frederick replied that he would be glad to see Lichnowsky and listen to what he had to say. No sooner, however, had the envoy reached Breslau than orders arrived from Vienna forbidding political discussions: the Emperor had arrived in the capital. "All my information," confided

Frederick to his nephew of Brunswick on December 13, "indicates the continuation of the war. The Emperor will not let go, and people say that he is ready for all risks in order to maintain his usurpation of Bavaria." Four days later he reported to St. Petersburg that Kaunitz was now believed to side with the Empress, adding that in such case agreement was not impossible. To his niece, the Princess of Orange, he wrote: "We swing between peace and war, but Mars will probably prevail." He explained the situation in a letter to Catherine on December 18. "The difficulty will be with the court of Vienna, not with me. The Empress Dowager, her daughters, and the whole nobility desire peace. But the Emperor, backed by Kaunitz, opposes, because this young prince desires to subject Germany to his despotic yoke, because he fears the charge of weakness, because in taking command of the army he increased his power, to which he expects his mother to yield, and because his subordinate position at Vienna has become unbearable, whereas at the front he is free." France, he added, was also impatient at his obstinacy. No one could charge Frederick with intransigence. When Hertzberg implored him to stand firm he replied that he must not lose the goodwill of France and Russia, both of whom were anxious to mediate and were striving to bring Joseph to reason.

After the issue had hung in the balance all the winter, Frederick wrote cheerfully to Henry on February 24, 1779. "Whatever the position of the Austrians, it is certain that they consent to restore the larger part of what they usurped in Bavaria, so it only remains to discuss the rest of the matter with the Elector Palatine and oblige him to pay the Saxons the four million thalers which are their due. The Russians and French undertake to see it carried out." The clearest indication of peace was that the Austrians were stopping all their arrangements for a new campaign. "So unless something unpredictable occurs, I believe peace is as good as made. The plenipotentiaries will meet at Teschen in a week; the armistice will follow the signing of preliminaries, and then we shall evacuate the enemy's territory the same day as they evacuate Bavaria." On February 26 he received a report from an agent in Vienna that the Emperor got drunk every afternoon, that there was no money, and that everyone sighed for peace. An uneasy peace of exhaustion was at last in sight. "We have had no striking advantage over the enemy that could humiliate him," he wrote to Henry on February 27. "They tell me that the Emperor, annoyed at having to disgorge his usurpations, desires to revenge himself at the first opportunity. So we must regard the coming agreement as a truce rather than a lasting peace." Yet Frederick was glad to see the end of the expensive struggle, all the more since the aid of his Russian ally, which would have had to be dearly bought, had not been required. "Though the restitution is not complete," he wrote to Henry on March 4, "this is the first project of the Emperor's unbridled ambition to be frustrated, and we gain the great advantage that in the Empire we shall be regarded as a useful counterpoise to Austrian despotism." Here, indeed, is the importance of the War of the Bavarian Succession, less spectacular than the rape of Silesia but scarcely less significant: Prussia was no longer a rebel, but a rival, the recognized champion of other German interests as well as of her own. Military glory there was none, but the political dividends were high.

March witnessed an armistice and the gathering of the diplomatists at Teschen. Prussia was represented by her ex-Minister at Vienna, who received frequent instructions from Frederick at Breslau. Even now he felt by no means sure that the disgruntled Emperor would not renew hostilities. The chief difficulty was the indemnification of Saxony by the Elector Palatine, who was nothing but a tool of Vienna. "If Saxony does not obtain an honorable satisfaction," he wrote to Henry on March 28, "no one in future will care to ally with Prussia. So I insist on this point: either Saxony receives an indemnity or I continue the war. So let us await patiently what the Congress will do; as I am prepared for all eventualities I have nothing to fear." The payment of the required indemnity to Saxony removed the most serious obstacle, and the Treaty of Teschen, an elaborate settlement in 124 articles, was signed on May 13, 1779. The Emperor had to content himself with a small fragment of Bavaria, the so-called Inn Quarter, and consented to the merging of the Franconian duchies of Anspach and Bayreuth in Prussia when their childless Hohenzollern ruler died. Hertzberg regretted the permission to Austria to retain even the smallest portion of a country to which she had no right, but his master was satisfied to have achieved his main purpose of checkmating Joseph.

Frederick had won the first round of the boxing-match, but

he realized that it was unlikely to be the last. "During the life of the Empress the coming peace in Germany, it is generally believed, will be stable, but to forecast the situation after her death is difficult. Anyhow it will not be easy for the Emperor to venture on the smallest enterprise, against either the Turks or Italy, so long as France, Russia, and I hold together." His debt to Catherine was acknowledged in a fulsome letter. "All Germany owes to Your Majesty the peace just concluded. A few words from you, madame, have sufficed to frustrate the whole ambition of Austria. When Your Majesty deigns to undertake difficult tasks, one is sure in advance that you will succeed." It was a further satisfaction that the Austro-French alliance had ceased to exist in anything but name.

When Maria Theresa passed away, in 1780, her gifted and headstrong son became the undisputed master of Austria, though the veteran Kaunitz remained at his side.[1] "A new phase begins," commented Frederick. He was prepared for further trouble, realizing as he did Joseph's fierce resentment of the Teschen compromise, and knowing from his own experience the temptations of a young ruler with a powerful army at his back. Moreover, the European landscape was constantly changing. Catherine now found a willing accomplice in her covetous designs against Turkey in the Emperor, who visited her in 1780. She concluded an alliance with him in 1781 and declined to renew the treaty with Prussia when it ran out. "The Emperor weighs on my septuagenarian shoulders," complained the King to his nephew of Brunswick in January 1782. "Perhaps he thinks me too old to draw the sword, but he sets my pen in motion. On all sides he gives me plenty to do, and I endeavor with equal energy to parry his attacks. Which of us will have Russia on his side is now the problem. They say in Vienna that he is seeking to isolate Prussia by drawing Russia away from us, for France will never unite with Prussia. In such an event we could only look to England, which would be less advantageous than our present position, but better than nothing. All these matters no longer concern me personally. My time is over, but my duty is to think of the welfare of the country and if possible to avert a destructive struggle like that of 1756. One escapes from such a danger only

[1] Ranke: *Die deutschen Mächte und der Fürstenbund,* Vol. I, is essential for the last six years of Frederick's reign.

by a miracle and one must do everything to avert it even when there is little hope of success." The advantages of adding Bavaria to Austria were so obvious that the attempt was certain to be renewed. As Kaunitz reminded his master, the Austrian Netherlands were too distant to be defended against France so long as the heart of Austria was open to Prussian attack, and the Emperor described Bavaria as perhaps the only means by which Prussia could be abased. Catherine's approval of his schemes was secured in 1784 by the argument that Austria would thereby be better able to combine with her in their designs on Turkey. Frederick's entente with Russia, which had begun in 1762, was at an end, and once more he found himself alone.

In this new phase of chilly isolation the King determined to cultivate the princes who had approved his attitude in the Bavarian crisis and to defend them as well as himself against further Hapsburg encroachments: no other policy was possible. In October 1784 he drafted a scheme for the sole purpose of maintaining established rights, which was worked out in detail by Hertzberg, to be ready for emergencies. They had not long to wait, for in 1785 Joseph renewed the proposal to Karl Theodor to exchange the whole of Bavaria and the Palatinate for the Austrian Netherlands with the glittering title of King of Burgundy. The Elector was not disinclined, but his heir, Duke Karl of Zweibrücken, indignantly rejected the offer of money and a royal title, for he knew that he could count on the strong arm of Prussia. The second attempt was even less successful than the first, and it was defeated without any addition to Austria's possessions and without an appeal to arms. "My God," wrote Frederick, "we are surrounded by cowardice and venality. Shall we alone be able to maintain the Constitution of the Empire? If France were to be won over by the Emperor's offer of Luxemburg, of which there are rumors, the only course would be to combine the voices of Saxony, Hanover, Mainz, Trier, and other princes in protest against all attempts by Austria against the Constitution of the Empire." France once again declined to take a hand in the Austrian game, and Frederick proceeded to construct the Fürstenbund or League of Princes, with fifteen member states. The Emperor believed, as he had believed in 1778, that Prussia would not fight, but this time there was no need to put his speculations to the test, for Prussia no longer stood alone.

When Hanover and Saxony joined, on July 23, the rest was easy. The Duke of Zweibrücken, the Archbishop of Mainz, chief of the three ecclesiastical Electors, Karl August of Weimar, the patron of Goethe, Gotha, Brunswick, Mecklenburg, Baden, Anspach, Hesse, and Anhalt came trooping in. The members agreed to co-operate in defense of the *status quo* in questions of common interest such as the election of an emperor. It was an imposing array, and for the second time in seven years Joseph found himself checkmated. His loss of prestige was Frederick's gain; more than ever Prussia was the rising sun in the German firmament, and his portraits were to be found in the cottages of the Bavarian peasantry, who had no desire to become Austrian subjects. The object of the Fürstenbund—to frustrate the ambitions of Vienna —was triumphantly achieved without bloodshed or expense. Since, however, the princes were agreed in opposing the schemes of Joseph but in nothing else, the ghost of the Holy Roman Empire lingered on till it vanished twenty years later at the touch of Napoleon's spear.

That Frederick had no vision of a European system or a concert of the powers is not surprising in the eighteenth century. The medieval idea of a *Respublica Christiana* was dead and no alternative formula of unification had been found; pioneers of the idea of a League of Nations like Penn and Saint-Pierre were voices crying in the wilderness. Yet he was no more a nationalist than an internationalist, for nationalism in our modern sense is the child of the French Revolution. Born into a Germany that, as Metternich said of Italy, was merely a geographical expression, he never dreamed of a nation state under a Prussian or any other head. German rulers were no more to him than anyone else, and there were more Germans than Frenchmen in the army routed at Rossbach. He was as eager to add Saxony to his dominions as he had been to snatch Silesia from the Hapsburgs or West Prussia from the Poles. His horizon was bounded by the interests of his little heritage as he conceived them. He anticipated Bismarck in his conviction that the power of Prussia could only wax if that of Austria waned, but Bismarck's conception of a Prussianized Germany and an Austro-German *Mitteleuropa* standing up like an impregnable fortress against attack from east or west was beyond his ken.

Frederick survived his final triumph over Austria by a year, during which he concluded the first commercial treaty with the United States. Working heroically to the last, despite asthma, dropsy, indigestion, and gout, he died in his chair at the age of seventy-four on August 17, 1786. He had signed his own death-warrant by sitting on horseback for hours in a deluge of rain during a review in Silesia in the summer of 1785, and he was never the same again. Mirabeau, who had been sent by the French Government on a secret mission in view of the anticipated change of ruler, reported the reception in Berlin of the news of the death of the monarch whom he described as the greatest man of his century. "Everyone is gloomy, no one sad. Not a face but indicates relief and hope; no regrets, not a sigh, no praise. So that is the end of all his victories and his glory, a reign of nearly half a century filled with great events. Everyone wished for the end and welcomed it when it came." Old General Möllendorf broke down when he addressed the officers. "You have lost the greatest of kings, the first of heroes. For myself I lose my master and, if I may say so, my friend." Beyond the frontiers there was a similar recognition of his stature and a similar sentiment of relief. "As a soldier," wrote Joseph to Kaunitz, "I regret the loss of a great man who will always rank high in the art of war. As a citizen I regret that his death did not occur thirty years earlier. Had he died in 1756 Silesia would have been recovered; now it is too late." His wish to be buried in the garden of Sans Souci near the graves of his dogs and his favorite horse was ignored, and he lies beside his stern father in the Garnison Kirche at Potsdam.

Frederick had never courted popularity, never asked for gratitude, never troubled about the feelings of his subjects towards himself and his work. He had been content to do his duty as he saw it, to plan and labor for the welfare and greatness of his state. He lived and died without much interest in the German race, without knowledge of the treasures of the German mind. Yet his impact on the political evolution of central Europe extended far beyond the limits of his little kingdom. The leading figure on the German stage since Charles V raised Prussia to the rank of a great power, not only by the flash of his sword but by his incomparable prestige, he developed the efficient and conscientious bureaucracy established by his father; he set the example of a working ruler, proud to deserve the title of the first

servant of the state; he inaugurated a system of religious toleration unknown elsewhere in Europe except in Holland; he sheltered the Jesuits when the order was suppressed in Catholic
countries; he subordinated private interests to what he believed
to be the good of the community; he left a fuller treasury than
he had found and an army of 200,000 men. *"Ein Heldenleben!"*
(a heroic life), exclaims the unemotional Ranke, and Carlyle
salutes him reverently as the last of the kings. In the words of
Mirabeau, he could have no successor.

All this is true enough, yet it is not the whole truth. The Re-
cording Angel finds as much to censure as to applaud—many
would say far more. In the domestic field Frederick completely
neglected the political education of his subjects, whose duty in
his eyes was to work, to fight, to obey. "The Prussian Monarchy,"
wrote Hugh Elliot, British Ambassador during the closing years
of the reign, "reminds me of a vast prison in the centre of which
appears the great keeper, occupied in the care of his captives."
The verdict is too harsh, since it ignores the autocrat's maxim
that his subjects might say what they liked so long as he could
do what he liked. A juster comparison would be to a school in
which, to use Mill's phraseology, the master does all his pupils'
lessons for them. In his *Lettre remise à Frédéric Guillaume II
de Prusse le jour de son avènement,* and in his eight-volume
treatise *La Monarchie prussienne,* published in 1788, Mirabeau
denounced almost every feature of the Frederician system—
military slavery, Mercantilism, the caste distinctions, the excise.
"Freedom of all citizens, of industry, of commerce, of religion,
of the press, more freedom of things and of men: that is the
whole art of government." Unfortunately, Prussia had to wait
for these reforms till the coming of Stein and Hardenberg
twenty years later. That the system could only be worked by a
superman no one realized better than Frederick himself, and it
collapsed when the guiding hand was withdrawn. The most
convincing argument against it is to be found in the picture
of his kindly but indolent and dissolute successor with piles of
unanswered letters on his desk. Prussia, in the celebrated words
of Queen Luise, went to sleep on the laurels of Frederick the
Great. Though he had doubled her size and trebled her population, he left her as he had found her, still essentially a feudal
state, the class barriers intact, the peasants serfs, the nobles un-

taxed. It was this stubborn and short-sighted refusal to share responsibility with his people that exposed him to the rebukes of such sturdy patriots as Stein and Arndt.[1]

In the sphere of high politics Frederick bequeathed a sinister tradition of successful aggression, justified, as he believed, by the doctrine of *Raison d'État*. He would have applauded the celebrated confession of Cavour: "If we did for ourselves what we do for our country, what rascals we should be!" The national industry of Prussia, complained Mirabeau, was war, and the blistering phrase has floated down the ages, though no Frenchman has a right to throw stones. It would be truer to say that since his accession in 1740 nowhere has the belief in arms as the natural method of settling disputes been so generally held, nowhere has the threat of war as an instrument of policy been so systematically employed, nowhere—with the shining exception of Kant—has there been so little sense of international solidarity or such scanty disposition to work for an interdependent world. Negotiations without arms, he declared, in a memorable aphorism, were like music without instruments. To hold the conqueror of Silesia solely responsible for this gospel of anarchy is absurd, but its prevalence and persistence may be fairly regarded as part of the price that Europe has had to pay for his victories and his fame. When Napoleon stood beside the coffin in the Garnison Kirche at Potsdam after the Battle of Jena, he observed to his generals: "If he were alive we should not be here." Is it surprising that his dauntless spirit lived on as the symbol of national glory and strength, an inspiration in the darkest hours, not merely while Prussia was a unit in a larger political structure, but when a Prussianized Germany had become the most formidable military power in the world?

[1] The state of Prussia at Frederick's death is described in Heigel: *Deutsche Geschichte seit dem Tode Friedrichs des Grossen*, Vol. I, and Martin Philippson: *Geschichte des deutschen Staatswesens vom Tode Friedrichs des Grossen*, Vol. I.

Chapter IV

THE CROWN PRINCE

ARIA THERESA used to speak of her terrible antagonist as "the evil man," and her Minister Bartenstein remarked that you might as well try to wash a black man white as to improve the King of Prussia. "I hate both those heroes and all such captains of banditti," wrote Horace Walpole on hearing of his death, bracketing him with the Emperor Joseph. Does he deserve such titles? Outside his own country the general verdict has been severe. "A repulsive and formidable person," remarks Lord Rosebery, and Lytton Strachey dismisses him as a knave of genius. One of his latest English biographers, Norwood Young, denounces him as definitely a bad man. Not even his ardent admirers have ventured to label him good. Happily the historian is not compelled to vote either for excommunication or for acquittal.[1] Men of action have a rough trade. To make omelets, as the French say, one must break eggs. For the rape of Silesia there is as little excuse as for the Massacre of St. Bartholomew, the expulsion of the Huguenots from France, or the three partitions of Poland. Yet the perpetrators of these crimes believed that they were rendering service to their state.

Frederick was among the most dynamic and audacious of rulers in any age, but he was far from being the worst. He possessed some shining qualities—above all, an unwearying devotion to what he felt to be his royal duty. While Napoleon, the perfect type of the complete egoist, cared far less for France than for his own career, Frederick dedicated his life to the service of Prussia and created a new standard of responsible kingship.

[1] The primary source for the study of Frederick's character during every phase of his career is the correspondence in *Œuvres de Frédéric le Grand*, Vols. XVI–XXVII, and *Politische Correspondenz*. The best accounts of his life before his accession are in Koser: *Friedrich der Grosse als Kronprinz*, and Lavisse, *La Jeunesse du Grand Frédéric*, and *Frédéric le Grand avant l'avènement*. Willy Norbert: *Friedrichs des Grossen Rheinsberger Jahre*, and Otto Gervais: *Die Frauen um Friedrich den Grossen*, are also useful. For his portraits see Koser and Seidel: *"Die äussere Erscheinung Friedrichs des Grossen,"* in *Hohenzollern Jahrbuch*, I, 87–117.

Trained in a harsh school, his gentler instincts frozen during the impressionable years of adolescence, he struck his contemporaries as a superman, ruthless and sarcastic, difficult to love and impossible to trust. He was capable of the meanest actions, and Bismarck charged him with vanity; yet he was by no means without softer feelings and he numbered men and women of lofty character among his intimate friends. A wiser upbringing would scarcely have affected his policy, but it might well have made him a happier and a better man.

Frederick the Great, like Henry VIII and Charles I, was a younger son, his two elder brothers dying in infancy. Such casualties in the nursery and the schoolroom have often changed the course of history. The first King of Prussia lived just long enough to welcome his arrival in 1712, and three younger brothers followed in the next twenty years. Yet though his parents had fourteen children, only one of them meant much to him throughout life: our dear Wilhelmina, as Carlyle calls her, three years older than himself, was his only playmate. His childhood was happy, for his mother was affectionate and intelligent and the brutal antagonism of his father was not yet aroused. The precocious boy enjoyed his lessons, learning from Mme de Rocoulle, the devoted governess of the royal children, and from his French tutor, Duhan de Jandun, son of a Huguenot exile, to write and speak the language of cultivated Europe better than his own. German, he confessed, he spoke like a coachman. Here is his first letter to Duhan that has survived, written from Potsdam at the age of fifteen, of course in French: "My dear Duhan, I promise that when I have my own money I will give you twenty-four hundred crowns a year and I will always love you, even a little more than now if that is possible." The promise of unchanging devotion to the good tutor who looked after him from four to sixteen and initiated him into French poetry was faithfully kept. Literature and music were his delight, and despite the parental veto he picked up a smattering of Latin in stolen hours. When the royal drill-sergeant, who demanded that his heir should be a pocket edition of himself, discovered the divergence of interests, he turned savagely against him and for many years darkened his life. The *Memoirs* of Wilhelmina are among the most untrustworthy of a class of works that at all times need to be studied with critical eyes, but their picture of the clash of generations and ideologies is true to life. Friction between the ruler and the heir is an old story, in Prussia and elsewhere, but in few cases has there been so much to quarrel about. Two ways of life were in conflict. The struggle never ceased, though in later years each became dimly aware of the merits of the other. Athens was ranged against Sparta, Weimar against Potsdam. Frederick's father was master of his fate but not of his soul.

All the fault was not on one side. Wilhelmina always speaks as if her father had little to do except to hunt, drink, and bully his family. That he was one of the hardest workers in Europe, a first-rate administrator, an upright servant of the state, she never understood. The ideal of this Old Testament Christian, as he has been described, was to be the *Landesvater,* the thrifty squire, the model soldier, the embodiment of discipline, the apostle of the strenuous life; but being ill-tempered, uncultured, and unrefined, his faults were better known than his virtues. To such a man it was infuriating to see his heir growing up, as he believed, an effeminate dilettante, wasting precious hours on poetry and the flute, indifferent to the army, caring nothing for the chase, loathing the drinking bouts and the horseplay of the *Tabagie.* Moreover, though the young man at this stage kept his religious convictions to himself, the stern Calvinist parent knew that the narrow Pietism to which he clung made no appeal. No one was ever less inclined than Frederick to take his beliefs on trust. It was still worse that he developed a weakness for the fair sex. The King drank to excess, but he was as faithful a husband as George III. For a short time after a ceremonial visit to Dresden with his father at the age of sixteen, it seemed to some observers as if the lad might take Augustus the Strong, Elector of Saxony and King of Poland, the most extravagant and dissolute ruler of his time, as his model. It was apparently on this occasion that temptation first came his way in the shape of the beautiful Countess Orczelska, at once the illegitimate daughter and the mistress of the Elector. The attraction to Doris Ritter, daughter of a Potsdam music-teacher, was more innocent, though the King, assuming the worst, had her publicly whipped and sent to prison. While his mother, herself a lover of books, encouraged him to follow his literary bent, his father could now hardly bear the sight of the rebellious youth. Even if we discount Wilhelmina's lurid anecdotes of "the pains of purgatory," we have the evidence of Frederick himself that for some years his life was almost insupportable.[1]

The crisis of the autumn of 1730 was as decisive for the shaping of his character as the seizure of Silesia ten years later for the evolution of his policy. Thoughts of flight began to take shape in his mind at the age of sixteen, as the British and French Ministers reported to their chiefs. He could bear anything, he declared, except blows, for there his honor and his pride were involved. His father, he complained, mistook the Crown Prince for a Prussian officer. The hazardous project was discussed with two young friends, Keith and Katte, and was whispered to Wilhelmina, who vainly strove to save him from the abyss. There was hardly a chance of success, for he was jealously watched and everyone dreaded the ungovernable temper of the King. The plan to slip across the French frontier during a journey with his father was discovered; Keith got away, but Katte was caught in the net. When Wilhelmina had reproved the latter for incautious talk, he denied that he had encouraged his master to fly, though he believed that no harm could come to a Crown Prince. "You are gambling for high stakes," retorted Wilhelmina; "I fear I am a good prophet." "If I lose my head," replied Katte, "it will be in a good cause, but the Crown Prince will not abandon me." Though he was a cultivated young man, his morals were lax, and he was not a wholesome influence for a sensitive youth of eighteen. The heir was deprived of his sword, assailed with blows, and cross-examined by his exasperated parent.

THE KING: Why did you wish to desert?

FREDERICK: Because you treated me not as your son but as a miserable slave.

THE KING: So you are only a cowardly deserter, with no sense of honor?

FREDERICK: I have as much as you.

The royal greeting to the Queen on his return to Berlin was a cruel lie: "Your unworthy son is dead." "What!" she cried, "you have been barbarous enough to kill him?" "Yes, but I want the casket." When she went to fetch the box of letters Wilhelmina

[1] The most authoritative account of the court is in Krauske: *"Vom Hofe Friedrich Wilhelm I,"* in *Hohenzollern Jahrbuch,* V, 175-210.

heard her moaning, "My God, my son!" The King's face, contorted by fury, was horrible to behold. Though he soon admitted that Frederick was alive, he poured forth terrible threats of death for his son and lifelong confinement for his daughter. Katte was beheaded in the fortress of Küstrin under the window of the Crown Prince, who was compelled to witness the grisly spectacle and fainted away. Whether his own life was only saved by foreign intervention we cannot be sure. While Ranke and Lavisse think that a death sentence was never seriously considered, Koser, a still greater authority, pronounces it not impossible. Frederick, at any rate, believed that his fate had hung in the balance. This shattering experience, which might have broken a weaker nature, forced him to face life from a new angle. Since the royal autocrat was master of the situation, the only course was to feign contrition and to play for time. After an interval of rigorous imprisonment, during which an army chaplain sent reports of his attitude to Potsdam and only books of devotion were permitted, he was allowed to live in a house of his own and ordered to serve his apprenticeship in the local administration of the Küstrin district. There was little society to be had except that of the attractive Frau von Wreech, the wife of an officer living not far away and already the happy mother of five children, who inspired a deep affection and to whom some of his earliest letters are addressed. He gradually regained his resilience, and after more than a year in the shadows he returned to Berlin. Terrified of his father and kept short of cash, he accepted money from Seckendorf, the Austrian Ambassador, to pay his debts. He had learned to think, to rely on himself, to conceal his emotions, to work hard. Suffering and reflection had matured him and at nineteen he was already a man. Starving for lack of intellectual nourishment, his overmastering desire was to get back to his friends, his music, and his books.

Frederick William I had married at eighteen, and the time had come to find a wife for his heir. There had been endless talk of a double match with the English cousins, Wilhelmina taking "poor Fred," the unloved son of George II, and her brother his sister Amelia. The Queen, a sister of George II, longed for the arrangement, while her suspicious husband, who detested his wealthier Hanoverian relatives, never desired an English wife for his son. The project was vigorously assailed by the court of

Vienna, and was dropped in 1730 after an angry scene between Hotham, the special envoy, and the King. Wilhelmina had to content herself with a distant cousin, a son of the Margrave of Bayreuth, while the colorless Elizabeth Christina of Brunswick, three years younger than himself, was selected for the Crown Prince.[1] The match was engineered by Seckendorf and Field-Marshal Grumbkow, the chief Minister of Frederick William I, who was in the Ambassador's pocket, in the belief that marriage with a niece of the Emperor would swing Berlin into line with Vienna. The notion that the wishes of his children should be consulted never entered the father's head. "You know, my dear son," wrote the autocrat, "that if my children are obedient I love them very much."

Having learned the bitter lesson that only slavish obedience would make life bearable, Frederick accepted his fate with grief in his heart. "They want to flog me into love," he complained to Grumbkow. "I pity the poor creature," he wrote even before he saw his Dulcinea, as he called her; "there will be one more unhappy Princess in the world." If we are to believe Wilhelmina, the Queen, embittered by the failure of her matrimonial ambitions, rubbed salt into the wound. "Your brother is in despair," she remarked at the family table. "She is just an animal. She replies to everything with Yes or No, accompanied by an inane laugh which makes one sick." Princess Charlotte chimed in with the remark that she exhaled an insufferable odor. Frederick changed color, and after supper Wilhelmina asked him about his future bride. He did not dislike her as much as it appeared, was his reply. She was nice-looking, but she lacked education and was very badly got up; Wilhelmina would doubtless be good enough to supply the polish. "I recommend her to you, my dear sister, and I hope you will take her under your wing." When the frightened girl arrived in Berlin and was presented to her future sister-in-law, she stood silent and motionless as a statue. Yet the companions in misfortune resolved to make the best of it. Though lacking personality, she was gentle, pious, and unpretentious; she played the harp and was fond of books. She tried her best to please her husband of twenty-one, and for the next seven years they were not unhappy. Though intellectual

[1] Hahnke: *Elizabeth Christine, Königin von Preussen,* paints a sympathetic portrait and provides selections from her correspondence.

comradeship was out of the question, she loved and admired him and won his enduring respect. "I should be the most contemptible of men," he wrote, "if I did not sincerely respect my wife; for she is the gentlest creature and is always seeking how to please me." Yet he could not love to order. At first they corresponded when he was away, and after the separation that followed his accession she recalled with wistful regret the brightness of the dawn. Though the mating of the eagle and the dove turned out a trifle better for the time than could be expected, her childlessness was a disappointment and the compulsion to marry a woman who shared none of his interests embittered a character already deeply seared by the tragedy of Kustrin.

Frederick's restoration to limited and precarious favor in 1732 was followed by his appointment as colonel of a regiment at Neuruppin, about forty miles north of Berlin; and on his marriage in the following year he was permitted to have a home of his own. Rheinsberg is as imperishably associated with the springtime of his life as Sans Souci with the middle and later years. The country was flat and uninteresting, but the house after its extension by Knobelsdorff and decoration by Pesne had a graceful and cheerful air, and the lake was a delight. "Do not form too lofty an idea of Remusberg," he wrote to a friend. "It is a retreat, a place for study, the home of friendship and repose. Everything is very simple; we avoid anything out of the common or pretentious." Here he could live his own life, keeping as far as possible out of his father's sight. "We lead a country life," he wrote to Count Manteuffel after settling down; "it seems to me more diverting and agreeable than the most brilliant courts. What a pleasure when one can give rein to one's talents despite all obstacles!" The evenings were enlivened by concerts and amateur theatricals in which the host took an active part. How they enjoyed themselves we can read in the *Memoirs* of Baron von Bielfeld.

˙ "I am always the same," he assured his old tutor Duhan in 1734, "but I am like a mirror that is obliged to reflect every object presented to it. I would say more but for the injunction of the sage to put a seal on one's lips." Under these circumstances study was his consolation, and in 1738 he reported that he was more buried in his books than ever. He read omnivorously, chiefly in Latin and French literature and modern history, dabbled in philosophy and science, formed an extensive library, and gathered round him a circle of congenial spirits. "I have a tender and sympathizing heart," he wrote, "and I feel the troubles of my friends as if they were my own." There was hardly a soldier among them except Baron de la Motte Fouqué, the son of a Huguenot refugee: the talk was of literature and the arts, not of politics or war. His special favorites were Jordan, a thoughtful, widely cultured, high-minded Huguenot, who entered his service as secretary and literary factotum in 1736 and was described by Voltaire as *bon garçon et discret;* Keyserlingk, a Kurland nobleman, affectionately described as *le cher Cesarion;* and Algarotti, a young Venetian interested in science. The despised German language was rarely heard in the house, and his writings, like his private letters, were in French. His first book, *Considérations sur l'état politique de l'Europe,* revealed how carefully he had studied the political landscape and how capable he was of forming his own opinions. *L'Antimachiavel,* published in the year of his accession and acclaimed by Voltaire as the best princely composition since Marcus Aurelius, enshrined his maxims of government, which in some respects approached those of the Florentine realist more closely than the title would suggest. His French verses, on the other hand, are described by Sainte-Beuve as his greatest sin, though he adds that they are no worse than others of the period once admired and now unreadable. They were composed purely for his own satisfaction, he explained to Wilhelmina, not with the ambition of securing a place on Parnassus. Neither in French nor in German could he spell correctly, and he liked his performances in both languages to be revised.

The choicest delight of the years of apprenticeship was the correspondence with French intellectuals—Fontenelle, Rollin, the historian of the ancient world, and, above all, Voltaire, which began in 1736 and continued with interruptions for over forty years. At first it was roses, roses all the way. The ardent disciple paid sincere and delicate homage by forwarding to the oracle his compositions in verse and prose to be criticized and improved. The *Henriade* and the early plays had taken Frederick by storm. The poet was flattered by the unstinted and indeed extravagant admiration of the heir to a throne, the only prince of the time who was seriously interested in things of the mind, and he responded with a cataract of compliments. *"Votre Majesté ou*

Votre Humanité" was the formula employed in his first letter after the pupil ascended the throne. In addition to the similarity of literary tastes, both were children of the *Aufklärung,* the Age of Reason, rejoicing in the thought that the reign of superstition and priestcraft was nearing its end. Prussia, they hoped, would be humanized and French culture grafted on its rugged strength. Like Voltaire, Frederick believed in a Supreme Being: "everything, even to the growth of a blade of grass, proves the Divinity." Yet his chilly Deism found no trace of a guiding hand in the tangled affairs of men. Among his favorite philosophical books were Bayle's *Dictionnaire historique et critique* and the writings of Wolff. In 1738 he became a zealous member of the first Masonic lodge to be established in Germany.

On his accession in May 1740 at the age of twenty-eight the character and ideology of Frederick were fully formed. The new ruler was aware of his exceptional gifts and was determined to employ them without delay. The transformation of Prince Hal into the hero of Agincourt was scarcely less dramatic than that of the young intellectual into the autocrat and soldier. "He will never be a general and a statesman," had been the verdict of Seckendorff, who had known him for years; yet he warned Vienna that he would need watching, owing to his deceitful nature. Close observers, indeed, expected him to abandon the limited-liability methods of his father and to strike out for himself. The scales fell from the eyes of the dying King when he exclaimed after the last talks: "I die contented since I leave such a worthy son and successor." Prince Leopold, the Old Dessauer, presuming on his age and military services in the first hours of the new reign to ask for the continuance of his authority, was sharply reminded that in Prussia all authority was in the hands of the King. The royal family, like the people, breathed a sigh of relief at the disappearance of the despot who had ruled them with a rod of iron, but they quickly discovered that they had exchanged one master for another. "I would give a hundred pistoles," sighed Pöllnitz, the Chamberlain, "to have our old ruler back." The Queen Mother, who had loved to dabble in politics behind her husband's back, was rigidly excluded from public affairs, though she was invariably treated with affectionate respect.

Frederick had sometimes thought of dissolving his marriage

when he was his own master, though he had no other partner in view, but his accession brought no immediate change. The new Queen was the hostess at Rheinsberg when Voltaire paid his first visit in the autumn of 1740, and perhaps she might have continued to share his home had she had children and had not her husband quickly plunged into war. What little affection there had been on his side melted away during his long absence, and the partnership, though never legally dissolved, came to an end. Henceforth they met only on official occasions and at family gatherings, and his rare letters became cold and impersonal. Solomon, he sadly remarked, had a seraglio of a thousand women and thought it was not enough. "I have only one, and that is too much for me." She received a moderate allowance, living at Schönhausen, just outside Berlin, in the summer and at the Schloss for the rest of the year. She continued to dream of a restoration to favor, but it was not to be. No word of reproach was uttered on either side, but her exclusion from his life and home nearly broke her heart. A nobler nature than that of Frederick would have saved something from the wreck. She never saw Sans Souci or the Neues Palais, for she dared not go without an invitation. She had the satisfaction of knowing that no one had taken her place, for the Barberina, the Italian dancer who took Berlin by storm in 1744, was only a nine days' wonder. Partial consolation was also derived from the sympathy and kindness of the royal family. Even the Queen Dowager, who had passionately opposed the match, softened and often invited her to Monbijou.

Her affection for her unloving husband survived decades of frustration and neglect. Writing to her favorite brother, Ferdinand of Brunswick, on the King's recovery from a stroke in 1747, she added that she had been terribly anxious and would have gone to Potsdam had she dared. A year later she poured out her heart. "From what I hear of the theater at Potsdam it must be very fine: happy are they who can see it. But it is not all the magnificence that would attract me, but the dear master of the place. Why is it that all is changed, that I have lost the old kindness and favors? I still think with pleasure of the time at Rheinsberg, where I was perfectly happy, being treated with honor by a cherished master for whom I would sacrifice my life. How I grieve it is all gone! Yet my heart will never change, and I shall always be the same for him and I still hope for better days. This is my only support. May the Supreme Being preserve this dear King in perfect health!" To her husband she never complained, though she occasionally reveals her bleeding heart. Here is an affectionate and anxious letter written on the eve of the Seven Years' War. "May God preserve you and soon give us peace and tranquillity, crowning with glory and happiness all your laudable enterprises and turning everything to your satisfaction. These are the very sincere wishes of a heart wholly attached and devoted to you and full of tender and sincere friendship but also filled with grief and affliction when I think that perhaps you are soon to be exposed to dangers once more; I cannot think of it without mortal grief. Forgive me for worrying you with my lamentations, but my mind and heart are so filled with them that I must break my vow of silence. I take courage to unburden my heart to the only person who causes my fears, and you are too gracious not to pardon me and not to understand my legitimate grief." The letter is signed in the usual way: "Your most humble, most obedient and faithful wife and servant Elisabeth."

The voluminous diaries of Lehndorff, her Chamberlain, reveal the lonely woman in her stuffy little court. Trivialities counted for more and more with advancing years, for she had no serious duties to perform and no intimate friends outside her own family. "I am extremely surprised at the Queen," is the entry on August 1, 1758, at the height of the Seven Years' War. "She sits two or three hours at table, talking of the petty disputes with the princesses at much greater length than of the big events concerning the welfare of the state. Never was I so bored at her table as today. It is impossible in a time of such danger to take part in such trifles." A few years later, at the marriage of the heir to the throne, we see her bustling about, "talking loudly, though she has nothing to say." A similar picture of excruciating boredom is painted in the well-known diary of Countess Voss, who was one of her ladies-in-waiting for thirty years.

After Wilhelmina's marriage and departure to Bayreuth, brother and sister met only at long intervals. He had introduced his fiancée to her future sister-in-law with the words: "The sister I adore," and indeed she was the only woman to whom in mature years he was ever deeply attached. It was not, however, an untroubled relationship, for each gave the other cause to complain. Her *Memoirs* were written during years of agonizing domestic grief, and she was so prone to exaggerate that we must take her testimony about her brother and everyone else with a grain of salt. Detesting loose living as she did, she was pained by his youthful escapades, and when this brief phase ended she noted with regret a growing cynicism and sharpness of tongue. Their first meeting after his liberation was at her wedding, when she found him surprisingly cold. He and her husband never took to each other, for the young Margrave lacked cultural interests. On returning from a brief campaign the latter reported that his brother-in-law was a changed man. It was only too true, as she discovered when he passed through Bayreuth on his way home. His sarcasms at the expense of "the little prince" and "the little court" were a shock. She felt that she had lost his affection and that he thought of nothing but his plans. During the Silesian War there was a breach of friendly relations, and some of his letters breathed an unusual sharpness of tone; but after three years the old affection returned and flowed in a tranquil current to the end.

The first Silesian conflict absorbed most of Frederick's attention for the first five years of his reign, and his character bore the marks of the fray. His baptism of fire at Mollwitz revealed the horrors of war. "A victory," he wrote, "but God save us from a second such murderous battle! My heart bleeds." His estimate of human nature, never very flattering, became ever lower. When the Inspector of Schools dilated on the beneficent influence of education and argued that human nature was now rightly regarded as inclined to good rather than to evil, as once supposed, the King acidly retorted: "My dear Sulzer, you do not know that accursed race." It was more probable, he added, that we sprang from evil spirits, if there were such things, than from a Being whose nature is good. Unlike most children of the *Aufklärung,* he disbelieved in his fellows and rejected the doctrine of perfectibility. Yet he knew good men from bad and entertained a genuine respect for their virtues. No one can read his early correspondence, particularly with Jordan, the most intimate friend of his early life, without feeling there was warmth and even gaiety in his heart. Here is a characteristic letter, dated January 14, 1741, when for the first time he found himself on the crest of the wave. "My dear Monsieur Jordan, my sweet Monsieur Jordan, my quiet Monsieur Jordan, my good, my benign, my peaceable, my most humane Jordan, I announce to Your Serenity the conquest of Silesia, I give you notice of the bombardment of Neisse, I prepare you for more important projects, and I inform you of the happiest success to which fortune has ever given birth. Be my Cicero in regard to the rightness of my cause, and I will be your Cæsar as regards its fulfillment. Adieu! You know if I am not, with the most cordial friendship, your faithful friend." And here is his last letter, written from camp in 1745 during the Second Silesian War, on learning that his friend was dying. "My dear Jordan, do not grieve me by being ill. You make me melancholy, for I love you with all my heart. Take care of yourself and do not worry about me. You will learn from the papers that affairs of state are going well. Adieu! love me a little, and try to comfort me by getting well." The letters to Duhan, both before and after his accession, were equally affectionate. He signs himself *"votre fidèle ami," "votre fidèle élève."* The last, written on the eve of his old tutor's death in 1746, concluded with the words: "Adieu, dear Duhan; believe me, I love you with all my heart." Sainte-Beuve, one of the few foreigners who have written of him in friendly terms, pronounces him a faithful friend.

Frederick usually visited his mother at Monbijou once a week and treated her with affectionate consideration, though there was little real tenderness. Of his sisters, Wilhelmina was always the favorite, but he was on affectionate terms with three of the others. Ulrike, who had brains and temperament, married the Crown Prince of Sweden, became Queen in 1751, strove for more power than her subjects allowed her, quarreled with her gifted son Gustavus III, and was not seen in Berlin again till as a widowed Queen she paid a long and happy visit to her old home.[1] Charlotte, Duchess of Brunswick, also possessed brains, and Brunswick was within easy range of Berlin. Frederike, unhappily married to "the wild Margrave" of Anspach, was a lightweight, and Sophie, the neglected wife of "the mad Margrave" of Schwedt, a drunken and dissolute boor, was even worse off. In later life the King saw most of Amelia, Abbess of Quedlinburg, the only unmarried member of the family, whose unhappy

---

[1] See Heidenstam: *Une Sœur du Grand Frédéric: Louise Ulrique.* Her letters to her mother, brothers, and sisters down to 1758 were published in two volumes by Arnhem in 1909–10.

romance with Baron Trenck, an aide-de-camp of the King, was to bring a dash of color into the domestic annals of the Hohenzollerns, but also to leave her permanently embittered.

Of the three brothers, the colorless Ferdinand, the youngest of the flock, never played or desired to play a part on the public stage, though he fought bravely in the Seven Years' War. Even the *Memoirs* of his daughter Louise fail to bring him to life. Henry was so gifted and so touchy that friction was inevitable, all the more since he regarded the King as too rash in both policy and war; he was not a member of the Round Table and they were never wholly at ease in each other's company. August Wilhelm alone, born in 1722, comes into the picture of the early years of the reign. The handsome and charming heir to the throne, who married a sister of the Queen and was created Prince of Prussia in 1744, was a feminine nature, lacking ambition, loving books, and happiest in the beautiful gardens of Oranienburg presented to him by the King. He had been his parents' favorite, and his relations with his elder brother were mildly affectionate till he grew to manhood and began to suffer from an inferiority complex. Except for urging him to safeguard the dynasty by a large family Frederick asked nothing of him and gave him no authority in the state. The marriage was unhappy, but his desire for a divorce and a second marriage to Sophie von Pannewitz, later Countess Voss, whom he adored, was vetoed by the King. The volume of correspondence between the brothers, edited by Volz in 1927, contains plenty of praise for the head of the family, "my best friend," but the adulation sounds a little forced. The Prince's conspicuous failure in the field in 1757 earned him a harsh and public rebuke. "My brother," wrote the King, "is intelligent and well-informed and he has the best heart in the world, but he lacks resolution, is very timid, and dislikes vigorous courses." The three younger brothers were inseparable companions, and Frederick resented the growing influence of Henry, who was overawed neither by his royal title nor by his world-wide fame. When August Wilhelm reported that Henry was deeply hurt at some lack of consideration, he received a sharp reply: "You swallow all he says. He is your demigod. Your uncritical friendship blinds you to his failings. He thinks he can lead the whole family by the nose."

The fullest account of the relations of the royal family is to be found in the diaries of Lehndorff, a Chamberlain of the Queen, which cover the years 1750–84.[1] He was intimate with the King's brothers, whom he calls the divine trio, but to his lasting regret not with Frederick himself. "I feel it is only done to hurt me," he wrote in 1756 when his request for permission to travel had been refused. "My God, how he could make himself loved! I brought into the world a heart full of love for my master, but he has never failed to cause me grief. He opposed a very advantageous marriage; he appointed me to the Queen's court against my wish; in a word, he has frustrated all my plans. I have always retained a son's affection for him, and I always hoped that he would be a father to me after so long being merely my King." "I have ceased to have great expectations," he wrote a few months later; "that is the only correct attitude for citizens in our country if they are not to fret to death. The moment one aims high or desires to be really useful to the fatherland, one must expect nothing but unnecessary annoyance. Here everything is a matter of luck. The King does not deign to take notice of young folk or to test their talents. He forms an opinion from the report of three or four people neither decent nor honorable. So we remain forgotten. The knowledge we acquire makes our situation appear even harder, and the end is total discouragement. I am an example. If ever a man was devoted to the King, it was I. I loved him like my father and would have sacrificed for him all I hold dear. But since I have always been rebuffed and insulted, only respect for him remains, whereas I should like to love him with all my heart."

Byzantinism was never tolerated by the Hohenzollerns till Bülow burned incense before William II. Confronted with the overwhelming personality of Frederick the Great, it was difficult for most people to find their tongues. Lehndorff describes a lunch party of forty on the birthday of the Prince of Prussia in 1753. Everyone was in the best of humor, when the arrival of the King turned the company into forty statues. On another occasion at a big dinner given by himself, the King denounced one of the female guests who had aroused his wrath, and proceeded to revile all the ladies of the court. The pretty ones married, he complained, and the ugly ones remained: "you can smell

[1] *Dreissig Jahre am Hofe Friedrichs des Grossen*, 3 vols., edited by Schmidt-Lötzen.

them ten miles away." Everyone was relieved when the meal was over. The guests hurried away "as if there had been an earth-quake, and each thought only of his own safety." The superman could do most things if he chose, but he scarcely tried to make himself loved. Yet he was grateful for loyal and efficient help. His political secretary Eichel, described by Lehndorff as kindly, modest, and hard-working, was the only person who knew all his master's secrets and enjoyed his entire confidence. In the course of years he came to feel something like veneration for the man whose extraordinary gifts he was in the best position to observe and whom he loyally served till his death in 1768.

Frederick's letters to Fredersdorff covering the years 1745–56 reveal a curious relationship and the softer side of a hardening heart.[1] Meeting him in the dark days at Kustrin, he took him to Ruppin and Rheinsberg, first as lackey, then as valet, finally, on his accession, as Keeper of the Privy Purse. Voltaire described him as *"le grand factotum du roi."* The King liked, trusted and cared for him like a father though Fredersdorff was four years older; he addressed him with the familiar *du,* gave him a small estate near Rheinsberg, and employed him in various confiden-tial affairs. In a letter written on the eve of Mollwitz he com-mended to the care of his brother August Wilhelm the "six friends whom I love best," of whom Fredersdorff was one. The faithful servant suffered from wretched health, and his frequent illnesses evolved expressions of tender and anxious sympathy. A few of the letters were published in a brochure in 1834 and a few more in the *Œuvres,* but it was not till the appearance of three hundred items in 1926 that the shadowy figure became a man of flesh and blood. He was too uneducated for cultural con-tacts or serious political services, and the letters deal with health, food, clothes, and other petty details of daily life. How far the valet returned his master's affection we cannot tell, but of his fidelity there can be no doubt. His death in 1758 was among the crowding afflictions of the Seven Years' War. Frederick in his time broke many hearts, but he could understand the meaning of bitter grief.

[1] *Die Briefe Friedrichs des Grossen an seinen vormaligen Kammerdiener Fredersdorff,* published 1926, reveal Frederick's complete inability to master the German language.

Chapter V

THE PHILOSOPHER OF SANS SOUCI

RHEINSBERG was presented to his brother Prince Henry in 1744, since Frederick desired a country house nearer the capital.[1] He had never cared for the huge palaces in Berlin and Charlottenburg, while gloomy Wusterhausen, with its unhappy memories, made no appeal to a man who did not hunt. He chose an attractive site near Potsdam in 1743, and Sans Souci, the masterpiece of Knobelsdorff, architect of the Berlin Opera House and the renovator of the Potsdam Schloss, was completed in 1747. Every detail of design and internal decoration, as well as the layout of the grounds, was discussed, and the elegant little building filled with pictures and statuary reflects the aesthetic side of the ruler's character. Watteau and Lancret were special favorites. Indeed, he pressed so hard for his own plans that his architects, one after the other, lost favor or resigned. Though plenty of hard work was done in the sunny rooms of the royal bungalow, it was intended mainly for refreshment of spirit and the claims of culture. Thrice in his life—at Rheinsberg, in the decade of peace, and after the Seven Years' War—Frederick gathered round him a select circle in which he could read his own and other poems, discuss the French classics, dilate on the supermen of history, and argue about immortality or free will. Though Wilhelmina described it as a monastery of which her brother

---

[1] Records of meetings and impressions are collected in Volz: *Friedrich der Grosse im Spiegel seiner Zeit*, 3 vols. Discriminating character studies by the diplomatists who knew him best are provided in *Mémoires des négotiations du Marquis de Valori* and *Memoirs and Papers of Sir Andrew Mitchell*. The pictures painted by Sir Charles Hanbury-Williams, Lord Malmesbury, and Hugh Elliot are of less value because they are based on less intimate knowledge. The vivid conversations with de Catt may be read in an English translation with a striking Introduction by Lord Rosebery. Frederick's relations to the Prussian Academy are described in Harnack: *Geschichte der Preussischen Akademie der Wissenschaften*, and Dilthey: *Friedrich der Grosse und die deutsche Akademie* (Dilthey: *Gesammelte Aufsätze*, Vol. VI). His debt to French culture is analyzed in Dilthey: *Friedrich der Grosse und die deutsche Aufklärung* (*Gesammelte Aufsätze*, Vol. VI). Zeller: *Friedrich der Grosse als Philosoph*, published on the centenary of his death, discusses his thoughts on ultimate problems.

was the abbot, there was plenty of refined entertainment. The host, an accomplished performer on the flute, often played his own compositions, with a son of John Sebastian Bach at the piano. After a visit in 1752 Winckelmann declared that he had found Sparta and Athens in Potsdam. In the words of Voltaire:

> *Il est grand roi tout le matin,*
> *Après diner grand écrivain,*
> *Tout le jour philosophe humain*
> *Et le soir convive divin.*[1]

Here, in "the feast of reason and the flow of soul," he was supposed to be the Philosopher of Sans Souci, as he described himself in a slender volume of verse and prose privately printed in 1750, not the King of Prussia. The assumption of equality, needless to say, could not be carried too far. His tongue was as sharp as a razor, and at times he seemed to take malicious delight in wounding the feelings of his friends. Conversation was in French, and almost all the Knights of the Round Table were imported from France. The Prussian Academy, founded by Frederick I under the auspices of Leibnitz and completely neglected by his philistine son, was revived under a new and wider title, Académie des Sciences et Belles-Lettres. Maupertuis, famous for his discovery that the poles are flat, accepted an invitation to become its president and to reside in Berlin. Euler, the famous Swiss mathematician, gave luster to the scientific section, and when he migrated to St. Petersburg he was succeeded by the no less eminent Lagrange. La Mettrie, a doctor and author, evicted successively from France and Holland for his truculent materialism, found shelter and a pension at Berlin till his early death. Formey, a Swiss Protestant, was appointed perpetual secretary, and the first volume of the *Transactions* was published in 1745. Among the King's many contributions were *éloges* of his friends and extracts from his historical writings. The proceedings were in French, and there was no thought of including the few German authors who might have qualified. Wolff, the King's favorite philosopher, was a member, and Hertzberg,

---

[1] *All the morning the great King,*
After dinner the great writer,
All day long philosopher,
In the evening host divine.

the learned lawyer who was one day to become Foreign Minister, was admitted as an expert in Prussian history.

The brightest star in the firmament was Voltaire, who paid four visits between 1740 and 1743 and only consented to seek a new home in 1750 after the death of "the divine Émilie." The intellectual atmosphere was so French that he could joyfully report that he was still in France. Yet it was a risky experiment, requiring for its success not merely mutual admiration, but mutual respect. The former was forthcoming in full measure, at any rate on the King's side, for the more Frederick knew of the mind and work of Voltaire, the more he recognized his unchallengeable supremacy. The guest talked as well as he wrote, and the host, himself an accomplished conversationalist, delighted in the cascade of epigrams and the flash of repartee. Their views differed as little in politics as in religion and philosophy, for the fastidious man of letters was scarcely more of a democrat than his host. That the humanitarian denounced the barbarism of war caused no embarrassment, for he was reminded that he knew nothing of such matters. Unfortunately, the liking of the two men for each other wilted under the acid test of daily intercourse. Each became acutely aware of the foibles of the other, and neither set a seal on his lips. The marvel is, not that the partnership broke down in less than three years, but that it lasted so long. The King was disgusted by Voltaire's financial speculations and incensed by his jealousy of rival intellectuals. The breaking-point was reached when *Doctor Akakia,* one of the most scintillating satires in literature, pilloried the pseudo-scientific absurdities of Maupertuis. The vitriolic attack on the president of his Academy was regarded by the King as damaging to the prestige of the crown, and the pamphlet was publicly burned. The time had come to part. In packing his luggage Voltaire took with him a presentation copy of the privately printed volume of his host's verses. Alarmed by the vision of his amateur efforts being scrutinized in the fastidious Paris salons, the author instructed the Prussian representative in the Free City of Frankfurt to retrieve the precious work. The instruction was carried out by a blundering official, and the traveler and his niece, who had come to meet him, were treated as prisoners in their hotel for several days. Poet and ruler never met again, but after an interval the correspondence was renewed and continued fitfully to the end.

An elaborate portrait of Frederick during the decade of peace was painted by the old soldier and diplomat Marquis de Valori, French Ambassador at Berlin from 1739 to 1750, who had accompanied him on his campaigns and earned his liking and respect. "His appearance is agreeable. He is small and distinguished-looking. He is irregularly built, the hips too high, the legs too long. He has fine blue eyes, a little too prominent, which reflect his feelings and differ greatly according to circumstances. When he is displeased they are fierce, but when he wishes to please, none are softer, more affectionate, more engaging. The mouth and nose are agreeable. The smile is amiable and intelligent, though often mocking and bitter. His sweetness of expression appeals to everyone when he is in tranquil mood. Who would not be attracted when he wishes it or terrified when he is angry? His health is precarious, his constitution is fiery, and his regimen contributes to the heating of his blood. He used to indulge in coffee to excess. Once I ventured to suggest he was taking too much. Now he had only seven or eight cups in the morning and one pot after dinner, was his reply. He is extreme in everything. His special failing is his contempt for mankind. He only admits intelligence in very few; he undervalues what is called good sense—that is, a sound, straightforward judgment independent of cleverness. He talks much and extremely well, but he is a bad listener and he meets objections with ridicule. It is difficult to be more rash in everything, hence his contempt for people. He denounces vices with surprising eloquence. It is the same with morality, the best features of which he seems to have learned by heart; but he is so inconsequent and so little convinced of what he is saying that in a quarter of an hour he is contradicting himself.

"Yet he has his principles in administration as well as in policy, though the latter are often subordinated to the moment, to caprice, to unconfirmed reports. Happily such decisions are not final and he usually returns to the truth. His course once decided, he cares nothing for forms. He is distrustful to excess. If he were less so, it would be enough for him to conceive the plan, leaving the rest to his ministers, who, wiser though less enlightened than he, would soften what is too severe in application. He thinks men are all made to obey without rejoinder or reflection, and this explains his excesses and astonishing inconsistencies. I have always tried to unravel the motives of his orders, his refusals, his reasons for mortifying or caressing those who approach him. I have been forced to the conclusion that in most cases they were good ones though the form needed improvement. His great vivacity leads him to precipitancy. He owes to his slapdash temerity the conquest of Silesia. Why should I not say so, since he confessed as much to myself? The high standard of his troops and magazines increased his audacity so long as he was only confronted with a small force dispersed over Silesia, but when he was up against an army, he realized all the risks and I think even exaggerated them. His constant good fortune nourished his self-confidence for a time, but later reflection convinced him that he owed much to luck. He always despised his enemies from afar, particularly the Saxons; it was they who gave him most anxiety in 1744, though he punished them in 1745. It was in this latter campaign that he revealed the talents of a great general. He believed himself to possess them all, as well as those of the King and the writer, a strange mixture. Wit became his hobby-horse, just as giant soldiers appealed to his father. He coveted a reputation for universality, the poet, the orator, the musician added to the great King. His large army necessitated great economy, but I think he carried thrift too far. No one had a more alert intelligence, though it might have been turned to better account. Nobody exercised such seduction when he chose, as was always the case when his *amour-propre* was involved. After winning you he ignored you, and he ended by regarding you as his slave for servile obedience to his caprice. He is hard and imperious with his brothers, keeping them in a state of dependence to which he never submitted in his father's days." Frederick liked Valori more than the Ambassador liked the King, but this analysis of his complex character is based on too close study during long years of sunshine and storm to be lightly dismissed.

This French portrait may be compared with the somber picture by another diplomatist, Sir Charles Hanbury-Williams in October 1750. "Now for a little about the completest tyrant that God ever sent for a scourge to an offending people," he wrote to his bosom friend Henry Fox. "I had rather be a post-horse than his First Minister, or his brother, or his wife. He has abolished all distinctions. There is nothing here but an absolute Prince and a People, all equally miserable, all equally trembling before him, and all equally detesting his iron government. There is not so much distance between your footman and you, or between an English soldier and his captain, or between a curate and a Bishop, as there is between the King of Prussia and his immediate successor the Prince of Prussia, who dares not go out of Berlin one mile without his tyrant's leave nor miss supping every night with his Mamma upon any account. Another of his brothers is at this moment sent into banishment in a country town; and the third is in frequent danger of being put in irons for daring in conversation sometimes to have an opinion of his own. It is known that Princess Amelia has a mind to be married to the Duke of Deux Ponts. But he, Nero, told her t'other day that she must never marry. His reason is that she is to be the Abbess of Quedlinburg, which is worth about 5,000£ per annum. He will have her to spend that money in Berlin. He makes a great rout with his mother, but people that know him well know that he does not love her. She is an old gossip, with all the tittle-tattle of that sort of people, and she is reckoned to have a large share of ill-nature. One would think that the wretched life that the King and Queen Mother led under the late King of Prussia's reign would have taught them humanity. Instead of which they seem only to have learnt the art of making those under them as miserable now as they themselves were formerly. The least that passes in a private family must undergo the royal inspection. He keeps several persons at Berlin who daily write journals of all that passes there and send them to Potsdam, and at the head of this tribe of news-writers is Her Sacred Majesty the Queen Mother. It is a melancholy sight to see the Queen. She is a good woman and must have been extremely handsome. It is impossible to hate her; and though his unnatural tastes won't let him live with her, common humanity ought to teach him to permit her to enjoy her separate state in comfort. Instead of this he never misses an opportunity of mortifying this inoffensive, oppressed Queen. And the Queen Mother assists her dearly beloved son in this to the utmost of her power by never showing her common civility or hardly ever speaking to her. He hates in general to see people happy. For his sway is founded on vexation, and in oppression is his throne established." In reading this slashing indictment we must remember that the writer only spent a few months in the Berlin Embassy and only met the King on a few official occasions.

The Seven Years' War crashed into the busy routine of Frederick's life and tested him, morally and physically, to the uttermost. He met the challenge with the resilience of a blade of Toledo steel, and indeed nothing but his unbending resolution could have carried him through. In the words of Napoleon, he was greatest when things were at their worst. His changing moods are mirrored in his correspondence and in the vivid dispatches of Sir Andrew Mitchell, who, at the wish of King George II, accompanied him on his campaigns and was sometimes under fire. The Ambassador, who held his post for fifteen years, was no flatterer, but his dominant impression was one of incomparable resilience and resource. "His superiority of talent," he reported in May 1759, "the readiness and fertility of his invention, fill me with confidence. No sooner does one project fail than he is ready with another; no disappointment discourages him, no success elates him beyond measure. It is impossible to describe the fatigue of body and mind which this hero King undergoes, and that with an appearance of perfect tranquillity, even in the most unfavourable and perplexing circumstances." In the autumn of the same year, after the terrible disaster at Kunersdorf, he reported to Pitt: "I cannot despair while the hero lives." Almost everyone despaired except himself. "The King will do everything man can do," wrote the Ambassador in January 1760; "but his country is exhausted, the instruments of action are exhausted, his best officers are either killed or prisoners; a general discouragement reigns through the whole army from the fatal effects of which he is perhaps the only person exempted." That a price had to be paid for this iron self-control was no surprise. "Ferocity has seized his mind and cruelty has steeled his heart." The Ambassador never loved him, but he respected and admired him to the last.

Resounding victories alternated with catastrophic defeats; but whereas no single triumph could bring him peace, for he could never dispose of all his enemies at the same moment, a sudden turn of the wheel of fortune might involve total collapse. "I am in purgatory," he wrote to de Catt in August 1760; "the burden often becomes insupportable. Nothing points to a decision; my patience wanes; it is enough to drive one mad." He poured out his heart in his letters to d'Argens, Keith, and other friends, complaining bitterly of the dog's life he was forced to lead, the physical privations, the loneliness, the crushing superiority of his enemies, the hopelessness of the military outlook. "Often I should like to drown my sorrows in liquor," he confided to his sister Amelia; "but as I do not drink, nothing helps except to make verses and then I forget my misfortunes for the time." Luck, he declared again and again, would settle it as it settled most things, though whether in his favor or otherwise he could not predict. "It's a dog's life," he wrote to Mme Camas in 1760, "which no one except Don Quixote has had to live." He added in 1762 that for the last six years he had envied not the living but the dead; to the Duchess of Saxe-Gotha he wrote that he would rather clean out the stables of King Augeas. The destiny of Prussia rested on the physical survival of a single man, and he knew that the eyes of the world were upon him. Never had he felt so lonely. His mother passed away in 1757, Wilhelmina in 1758. Her last letter was to him. "The most affectionate, the most faithful friendship united the King and his noble sister," he wrote in his *Memoirs*. She was a princess of rare worth, he added, with a fine intellect, a special talent for the arts, and a generous heart. The Margravine had her failings, but these carefully chosen words are strictly true.

A tragedy of another kind was the violent breach with the Prince of Prussia, who had disapproved the attack on Saxony which opened the desperate struggle and who at first received no command. His gentle nature was shocked by the rough processes of war as it was waged by his brother in Saxony. "We live in a century which has given birth to Prussian power," he wrote on April 15, 1757 to Princess Henry, from whom he had no secrets. "Luck and wise governments have brought it to the state we see. Beware lest folly, pride, and caprice do not destroy this fine edifice. If providence concerns itself with our proceedings in Dresden, what are we to expect?" He proceeded to lament his own fate. "My position is most disagreeable. No one takes notice of me and I am conscious of a chillness bordering on contempt. You know me, so you will understand that my heart is broken." He complained of neglect; but when on the death of the veteran Schwerin in battle in 1757 he succeeded to the command of an army, he failed to save Gabel and Zittau from the Austrians after the disaster at Kolin and was forced to retreat to Bautzen, where he met the King. Frederick was in his most terrifying mood, refusing even to speak to his luckless brother. "After this," he wrote, "it is impossible to entrust you with an army. You will always be a wretched soldier." The verdict, though severe, was not unjust; August Wilhelm was no soldier. He resigned his command and retired to Oranienburg with bitterness in his heart. He had a good conscience, he declared; the King had made him a scapegoat for his own mistakes. "Our great man is so full of himself," he wrote to Princess Henry, "he asks nobody's advice, he is so impulsive, he refuses to believe truthful reports, and when the luck turns he throws the blame on the guiltless." A year later, in the summer of 1758, August Wilhelm died at the age of thirty-six. Though not apparently the direct result of his disgrace, the public humiliation undoubtedly helped to devitalize him. When he was gone the King regretted his harshness, spoke gently of him in his *Memoirs,* and did his best for the children, the eldest of whom, Frederick William, a boy of fourteen, became heir to the throne. With Wilhelmina, who married Prince William of Orange, her uncle corresponded affectionately for twenty years.

The next brother, Prince Henry, who had been too young to play a part in the first two Silesian Wars, now began to reveal the talent which earned him the King's compliment that he was the only one of his generals who never made a mistake. Yet the brilliant soldier who was so useful in the field gave little moral support in critical times and was never a real friend. "My adored Prince Henry," writes Lehndorff, the Queen's Chamberlain, "deserves to be the master of the world." Even Lehndorff, however, confessed that there were spots on the sun. He was inclined to extravagance and, even when loaded with rewards, always dissatisfied. Mitchell, the British Ambassador, described him as very vain and jealous of his brother's greatness.

Koser's publication in 1884 of the conversations and diaries of Henri de Catt during the years 1758–60 was a landmark in the history of Frederician studies. He and Frederick had met on a Dutch canal boat when the young student from French Switzerland was at the University of Utrecht and the King of Prussia was traveling incognito as First Musician to the King of Poland. The royal tourist, attracted by his obvious intelligence, his love of French literature, and his refined manners, revealed his identity and offered him the vacant post of *Lecteur.* The first *Lecteur,* Darget, had returned to France, and his successor, the Abbé de Prades, had been dismissed and imprisoned on the ground that he had betrayed military secrets. De Catt readily accepted and remained in his service for over twenty years, but for some reason his records embrace only the first two. He was more than a *Lecteur,* for he drafted, revised, or copied letters in French, bore the infliction of his master's verses, and played the part of sympathetic listener whenever the superman was in the mood for talk. The partnership opened happily, for they liked and respected each other. Frederick's letters to him are charming, and his references in the correspondence with Voltaire, d'Alembert, and other friends are always laudatory. The new recruit was a cultivated and tactful man, equally free from embarrassment and familiarity. He became a member of the Berlin Academy and settled down happily in his second home. Even when he lost his post in 1780, owing apparently to unproved charges of bribery, he remained in Potsdam till his death in 1795. Like other French-speaking visitors for long or short periods, he never learned German. His manuscripts were bought by Frederick William III in 1831 and used by Preuss in the first documentary history of the reign. The diary entries, which are brief and colorless, are omitted in the English translation published in 1916 with a sparkling Introduction by Lord Rosebery; for the conversations offer a great deal more than the notes, sometimes touching them up, sometimes contradicting them, often adding materials from other sources. Though compiled or at any rate revised after the loss of favor, there is no trace of resentment in the finished work. "The more I see of this prince," he wrote after a month's experience, "the more reason I have to love and honor him." For twenty-four years the King honored him with his entire confidence, he declares in the Introduction, written thirty years later, when his old master was in the grave. "The estrangement, so little deserved, will not influence me." All is admiration and respect. The conversations are doubtless *Dichtung und Wahrheit,* artistic renderings rather than exact reports, and the chronology is very confused; yet there is no reason to doubt the substantial accuracy of the picture. The chief points, he tells us, were written down every evening.

The *Lecteur* started work at Breslau in March 1758, at the height of the Seven Years' War. The sensational victories of Rossbach and Leuthen in the previous year had made Frederick the most famous man in Europe, but the worst was still to come. The iron warrior appears in a softer light than we might expect. Plagued not only by anxiety but by gout, indigestion, and sleeplessness, he relieved his feelings in tears, in the composition and recitation of poetry, and in the unfailing companionship of his flute. Producing a little gold box on a chain on his bosom that contained eighteen opium pills, he remarked: "There, my friend, is all that is required to put an end to this tragedy." Yet the mood of black depression never lasted very long. De Catt was never a guest at the royal table and could hardly be reckoned as a friend, but he was often summoned for an hour's talk in the late afternoon at the most tragic moments of the campaign.

The King loved to speak of past times. His father, he declared, was a terrible man, but a just man. "His work made mine possible." The tragedy of Kustrin, when "the grenadiers held my head at the window," was often in his thoughts. At Rheinsberg, he declared, he studied day and night, reveling in Cicero and Plutarch, Lucretius and Tacitus, but above all in Racine. Voltaire, of whom he constantly spoke, was dismissed as "that weasel": "if his heart equalled his genius he would have towered over everyone." Maupertuis had an honest heart; La Mettrie was humorous but credulous; Algarotti had a fine brain, but was very selfish. "The good and worthy Jordan was the friend I preferred." Sir Andrew Mitchell was described as "an excellent man, with a good heart, widely cultivated, and attached to me." Maria Theresa was always mentioned with respect. "She is my enemy, but I must do her justice. Princesses like her are rare." The passing of Wilhelmina cut him to the heart. "She was infinitely dear to me. To her I owe for the most part the little I am worth. She urged me to work, to study, to take my position seriously." The death of Marshal Keith in action moved him more than that of Schwerin. He talked longingly of Sans Souci, regretting that fate had not allowed him a quiet life. Once he observed that the death of the Prince of Prussia had destroyed the dream of abdicating in his favor and withdrawing to the delightful society of chosen friends, but de Catt was not impressed. Everyone knew that August Wilhelm was unfitted for the burden of rule, and nobody imagined that the ablest autocrat of the eighteenth century would follow the example of Charles V. Epicurus, declared the King, appealed to the young and the fortunate; riper years and the experiences of life made him a Stoic. Yet the Stoic always kept a warm place in his heart for the friends of his youth. "If it all ends well," he wrote in 1762 to Mme Camas, aged seventy-six, "how I shall thank heaven to see you again, *ma bonne maman,* and to embrace you. Yes, I say embrace you, for now you have no longer any lover but me, you can no longer make me jealous, and I have a right to demand a kiss as the price of my constancy and attachment. So you must prepare yourself."

When Frederick returned from the Seven Years' War, the hands of the clock seemed to slow down. The pilot had weathered the storm, but the fire of youth had burned itself out and the era of adventure was followed by the era of routine. Every penny was needed for his suffering land. "The King's economy," reported Mitchell in 1764, "has increased of late to such an extent as to deserve another name; it extends to the meanest trifles. He is often rough and out of humour." Two years later the Ambassador wrote to Chatham: "Great men have their failings. His is that of vanity, and a desire on every occasion to have the lead." Though still full of mental and physical vigor, he looked and felt like an old man. More than ever he was *le premier domestique de l'État,* the father of his country, toiling on *ohne Hast, ohne Rast.* While individuals meant less and less to him, the figure of Old Fritz in his faded blue snuff-soiled uniform and cocked hat grew ever more familiar as he moved about his provinces with the regularity of the seasons. Prussia, he was resolved, should be both a *Rechtsstaat* and a *Kulturstaat.* So anxious was he that the meanest of his subjects should have fair play that in the celebrated case of Miller Arnold he angrily dismissed and imprisoned the Grand Chancellor and the other magistrates whom he believed to have favored the richer side, though, as it turned out, they had done no more than their duty and were reinstated in the following reign. Everyone knows the story of the King finding a crowd gazing at a picture in the street. In answer to his inquiry he learned that it was a caricature of himself grinding coffee inspired by detestation of the French excisemen. "Hang it lower," came the order, "so that they can get a better view," and he drove on amid cheers. "That arrangement suits me very well," was his terse comment; "they say what they like and I do what I like." While his entourage had often to complain of his temper and his tongue, the little man was inclined to regard him as a protector and a friend.

A vivid and not wholly unsympathetic portrait of the King soon after the return of peace is painted in the well-known volumes of Thiébault: *Mes Souvenirs de vingt ans de séjour à la cour de Berlin.* When the Professor of Literature at the Academy, who had been selected by d'Alembert, arrived in 1765, he was summoned to Potsdam.

THE KING: You do not know German?

THIÉBAULT: No, sir, but I hope soon to master it.

THE KING: You are fortunate in your ignorance. Give me your word of honor that you will not learn our language.

The promise regretfully given was faithfully kept. Frederick took to him and summoned him occasionally for a talk. It was not always an unmixed pleasure, for the host was mistrustful and the Frenchman never felt entirely at ease. Great tact and self-control were needed when the King indulged his unpleasant propensity for gibes to which argumentative replies were impossible. In conversing with literary men, declares Thiébault, he liked to forget that he was King, but he would not have been pleased if it were forgotten by his guests. Loving philosophic discussions, he would encourage visitors to express their opinions, particularly on the subject of religion, and would then launch out in sarcastic comment. When the embarrassed guest took refuge in silence, he was annoyed. Had he a heart? Thiébault asked himself. For a time he could not answer the question, but the problem was solved when the death of his nephew Prince Henry, a promising lad of eighteen, moved him to almost uncontrollable grief. Among Thiébault's duties was that of revising and sometimes reading to the Academy his master's dissertations, a task beset by many pitfalls. Once the royal author lost his temper when a bad mistake was pointed out and a second attempt was pronounced even worse. "This new criticism was too much for him. His face became red with anger and wore a menacing look. It was a tense moment, but the danger quickly passed." The correction was accepted, for the royal author prided himself on his French and felt that he had a reputation to lose. De Catt, we are told, despite his official title, never read to his master, who preferred to read aloud himself. Once when the King's eyes were bad, Thiébault read *Figaro* to him, but Beaumarchais pleased the Prussian autocrat as little as Louis XVI. Five copies were bought of every book that he desired to read, since he possessed identical libraries at Potsdam, Sans Souci, Charlottenburg, Berlin, and Breslau. Possessing only a smattering of Latin and no Greek, he studied the classics in French translations. From the beginning to the end of his life France was his spiritual home.

Chapter VI

AUTUMN SHADOWS

THE NEGLECTED Queen had faded out of her husband's life. Though he always treated her with outward consideration and they met on ceremonial occasions, she bored him and he could bear anything better than ennui. She, on the other hand, kept a warm place for him in her heart, and her letters to her brother Prince Ferdinand of Brunswick, the distinguished soldier, are full of allusions to "our dear King." That of July 12, 1757, on the death of the Queen Mother, brings us very close to the lonely woman. "Only time can help. The loss is too great and I can never forget the friendship she showed me in recent years. She had real confidence in me and did justice to my attitude to her and the dear King. If anything could console me it is that I never failed in my duty to her and that she recognized it. She often gave me her blessing; if all her wishes are fulfilled I shall surely be happy. So I shall if God preserves him and arranges everything for the best, and if the King renders me a little more justice, this dear prince whom I love and adore as I shall to the end. What a satisfaction it used to be when I was with the dear departed and talked with her about this dear King and wished him every blessing! None of her children could regret her more than I." A single tender word from her husband, an occasional invitation to Potsdam, would have been balm to her heart, but it never came. His few letters are brief and impersonal, and she is never mentioned in his correspondence with friends and relatives. "Madame is fatter" was his chill greeting after the long separation of the Seven Years' War. Yet she never ceased to enjoy his respect. In his will drawn up in 1769, he begged his successor to allow her a suitable residence in the Palace at Berlin, and to show her the deference due to the widow of his uncle and a princess "whose virtue never varied." But he wanted personality as well as virtue, and personality she did not possess. He found it in her younger sister Juliana, Queen of Denmark, with whom he exchanged delightful letters in the closing years of his reign.

Frederick had long reconciled himself to a bachelor existence, but it was an unending grief to discover that his nephew and heir, afterwards Frederick William II, possessed neither the public nor the private virtues needed for his lofty station.[1] "This animal is incorrigible," he complained to Prince Henry. The Prince of Prussia, like his father before him, fulfilled the demand to supply the dynasty with princes, but he was useless for the serious tasks of government. There was little to be said for him except that he was good-natured and musical. The King was disgusted by his dissolute ways and by his dabbling in occultism under the guidance of his bosom friend Bischoffwerder. Prince Henry was too much of a *frondeur,* Prince Ferdinand too insignificant to be much of a help. Old friends of his youth—Fouqué and Algarotti, companions of the happy Rheinsberg days, his *liebes Mütterchen* Countess Camas, Sir Andrew Mitchell, Schwerin, Winterfeldt and Seydlitz, heroes of the Seven Years' War, were gone. Yet he was too occupied as well as too much of a stoic to complain of loneliness. Though he was often irritable and sometimes lost his self-control, the hermit of Sans Souci, as he described himself, seldom gave way to low spirits. There is a pleasant family picture in a letter written during the summer following the return of peace in 1763. "I am expecting here a whole swarm of nephews and nieces in a few days. I am becoming the uncle of all Germany." Four years later he reports that he is surrounded by a whole brood of nephews and nieces. "They are good children and I am very fond of them. When I am with them I feel like a hen who has brought up some chickens and finally persuades herself that they are her own." His favorites were Henry and Wilhelmina, the younger children of August Wilhelm. "I resolved to please him," writes Wilhelmina in her unfinished *Memoirs,* "and that gave me a feeling of confidence the first time I saw him [after the return of peace] which I had never had with anyone before, as I am excessively timid. But from the first day of his arrival I answered his questions without embarrassment. That pleased him and he showed me a thousand kindnesses. From that moment I can truly say he was a second father to me, and his affection for me lasted till his death."

Frederick never lacked attached friends during the long evening of his reign. That he disliked the society of women is a legend: no woman ever influenced his policy, but if they were rea-

[1] Gilbert Stanhope: *A Mystic on the Prussian Throne,* is a popular biography.

sonably intelligent he was only too glad to cultivate their acquaintance. The lively correspondence with the Bavarian princess Marie Antonie, Electress of Saxony and daughter of the Emperor Charles VII, extends from the close of the Seven Years' War till her death in 1780 and reveals both parties in a pleasant light. Though there are too many compliments for our modern taste, they are the expression of a genuine liking, for neither wanted anything from the other. The King saluted her as the most erudite and enlightened princess in Europe. She loved literature and music, and her two visits to Potsdam gave both parties unfeigned satisfaction. Prussia and Saxony had been foes, but Frederick had had his fill of glory and battle. "War is a scourge," he wrote in 1765. "It is a necessary evil because men are evil and corrupt, because it has always existed, and perhaps because the Creator desires revolutions to convince us that there is no stability under the sun. Sovereigns are sometimes compelled to oppose their open or secret enemies, as in my own case. If I have made people unhappy, I have been no less unhappy myself. But happily these wars are finished, and there is no sign of their speedy recurrence. While the coffers and the great powers remain empty we can cultivate the sciences at our ease. The recent blood-letting was so copious that I expect to finish my course in peace." Rulers, however, he explains in a later letter, were not wholly their own masters. "Men ought by nature to live in harmony: the earth is big enough to hold them, nourish them, occupy them. Two unhappy words, 'mine' and 'thine,' have spoiled everything; thence came interest, envy, injustice, violence, all the crimes. If I had had the good luck to be born in a private station, I would never have gone to law. I would have given even my shirt and made my living in some honest industry. With princes it is different. The opinion prevails that if they give way it is because they are weaklings and that if they are moderate they are dupes or cowards. Some easy-going and kindly rulers have been despised by their peoples. I admit that such false judges deserve disdain. Yet public opinion decides reputations, and however much one is inclined to brave the verdicts of this tribunal, one must sometimes pay it respect."

The Frenchmen who had enlivened the royal circle during the first half of the reign were gone. Voltaire was far away, Maupertuis and La Mettrie were dead, the eccentric d'Argens returned to his native land in 1768. Though rivers of blood had flowed during the Seven Years' War, Frederick still looked to France as the land of sweetness and light. He longed for another glittering star, but most of the celebrities were ruled out by their commitments, their character, or their ideology. Grimm's visits were welcome, but this Frenchified Teuton was too deeply pledged to Catherine the Great. Frederick disliked what he felt to be the arrogance of Diderot, though they had never met. He detested the dogmatic atheism of Holbach and Helvétius, though the latter spent a year as his guest while initiating the excise. Rousseau, the only man of genius except Voltaire, was personally and politically impossible. "We must succor this poor unfortunate," wrote the King to Lord Marshal Keith in 1762. "His only offense is to have strange opinions which he thinks are good ones. I will send 100 crowns, from which you will be kind enough to give him as much as he needs. I think he will accept help in kind rather than in cash. If we were not at war, and if we were not ruined, I would build him a hermitage with a garden, where he could live as he believes our first fathers did. I confess that my ideas differ from his as much as the finite and the infinite. He would never persuade me to feed on grass and walk on all fours. It is true that all this Asiatic luxury, this refinement of good cheer, indulgence, and effeminacy, is not essential to our survival, and that we could live with more simplicity and frugality than we do; but why should we renounce the pleasures of life when we can enjoy them? True philosophy, I feel, is that which allows the use and condemns the abuse; one ought to know how to do without everything without renouncing anything. I must confess that many modern philosophers displease me by their paradoxes. I stick to Locke, to my friend Lucretius, to my good Emperor Marcus Aurelius. They have told us all we can know and all that can make us moderate, good, and wise. After that it is a joke to say that we are all equal, and that therefore we must live like savages, without laws, society, or police, that the arts have corrupted our morals, and similar paradoxes. I think your Rousseau has missed his vocation; he was obviously born to become a famous anchorite, a desert Father, celebrated for his austerities and flagellations, a Stylites. He would have worked miracles and become a saint; but now he will be regarded merely as a singular philosopher who revives the sect of Diogenes after two thousand years. Maupertuis told me a characteristic story of him. On his first visit to France he lived in Paris by copying music. The Duke of Orléans, learning that he was poor and unhappy, gave him music to copy and sent him fifty louis. Rousseau kept only five, saying that his work was not worth more and that the Duke could employ it better in giving it to people poorer and more lazy than himself. This great disinterestedness is surely the essential foundation of virtue; so I conclude that the morals of your savage are as pure as his mind is illogical." One of the first books he read on the return of peace was *Émile,* and he was not impressed.

Why should he not try d'Alembert, mathematician and philosopher, author of the famous Introduction to the *Encyclopédie,* which embodied the ripe wisdom of the Age of Reason? He had been a member of the Prussian Academy since 1746, and had met Frederick at Wesel in 1755. "He seems a very nice fellow," reported the King to Wilhelmina, "gentle, clever, profoundly learned, unpretentious. He promised to come next year for three months and then perhaps we can arrange for a longer stay." The Seven Years' War intervened, but directly it was over he spent two months at Potsdam. The two men were strongly attracted to each other. Though no one could fill the place of Voltaire, the visitor was a first-rate conversationalist, and he combined high intellectual distinction with a nobility of character that the Patriarch of Ferney lacked. The guest, however, had no wish to be tied, and in the same year he declined an invitation to be tutor to the Grand Duke Paul, heir to the Russian throne. There was no society to be found in Prussia, he complained, except with the King himself. Voltaire's experience could not be ignored, his health was poor, and Paris meant the salon of Mme Geoffrin and the loving heart of Mlle de Lespinasse. Though he greatly enjoyed the visit, he declined the flattering invitation to make Prussia his permanent home. "More penetrated than ever by admiration for your person and gratitude for your kindness," he wrote, "I should like to inform the whole of Europe what I have had the happiness of seeing in Your Majesty, a prince greater even than his fame, a hero at once *philosophe* and modest, a King worthy and capable of friendship—in fact, a true sage on the throne."

The host's reply was in equally vibrant tones. "I shall never forget the pleasure of having seen a true philosopher. He departs, but I shall keep open the post of president of the Academy, which he alone can fill.[1] A certain presentiment tells me that it will come, but that we must await the appointed hour. I am sometimes tempted to wish that the persecution of the elect may redouble in certain countries. I know this desire is in some measure criminal, since it involves the renewal of intolerance, of tyranny, of the brutalities of the human race. That is how I feel. You have had it in your power to put an end to these culpable desires which offend the delicacy of my sentiments. I do not and will not press you. I will await in silence the moment when ingratitude will compel you to settle in a country where you are already naturalized in the minds of those who think and are sufficiently cultivated to appreciate your merit." The King wrote from his heart, but his blandishments were in vain.

An affectionate correspondence, scarcely inferior in interest to that with Voltaire, continued till d'Alembert's death twenty years later, though they never met again. From beginning to end of this fascinating exchange there is not a jarring note. "Your works will live," wrote the King, "mine will not; I am only a dilettante." He apologized for his bad verses, but hoped they would send his friend to sleep. Though both men believed in the supremacy of reason, Frederick had far less expectation of its ultimate triumph: the average man, he felt, had no use for it. In some long and striking letters written in 1770 he explained his intellectual position in detail. "I think that a philosopher who set out to teach the people a simple religion would risk being stoned. Men desire objects that strike their senses and appeal to their imagination. Even if you could rescue them from so many errors, it is doubtful if they are worth the effort to enlighten them." Even skeptics were not beyond temptation, for the tendency to superstition was inborn in the human race. "If one founded a colony of unbelievers, in the course of years we should witness the birth of superstitions. Marvels seem to be made for the people. If one abolishes some ridiculous religion, something still more extravagant takes its place. I think it is good and most useful to enlighten man. To combat fanaticism is to disarm the most cruel and sanguinary of monsters. To protest against the abuses of monks, against vows so contrary to the designs of nature and the

[1] A successor to Maupertuis was never appointed.

146

increase of population, is only to serve one's country. But it would be unwise and even dangerous to suppress those elements of superstition which are provided for children and which their fathers desire them to be taught."

The old King found the world as full of interest as ever, but he did not cling to life. When the Queen of Sweden lost her husband in 1771, he reminded her that this was not the best of all possible worlds, as Leibnitz had argued, but the worst. "When we enter our seventieth year," he wrote in 1781, "we should be ready to go directly the signal sounds. When one has lived a long time one ought to realize the nothingness of human things and, weary of the unceasing ebb and flow of good and evil fortune, should depart without regret. Unless we are morbid we should welcome the close of our follies and torments and rejoice that death delivers us from the passions that destroy us. After having maturely reflected on these grave matters, I expect to keep my good humor so long as my frail machine holds out, and I advise you to do the same. Far from complaining that my end is near, I ought rather to apologize to the public for having had the impertinence to live so long, for having bored it and wearied it for three quarters of a century, which is past a joke." D'Alembert, though the younger of the two, passed away in 1783, and Frederick's last letter restated the outlines of the blend of skepticism, epicureanism, and stoicism that formed his creed. "Man, it seems to me, is made rather for action than for thought; fundamental principles are beyond our reach. We pass half our life in shedding the errors of our ancestors, but the same time we leave truth resting at the bottom of the well from which posterity will not extract it despite all our efforts. So let us enjoy wisely the little advantages that come our way, and let us remember that learning to know is often learning to doubt."

While the Electress of Saxony, Queen Juliana of Denmark, and d'Alembert shed their radiance from afar, Frederick was not without pleasant companionship nearer home. The Jacobite brothers George and James Keith had left Scotland in their youth after the failure of the Old Pretender in 1715, and after many wanderings had come to anchor in Prussia. James, the Marshal, fell in the Seven Years' War. George, "Milord Marischal," after filling the posts of Prussian Minister at Paris and Governor of Neuchâtel, was provided with a house in the grounds of Sans Souci. When the old man, who lived to the age of ninety-two, was no longer able to climb the hill, the King walked beside his invalid chair. Keith had seen much of the wider world which Frederick had always longed to visit, and he was a man of wide culture and lofty character; among the ornaments of the Round Table none was more welcome. Since the death of Jordan and Wilhelmina no one came so close to the heart of the lonely ruler who, for all his stoicism and reserve, craved for a little human warmth. "I thought you knew you would always be well received," he wrote in 1764; "by night and day, in all seasons, weather, and hours, you will be received with open arms by your faithful friend."

Old men prefer the friends of their prime, but with the death of Keith and Pöllnitz, an entertaining old chatterbox, the last of Frederick's elder contemporaries were gone. The faithful Eichel left no successor of the same stature to perform the confidential work in the royal chancery, but Hertzberg was not only a valued counselor but a welcome guest at Sans Souci, often for weeks at a time. Only one new figure crosses the darkening stage. Lucchesini, a Marchese of twenty-eight, then at the beginning of his distinguished career, attracted the King's attention while traveling through France and Germany in 1779, and accepted an invitation to settle down as Chamberlain. From 1780 onwards they met almost daily at the Round Table, where the talk sometimes lasted for hours. Students have reason to be grateful to this cultivated Italian whose diary, covering the period May 1780 to June 1782, is our best source for Frederick's later table talk.[1] That the host did most of the talking and repeated his anecdotes did not matter, for Lucchesini was a good listener and their scope is described as immense. The Prince de Ligne, who knew everybody and was himself one of the wittiest of men, has given us a vivid report in his memoirs of the King's conversation when he accompanied the Emperor Joseph to the meeting of the monarchs at Neustadt in 1770 and when he spent a week at Potsdam in 1780. "The King's encyclopedic range enchanted me. The arts, war, medicine, literature, religion, ethics, history, and legislation were discussed: the great epochs of Augustus and Louis XIV, good society among the Romans, the Greeks and the French; the

[1] *Das Tagebuch des Marchese Lucchesini,* edited by Oppeln-Bronikowski and Volz.

chivalry of Francis I; the frankness and valor of Henri IV; the renaissance of letters since Leo X; anecdotes of clever men; the slips of Voltaire, the touchiness of Maupertuis, the charm of Algarotti, the wit of Jordan, the valetudinarianism of d'Argens, whom the King could send to bed for twenty-four hours by remarking that he looked ill. He talked of everything imaginable in a rather low voice."

An incisive analysis of this complicated veteran by Sir Andrew Mitchell's successor, Sir James Harris (afterwards Lord Malmesbury), in a dispatch dated March 17, 1776, emphasized "that motley composition of barbarity and humanity which so strongly mark his character. I have seen him weep at tragedy, known him to pay as much care to a sick greyhound as a fond mother to a favorite child; yet the next day he has given orders for the devastation of a province or by a wanton increase of taxes made a whole district miserable. He is so far from being sanguinary that he scarce ever suffers a criminal to be punished capitally, unless for the most notorious offense; yet in the last war he gave secret orders to several of his army surgeons rather to run the risk of a wounded soldier dying than by the amputation of a limb increase the number and expense of his invalids. Thus, never losing sight of his object, he lays aside all feelings the moment that is concerned. And although as an individual he often appears and really is humane, benevolent, and friendly, yet the instant he acts in his royal capacity these attributes forsake him and he carries with him desolation, misery, and persecution wherever he goes. Though they feel the rod of iron with which they are governed, few repine and none venture to murmur." The Ambassador, like various other people, hints at unnatural vice, but there is no foundation for such scandalous talk.

While Frederick was writing the story of his campaigns and rereading his favorite French authors, the Augustan Age in Germany was dawning; Lessing and Klopstock, Herder and Wieland, Goethe and Schiller were beginning to fill the world with their fame. The romantic productions of the *Sturm und Drang* period, with *Götz* and *Die Räuber* at their head, could hardly be expected to appeal to the lover of classical tradition; the *Messias* was remote from his ideology, and Herder's cult of the *Volk* conveyed no meaning to an autocrat. Lessing and Wieland, on the other hand, children of the *Aufklärung,* spoke

149

a language that he could well have understood. The former spent several years in Berlin and Breslau, and, though a Saxon, applauded Prussian victories. Through the mouth of Tellheim, in *Minna von Barnhelm,* he preached the gospel of military honor, and the noble plea for toleration in *Nathan der Weise* would have gone straight to the ruler's heart. Yet Frederick, who knew the name from his fleeting association with Voltaire, had no idea of his solid merits, and twice rejected the suggestion of his friends that he should be appointed Royal Librarian and Keeper of the Gem Collection.

"Since my youth I have not read a German book, and I speak it badly," confessed Frederick to Gottsched during their conversations at Leipzig in 1757; "now I am an old fellow and I have no time." Yet his neglect of the intellectual springtime of his country, however regrettable for himself, may be regarded on balance as a blessing. He had commenced his reign by allowing uncensored liberty to the Berlin press, but the privilege had been quickly revoked. "Do not talk to me of your liberty of thought and the press," wrote Lessing to Nicolai in 1769. "It reduces itself to the permission to let off as many squibs against religion as one likes. Let somebody raise his voice for the rights of subjects or against exploitation and despotism, and you will soon see which is the most slavish land in Europe." Wieland declared that, while he felt the greatest admiration for the King of Prussia, he thanked heaven that he did not live under his stick or scepter. He had always had a heavy hand, and it was far better for the mind of Germany to develop on its own lines than to be cramped by the patronage of the crown. That was also his own view, as he explained to Mirabeau at their second and last meeting on April 17, 1786. Why was the Cæsar of the Germans, asked the visitor, not Augustus as well? Why did he not think it worth while to share in the fame of the literary revolution of his time, to quicken its tempo, to support it with the fire of his genius and his power? "What could I have done to favor German writers," replied the King, "compared with the benefit I conferred by letting them go their own way?" On reflection Mirabeau agreed. "I regard it as a very minor misfortune," he wrote in his *Monarchie prussienne,* "that German literature lacked the support of the great. It is the same with writing as with trade: it detests compulsion, and compulsion is the inseparable companion of the great."

The interesting little treatise, *De la littérature allemande, des défauts qu'on peut lui reprocher, quelles sont les causes, et par quels moyens on peut les corriger*, published in 1780, is the only one of Frederick's writings that continues to be widely read. The root of the trouble, he argues, is in the language, *à demi barbare*, which it is impossible even for a genius to handle with effect. "I seek in vain for our Homers, our Virgils, our Anacreons, our Horaces, our Demostheneses, our Ciceros, our Thucydideses, our Livys. I find nothing. Let us be sincere and frankly confess that so far belles-lettres have not prospered on our soil." Germany had produced philosophers, but not poets or historians. German culture had been thrown back by the Thirty Years' War. "To show you how little taste there is in Germany you have only to go to the play. There you will see the abominable pieces of Shakespeare translated into our language, and the whole audience in transports as they listen to these ridiculous farces worthy of Canadian savages. I thus describe them because they sin against all the rules of the theater. These rules are not arbitrary: you find them in the *Poetics* of Aristotle, where the unity of place, time and action are prescribed as the sole means of making tragedies interesting. One can pardon his strange digressions, for the birth of the arts is never the time of their maturity. But here is a *Götz von Berlichingen* on the stage, a detestable imitation of these bad English pieces, and the audience demands the repetition of these disgusting platitudes." That the critical standards of the public might be superior to his own never entered his head. Goethe's name is not mentioned, and Lessing, then in his last year, is ignored.

What could be done? The royal critic refused to despair, for Germany had produced great men, among them Leibnitz who had filled Europe with his fame. The first task was to perfect the German tongue. The classics of all languages, ancient and modern, should be translated, so that writers and readers might learn from the best models. France had shown the world what could be achieved. The "crude and graceless works" of Rabelais and Montaigne had only bored and disgusted him, but in the seventeenth century her authors set the standard for the whole continent. Secondly, university methods must be reformed from top to bottom. Philosophy should be taught in its historical evolution from the Greeks to Locke, with comments on the various schools. Professors of law should trace the growth of their science. Professors of history should devote special attention to the fortunes of Germany, particularly since Charles V, and should emphasize the significance of the Treaty of Westphalia, "because it became the basis of Germanic liberties and restrains the ambitions of the Empire within just limits."

After all this fault-finding and the astonishing revelation of ignorance it is a pleasant surprise to find the old man lifting up his eyes to the hills. Various handicaps had prevented the Germans from advancing as speedily as their neighbors, but latecomers sometimes pass their predecessors in the race. This might happen in Germany quicker than they expected if the rulers had a taste for literature and encouraged the best writers with praise and rewards. "Let us have some Medicis, and we shall see some geniuses. An Augustus will make a Virgil. We shall have our classical authors; everyone will wish to read them and profit by them; our neighbors will learn German; the Courts will speak it with pleasure, and our language, refined and perfected, will spread all over Europe thanks to our good writers. These bright days of our literature have not yet come but they are drawing nigh. I announce to you that they will appear, though I am too old to witness them. I am like Moses and I gaze from afar at the Promised Land." When these words were written the partnership of Goethe and Karl August was five years old, all Europe was reading the *Sorrows of Werther,* and the *Urfaust* was in manuscript; but at the time of Frederick's death only five of the eighteen academicians were Germans. The best of several rejoinders came from the sturdy old champion of Germanism, Justus Möser, author of the *Patriotische Phantasien* and the *History of Osnabrück.*

Frederick's mood in the last year of his life was one of tranquil resignation. "I have lived over seventy years in this world," he wrote to Charlotte, Duchess of Brunswick, who had lost a son; "and during that time I have seen nothing but the strange freaks of fortune that mingles many painful happenings with a few that are favorable. We toss without ceasing between many anxieties and certain moments of satisfaction. That, my dear sister, is the common lot of man. Young folk ought to feel the loss of their relatives and friends more than the old; for the former have long to dwell on their sorrow, whereas people of our age will soon be gone. The dead have the advantage of being sheltered from the strokes of fortune, while we who remain are exposed to them day by day. These reflections, my good sister, are not exactly consoling. Fortunately your wisdom and your disposition have given you strength to bear a mother's grief. May heaven continue to help you and to preserve a sister who is the happiness of my life."

We are indebted to Zimmermann, the celebrated Swiss author and doctor, for our last glimpses of the old ruler a month before his death.[1] Having lost faith in his own medical advisers, he besought the Court Physician at Hanover to pay him a visit. "Eight months ago I was violently attacked by asthma. The doctors here gave me all kinds of drugs, which make me worse instead of better. Your reputation having spread throughout northern Europe, will you come for a fortnight? I am sure the Duke of York will allow it." Zimmermann paid his first visit on June 24, and for over a fortnight he saw the patient twice a day. He found him at Sans Souci in an easy chair with an old hat on his head, his blue coat stained yellow and brown with snuff, a terribly swollen leg resting on a footstool. "All the fire and all the power of his best years shone in his eyes and often made visitors forget his wasted body." "You find me very ill," remarked the King, and it was obvious that the end was near. Yet he proved a most refractory patient, sometimes flatly refusing to take the prescribed medicines, sometimes devouring large quantities of indigestible and highly spiced foods in which he had always delighted. His mood varied with his health, sometimes gentle and winning, more rarely terrible and harsh. The two men took to each other from the first, and the doctor was deeply moved when the time came to part. Removing his hat and speaking with indescribable dignity and friendliness, Frederick said: "Adieu, my good, my dear Mr. Zimmermann. Do not forget the good old man you have seen here." We would gladly exchange some of the realistic medical details for more of the talk that enlivened their meetings on the better days.

[1] *Über Friedrich den Grossen und meine Unterhaltungen mit ihm kurz vor seinem Tode.* Leipzig, 1788.

When Goethe visited Berlin in 1778 he was disgusted by the abuse of the ruler to which he had to listen; yet there was a pervading sense that he was not as other men, and the rough military verses of old Gleim were current coin. The memoirs of General von der Marwitz contain a striking snapshot of Frederick in the year before his death as he appeared to an eager schoolboy. Returning from a review of his troops, he was received by Princess Amelia before her palace in the Wilhelmstrasse. The crowd, having accompanied him with acclamation as he rode on his white horse, stood bareheaded at the door through which he had passed. "Yet nothing had happened: no pomp, no salvos, no music, no recent event. Only a man of seventy-three, badly dressed and covered with dust, returns from his exhausting daily task. Yet everyone knew that this old man was working for him, that he had given his life to this task, that he had not missed a day for forty-five years. Everyone saw also the fruits of his labors, near and far and all around. When one looked at him, reverence, admiration, pride, confidence, in fact all the nobler sentiments were experienced." The old stoic neither expected nor craved for survival after death. He was content in the knowledge that he had spent himself to the uttermost in the service of his country and that he had won fame far beyond the visions of his flaming youth.

Chapter VII

VOLTAIRE : THE HONEYMOON

FREDERICK THE GREAT described himself as "philosopher by inclination, politician by duty." His range of interest as a young man was astonishing and his appetite for knowledge never flagged. Throughout life he studied the cultural activities of Europe with scarcely less, attention than the political scene, not as an outsider, but as one who was proud to take his place as a laborer in the vineyard. His respect for scholars and thinkers was unfeigned, and literary talent aroused his unalloyed delight. The classics, ancient and modern, were his familiar companions, and his resilience in desperate situations was partially due to the refreshment of spirit derived from his devotion to the things of the mind. How could this Hohenzollern prince fail to be fascinated by the most brilliant writer of the age, the uncrowned king of the republic of letters for half a century, the wittiest and most versatile man in Europe, poet, dramatist, novelist, historian, *philosophe,* student of science, pamphleteer, a soldier in the army of humanity and a citizen of the world? The story of this unique relationship is enshrined in the three massive volumes of their correspondence edited by Koser and Droysen in 1908, which supersedes the imperfect editions offered to the public since the close of the eighteenth century.[1] While most of Frederick's letters can now be read in their first draft and their final form—for at first he took great pains in their composition and asked Jordan to revise them—those of Voltaire have for the most part been taken from printed editions since the originals have disappeared. Though there are gaps in the correspondence, 654 items covering forty-two years have been preserved. There

[1] *Briefwechsel Friedrich des Grossen mit Voltaire,* ed. Koser and Gustav Droysen (3 vols. 1908–11) and *Nachträge zu dem Briefwechsel Friedrichs des Grossen mit Maupertuis und Voltaire* (1917), supersede all previous collections. The fullest account of their relations is in Desnoiresterres: *Voltaire et Frédéric le Grand.* Abbé Bénard: *Frédéric II et Voltaire* (1878), Duc de Broglie: *Voltaire avant et pendant la Guerre de Sept Ans* (1898), Henriot: *Voltaire et Frédéric le Grand* (1927), and Lytton Strachey's essay "Frederick the Great and Voltaire," in *Books and Characters,* are useful, though the last only deals with the quarrel.

is nothing like it in the history of literature, for the exchange between Grimm and Catherine the Great reflects the contact not of intellectual equals but of patron and servant.

The first volume contains the material of the four years preceding the death of Frederick William I in 1740, and is by far the most attractive. It is the honeymoon period: each saw the other through a golden haze, for personal contact had not revealed the spots on the sun. When the first letter was written from Berlin on August 8, 1736, the Crown Prince was twenty-four, the author of *Œdipe* and *Zaïre,* the *Henriade,* and the *Lettres sur les Anglais* forty-two. The heir to the throne, starving for intellectual companionship, offers his homage on bended knee. "Though I have not the pleasure of your personal acquaintance, you are none the less known to me by your works. They are treasures of the mind, composed with such taste, delicacy, and art that one discovers new beauties at every reading. I believe that they mirror the character of their author, who does honor to our century and to the human spirit. If the discussion of the respective merits of the ancients and moderns is ever renewed, you and you alone will tilt the balance to the latter side. To your excellence as a poet you add numberless other accomplishments that have some affinity to poetry but have been connected by your pen alone. You are the first poet to put metaphysical ideas into verse. Your indulgence for all who devote themselves to the arts and sciences leads me to hope that you will not exclude me from the number of those whom you consider worthy of your instructions. I venture to assert that there is no one in the world whose master you could not be." The disciple proceeds to applaud the *Henriade, César,* and *Alzire.* "If the great Corneille came to life again, he would see with astonishment and perhaps with envy that the tragic goddess has lavished on you the favors of which she was less generous to him." Would Voltaire be good enough to forward all his works, published or in manuscript? "I should think myself richer in possessing them than in all the ephemeral and contemptible gifts of fortune that chance provides and takes away. Your poems merit the study of honest men. They are a school of morals in which one learns to think and act. Virtue is painted in the brightest colors. The idea of true glory is defined, and you insinuate the taste for the sciences so skillfully that your readers are stirred to follow your lead. If I am not privileged to possess you, I may at least hope one day to see him whom I have long admired from afar."

This effusive eulogy, signed *Votre très affectionné ami Frederic, P.R. de Prusse,* and obviously written from the heart, was described by Voltaire to a friend as a very strange letter. "He invites me to visit him, but I am explaining that one should never quit one's friends for princes." He had just settled down with the Marquise du Châtelet in her château at Cirey in the independent Duchy of Lorraine, and for the first time in his roving life he had a real home of his own. Occasional visits from the accommodating husband, from whom she was practically though not legally separated, never disturbed the harmony of the ménage. "The divine Émilie," who wrote treatises on physics and translated Newton's *Principia,* had a bad temper, but their frequent quarrels were compatible with genuine affection. The reply is a skillful blend of flattery and caution. "You are too flattering; but it is a pleasure a thousand times purer to find a prince who thinks like a man, a philosopher prince who will make men happy. The only really good kings are those who, like yourself, begin by instructing themselves, by knowing their fellows, by loving truth, by detesting persecution and superstition. A prince with such ideas can restore the golden age in his state. Why do so few kings seek this advantage? Because almost all of them think more of royalty than of humanity, whereas with you it is just the reverse. Be assured that if some day the confusion of events and the perversity of man does not spoil so divine a character, you will be adored by your peoples and cherished by the whole world. Philosophers worthy of the name will flock to your territories, and, just as the celebrated artists crowd to the land where their art is most favored, thinkers will come and surround your throne." While promising to forward his works, Voltaire politely declines a meeting. "I should regard it as a great happiness to come and pay my respects to Your Royal Highness. People go to Rome to see the churches and the pictures, the ruins and the bas-reliefs. Such a prince as you is far better worth a journey, for here is a much more wonderful and exceptional sight. The friendship that attaches me to my retreat does not permit me to move. You will doubtless agree with

Julian, that great and maligned man, who said that friends should always be preferred to kings. My heart will be at your command, your glory ever dear to me. I hope that you will always be true to yourself and that other kings will follow your example." The letter was accompanied by a poem on "Kings and Kingship."

Frederick's delight at the response to his advances was expressed in an exuberant letter of immense length written from Rheinsberg on November 4, 1736. Though unable to recognize himself in Voltaire's portrait of the perfect prince, he would take it as a model and strive to become worthy of a master who knew how to teach so divinely. "I cannot but admire this generous character, this love of mankind, which deserves the homage of all nations. I venture to affirm that their debt to you is even greater than that of the Greeks to Solon and Lycurgus. Authors are in a certain sense public men; their ideas spread through the world. You form good citizens, faithful friends, subjects zealous for the public weal. Regard my actions forthwith as the fruit of your teachings. My heart is touched and I have solemnly resolved to follow them throughout life. If there is one thing I desire above others it is to have men of learning and ability around me." After dilating on the merits of Wolff's philosophy, the intolerance of theologians, and the wide sweep of Voltaire's genius, the Crown Prince bows to the inevitable. "I respect the bonds of friendship too much to wish to tear you from the arms of Émilie. Only a hard and unfeeling heart would exact such a sacrifice. I beg you to convey my homage to this prodigy of mind and learning. How rare are such women! There is no happiness that I do not wish for you and none of which you are unworthy. Cirey will henceforth be my Delphi, and your letters, which I beg you to continue, my oracles." This bouquet with its homage to Mme du Châtelet, who was described by Voltaire as "more to me than a father, a brother, or a son," seemed to him even kinder than the first. It was followed three days later by a poem ending:

Et votre nom, fameux par de savants exploits,
Doit être mis au rang des héros et des rois.[1]

[1] *Your name, illustrious by your learned works,*
Deserves a place with heroes and with kings.

Its greatest merit, explained the author, was that it was adorned with the name of Voltaire. "I know it has faults and is unworthy of its object. I have read your works and those of the most celebrated authors, and I assure you that I realize the infinite difference between their verses and mine. Criticize, condemn, disapprove, on condition that you spare the last two lines."

Posts were slow and irregular, and Voltaire's reply, even warmer in tone than the first, was dispatched from Leiden in January 1737. In reading the letter he had shed tears of joy, for he recognized in the writer a prince who would be the darling of mankind. "You think like Trajan, you write like Pliny, you talk French like our best writers. Louis XIV was a great King and I respect his memory; but his voice was not so human. I have seen his letters; he could not spell. Under your auspices Berlin will be the Athens of Germany, perhaps of Europe. I confess that I should think myself most unfortunate were I to die without seeing the model of princes and the marvel of Germany. I do not wish to flatter you; that would be a crime. I could not do it, and it is my heart which speaks. Happy is he who can serve you, happier still he who enters your presence. If I were not concerned with the happiness of mankind I should regret that you are destined for the throne. I should like you to remain in a private station, so that our souls could meet in all freedom; but my wishes must yield to the public good." Frederick's anxiety to see his new friend waxed from day to day. "I confess I am eager to meet in your person the finest product of this century and of France, but philosophy teaches me to restrain my ardor. I love my friends with a disinterested friendship, and I shall always prefer their interests to my pleasure. In any case leave me the hope to see you some day. Your letters will be a compensation: Holland, which I have never liked, will become for me a holy land since you are there. My entire esteem, based as it is on your merit, will only cease with my life."

This full-throated pæan was repaid in kind.

Les lauriers d'Apollon se fanaient sur la terre,
Les beaux-arts languissaient ainsi que les vertus,
La Fraude aux yeux menteurs et l'aveugle Plutus
Entre les mains des rois gouvernaient le tonnerre.
La Nature indignée élève alors sa voix:

159

Je veux former, dit-elle, un règne heureux et juste,
Je veux qu'un héros naisse et qu'il joigne à la fois
Les talents de Virgile et les vertus d'Auguste,
Pour l'ornement du monde et l'exemple des rois.
Elle dit; et du ciel les Vertus descendirent,
Tout le Nord tressaillit, tout l'Olympe accourut;
L'olive, les lauriers, les myrtes reverdrent,
Et Frédéric parut.[1]

Every letter brought its glowing tribute to the young Solomon. Frederick's vigorous championship of Wolff against the machinations of his enemies in Prussia earns the highest praise. "You immortalize your name in protecting the enlightened philosopher against absurd and intriguing theologians. Continue, great prince, great man; destroy the monster of superstition and fanaticism, this enemy of the divinity of reason. Be the king of the philosophers, while other princes are only the kings of men. I thank heaven every day that you exist."

The Crown Prince was attracted not only by the genius and celebrity of his correspondent, but by agreement on some of the deepest problems of life. Here is his confession of faith. "Metaphysical questions are beyond us. We strive in vain to guess what passes our comprehension, and in this world of ignorance the likeliest conjecture passes for the best system. Mine is to adore the Supreme Being, uniquely good, uniquely merciful, and thereby alone deserving our homage; to succor to the best of my power my fellow creatures, of whose miserable condition I am well aware; for the rest, to trust to the will of my Creator, who will dispose of me as he pleases and from whom, whatever hap-

---

[1] *The laurels of Apollo faded fast,*
The fine arts languished and the virtues too,
Deceit in lying eyes and Plutus blind
In royal hands controlled the thunderbolts.
Indignant nature lifted up her voice:
I plan, said she, a just and happy reign,
I need a hero, one who will combine
Augustus' virtues with all Virgil's gifts,
To adorn the world and be a model for kings.
She spoke; and Virtues floated from the skies.
The whole north trembled, Olympus hurried up;
The olive, laurel, myrtle donned their green,
And Frederick appeared.

pens, I have nothing to fear. I imagine your creed is much the same." Voltaire replied that he was delighted to share his opinions in everything, including his recognition of the limitations of our knowledge. "All I know is that whether matter is eternal (which is incomprehensible) or whether it has been created in time (which presents great difficulties), whether our soul perishes with us or enjoys immortality, one cannot amidst these uncertainties pursue a course wiser or more worthy than that which you adopt—to furnish your soul, immortal or not, with all the virtues, all the enjoyment, all the instruction of which it is capable, to live as a prince, a man, and a sage, to be happy and to make others happy. I regard you as a gift from heaven. I admire the fact that at your age the pursuit of pleasure has not mastered you, and I congratulate you that philosophy leaves you the taste for pleasures. We are not born solely to read Plato and Leibnitz, to measure curves, to arrange facts in our head. We are born with a heart needing to be filled with passions which we must satisfy without being ruled by them. One of your greatest boons to mankind will be to overthrow superstition and fanaticism, to prevent those in authority from persecuting others who think differently. Assuredly philosophers will never disturb states: why, then, disturb philosophers? You see, worthy heir of the spirit of Marcus Aurelius, with what freedom I speak to you. You are almost the only person who deserves such an approach."

Frederick confesses and laments the intellectual stagnation of Germany. "Our universities and our Academy of Sciences are in a sorry state; it seems as if the Muses wish to desert these regions." Frederick I, generous to extravagance and a lover of splendor, had patronized the arts, and in choosing Louis XIV for his model he believed he would receive similar praise. His gifted wife, Queen Charlotte, summoned Leibnitz to Berlin, where he founded an Academy, but it was a false dawn. "The arts are perishing. I weep as I watch the disappearance of knowledge, while arrogant ignorance and boorish manners take its place. The Germans are not stupid. They possess good sense and their character resembles that of the English. They are hardworking and thorough; when they take up anything they concentrate on it. Their books are terribly diffuse. If they could be purged of their clumsiness and familiarized with the Graces,

I should not despair of my nation producing great men." Unfortunately a certain difficulty would always prevent them from having great books in their own language, for in Germany there were many rulers and there was no means of getting them to submit words to the arbitrament of an academy. "So our savants must write in foreign tongues; and as these are very difficult to master, it is to be feared that our literature will never make great strides." There was another grave disadvantage: princes usually despised men of learning, and the courtiers followed their lead.

A visit to Cirey by the faithful Keyserlingk, bearing a letter, a portrait of the Crown Prince, and other offerings, seemed to bring the friends still closer to each other, and the envoy reported that Voltaire surpassed all expectations. Frederick gratefully accepted corrections of his verse, but in questions of history and philosophy he was never a mere disciple. An exchange of ideas on the freedom of the will revealed a difference of outlook, though the younger thinker, a convinced determinist, admitted that we could only guess. "I think that man is not made to reason profoundly on abstract matters. God has given him sufficient knowledge to do his work in the world, but not enough to satisfy his curiosity. We are made for action, not for contemplation." This ideology, he explained, in no way clashed with a lofty view of God or man. "Believe me, you are the strongest possible argument in favor of mankind. I find it easier to believe in human perfection when I think of you. I feel that only a God or something divine could combine in a single being all your perfections. You act according to a principle, according to sublime reason, and therefore according to necessity. This system, far from being contrary to humanity and virtue, is most favorable to them, since in finding our interest, our happiness and satisfaction in the exercise of virtue, it is a necessity for us always to lean towards what is virtuous." The letter contained the usual bouquet for Mme du Châtelet. "If I were to approach the divine Émilie I would say to her, like the angel of the annunciation: You are blessed among women, for you possess one of the greatest men in the world." The learned lady sent him her treatise on Fire, and received a flattering letter of thanks, signed *"Votre très affectionné ami et admirateur."* A poem entitled *"A la divine Émilie,"* composed in November 1737, heaped incense on the altar of *"sublime Émilie," "charmante Émilie."* The exchange of compliments contined till his accession, after which the absence of an invitation to accompany her friend chilled the atmosphere.

During the first two years of the correspondence there are no references to politics, domestic or foreign: Frederick writes to "the Apollo of France" as an Intellectual who happens to be heir to a throne. It was too dangerous to trust his thoughts to the post, for the eye of a suspicious parent was upon him. In April 1738, however, he announces the dispatch of his first political treatise, *Considérations sur l'état présent du corps politique de l'Europe,* begging Voltaire to hide the secret of his authorship. "I was astonished," was the reply, "to find in you a metaphysician so sublime and so wise, so graceful a poet. I am not surprised that you write like a great prince, a real statesman. Is it not right that Your Royal Highness should be master of his trade? I believe that if the *Considérations* had been printed under the name of an English Member of Parliament I should have recognized your work, and have said: Here is the great prince hidden beneath the great citizen! There is an air of a member of the Empire about it that no English citizen possesses, for no English statesman takes so much interest in German liberties. Still more should I have recognized the author in the greatness of soul and the humanity which suffuse all your pictures. Mme du Châtelet and I have read it several times and she pronounces it the best of your works. I agree, but the most recent of your favors is always the most prized." Voltaire proceeded to discuss the work, and suggested that, in view of the approaching extinction of the male Hapsburg line, the Imperial title, like certain bishoprics, should alternate between Lutherans and Catholics. All princes should engrave on their council tables and the blade of their swords: "It is a disgrace to lose one's states; it is punishable rapacity to invade those to which one has no right." These were the words of a great man and the guarantee of the happiness of his people.

The professional and the amateur exchanged poems vying with each other in the ingenuity of their compliments. "Your Royal Highness," wrote Voltaire, "is more Frederick and more Marcus Aurelius than ever." Only a Voltaire was lacking at Rheinsberg, rejoined the Crown Prince, in order to enjoy perfect happiness; yet he was always in his heart. "Your portrait occupies the place of honor in my library, immediately above your books, opposite my chair, so that you are ever before my eyes." New works were discussed, new plans explained. Frederick's range became ever wider, and in May 1739 he announces the most ambitious of his projects. "At the moment I am busy with Machiavelli. I am making notes on *The Prince,* and I have begun a work that will entirely refute his maxims, which are the enemies of virtue and of the true interests of princes. It is not enough to point out the way of virtue to men; one must set in motion the springs of interest, without which very few are inclined to follow reason. I hope to send you the manuscript within three months." If he deigned to write against Machiavelli, rejoined Voltaire, it would be Apollo slaying the serpent Python. The promise of a present of wine brought the gallant reply: "I hope to drink it to the health of my dear sovereign, the real master of my soul, whose subject I am more truly than of my own King." A month later Frederick wrote that his task would take longer than he had expected. To know everything that had been written on Machiavelli he needed an infinity of books, and after digesting them he would require some time. His attack would be a sequel to the *Henriade,* that terrible picture of the wars of religion, the malice of priests, the fatal effects of false zeal. "It is on the noble sentiments that I shall forge the thunderbolt that will annihilate Cæsar Borgia." It would only be published, however, if approved by Voltaire.

A report from distant Insterburg in East Prussia in the summer of 1739 displayed the heir to the throne in a new and attractive light. Hitherto his letters had been as silent about his official duties, slight as they were, as about his cross-grained father and his unloved wife. Here at last was an anticipation of *le premier domestique de l'état,* who was to rival Frederick William I in his care for the material welfare of his subjects. "Here we are, after journeying for three weeks, in a country that I regard as the outermost fringe of the civilized world. It is little known in Europe, but it deserves more attention since it can be regarded as the creation of the King." The duchy, described as Prussian Lithuania, had been ravaged by plague at the beginning of the century. The fields were uncultivated, the beasts perished, and the most flourishing of Prussian provinces was transformed into a terrible wilderness. Meanwhile Frederick I died and his false grandeur was buried in his grave. "My father, who followed him, was touched by the public misery. He came and saw for himself this vast devastated territory, with all the fearful traces of pestilence, famine, and the sordid avarice of the ministers. Twelve or fifteen depopulated towns, four to five hundred derelict villages, were the sorry spectacle that met his eyes. Far from being repelled by such unpleasant objects, he felt the liveliest compassion and resolved to restore the population, prosperity, and commerce. He spared no expense; he reconstructed everything that the pestilence had destroyed, and brought thousands of families from all parts of Europe. The land was cleared, population increased, commerce flourished anew, and today this fertile country is more prosperous than ever. There are over half a million inhabitants, more towns than before, more livestock, more fertility than in any other part of Germany. All this is due to the King, who not only gave orders, but supervised their execution; who made the plans and carried them out quite alone; who spared neither thought nor pains, nor immense expenditure, nor promises, nor rewards, to ensure the happiness of half a million human beings. I hope you will not be bored by these details. Your humanity should extend to your Lithuanian as to our French, English, and German brothers. I find something heroic in the King's generosity and energy in repeopling this desert and making it fertile and happy, and I thought you would share my feelings." This testimonial cannot be dismissed as intended for his father's eye, for the friendship with Voltaire was a jealously guarded secret. He had begun to understand that the man who had darkened his life was in some ways worthy of respect and imitation.

In November 1739 Frederick reports that the refutation of Machiavelli was finished, that revision had begun, and that he was sending it to be polished up. "Though I do not wish to put my name to it, I should not like it to injure me if the authorship were suspected. So I beg you to tell me what needs correction. You understand that in this case your indulgence would be fatal." He had kept silence when prudence dictated caution. He was acquainted with a multitude of anecdotes on the courts of Europe, which would have amused his readers, but that would have produced a satire all the more damaging because of its truth. That he would never do. He was not born to annoy princes. He would prefer to make them wise and happy. Voltaire's response was prompt and flattering. "Monseigneur, the welfare of the world demands the publication of this book; people must see the antidote presented by a royal hand. It is strange that princes have not written on such subjects. It was their duty, and their silence on Machiavelli indicates tacit approval. Here at last is a book worthy of a prince, and I do not doubt that an edition of Machiavelli, with this refutation at the close of each chapter, would be one of the most precious monuments of literature." There were very few mistakes in French, he added, and he begged to be allowed to contribute a preface and bring it out, as Frederick had sponsored an edition of the *Henriade*. "My task will be more agreeable than yours, for while the *Henriade* may interest some people, the *Antimachiavel* must be the catechism of kings and their ministers." The work, in his opinion, would benefit by a little less invective. "Zeal against the teacher of usurpers and tyrants has devoured your generous soul and sometimes carried you away. If it is a fault, it also resembles a virtue. When one has soundly belabored Machiavelli one can confine oneself to the argument." Since Frederick had no material interest in flattering his celebrated correspondent, there is no reason to doubt the sincerity of his youthful exuberance. Can we say the same of the middle-aged and experienced Voltaire? That he was attracted by the unaccustomed spectacle of an intellectual on the steps of a throne and delighted by his homage is natural enough. But was there also perhaps a calculation that Prussia might one day serve as a harbor of refuge if France were to become too hot for the pugnacious heretic? His whole life was a battle, and perhaps it was wise to look ahead.

Chapter VIII

VOLTAIRE: DISENCHANTMENT

THE second volume of the correspondence covers the years from 1740, when the friends met for the first time, to 1753, when they parted forever. A short letter of June 6, 1740 reported the long-awaited event. "My dear friend, my lot is changed and I have been present at the death-bed of a King. In ascending the throne I did not require this lesson to be sickened of human vanity and grandeur. I had planned a little work on metaphysics, but it has turned into a political treatise. I expected to joust with the friendly Voltaire; now I must cross swords with the old mitred Machiavelli [Cardinal Fleury]. So, my dear Voltaire, we are not masters of our fate: the whirlwind of events drags us along. Think of me, I beg you, merely as a zealous citizen, a somewhat skeptical philosopher, and a truly faithful friend. In God's name, write to me as man to man, and share my contempt for titles. Busy though I am I have always time to admire your works and to sit at your feet. Adieu! If I live I shall see you this year. Love me always and always be sincere with your friend Frederic." Voltaire responded with an ode, which he described to a friend as coming from his heart. The first and last stanzas convey a sufficient idea of this act of homage.

> Enfin voici le jour le plus beau de ma vie,
> Que le monde attendait et que vous seul craignez,
> Le grand jour òu la terre est par vous embellie,
>   Le jour òu vous régnez.
> Quelle est du Dieu vivant la véritable image?
> Vous, des talents, des arts et des vertus l'appui,
> Vous, Salomon du Nord, plus savant et plus sage,
>   Et moins faible que lui.[1]

[1] The best day of my life has dawned at last,
The world was waiting, you alone felt fear,
The great day when the earth received your light,
    The day of your accession.
Who is the image of the living God?
You, the support of talents, virtues, arts,

The King's second letter, a week after the first, began with a short poem on his new tasks.

> *Désormais ce peuple que j'aime*
> *Est l'unique dieu que je sers.*
> *Adieu mes vers et mes concerts,*
> *Tout les plaisirs, Voltaire même;*
> *Mon devoir est mon dieu suprême.*[1]

"You see, my dear friend," he added, "that the change of fortune has not cured me of my versifying mania; perhaps I never shall be cured. I think too highly of the art of Horace and Voltaire to renounce it, and everything in life has its appropriate time." He hoped to be in Wesel in August or perhaps even farther west. "Promise to join me, for I could neither live happy nor die in peace without having embraced you. A thousand compliments to the Marquise. I labor with both hands, one for the army, the other for the people and the arts." It was the first time that he expressed interest in what his father had regarded as the main pillar of the state.

Voltaire's first letter, dated June 18, was a cascade of compliments. "Sire, if your lot is changed, your noble soul is not; but mine is. I was somewhat of a misanthrope and the injustices of men weighed on me. Now, like everyone else, I rejoice. Thank heaven Your Majesty has already fulfilled almost all my predictions. You are already beloved, both in your state and in Europe. You command me to write less to the King than to the man, an injunction after my own heart. I do not know how to approach a king, but I am quite at ease with a real man, a man who has the love of the human race in his head and heart." Had his father recognized the full merit of *"mon adorable prince?"* How did he spend the day? Was he overworking? "In the name of the human race, which has need of you, take care of your precious health." He longed to meet him, and the Queen of Sheba (Mme

---

> *You, Solomon of the north, more learned, more wise,*
> *   Without his frailties.*

[1] *Henceforth this people that I love*
Shall be the only god I serve.
Farewell my music and my verse,
Farewell delights, farewell Voltaire.
My duty is my supreme god.

du Châtelet) looked forward to seeing Solomon in his glory. In a few weeks he hoped to dispatch the best and most useful book ever written (the *Antimachiavel*), "worthy of you and your reign." He pronounced it superior to the *Prince* even in style, and as the only book worthy of a king for the last fifteen hundred years (since Marcus Aurelius). Mme du Châtelet added her tribute to "this incomparable work." The author, now living in a glass house, was terrified of publicity and adjured Voltaire to buy up the whole edition, but on receiving the assurance that every dangerous passage had been eliminated he authorized his editor to proceed.

In reply to the request for personal details Frederick began with a description of the death-bed of the late King. He had talked at length of affairs of state, foreign and domestic, with the greatest clarity and good sense; had handed over the reins in his last hours; had borne his sufferings like a stoic; had died with the curiosity of a doctor about his experiences and with the heroism of a great man. The new ruler proceeded to describe the measures of the first three weeks of his reign. He had increased the army. He had laid the foundations of the new Academy, which he had invited Wolff, Maupertuis, Euler, and other celebrities to join. He had established a college for commerce and manufactures. He had engaged painters and sculptors. His most urgent task was to accumulate a store of grain in every province sufficient for eighteen months.

After four years of literary contact the friends met near Cleves in September 1740. "I have seen this Voltaire whom I was so eager to know," he reported to Jordan; "but I had fever and my head was as insubordinate as my body was weak. With persons of this sort one ought not to be ill; one should be very fit—indeed, better than usual. He possesses the eloquence of Cicero, the gentleness of Pliny, and the wisdom of Agrippa; in a word he combines the virtues and talents of three of the greatest men of ancient times. His mind works incessantly. He declaimed *Mahomet,* his admirable tragedy, holding us spellbound, and I could only admire in silence. The Châtelet is lucky to have him; someone with a good memory could make a brilliant book of the gems that fell from his lips." Voltaire was equally pleased with the encounter. "I saw one of the most amiable of men," he reported to a friend, "a man who would shine in society, who would be everywhere in demand even were he not a king, a philosopher without austerity, full of gentleness and consideration, forgetting his rank when he is with friends, forgetting it indeed so completely that he almost made me forget it too. It needed an effort to remember that the man sitting at the foot of my bed was a sovereign with an army of 100,000 men." Another friend was informed that he talked as he wrote. "I do not yet know if there have been greater kings, but no more amiable person has ever lived. It is a miracle of nature that the son of a crowned ogre, educated with fools, should have acquired in his wilderness the finesse and all the natural graces that in Paris are the accomplishments of a small number and yet make its reputation."

A few months after his accession Frederick received unexpected but by no means unwelcome news from Vienna. "The Emperor is dead," he reported. "This upsets all my peaceful ideas, and I think that in June it will be guns, soldiers, and trenches rather than actresses, ballets, and the theater, so that I must cancel our arrangement [to bring an acting company to Berlin in June 1741]. This is of the greatest consequence for Europe, the signal for the complete transformation of the old political system." Though the Frenchman knew nothing of the plan for the seizure of Silesia it was generally believed that important events were at hand, and Cardinal Fleury desired him to find out as much as he could about his host's plans, a task beyond the capacity of the French Ambassador. It was also to prove beyond the capacity of Voltaire, even though he redoubled his flatteries. "The greatest epochs follow close on your coronation. You are about to make or to become an Emperor. It would be only just that he who possesses the soul of Titus, Trajan, Antoninus, and Julian should also occupy their throne. Be Your Majesty emperor or king, you are born only to do good."

The long-awaited visit of a week in November 1740, despite the delights of conversation, witnessed a slight fall of temperature. Frederick felt that Voltaire had made too many changes in the *Antimachiavel* and had put forward excessive demands for the expenses of the journey. "Your miser," he reported to Jordan, "will drink the dregs of his insatiable desire for riches—he will have thirteen hundred crowns. I flatter myself that the seduction of Berlin will soon bring him back, all the more since the purse of the Marquise is not always so full as mine." When a rumor found its way into print that they had quarreled Voltaire wrote to a friend that it was false: "he does me the honor to write as often and with the same kindness as before." Poems and flatteries continued to be exchanged and the tone of the King's letters is friendly enough, but the springtime of discipleship is over. Henceforth, except in the sphere of French poetry, they met on equal terms.

The first battle of the Silesian War stirred mingled feelings in the victor. "On this happy and unhappy day," he wrote from camp at Mollwitz, "we have lost a quantity of good subjects. I tenderly regret some friends whose memory will ever dwell in my heart. The grief for fallen friends is the antidote that providence has joined to all the triumphs of war in order to temper the immoderate joy of victory. My situation will soon lead me to face new hazards. After felling a tree it is desirable to destroy the roots lest they sprout again." Voltaire hated war, and the unprovoked attack on Austria revealed his young admirer in a new light, but he tactfully confined himself to encouraging the King to record his activities. "It is for Cæsars to write their commentaries. I foresee that Your Majesty will one day amuse yourself describing your two campaigns. Happy will be your secretary and most happy your readers." On his return to Berlin at the end of 1741 the King reported the coming of Euler and the expected arrival of other scholars. "So you see that war has not killed my taste for the arts, and that, as the Romans in their chariot races drove several horses abreast, one can engage in war, the sciences, and pleasure at the same time without a clash." That an invitation through Jordan to revisit Berlin "if he has nothing to do in Brussels" was declined made no difference to the flow of letters and verses. "Your Majesty has done much in a little time," wrote Voltaire at the close of 1741. "I believe that no living person is busier or occupied with a greater variety of tasks. But with this devouring genius, which embraces so many fields you will always retain the superiority of reason which raises you above yourself and above your achievements. My only fear is that you may come to despise men too much. The millions of two-legged animals without feathers who inhabit the earth are at an immense distance from you in soul and station. I detect another shadow—that Your Majesty describes the rascality of politicians and the self-seeking of courtiers so well that you will end by mistrusting the affection of men of every kind and will believe that a king is never loved for his own sake." The keen eyes had detected the beginning of the hardening process that was one day to condemn the Nestor of European rulers to a lonely old age.

Frederick's reply reveals that Voltaire's apprehensions were not unfounded. "I am so busy with great affairs, which philosophers call trifles," he wrote at the beginning of 1742, "that I cannot think of my own pleasure, the only solid good in life. Here I am, arguing with a score of more or less dangerous Machiavellis. Poetry waits on the threshold without obtaining an audience. One person talks to me of boundaries, others of rights, compensation, marriage contracts, debts, intrigues, recommendations. It is publicly announced that you have done something you never thought of; people think you are vexed by something at which you rejoice; a voice from Mexico declares that you are about to attack someone whom it is your interest to conciliate; you are ridiculed and criticized; a journalist writes a satire; your neighbors tear you to pieces; all of them send you to the devil while smothering you with assurances of friendship. Such is the world and such for the most part are the matters that occupy me. Would you care to exchange poetry for politics? The only resemblance is that both politicians and poets are the laughing-stock of the public and the butt of their *confrères.*" Almost every letter at this period breathes lamentations. "I am reading or rather devouring your *Siècle de Louis le Grand*. If you love me, send me the latest installments; it is my only consolation and recreation. You who work mostly for your own satisfaction should pity a practitioner of politics, who works because he must. Would anyone have foretold that a child of the Muses would be destined, jointly with a dozen grave lunatics who are called statesmen to turn the great wheel of events in Europe? Yet so it is, though it does not say much for providence. Deceit and duplicity are unfortunately the dominant traits of most of the men at the top, who should set an example. The study of the human heart in these spheres is very humiliating; it makes me regret a thousand times my dear retreat, the arts, my friends, my independence."

Describing himself as a deserter from Apollo to Bellona, Frederick writes with a mixture of cynicism and apology from the front. "If I were to tell you that two countries in Germany have started a cut-throat competition with other people whose name was unknown to them, and have gone to a distant land because their master has made a contract with a prince to murder a third, you would reply that these people are madmen and fools to lend themselves to the caprices and barbarity of their master. If I told you that we are carefully preparing to destroy some walls erected at great expense, that we reap where we have not sown, that we are the masters where no one is strong enough to resist us, you would exclaim: You barbarians, you brigands, you inhuman beings! Knowing your response I will not talk of such matters. I will merely inform you that the King of Prussia, learning that the territories of his ally the Emperor were being ruined by the Queen of Hungary, flew to his aid, joined forces with the King of Poland to make a diversion in Lower Austria, and was so successful that he expects shortly to meet the principal forces of the Queen. What generosity! you will say; what heroism! Yet the two pictures are identical. It is the same woman who appears first in her night-cap, then with her paint, her plate, and her top-knot." When the Abbé Saint-Pierre tried to interest him in his plan for the organization of peace, the King acidly observed that it merely required for its success the consent of Europe and some other trifles. Yet despite his grueling experiences he assured Voltaire that his character and outlook were unchanged. "I love Remusberg [Rheinsberg] and tranquil days, but one must accept one's station and make duty a pleasure."

If compliments are to be taken at their face value, the friendship remained intact.

> Accoutumé de vous entendre,
> De vos œuvres je suis jaloux;
> Cher Voltaire, donnez-les-nous.
> Par cœur je voudrais vous apprendre;
> Il n'est point salut sans vous.[1]

The homage was sincere enough, though campaigning had not improved the quality of the verse, and Voltaire played up gallantly. "I hope Your Majesty will stabilize Europe as you have

[1] *I am used to the sound of your voice,*
I am eager for all your books.
Give us some more, dear Voltaire.
I should like to learn you by heart;
For without you we are lost.

shattered it, and that my brother mortals will add their blessings to their admiration. You have restored the dignity and the prerogatives of the Electors. You have made an Emperor, and it is only the title that you lack. You possess 120,000 men, sturdy, well armed, well clad, well fed, well disposed; you have won battles and cities at their head. Your glory will be complete if you compel the Queen of Hungary to accept peace and the Germans to be happy. You are the hero of Germany and the arbiter of Europe. You will also be the peacemaker."

While Frederick was taking the waters at Aix-la-Chapelle in the summer of 1742 after the First Silesian War, Voltaire was his guest for an enjoyable week. Once again he received and declined tempting offers of a house in Berlin in conditions of perfect freedom, though the divine Émilie was never included in the invitation. He reported to Fleury that it should not be difficult to lead his host back to the French alliance, since he realized that Austria would strive to recover her lost province. At the end of the year fresh peaks of flattery were scaled. "Your Humanity is more adorable than ever. It is no longer fitting always to say Your Majesty. That is enough for the princes of the Empire, who see in you merely the King. But I, who see the man, forget in my transports the monarch and his power and think only of this human enchanter."

The preference of a bishop to Voltaire in an election to the Académie Française in June 1743, caused by the death of Cardinal Fleury, prompted a fresh invitation from Potsdam. "I wish you would settle in Berlin and rescue your little bark from the tempests that have so often battered it in France. How could you bear to be ignominiously excluded from the Academy when you are applauded in the theater, disdained at court, and adored in the capital? I would not tolerate such discrimination. Moreover, the levity of the French makes them inconstant alike in homage and contempt. Come hither to a nation that will not change its verdict, and leave a country where the Belle-Isles [the Marshal], the Chauvelins [the diplomatist], and the Voltaires receive no promotion."

Voltaire was now at last inclined to revisit Prussia, for a new motive was at work in a confidential commission from the French Government. His task was to discover the secrets of Prussian policy between the first two Silesian Wars while masquerading as a malcontent refugee. This curious incident was fully revealed more than a century later by the Duc de Broglie in the course of his researches on the diplomacy of Louis XV, and the story is told in the second volume of his *Frédéric II et Louis XV*. No one knew what Frederick was planning, but perhaps a *persona grata* might find out. "The King is determined to send you," wrote the Minister of Finance. "I am issuing instructions to pay you 8,000 francs and a year of your pension, which M. Amelot [the Foreign Minister] tells me is what you ask." In collusion with the author the performance of the new drama *La Mort de Cæsar* was forbidden at the eleventh hour in order to give substance to the rumor of a break with the court. It was a risky game, and Mme du Châtelet, already conscious of a slight fall of temperature at Cirey, wept at the thought that her partner, once anchored at Berlin, might not return. Voltaire, on the other hand, was eager to play the unaccustomed part for which he believed his fame and conversational powers to fit him like a glove. "Sire," he wrote effusively to Frederick from Paris in June, "console me for all I see. When I am ready to weep over the decadence of the arts I say to myself: There is a monarch in Europe who loves them and cultivates them and is the glory of his century. Then I say: I shall soon see him, this charming monarch, this King who is also a man, this crowned Chaulieu, this Tacitus, this Xenophon. Yes, I wish to start. Mme du Châtelet cannot stop me. I shall leave Minerva for Apollo. You, Sire, are my *grande passion*. I have much to tell Your Majesty. I will lay my heart at your feet, and you will decide if it is possible for me to pass my life at your side. You will be the arbiter of my destiny. If only you would honor me with a little portrait as like you as two drops of water! Do not forget me, my adorable sovereign." Voltaire's letters had always been flattering, but the tone was now so different from the customary protestations of unwillingness to leave home that it was bound to arouse suspicion. The King politely replied that he would be received with open arms.

Voltaire's first discovery was that Frederick had recently raised a loan in Amsterdam. Was this an indication of coming activities? If so, he might be glad of a little more cash. What about offering French money? "I should take care not to compromise anyone nor to let him suspect that I know you. He has written to me thrice since I have been at The Hague, advising me to settle at his court and to forget France." Amelot saw no harm in suggesting a subsidy, but begged that the object of the visit should be carefully concealed. "I hope to serve you faithfully and send accurate reports," was the reply, "even if people entertain suspicions about my journey, which I believe is not the case." Through Podewils, the Prussian Minister at The Hague, an old friend and now his host, he hoped to win his uncle, the Prussian Foreign Minister, for his purpose: namely, to secure Prussian support in France's duel with England. The King, it was true, had deserted his ally in 1742, but perhaps he might renew the tie. Despite all precautions Amelot heard that a Cologne paper was on the track. He was not surprised, for it was difficult to combine the roles of injured innocent and official envoy. Frederick however, was equally ready to play a double game, and an indiscreet criticism by Voltaire of the newly appointed tutor to the Dauphin placed a weapon in his hand. He had denounced his avarice and fanaticism and transcribed *"l'a ancien évêque de Mirepoix"* ("the former Bishop de Mirepoix") into *"l'âne évêque"* ("the ass Bishop"). "Here is part of a letter of Voltaire," wrote the King to his representative in Paris, "which I beg you to convey to the Bishop of Mirepoix by a roundabout way without you and me appearing in the matter. My intention is to make it so hot for him in France that he will have to come to Berlin." The two men were as slippery as eels, but each saw through the other's game.

The envoy reached Berlin from The Hague on August 30, 1743, and presented the usual poetical bouquet.

> *Grand roi, tous les dieux sur ta tête*
> *Ont versé leurs dons à la fois.*[1]

After some talks on general topics he came to business with a questionnaire, begging for replies on the margin which would be agreeable to the French court. Was not France displaying vigor and wisdom? If Frederick took the lead among the princes of the Empire in forming an army of neutrality, would he not snatch the scepter of Europe from the hands of the English? Since

[1] *Great King, upon thy head the gods*
Have lavished all their choicest gifts.

Austria was burning to renew the struggle for Silesia, had he any other ally than France, and, however powerful he might be, was not an ally of use? Frederick declined to commit himself in his replies. "The commission I can give you," he concluded, "is to advise France to behave more wisely than hitherto." A letter of September 7 adroitly indicated that he did not take the mission very seriously, partly because Voltaire had no credentials, partly because his opinion of French diplomacy and arms was low. "This nation is the most charming in Europe, and if it is not feared it deserves to be loved." Perhaps Louis XV might restore its fortunes. "I shall admire all that this great man does, and no sovereign will be less jealous of his success; but I am not inclined to talk politics with you, which would be like offering a glass of medicine to his mistress. I think I shall do better to talk poetry." He described his guest later as "the man of all men least born for politics," adding that his negotiations were a joke.

When Voltaire accompanied the monarch on a visit to Bayreuth he secretly urged the Margrave to influence his brother-in-law, but the harmony was disturbed by the discovery of Frederick's little game. "Unable to catch me in any other way," reported the envoy to Amelot on October 5, "he thinks it can be done by embroiling me with France; but I swear that I would rather live in a Swiss village than enjoy at this price the dangerous favor of a King capable of mixing treachery with friendship. To please him in this case would be too great a misfortune." Frederick was partially aware of the sentiments of his guest. "Voltaire has somehow discovered our little stratagem and is extremely annoyed," he wrote on October 14; "I hope he will get over it." He was promised all that he asked. "France has hitherto passed for the refuge of unfortunate kings," wrote the King. "I desire my capital to become the temple of great men. Come, dear Voltaire, and say what you would like. I wish to please you. Choose your house, and decide what is needed for your happiness. I will do the rest. You will always be entirely your own master." He would receive a pension of twelve thousand francs.

Before leaving Berlin on October 12, 1743, Voltaire promised to return when he had arranged his private affairs. He begged for a few lines in writing to take home to say "that you are now satisfied with the dispositions of France; that no one has ever drawn such an advantageous portrait of his King; that you believe me all the more since I have never deceived you, and that you are resolved to combine with a prince so wise and so firm. These vague words commit you to nothing, and I venture to say that they will have an excellent effect. If you have received disparaging accounts of the King of France, I must tell you that you have been described in the darkest colors to him; justice has been done to neither of you. Forgive me therefore for seizing this occasion to reconcile two monarchs so dear and so estimable; it will be the happiness of my life. I will show my letter to the King, and I shall be able to secure the restoration of part of my possessions of which the Cardinal [Fleury] deprived me. The money that I shall owe to you I will come and spend here. My second great day will be when I can tell the King all that I think of you. The first will be when I come and settle at your feet and begin a new life which will be wholly yours." The appeal was in vain, for the envoy left with empty hands, knowing no more of Frederick's plans than when he arrived. As a matter of fact, the King had already made up his mind to renew co-operation with France, and when Voltaire was gone he summoned the French Ambassador to talk business.

On returning to Paris the amateur diplomatist reported that his mission had been a success; Frederick's bad impressions and prejudices had rapidly diminished. He had spoken of Louis XV with respectful esteem, very different from his attitude to other rulers, and every chance of singing the praises of France had been seized. There had been difficult moments. "On the eve of his departure for Bayreuth he was told that I had come to spy on his conduct. It was also bad luck that someone wrote to M. de Valory [French Minister at Berlin] that I was charged with a secret negotiation behind his back. My good faith dispersed these clouds. I told the King, when he reproached me, that I had had the honor of speaking with you before my journey, and that you had simply advised me to cultivate a good understanding between the two monarchs, advice that my zeal did not require. He told me several times that I ought to have letters of credence. I replied that I had not troubled to ask for them; my only purpose and duty was to help M. de Valory to succeed. I preferred talking to the King of Prussia as a friend rather than an envoy, and I thought it was also to his advantage as well."

Voltaire's promise to return after arranging his affairs was not seriously meant, and in April 1744 Frederick announced that the furniture was being removed from the house destined for him in Berlin. There was no longer a patriotic reason for migration, for in June 1744 a fresh treaty of alliance for twelve years was concluded between Prussia and France. Moreover, after their latest experiences neither monarch nor poet trusted each other. The flow of letters and verses, so steady during the first seven years of friendship, almost ceased between 1744 and 1748. Mme du Châtelet, who had been terrified at the prospect that her companion might settle in Berlin, exerted all her influence to keep him at Cirey. "I was in Lorraine at the court of King Stanislas," he reported to Frederick in January 1749. "I know that everybody will ask why I am at the court of Lunéville, not at that of Berlin. Sire, it is because Lunéville is near the waters of Plombières, where I often go to preserve for a few days longer an unfortunate machine containing a soul devoted to Your Majesty. Besides, could you bear with me? I have a malady that makes me deaf in one ear and lose my teeth. The waters of Plombières have left me tired. There is a nice corpse to drag to Potsdam! If I improve a little this winter it will be a pleasure to come and pay my respects in the summer."

Frederick replied in May that he expected him in July. "You will find me here, a peaceful citizen of Sans Souci, living the life of a philosopher. If you love tumult or show, I advise you not to come; but if quiet and harmony attract you, fulfill your promises." "I am crazy to see you," he added in June; "it would be treason if you decline. I wish to study with you. This year I have leisure, and God knows if I shall have it again. I shall see if you really care for me or if it is all words." In July Voltaire promised a visit in September, well or ill. "After that I shall die content, and I could be buried in your Catholic church [the newly erected Hedwigskirche in Berlin]. An Englishman put on his tomb: 'Here lies the friend of Sidney.' I will put on mine: 'Here lies the admirer of Frederick the Great.' Believe me, Sire, my enthusiasm for you has never changed, and if you were King of the Indies I would go to Lahore or Delhi." In July he fixed October for his arrival. "Believe me," he wrote on August 17, "my heart has often made the journey to Berlin while you believed it elsewhere. You have aroused fear, admiration, interest. Allow me to say that I have always taken the liberty to love you." A rumor that he had lost favor evoked a request for the order *Pour le Mérite*. These protestations of devotion had long ceased to be taken at their face value in Berlin. "It is a pity," wrote Frederick to Algarotti on September 19, "that such a mean soul is mated to such a fine genius. He has the pretty little tricks and the malice of a monkey. But I shall say nothing, for I need him for my French studies." The King's letters became ever more pressing. "I feel my extreme need of you and the great help you could be to me. The passion for study will last all my life. I can acquire all sorts of knowledge if I try, but that of the French language I owe to you."

The death of Mme du Châtelet in childbirth in September 1749 facilitated the long-contemplated migration to Berlin. "I have lost a friend of twenty-five years," moaned Voltaire, now aptly described by Carlyle as a quasi-widower, "a great man whose only failing was to be a woman, regretted and honored by the whole of Paris. Perhaps justice was never done to her in her lifetime, and you might have judged her differently had she had the honor to know you. But a woman able to translate Newton and Virgil and possessed of all the virtues will doubtless be regretted by you also. My condition during the last month leaves me no hope of seeing you again." He did not mention the fact, which mitigated his grief, that his old partner had transferred her affections to Saint-Lambert, whom she had met at the court of Lunéville, the father of her unwanted child. "Voltaire declaims too much in his affliction," wrote Frederick to Algarotti, "which makes me think he will soon get over it."

In June 1750, having received a substantial sum for the journey and the promise of a generous allowance for himself and Mme Denis, his niece, a childless widow, Voltaire set out for Berlin for his fifth meeting with the King. "The days I shall pass with Frederick the Great will be the best in my life," he wrote from Compiègne, where he sought leave from Louis XV to migrate. He was welcomed with an indifferent Frederician quatrain:

> *Les destins ont sur votre vie*
> *Répandu les talents avec profusion;*

Votre prose et vos vers, voilà mon ambroisie:
Voltaire est mon seul Apollon.[1]

On learning that Mme Denis judged it a risky experiment, the royal host presented his prospective guest with a charter of liberty. "I have seen your niece's letter from Paris and her friendship for you earns my esteem. If I were she I should think the same, but, being what I am, I disagree. I should grieve to cause misfortune to my enemy; how, then, could I wish it for one whom I esteem and love, who sacrifices his country and all that man holds most dear? No, my dear Voltaire, if I could anticipate that your transplantation could be the slightest disadvantage to you I should be the first to dissuade you. Yes, I should prefer your happiness to my own. But you are a philosopher and so am I. What more natural or simple than that philosophers, made to live together, united by the same studies, tastes, and ideas, should indulge in this satisfaction? I respect you as my master in eloquence and knowledge; I love you as a virtuous friend. What slavery, what sorrow, what reverse of fortune is to be feared in a country where you are as much esteemed as in your own and as the guest of a friend with a grateful heart? I am not presumptuous enough to believe that Berlin is the same as Paris. If weather and grandeur make a city attractive, we take second place. If good taste is to be found anywhere, I agree it is there, but do you not carry it with you wherever you go? Our resources suffice to applaud you, and as to our feelings, we yield to no country. I respected your friendship with Mme du Châtelet, but after her I was one of your oldest friends. What! Because you retire into my house it will be said that it became your prison! Because I am your friend I shall be your tyrant! Such logic I do not understand. I am convinced you will be very happy here as long as I live, that you will be regarded as the father of letters and of people of taste, that you will find in me all the consolations that a man of your merit can expect from one who holds you in esteem." Voltaire forwarded this letter to his niece

---

[1] *The fates have showered on thy life*
All talents with a generous hand.
Your prose and verse are my delight.
Voltaire alone is my Apollo.

with the injunction to preserve "this precious monument," to allow no copies, and to show it only to a few real friends. He was welcomed in verse as well as in prose:

> Soutien du goût, des arts, de l'éloquence,
> Fils d'Apollon, Homère de la France.[1]

The partnership opened under favorable auspices, and the visitor was assigned apartments in the palaces of Potsdam and Berlin. "The King has made me his Chamberlain," ran the report to his niece, "gives me one of his orders [the coveted *Pour le Mérite*], a pension of 20,000 francs, and 4,000 francs to you for life if you will run my house in Berlin." Permission was obtained from the French court to resign his posts as Historiographer and Chamberlain (*Gentilhomme Ordinaire*). To judge by his first brief notes the guest was content. "My health is no worse here than elsewhere," he wrote in October, "and I am much happier. You, Sire, and work: that is all a thinking creature needs. I prostrate myself before your scepter, your lyre, your pen, your sword, your imagination, your universality. I have abandoned everything to attach myself solely to you. You make me happy. I count on passing the brief remainder of my life at your feet." It looked like a permanent transplantation, and a picture was hawked about Paris with the caption *Voltaire le Prussien*. He described Sans Souci as his philosophical paradise. "Nature has created Frederick the Great for me," he reported to Paris. "Only the devil himself can prevent me spending the last years of my life happily with a prince whose thoughts are mine and who is good enough to love me, so far as a king is capable of love." Yet there were soon clouds in the sky, and the feelings of the visitor are much more accurately described in the sparkling letters to his niece. "The royal suppers are delightful," he wrote on November 6; "we talk reason, wit, science; liberty reigns, he is the soul of it all; no ill humor, no clouds, at any rate no storms. My life is free and full of work; but—but—opera, comedy, festivities, suppers at Sans Souci, military maneuvers, concerts, studies, readings; but—but— Berlin, big, much better laid out than Paris, palaces, theater, affable queens, charming princesses, maids of

---

[1] *Pillar of taste, of arts, of eloquence,*
Son of Apollo, Homer of fair France.

honor beautiful and well got up; but—but— My dear child, the climate is becoming pretty chilly." Vain and jealous, grasping and quarrelsome, he complained to the King of mischiefmakers, but he was his own worst enemy.

A few months after his arrival Voltaire arranged with a shady Berlin Jew named Hirsch for the purchase of over two thousand pounds' worth of Saxon exchequer bills, which by the recent Treaty of Dresden were payable at par to Prussian subjects. Since they had lost much of their value in Saxony there would thus be a very substantial profit; but Voltaire was not a Prussian, and the transaction was therefore illegal. There were other complications. He gave a draft on Paris to Hirsch, who handed over some jewels in pledge till the stocks were delivered. He failed to produce them; Voltaire stopped the payment of the draft; Hirsch demanded the return of the jewels and charged his client with changing some of them; Voltaire went to law, and Hirsch failed to prove that the jewels were changed. The visitor won on most points of the case, but his reputation never recovered from this washing of dirty linen. The moral, declared Lessing, was that it was difficult to decide a quarrel when both parties were rogues, and he spoke with authority since he had been employed as a translator by Voltaire in connection with the case. "His avarice was known in Berlin while I was there," wrote Wilhelmina to her brother, "but I should never have thought him capable of cheating. I should be sorry if his misconduct deprived you of a piece of furniture most useful for your diversion and amusement. What is the good of mind and talents if one uses them so ill? I hope he will earn your pardon by more prudent conduct, for he is irreplaceable." The King's rejoinder was in the same critical vein. "The lawsuit of Voltaire and the Jew is coming on, and from what I hear it is a case of a rogue trying to deceive a cheat. It is a great pity that mind has so little influence on morals, and that a celebrity in the republic of letters should be so contemptible in character."

Since genuine affection had never existed and respect had now disappeared, it is hardly surprising that the partnership lasted less than three years. During the first winter they rarely met, for the guest lived at Berlin and the host at Potsdam. Complaints of persecution and appeals for protection produced a chilling reply dated February 24, 1751. "I was glad to receive you as my guest.

I esteemed your intellect, your talent, your knowledge. I naturally believed that a man of your age, weary of literary feuds and of exposing himself to the storm, came here to find refuge as in a tranquil harbor." The King proceeded to complain of interference in matters that did not directly concern him, in addition to the affair with the Jew. "I kept the peace in my house till you arrived, and I warned you to avoid intrigues and cabals. I like gentle and peaceful people who do not import the passions of tragedy into their conduct. If you can make up your mind to live like a philosopher I shall be happy to see you, but if you give rein to your passions and quarrel with everybody, it would be just as well to remain in Berlin."

Two penitent letters from Voltaire brought a slight *détente*. He could come to Potsdam, replied his host, but there must be no talk of lawsuit. "Since you have won I congratulate you on your victory, and I am very glad this miserable business is over. I hope you will have no more quarrels, either with the Old or the New Testament. Even the finest intellect in France will not hide the stains that in the long run your conduct would leave on your reputation. I write this letter with the robust good sense of a German who says what he thinks; it is for you to profit by it." The reply was almost abject. "Your Majesty is absolutely right. I have never cured myself of the accursed notion of always forging ahead in everything; and though I realize that there are a thousand occasions when one should know how to hold one's tongue, I longed to vindicate myself against a man unworthy even of defeat. Believe me, I am in despair and have never felt such profound and bitter grief. I have thoughtlessly deprived myself of the sole object of my coming; I have forfeited the conversations that provide enlightenment and inspiration; I have displeased the only man whom I desired to please. If the Queen of Sheba had been in disgrace with Solomon she would not have suffered more. I assure the modern Solomon that all his genius cannot make me feel my fault as keenly as my own heart. I suffer from a cruel malady, but it is nothing compared with my affliction." Voltaire, wrote Frederick to his brother, was now as gentle as a lamb and as amusing as a harlequin.

The visitor appeared to have learned his lesson and his letters continued in a minor key. "I do not flatter you," he wrote in

May 1751, "and you know from my audacities whether I love and tell the truth. I admire you as the greatest man in Europe and I am bold enough to cherish you as the most amiable. Do not believe that I am here for any reason but these. You know I am sensitive. Be assured that I am warmly appreciative of all your kindnesses and that your person is the happiness of my life. After you I love work and a quiet life. No one here complains of me. I beg Your Majesty one favor; namely, to leave me my apartment in Berlin till my journey to Paris. If I quitted it the papers would say that I had lost favor, and that would be a fresh bitterness. I will clear out when some prince arrives, and then it will seem all right." The letter closed with the wish that the King would look into his lawsuit. "Your Majesty would see that I acted like a man worthy of your protection and worthy to be your guest." He was well aware what the world would say if he left Prussia so soon after his arrival had been heralded with drums and trumpets.

The paucity of letters during the summer of 1751 is doubtless due to the fact that the guest had migrated to Potsdam. His chief task was to revise the products of his patron's busy pen, each of which provided the occasion for the most extravagant laudations. *The History of the House of Brandenburg,* he declares, would have given the author an eminent reputation even had he done nothing else. "But this work, unique of its kind, added to others, to say nothing of five victories, makes you the most extraordinary man who ever lived. *Grand Dieu!* How clear, elegant, precise and, above all, philosophic it all is! Here is a genius that is always master of the subject. The history of society, government, and religion is a masterpiece. Sire, you are adorable. I will spend my days at your feet. Do not put me in a niche. If the Kings of Denmark, Portugal, Spain, etc., did so, it would mean nothing to me: they are only kings. But you are perhaps the greatest man who has ever occupied a throne." Such gross flattery can hardly have given much pleasure to its recipient, who preferred the poems from which at any rate he might learn the art of writing French verse.

Voltaire, never easy to please, was far from happy; the spell was broken, his health was poor, and there was little society when the King was away. "I am absolutely alone from morning till night; my only consolation is the necessary pleasure of exercise. I wish to walk and work in your garden. I assume it is permitted, but I find some big grenadiers who hold their bayonets to my stomach. So I flee before them like the Austrians and Saxons. Did you ever read of a poor devil of a poet invited by Their Gracious Majesties being chased from the garden of Titus or Marcus Aurelius at the point of the bayonet?" He asked for a sunnier room. "Perhaps it is a sick man's fancy, but if so Your Majesty will have pity. You promised to make me happy." Frederick confined his communications to the sphere of literature, in which his troublesome guest was supreme. "I tell you nothing of my occupations," he wrote from Silesia early in September, "because these are things in which you are not interested. Camps, soldiers, fortresses, finances, lawsuits are found in all countries, and the papers are full of these miseries. I hope to see you on the 16th, and I wish you health, tranquillity, and contentment." Compliments were now reserved for verse.

> *Quel avenir t'attend, divin Voltaire!*
> *Lorsque ton âme aura quitté la terre,*
> *A tes genoux vois la postérité.*
> *Le temps qui s'élance*
> *Te promet d'avance*
> *L'immortalité.*[1]

The conversation of the magician remained a sheer delight. "Voltaire made us laugh at supper," he reported to his brother in November; "he was more original than I ever saw him."

Could these joys be expected to last? In September 1751 Voltaire received a staggering blow. The King, he was informed by La Mettrie, had said: "I shall want him for about another year. One squeezes the orange and throws away the skin." Was it really true? He could hardly ask and he was tormented by the doubt. But the sharpest tongue in Europe could give as good as he got, and there was talk of a suitable riposte. Maupertuis, he complained to his niece, quoted him as saying that the King sent him his dirty linen to wash. The story, needless to say, reached

---

[1] *Your fame is safe, divine Voltaire.*
For when your soul has left our earth
I see posterity at your feet.
Already the advancing years
Assure your immortality.

the ears of the King, who knew from experience that Voltaire's denials were not always to be taken seriously. These celebrated mots were so characteristic of their presumed authors that they may well be authentic, but we cannot be sure. The garment of friendship was wearing thin, and the guest felt the more uneasy about his prospects because he had no longer a home in France. Whatever hopes he had cherished of exerting political influence or playing the part of an amateur diplomatist at the Prussian Court had long disappeared, for Frederick's keen eye had taken his measure. On returning to Sans Souci after a long absence he found the walls of his room painted in yellow, the color of disfavor, and the furniture covered with needlework depicting the fables of a fox.

The year of the quarrel (1752) opened with the dispatch to Potsdam of an advance copy of *Le Siècle de Louis XIV*. He would have brought it himself, the author explained, had his health allowed. "I only ask to see you and hear you talk. You know it is my sole consolation, the sole motive that made me renounce my country, my King, my appointments, my family, my friends of forty years. All that is left is your solemn promises, which sustain me against the fear of your displeasure. As it is announced from Paris that I am in disgrace, I implore you to tell me if I have displeased you in any way. I may err from ignorance or *empressement,* but my heart will never offend. I live in utter solitude, devoting to study such time as my cruel maladies permit. I write to my niece, but to no one else. My family and friends are only fortified against their own predictions by your assurances. To her I speak only of your kindness, of my admiration for your genius, of the happiness of living with you. It is cruel that the talk in Paris has turned her against the idea of coming here and witnessing my last hours. Once more, Sire, deign to tell me if you have anything to blame. I should count it among your greatest favors. I deserve it, having given myself to you without reserve. The happiness of feeling myself less unworthy of you will enable me to bear patiently the ills with which I am overwhelmed." The note was too fawning to be impressive and the analysis of the situation was not altogether correct. Mme Denis was far from being his sole correspondent, and she had never dreamed of exchanging the delights of Paris for the boredom of Berlin. The King's replies, ignoring the appeal for a testimonial of good conduct, are confined to literary matters such as his enjoyment of the *Siècle de Louis XIV* and the first installment of the *Dictionnaire philosophique*. "Your flame, like that of the vestals, never goes out. The small portion that has fallen to my lot needs a good deal of stirring, and often nearly expires amid the cinders." This was not a mere pose, for Frederick described himself as a dilettante in every genre. Literary compliments were no compensation for the loss of the King's favor. "Voltaire is isolated," reported old Pöllnitz to Wilhelmina; "tired in mind and body, and hardly recognizable. Yesterday he spent two hours with me, but our conversation was scanty. He was silent from low spirits, I from awe at his genius."

The most satirical of men had skated on thin ice almost from the moment of his arrival in the autumn of 1750, and two years later he plunged into the depths. As Lytton Strachey observes in his sparkling essay "Voltaire and Frederick," he was restless, he was reckless, he was spoiling for a fight. He and Maupertuis, the only stars of the first magnitude in the Frederician firmament, had once been friends, but they had got on each other's nerves. The opportunity of the most brilliant pamphleteer in Europe arrived when a Dutch scientist named König courteously challenged the claim of Maupertuis to have discovered the mathematical principle of least action, adducing an unpublished letter of Leibnitz in support of his criticism. Maupertuis was furious and persuaded the Academy to declare König, who was a member of the Academy, guilty of forgery and to expel him from its ranks. Though the original letter of Leibnitz had disappeared, there was no reason to doubt its authenticity, and such high-handed action invited reprisals. Voltaire was a friend of König and, though no mathematician, plunged gaily into the fray with a restatement of his case and an exposure of the methods of Maupertuis. The *Lettre à un Académicien de Paris* was anonymous, but a signature was as superfluous as that of Macaulay in the *Edinburgh Review*. Incensed by the exposure of the president of his Academy, the King retorted in an anonymous brochure, exalting Maupertuis and flagellating his assailant in unmeasured terms. When the second edition bore on the title-page a crown, a scepter, and the Prussian eagle, the secret was revealed. "All the world will know that none of our sons is so unnatural as to raise his arm against his father, and that none of our academicians is vile enough to become the mercenary tool of jealous fury. No, sir, we all render to our president the admiration due to his learning and his character; we even venture to appropriate him, to claim him from France. Here he enjoys during his life the glory to which Homer attained long after his death. Berlin and Saint-Malo dispute which is his true fatherland. We regard his merit as ours, his knowledge as conferring the greatest splendor on our Academy, his writings as works of which the use accrues to us, his reputation as that of the Academy, his character as the model of a man of honor and a true philosopher." The King was right to hold his shield over the president, but the eulogy was too shrill to convince. The victim was as vain as his assailant and he had started the whole trouble by his monstrous treatment of König.

Voltaire was not the man to turn the other cheek, for as he wrote to his niece, though he lacked a scepter, he possessed a pen. This time he traveled far beyond the original dispute, tearing to pieces a volume of Maupertuis's pseudo-scientific miscellanies in the sparkling *Diatribe du Docteur Akakia, Médecin du Pape,* in which the imaginary doctor lays some of the more grotesque conclusions before the Inquisition with critical comments. Frederick, to whom it was shown, enjoyed the incomparable wit, but forbade publication. Despite the author's promise, the satire was published simultaneously in Leipzig and Paris under a license granted for another work. The King gave orders for it to be publicly burned and the ashes to be sent to Maupertuis, and for all copies to be bought up. He was too late and soon all Europe was joining in the fun. A stern royal admonition produced the usual paper assurances, but nothing else. "I promise Your Majesty," wrote the culprit on November 27, "that so long as I am your guest I will not write against anyone, neither the government of France, nor the ministers, nor other sovereigns, nor literary celebrities, whom I will treat with due respect. I will not misuse Your Majesty's letters, and I will conduct myself in a manner befitting a writer who has the honor to be Chamberlain to Your Majesty. I will fulfill all your orders and obedience will not be difficult. I beg you once more to bear in mind that I have written against no government, still less against that of France, which I only left to finish my life at your feet. I beg you to look into the Maupertuis dispute and to believe that I forget it since that is your command. I submit to all your wishes. If Your Majesty had ordered me not to defend myself and not to take part in this literary encounter I should have obeyed. I beg you to spare an old man crushed by sickness and grief, and to believe that I shall die as attached as on the day I arrived at your court."

The King was too incensed to be placated by specious promises of amendment and obedience. Voltaire had behaved like a madman, he wrote to Wilhelmina. "He has cruelly attacked Maupertuis and played so many pranks that, but for the abiding seduction of his intellect, I should have been obliged in honor to dismiss him." The reply to his exasperating guest was short and sharp. "Your effrontery astonishes me. After what you have done, which is as clear as day, you persist instead of avowing your guilt. Do not imagine you will make people believe that black is white; if one does not see it, it is because one has not the wish. If you continue the affair I shall publish everything, and it will be recognized that if your works deserve statues your conduct would deserve chains." The offender's response to Jove's thunderbolt was confined to four agonized lines: "My God, Sire, in my condition! I swear to you on my life, which I renounce without a pang, that it is a hideous calumny. I implore you to interrogate all my staff. What! You will judge me unheard! I demand liberty or death."

The time for explanations had passed, and the monarch demanded the return of the order *Pour le Mérite* and the Chamberlain's key. They were dispatched on New Year's day 1753 with lamentations in verse and prose.

Je les reçus avec tendresse,
Je vous les rends avec douleur;
C'est ainsi qu'un amant dans son extrême ardeur
Rend le portrait de sa maîtresse.[1]

The letter was a shrill cry of distress. "Nothing is left but to hide myself forever and to deplore my misfortune in silence. How shall I live? I have no idea. I ought to be dead with grief. What

[1] *Received with tenderness, returned with pain.*
'Tis thus that lovers in their ardor fierce
Hand back the portraits of their mistresses.

do you wish me to do? I know not. I know only that you have attached me to yourself for sixteen years. Dispose of a life that I have consecrated to you and the close of which you have rendered so bitter. You are kind and indulgent; I am the unhappiest man in your dominions. Decide on my fate." Desiring to minimize the public scandal, the King allowed his discredited guest to retain the order and the key and to remain in Berlin till the end of March. Despite some friendly talks at what he described as *soupers de Damoclès,* he had resolved to fly and never to return. He received permission to leave Prussia in order to take the waters at Plombières, and on March 26 he set out for Leipzig. The failure of the experiment was almost wholly his fault. Nothing need be added to the verdict of his admiring niece on the morrow of the breach. "My uncle is not made to live with royalty. He is too lively, too inconsequent, too self-willed. I foresaw all this years ago." Frederick was difficult enough, but Voltaire was frankly impossible.

Chapter IX

VOLTAIRE: THE AFTERMATH

 THE third volume of the correspondence covers the last twenty-five years of the life of Voltaire. The two men had learned to know each other only too well, and it was as clear to themselves as to everyone else that they were best apart. Voltaire's sentiments were a blend of admiration and fear, Frederick's a mixture of admiration and contempt. Of affection on either side there was not the slightest trace. Despite his promises, the incorrigible offender published new editions of *Doctor Akakia,* even more virulent than the first. Maupertuis, who had brought it on himself, collapsed, left Berlin, made no reply to his merciless enemy, and died in Switzerland a few years later.

"Voltaire is the most malevolent madman I ever met," wrote the angry monarch to Darget, "he is only good to read. You cannot imagine all his duplicities, knaveries and infamies here. I am disgusted that so much wit and learning do not make people better. I took the side of Maupertuis because he is a thoroughly decent fellow and because Voltaire tried to ruin him. A little too much *amour-propre* made him too vulnerable to the attacks of a monkey who deserved contempt after his whipping."

Frederick's first letter after the departure of his guest, dated April 19, 1753, was written with a pen of gall. "I was told of your plan to go to Leipzig in order to launch new insults against the human race. You should know better than anyone else that I do not revenge myself for abuse. I see the evil deed and I pity those who are base enough to commit it. I laugh at your impotent wrath. I know not whether you regret Potsdam; to judge by your impatience you must have had good reasons to be gone. I will not examine them and I appeal to your conscience if you have one. Confess that you were born to be the prime minister of Cæsar Borgia. For myself, who am only a good German and am not ashamed of the reputation for candor attaching to this nation, I do not write to you with my own hand, because I am not skillful enough to compose a letter that might not be misused.

You possess the art of amending dates and transposing events according to taste, and you correct phrases to fit your purpose. All your great talents, which I know so well, compel me to be cautious, and you will not be surprised if by the hand of my secretary I commend you to God's keeping when you are abandoned by men." A postscript ironically authorizing publication contained a warning against manipulation since the original text had been verified in legal form.

This stinging letter was crossed by one from Gotha written in Voltaire's most self-righteous vein. "I have always told you the truth and I always will. I shall always be tenderly devoted to you. I have never failed you and I never will. I will return to your feet in October. My heart is still yours. You know the enthusiasm that led me to you and will lead me again. When I begged you not to attach me by pensions you know that it was because I preferred your person to your benefactions. You ordered me to receive them, but the sole attraction will always be yourself. I swear to you between the hands of the Margravine of Bayreuth, whom I am begging to forward this letter, that I shall carry to the tomb the sentiments that led me to your feet when I quitted everything I held most dear and when you vowed to me eternal friendship." Such assurances of lifelong devotion excited nothing but derision. "Our rascal of a poet," wrote the King to Wilhelmina, "is still at Gotha, where he is trying to hook the Duchess. If he stays there long his tricks will soon be his undoing. It is not the authors' quarrel that I mind, for that was a small matter. It is the ferocity with which he persecutes Maupertuis, it is his abominable character, his falsities, his cheatings, and all his naughtiness here that make me detest him. I never took him for a very honest man, but I thought at least that he would save appearances. After what has passed and all I have seen with my own eyes, I thank my stars to have got rid of him, and he certainly will not catch me again." His angry disgust overflowed into a poem classing him with an infamous poisoner at the court of Louis XIV.

Voltaire, des neuf sœurs l'indigne favori,
Est enfin démasqué détesté de Paris.
On le brûle à Berlin, on le maudit à Rome.

Si pour être honoré du titre de grand homme
Il suffit d'être fourbe et trompeur effronté,
Avec la Brinvillers son nom sera cité.[1]

The peak of the quarrel was reached a few weeks later. Voltaire arrived in Frankfurt with Collini, his Italian secretary, on May 30. Next day Freytag, the Prussian Resident in the free city, acting on instructions from Berlin, entered his hotel to demand the order, the Chamberlain's key, and, above all, the privately printed edition of Frederick's poems, of which there were only twelve copies. The departing guest had been allowed to take the little volume, presented to him in happier times, but after the renewed attack on Maupertuis the King feared that his poetical effusions might reach the public without permission. The traveler promised to remain till his luggage arrived from Leipzig, and when the required articles were handed over a fortnight later he naturally expected to proceed. Unfortunately, however, Freytag decided to detain the traveler pending further instructions, and two days later he frustrated an attempt to leave. This incident, which he interpreted as an insult to his sovereign, was reported to Berlin, and meanwhile, despite the arrival of permission to depart, the traveler was detained. The matter was complicated by the fact that Mme Denis had joined her uncle and was compelled by Freytag to share his fate. A brief letter of June 26 contained a piteous appeal. "Sire, if, as I fear, my letters have not reached you, deign at least to read this. Deign to consider the horrible position of a respectable woman who has nothing on her conscience and who has been treated with the greatest violence and ignominy. What a fatal sequel to fifteen years of kindness! Sire, if I have erred, I beg a thousand pardons. I will forget Maupertuis. But in the name of your humanity save the life of a woman who has traveled two hundred leagues to look after an unfortunate invalid, and do not let his terrible death be the price of her noble act. Pardon me, Sire, I beg you."

[1] *Voltaire, unworthy favorite of the Muses,*
Is now unmasked, and Paris hates his name.
Berlin his writings burns, Rome curses him.
If to deserve the title of great man
It is enough to be both liar and rogue,
His name will join Brinvillers on men's lips.

A highly colored account of the ill-treatment of himself and his niece was dispatched from Mainz after they had been allowed to leave. To Voltaire the King made no reply, but he informed Mme Denis that the severity of his agent was unauthorized. Though the victims had every right to complain of the five weeks' detention in a free city over which the King of Prussia had no jurisdiction, Frederick was not seriously perturbed. Having given orders to retrieve the poems, he had gone to Silesia and knew nothing of Freytag's blunders till it was too late to intervene. "Voltaire's niece," he wrote to Wilhelmina, "makes him out to be so ill because I requested the return of the cross and his key and a book of poetry I had confided to him. He is acting—I know all about his maladies. Apart from some cramp in the stomach and a little skin trouble it is only a grimace."

After eight months of silence Voltaire wrote in March 1754 to disclaim the authorship of a lampoon. He added that the cruel enemy who had caused the breach (Maupertuis) could not destroy his feelings of respect. Frederick replied in a long and conciliatory letter. "I never believed you were the author of these libels; I know your style and thought too well. Even if you were, I would gladly forgive you. You will remember that, when you came to say good-by at Potsdam, I assured you I would forget everything if you promised to leave Maupertuis alone. If you had kept that promise I should have been pleased to see you back; you would have passed your days tranquilly at my side and, in ceasing to fret yourself, you would have been happy. But your stay in Leipzig revived my memory of the traits I had wished to efface. I thought it wrong that, despite your promise, you continued to attack him, and, despite my patronage of the Academy, you wished to cover it with the same ridicule as its president. Those are all my complaints, for as regards myself I have none to make. I shall always disapprove your attacks on him, but I shall none the less recognize your literary merit and admire your talent as I have always done. You honor humanity by your genius too much for me to be indifferent to your fortunes. I wish that you would drop these disputes and that, restored to yourself, you should be the delight of every company as of old." Yet Frederick had had quite enough of him. "Would you believe," he wrote to Darget in the spring of 1754, "that

195

Voltaire, after all the tricks he has played me, has made approaches with a view to return? Heaven preserve me! He is good to read, but dangerous to meet. You will laugh, despite your low spirits, when I tell you that I received letters from Maupertuis and Voltaire on the same day, both filled with recriminations. They take me for a drain-pipe into which they discharge all their filth. Thank heaven I have not such lively passions, else I should be at war all my life."

In August 1754 Voltaire dispatched from his new home near Geneva the concluding volumes of his *Annales de l'Empire,* the dullest of his books, but he had no intention of standing in a white sheet. "It will show you that my life is consecrated to work and truth. This life, always retired and busy despite my maladies, and my conduct till death will prove to you that my character is not unworthy of the favors with which you honored me during fifteen years. I appeal to the generosity of your heart not to fill my last days with bitterness. I beg you to remember that I forfeited my posts to have the honor of being with you and that I do not regret them; that I devoted my time and thoughts to you for three years; that I gave up everything for you and never failed you. My niece, who has been rendered unhappy by you alone, assuredly without deserving it, and who consoles my old age, ought at least to be an object of your kindness and justice. She is still ill from the horrible treatment inflicted in your name. I feel sure that you will deign by a few kind words to make up for what is so contrary to your humanity and your glory. I implore you by my sincere respect for you. Deign to hearken to your character even more than to the prayer of a man who has always loved you for yourself and who is unhappy only because he loved you sufficiently to sacrifice his country to you. I need nothing on earth but your favor. Believe that posterity, whose admiration you desire and deserve, will find nothing to blame in an act of humanity and justice. In truth, if you will recall my conduct during our long association, you will see how strange it is that you should be the cause of my unhappiness."

Every communication was now as carefully considered as a move at chess. Voltaire wrote letter after letter in the hope of eliciting a reply that he could utilize, but Frederick was not to be caught and replied in the third person through his secretary, the Abbé de Prades. Wilhelmina, who chanced to meet Voltaire while traveling in France in the autumn of 1754, was struck by the change. "He wept when he saw me. He said that he adores you, that he was to blame, that he recognizes his mistakes, that he is the unhappiest man in the world. His condition, his talk, and his countenance aroused my pity. I reproached him for his conduct, but I had not the courage to rub it in." A year later, in August 1755, he accompanied the gift of a new drama with the stereotyped formulas of devotion, without, so far as we know, extracting a response. He told his friends that he had declined offers of restoration to favor, but no confirmation of this statement has come to light. That the King was in no melting mood is indicated by a letter to Keith in June 1756. "I have not written to Voltaire, as you seem to think. The Abbé de Prades is charged with the correspondence. I know the madman and take care not to expose myself in the slightest degree." Yet Frederick's delight in his writings was undiminished. *La Pucelle,* which he knew in manuscript, appeared in 1755, the memorable poem on the Lisbon earthquake in 1756, *Candide,* the most characteristic and the most enduring of his works, in 1759. After all, there was only one Voltaire in the world.

On the outbreak of the Seven Years' War, though France and Prussia were now enemies, the King resumed the practice of writing with his own hand. In September 1757, after the catastrophe at Kolin, he describes his sorry plight. "If fortune turns her back on me and I am crushed, my fall will not merely furnish you with a good theme for a tragedy. This fatal event will add to the catalogue of the wickedness and perfidy of the class of men and women who govern the civilized peoples of Europe in a century in which a private citizen would be broken on the wheel for having done the hundredth part of the evil that ministers commit with impunity. I should say too much if I let myself go. Adieu! You shall soon have news of me, good or bad." The old signature Frederic reappears, and a postscript adds a couplet from *Mérope:*

Quand on a tout perdu, quad on n'a plus d'espoir,
La vie est un opprobre et la mort un devoir.[1]

[1] *When all is lost, when even hope is gone,*
Life is a shame, the only duty death.

Voltaire was delighted and replied with a long letter of homage and consolation. "With the valor of Charles XII and a better brain you have more enemies to confront than he. Your reputation will be greater, for you have won as many victories over better-trained foes and you have conferred benefits on your subjects in reviving the arts, planning settlements, embellishing cities. I do not mention other talents that would have sufficed to immortalize your name. Your greatest enemies cannot rob you of these merits; your glory is secure. Even if fortune frowns, you will always have enough territory to ensure an outstanding position in Europe. The Great Elector was not the less respected for ceding some of his conquests." Suicide, he added, would not be approved. "Your adherents would condemn it and your enemies would triumph. Think of the insults that the bigots would heap on your memory. But happily we are very far from seeing you reduced to such extremities, and I have high hopes of your courage and resource. It will be a consolation for me on my death-bed to leave behind me a philosopher King." Like most other onlookers the writer expected the downfall of Prussia, but he regarded the talk of suicide as a pose.

The military situation now changed with dramatic rapidity. "Sire," wrote Voltaire on receiving the news of Rossbach, "I must fulfill my duty as a citizen, and also the dictates of a heart ever attached to Your Majesty, to be grieved by the misfortune of the French and to applaud your admirable actions, to pity the vanquished and to congratulate you. I am no prophet, but I predict your happiness since it is so well deserved." After a second triumph at Leuthen a month later Frederick wrote from Breslau in January 1758 to thank his old comrade for his interest in a campaign where all seemed lost. "Live happily and tranquil at Geneva; that is all that matters. And hope that the high heroic fever of Europe is soon cured, that the trimumvirate [Austria, France, and Russia] collapses, and that the tyrants may not impose on the world the chains they are preparing. O Austrians! Your ambition, your desire for domination, will soon raise up other enemies, and the liberties of Germany and Europe will never lack defenders." The next letter gaily encouraged Voltaire to bite the mischievous politicians if a tooth remained in his head. The Duchess of Gotha, who was on excellent terms with both, wrote to express her pleasure at the reconciliation. "I am not surprised that the King of Prussia has resumed correspondence, for he told me here that he had a soft place for you in his heart."

The autumn of 1758 proved as critical as that of 1757. "I am much obliged to the hermit of Les Délices," wrote Frederick in October after the butchery at Zorndorf, "for his interest in the adventures of the Don Quixote of the north. This Don Quixote lives the life of a traveling comedian, playing now in one theater, now in another, sometimes hissed, sometimes applauded. His last piece was the *Thébaïde* [Racine's tragedy in which all the protagonists die]; there was scarcely anyone left to snuff the candles. I know not how it will all work out, but I believe with our good Epicureans that the onlookers have the best of it. Though I am on the move I hear of events in the republic of letters, and gossip says nothing of what you are doing. I feel inclined to exclaim: *Tu dors, Brutus!* For three years there have been no new editions of your works. What are you doing? If you have written something, please forward it. Meanwhile I wish you the tranquillity and repose that I lack."

At the close of 1758 Frederick turned to Voltaire for a tribute to Wilhelmina. "Never forget her, and summon all your forces to raise a monument in her honor. You have only to do her justice. Without departing from the truth you will find excellent material." When the poet responded with a few eloquent stanzas, the King explained that he wanted something for the public. "All Europe must partake of my grief, though I must not share in the tribute. Everyone must know that she is worthy of immortality and it is for you to confer it." He himself had not sufficient imagination; his French was not good enough for good verses, and bad ones were detestable. Prose or verse would do equally well. "Since you are the first man of your century I can only look to you." He was pleased with the revised and enlarged version of the ode, declaring that it brought him the first consolation since his loss. "Publish it and circulate it all over the world."

Though the correspondence seemed to have regained its old cordiality the past was unforgiven. The surrender of the order *Pour le Mérite* and his Chamberlain's key rankled in Voltaire's bosom, as he frankly informed the King. "I confess that I am very rich, very independent, very happy," he reported from

199

Geneva in 1759. "But you are lacking to my happiness, and I shall soon die without seeing you. You do not care, and I try to imitate you. I love your verse, your prose, your intellect, your bold and firm philosophy. I have been unable to live without or with you. I do not speak to the King, to the hero; I speak to him who enchanted me, whom I have loved, and against whom I still have a grievance." Letters to other friends show that he was on his guard, for political as well as personal reasons. "The King sends me more verses than he has battalions and squadrons," he complained. "Dealings with him are a little dangerous now that he is an ally of the English; he spares us as little with his pen as with his bayonets. He tries hard to recapture me. He is an exceptional man, very attractive at a distance." "I do not love Luc [Frederick], far from it," he wrote to another friend. "I will never forgive him for his infamous treatment of my niece or his audacity in writing me flatteries twice a month without reparation for his errors. I greatly desire his profound humiliation, the punishment of the sinner; I am not sure if I desire his eternal damnation." Frederick's feelings were less unfriendly. "For the sake of your genius I pardon all the annoyances of Berlin, all the libels of Leipzig, all the things you have said or published against me, which are strong, harsh, and numerous, without retaining the least rancor. I know I idolized you when I thought you were neither troublesome nor malicious, but you have played me so many tricks. We will not speak of them; I have forgiven everything with a Christian spirit. After all, you have brought me more pleasure than you have done me harm."

Frederick's letters throughout the Seven Years' War contain more politics than ever before or after. The tone is grim, for the burden of fighting half Europe was heavy to bear. His writings, he explained, were composed in the intervals between battles. "I utilize all my weapons against my enemies, like a porcupine, who defends itself at every point. I do not say they are all good, but one must employ all one's faculties. In this conflict all the rules of fair play and decency are forgotten. The most civilized nations fight like wild beasts. I am ashamed for humanity and I blush for my century. Let us be frank: the arts and philosophy are the property of the few. The great mass of the people and the common herd of the nobility remain what nature made them— namely, evil animals. Do you imagine that I enjoy this dog's life, witnessing and ordering the butchery of unknown people, losing friends and acquaintances every day, exposing my reputation to the caprice of chance, passing the whole year in anxiety, forever risking life and fortune? Despite the schools of philosophy man will remain the wickedest of animals; superstition, self-interest, vengeance, treason, ingratitude, will always produce bloody and tragic scenes, for the passions rule us, scarcely ever reason. There were and always will be wars, lawsuits, devastations, plagues, earthquakes, bankruptcies. Those are the themes of history. I suppose it is necessary. Pangloss will explain it to you. I, who have not the honor to be a doctor, confess my ignorance· Yet it seems to me that if a beneficent being had made the universe he would have made us happier than we are."

After the shattering blow at Kunersdorf Voltaire, like most other people, expected his old patron to collapse. "I believe he is in a very tight place," he wrote to Mme du Deffand on September 15, 1759. "Unless a miracle occurs he will be an example of the evils of ambition; if he succumbs he will not be able to put it down to the French." The old warhorse, however, had no thought of surrender. "My position," he wrote on September 22, "is not so desperate as my enemies think. I shall finish my campaign well. I am not disheartened, but I realize that peace is necessary. All I can say is that I have honor enough for ten, and that, whatever my plight, I am incapable of any action unworthy of a valiant knight, though that is a trifle to infamous politicians with a huckster mentality. To make peace there are two indispensable conditions: first, to act in union with my faithful allies; secondly, that it be honorable and glorious. You see I have only honor left and I will keep it at the price of my blood. If they want peace let them propose nothing contrary to the delicacy of my feelings. I am in the whirlpool of military operations, like an unlucky player who stands up to fortune. More than once I have compelled it to return to me like a flighty mistress. I have to deal with such fools that I am bound to triumph over them, but I am not worrying about what *Sa sacrée Majesté le Hasard* decides. So far my conscience is clear as regards my misfortunes. I ask nothing better than peace, but not a peace of humiliation. After having waged war successfully against all Europe, it would be a disgrace to lose by a stroke of the pen what I have preserved by the sword. If I were a private citizen I would yield anything for peace, but one must think of one's station." This declaration, like all other letters touching on politics, was forwarded to Choiseul, the Foreign Minister of Louis XV.

Though Voltaire never told his royal correspondent how meanly he thought of his verses, he spoke his mind on the old quarrels with notable frankness. Taking as his text one of the King's many reproaches for the vendetta against Maupertuis, he retaliated sharply in a letter in April 1760. "I think only of death, and my hour approaches, but do not sadden it with unjust accusations. You have done me enough harm; you have compromised me irrevocably with the King of France; you have caused me to lose my posts and pensions; you maltreated me at Frankfurt, myself and an innocent and respected woman who was dragged in the mud and imprisoned; and then, in honoring me with your letters, you spoil the sweetness of this consolation by bitter reproofs. The worst result of your writings is to make the enemies of philosophy throughout Europe say: "Philosophers cannot live in peace or live together. Here is a King who does not believe in Jesus Christ. He summons to his court a man who also does not believe and maltreats him. There is no humanity in these pretended philosophers, and God makes them punish one another." That is what people say and write on all sides; while the fanatics are united, the philosophers are divided and unhappy. While at the court of Versailles and elsewhere I am accused of encouraging you to write against the Christian religion; you reproach me and add this triumph to the insults of the fanatics. It makes me sick of the world, but happily I live in retirement on my domains. I shall bless the day when death brings my sufferings to an end, sufferings above all inflicted by you; but I shall wish you happiness, which in your position is perhaps beyond your grasp and which philosophy alone can procure in your stormy life. Pardon an old man whose days are numbered the utterance of these truths. He speaks more frankly because he is convinced that his own failings are infinitely greater than yours."

Frederick's reply was a blend of confession and severity. "I know I have failings, great failings. I assure you I do not spare myself. But this task would be more fruitful if I were not exposed to such buffetings and agitations. I will not reopen the past. Your offenses against me are grave. No philosopher would have tolerated your conduct. I have forgotten everything and I wish to forget everything, but if you had not been dealing with a madman in love with your genius you would not have escaped so easily. Understand that I will not listen to anything more about this niece, who bores me and who has less merit than her uncle to cover her failings. We talk of Molière's maid, but no one will remember the niece of Voltaire. Adieu! live peacefully in your retreat, and do not speak of dying. You are only sixty-two [Voltaire was sixty-six], and your soul is still full of the fire that sustains the flesh. You will bury me and compose a malicious couplet on my tomb. I shall not mind and I give you absolution in advance." Despite the milder tone of the correspondence, the King's judgment of the man was unchanged. "Whenever Voltaire's name is mentioned," reported the British Ambassador, "he says he has the worst heart and is the greatest rascal alive."

Frederick's letter of October 31, 1760 reflects the deepening gloom. The Russians and Austrians had occupied Berlin, and there were two more months ahead of the most arduous of his campaigns. His health and spirits were declining, and his description of mankind would have won the approval of Hobbes. "Your zeal burns against the Jesuits and superstitions. You are quite right to combat error, but do you believe the world will change? The human spirit is weak. More than three quarters of mankind are made to be slaves of the most absurd fanaticism. The fear of the devil and hell bewitches them, and they detest the sage who wishes to enlighten them. The majority of our species is stupid and evil. I search in vain for the image of God of which the theologians speak. Everyone has a wild beast in him and few know how to chain it up. Most give way to it when they are not restrained by the fear of the law. Perhaps you think me too much of a misanthrope. I am ill, I suffer, and I have to deal with half a dozen rogues of both sexes who would upset a Socrates or an Antoninus. You are lucky to be able to follow Candide's advice, to cultivate your garden. Not everyone can follow suit. The ox must plow, the nightingale sing, the dolphin swim, and I make war. The more I ply this trade, the more I feel that fortune plays the chief part. I do not think it will be long. My health is failing visibly. I shall soon be conversing with Virgil about the *Henriade,* descending into the regions where worries, pleasures, and hopes do not follow us, where your genius and that of a servant are reduced to the same level—in a word, where we return to the state of things before we were born. Perhaps you will soon be amusing yourself with my epitaph. You will say that I loved good verses and made bad ones; that I was not so stupid that I did not recognize your talents. Adieu! Live happily, and say a little *Benedicite* for poor philosophers in purgatory." In February 1761 Voltaire confided to his friend the Duchess of Gotha that he no longer wrote to Frederick, adding severely: "I renounce him." We have only one short letter from the King during that year, closing with the words: "Pray for a Don Quixote who has to wage war without ceasing and without hope of repose so long as the fury of his enemies pursues him." Voltaire was never inclined to shed tears over the misfortunes of the King of Prussia, least of all during the Seven Years' War, in which his sympathies had been entirely on the side of France.

It was not till almost two years after the Treaty of Hubertusburg, so far as we know, that the correspondence was resumed, after an interruption of over three years. At the end of 1764 Voltaire wrote a letter of condolence, unfortunately lost, on the occasion of an illness. A friendly but rather distant rejoinder, dated January 1, 1765, was in the King's lighter vein. "I thought you were so busy with destroying *l'infâme* that I could not imagine you would think of anything else. Your blows would have floored it long ago had not this hydra renewed itself incessantly from the stock of superstition spread all over the earth. For myself, long disillusioned of the charlatanries that seduce mankind, I place the theologian, the astrologer, the adept, and the doctor in the same category. I have infirmities and maladies, but I cure myself by regimen and patience. So you can console Europe for the important loss of my person, which it expected, though I count it a trifle; for, though my health is poor, I am alive. I appreciate your interest in my health and the obliging things you say; and I regret that your age makes me fear that with you will end that breed of great men and geniuses who adorned the age of Louis XIV."

Frederick's reply to another lost letter shows that, on Voltaire's side at any rate, past wounds were unhealed. "Wishing to keep the peace in my house, I did my best to prevent you hitting out. Ignoring my admonitions, you composed a libel [the attack on Maupertuis] almost under my eyes and used my permission for another work to publish it. In a word, you have wronged me in every way; I have borne all I could, and I suppress all other just complaints because I feel able to forgive you." The remainder of the letter was in the King's usual friendly and sparkling style. "You have lost nothing in leaving this country. There you are at Ferney, with your niece and your favorite occupations, respected as the divinity of the arts, as the patriarch of the *écraseurs,* covered with glory, and enjoying your reputation in your lifetime, all the more since at a hundred leagues from Paris they consider you dead and do you justice. An Englishman who had seen you told me that you were a little bent, but that the Promethean fire still burns within. It is the oil in the lamp and it will sustain you. You will reach the age of Fontenelle (ninety-nine) and compose an epigram on your own centenary. At last, full of years, satiated with glory, the conqueror of *l'infâme,* I see you scale Olympus, sustained by Lucretius and Sophocles, Virgil and Locke, placed between Newton and Epicurus on a bright cloud."

Voltaire's lost response must have contained some belated expressions of regrets. "If you had said ten years ago what you say at the close of your letter," wrote the King in January 1766, from Berlin, "you would still be here. Of course, mortals have their failings; perfection is not their lot. I know it from myself, and I am convinced of the injustice of asking more from other people. I would have loved you despite your faults because you have enough great talents to cover them. Only talents distinguish great men from the crowd. It is your special task to destroy *l'infâme* with your formidable club, for the ridicule you pour on it hits harder than any arguments. Few can reason, but everyone fears ridicule. Decent folk in all countries are beginning to think. In superstitious Bohemia, in Austria, an old haunt of fanaticism, the upper classes are beginning to open their eyes. The images of saints have less vogue. Despite the barriers placed by the court against the entry of good books, the truth finds its way. Though progress is slow, it is a great thing to see certain circles tearing down the bandage of superstition. In our Protestant countries the pace is quicker. Of the vast domain of fanaticism there remain only Poland, Portugal, Spain, and Bavaria, where crass ignorance and torpor keep superstition alive. As for your Genevese, since you are there not only are they unbelievers but they have all become *beaux esprits*. They talk in antitheses and epigrams. You have wrought a miracle. What is raising from the dead compared to giving imagination to those without it? In France the Swiss are butts, and in Germany, though we are not intellectual athletes, we joke about them. You have changed everything. You are the Prometheus of Geneva. If you had remained here we should have been something by now. Fate did not grant us such a boon. Scarcely had you quitted your country than belles-lettres decayed. Good taste in Rome was buried in the tomb of Virgil, Ovid, and Horace. I fear that in losing you, France may have the same fate. Whatever happens, I have been your contemporary. You will live as long as I, and I care little about the taste, the sterility, or the abundance of posterity."

Voltaire's championship of the principle of religious toleration in the famous cases of Calas, Sirven, and La Barre brought the old gladiators closer together. The battle-cry *Écrasez l'infâme* denoted the destruction, not of any church or creed, but of the system of intolerance in high places. The correspondence of 1766 is filled with atrocities. "Your old age," wrote the King, "is like the infancy of Hercules. That god destroyed serpents in his cradle; you, bent with years, destroy *l'infâme*. The progress of human reason is slower than one thinks, and here is the cause. Nearly everyone is content with vague ideas; few have time to examine them thoroughly. Some, strangled by the chains of superstition from infancy, do not wish or are not able to break them. Others, immersed in frivolities, enjoy life without a moment of reflection interrupting their pleasures. Add the timid souls and frightened women and you have society. It is much if you find one man in a thousand: you and those like you write for him. The others are shocked and curse you."

The King sent a contribution to the support of the Sirven family, but the case of La Barre, who was executed for damaging a crucifix and refusing respect to a procession, provoked criticism as well as sympathy. "It is tragic, but is it not partially the fault of the victims? Is it necessary to make a frontal attack on prejudices consecrated by time? And if one wishes to enjoy liberty of thought, must one insult an established belief? People who keep quiet are rarely persecuted. Remember what Fontenelle said: "If my hand was full of truths I should think twice before I opened it." The crowd does not deserve to be enlightened. If you ask me whether I should have pronounced a verdict of such severity, I answer no. I should have fitted the punishment to the offense. I should have said: You broke the statue, so you must restore it. You did not remove your hat before the village curé who was carrying you know what, so you must present yourself every day for a fortnight at the church without a hat. You have read the works of Voltaire, so you must study the *Summa* of St. Thomas under the guidance of the curé. The giddy fellow would have been punished more severely in this way than by his judges, for boredom is a century and death a moment."

This theme of the limits of toleration was pursued in further letters, which enshrine a declaration of policy no less than a personal confession of faith. Since Calas was innocent his execution was unjust, but with La Barre it was different. "You will agree that all citizens must obey the law, and penalties are fixed for those who disturb the national cult. Discretion, decency, above all, respect for the laws, forbid insults and scandal. These sanguinary laws need reforming and adjusting to the offense, but while they remain, the magistrates must carry them out. I, a cool child of reason, desire that men should be reasonable and, above all, live in peace. We know the crimes of religious fanaticism. Let us take care not to introduce this fanaticism into philosophy, the character of which should be gentleness and moderation. It should deplore the tragic end of a young man who committed an extravagance and point out the excessive rigor of the law made in a rude and ignorant age, but it must not encourage similar actions nor rail at judges who had no choice. Toleration should ensure to each the liberty to believe what he will, but it should not authorize the insults of giddy young men to what the people revere. There are my sentiments, which are calculated to assure liberty and the public safety, the first object of all legislation. I wager you will think: That is very German, reflecting the phlegm of a nation with moderate passions. We are, it is true, vegetables compared with the French. We witness the survival of old-time ferocity in the most polished nations. It is very difficult to make the human race good, to complete the taming of this animal, the most savage of all. This confirms my view that opinions have little influence on action, for I observe that passion prevails over reason everywhere. If you managed to make an ideological revolution, the sect you would form would be small, for thinking folk are few. And you ignore those who are opposed to the rays of light that reveal their turpitude; and the princes, who are taught that they can only keep their thrones so long as the people are attached to religion; and the people, who possess only prejudices, detest novelties, and cannot understand those in need of metaphysicians. Here are grave difficulties which I submit to you, and which, I believe, will always confront those who would desire to proclaim a similar reasonable religion. Superstition is a weakness inherent in the human mind; it has always existed and it always will. The objects of adoration may change like your French fashions, but what does it matter if one prostrates oneself before a piece of unleavened bread, or the bull Apis, or the ark of the covenant, or a statue?" Voltaire melted at last. "I have received charming letters, truly philosophic letters," he wrote to a friend in October 1766; "I forgive him everything."

Though Frederick was now writing in the friendliest way to "the patriarch of Ferney" and admiration for his gifts was undiminished, he never recovered the respect for his character that he had felt in the days of his youth. "You are right in saying that the death of Voltaire would be a loss for the republic of letters," he wrote to his sister Ulrike, Queen of Sweden. "He is the finest genius since Cicero and Virgil, and it is a pity that his heart is not equal to his head and that a man with such shining talents has so few virtues. But perfection is not for our species, and he would have been perfect had his soul not been perverse." A break in the correspondence between 1767 and 1769 led the King to complain to d'Alembert that Voltaire no longer wrote. "He will never forgive me for having been the friend of Maupertuis—an unpardonable crime." In 1769 the exchange was resumed and continued without interruption to the end. Voltaire's health was never good, and the first letter announced that he had been for more than a year in bed. "You are too modest," replied the King, "if you could have thought that your two years of silence could be patiently borne. Everyone who loves literature must be interested in your preservation and be glad when you send news. What interests me is to know what is being done by the hero of reason, this modern Prometheus who brings celestial light to cure the blind of their errors and prejudices. I adore literature, which alone charms our leisure hours and affords real pleasure. I should love philosophy as much if our feeble reason could discover hidden truths. So I pass my old age tranquilly and try to procure all the brochures of "the nephew of Abbé Bertin" [a nom de plume of Voltaire], for one can read no books but his."

In 1770, when Voltaire was seventy-six, a number of his French admirers commissioned a bust by Pigalle. The moving spirit was d'Alembert, who informed his friend of the plan. "It would be good if Frederick were among the subscribers," was the reply. "He owes me reparation as a King, a philosopher, and a man of letters." The invitation provoked a ready response. Greece, wrote Frederick to Grimm, would have made him a god or erected a temple in his honor. "The finest monument has been erected by himself in his own works, which will last longer than St. Peter's, the Louvre, and all the buildings consecrated by human vanity to eternity. You have only to tell me what is expected." D'Alembert replied that a crown and his name was enough. "Marshal Richelieu has given twenty louis d'or, and subscriptions are coming in, but they would be nothing without yours." The King's handsome contribution of two hundred louis d'or produced a letter of warm gratitude from Ferney. "Sire, the philosopher d'Alembert tells me that the great philosopher of the school and species of Marcus Aurelius, the cultivator and protector of the arts, has been good enough to encourage anatomy in deigning to head the list of the subscribers for a skeleton. This skeleton possesses a very sensitive old heart, which is penetrated with the honor done to him by Your Majesty. I thought that the idea of this caricature was a joke; but now that the chisel of the famous Pigalle is to be employed and that the name of the greatest man in Europe adorns the enterprise of my fellow citizens, I take it very seriously. I feel how unworthy of the honor I am, and at the same time I am deeply grateful." Yet, though nearly twenty years had elapsed since the quarrel with Maupertuis, the memory of that fierce encounter still rankled. "I still feel the irreparable harm he has done me. I shall never think of the calumny about the dirty linen, as stupid as it was deadly, and of all that followed except with a grief that will poison my last days. Yet all that d'Alembert tells me of the kindness of Your Majesty is such balm to my wounds that I am ashamed of my grievance. Pardon it in a man whose only ambition has been to live and die near you and who has been attached to you for thirty years. Deign to accept the tender respect of the old hermit."

The King's reply, though less emotional, was very friendly. "I do not regret that my feelings about your statue have become known. They are truths of which I have always been convinced and which neither Maupertuis nor anyone else has effaced from my mind. It was quite right that you should receive public gratitude in your lifetime and that I should have some share in this demonstration, since your works have given me so much pleasure. My trifling productions are not of this kind: they are my pastime. My principal occupation is to combat ignorance and prejudice in the territories of which the accident of birth has made me the ruler, to enlighten minds, to refine manners, to make people as happy as human nature and my means allow." He had just returned from a second meeting with the Emperor Joseph, who was preparing to play a great part in Europe. "Born in a bigoted court, he has shaken off superstition; brought up in luxury, he has adopted simple ways; fed on incense, he is modest; consumed by the desire for glory, he sacrifices his ambition to filial duty, which he scrupulously performs; and, not having had pedants for his teachers, he has the taste to read Voltaire and to esteem his merit. Moreover, he knows Italian literature well. One must always begin there. After belles-lettres comes philosophy; and when we have carefully studied it we have to ask, like Montaigne: What do I know? What I do know is that I shall have a copy of Pigalle's bust. That is little enough when I remember that once I possessed this divine genius itself. Youth is the time for adventure; the old and decrepit have to renounce *beaux esprits* and mistresses. Take care of yourself so that in your old age you can still enlighten the close of the century which is proud to have you and knows the value of its treasure." Verses were once more exchanged, a portrait was sent to Ferney, and the old man drank his morning coffee in a cup from the Royal Porcelain Factory at Berlin.

Differences remained, but the sparks no longer flew. The King was annoyed to find yet another attack on Maupertuis in the *Questions sur l'Encyclopédie* and begged d'Alembert to point out the impropriety of this vendetta against a dead man. D'Alembert replied that he had done so and would try again, though he expected no result. "I conclude from Voltaire's conduct," commented Frederick, "that if he were a sovereign he would be at daggers drawn with all his neighbors. His reign would be a continual war, and God knows what arguments he would employ to prove that war is the natural condition of society." Yet the octogenarian offender was admonished more gently than of old. "This Maupertuis, whom you continue to hate, had good qualities. He was a decent fellow; he possessed talents and learning. I admit he was brusque; it was that which caused the breach. I do not know by what fatality it is that two Frenchmen abroad are never friends; millions of them get along at home, but they change when they cross the Pyrenees, the Rhine, and the Alps. Well, it is time to forget mistakes when those who have committed them are no more. You will only meet Maupertuis in the valley of Josaphat, where there is no hurry for you to arrive. Continue for a long time to enjoy your glory here where you triumph over rivalry and envy. Let the setting sun diffuse those rays of taste and genius you alone can transmit from the age of Louis XIV, to which you are so intimately bound. Spread them on literature, arrest its decline, try to revive the taste for the sciences and letters, which seems to be going out of fashion. That is what I expect from you. Your career will surpass that of Fontenelle, for you have too much of the flame of life to die so early. We have here milord Marishal [Keith], aged eighty-five almost as fresh as a young man; we have Pöllnitz, who counts on another ten years of life. Why should not the author of the *Henriade, Mérope,* and *Semiramis* last equally long? Plenty of oil in the lamp keeps the light alive, and who had more of it than you? Besides, Apollo has revealed to me that we shall keep you with us. I have made my humble prayer to him and said: 'Oh, my only divinity, preserve thy Ferney son for many years, to the benefit of letters and the satisfaction of the hermit of Sans Souci!' "

Voltaire was equally gallant. "Live long, Sire, not for your glory, for that requires no addition, but for the happiness of your state, and continue the kindnesses that console me for all my troubles." On receiving a porcelain bust from Berlin inscribed *Immortalis* in January 1776, the patriarch composed the most graceful and elaborate of his many tributes.

Epictète au bord du tombeau
A reçu ce présent des mains de Marc-Aurèle.
Il a dit: mon sort est trop beau;
J'aurài vécu pour lui, je lui mourrai fidèle.

Nous avons cultivé tous deux les mêmes arts
  Et la même philosophie;
Moi sujet, lui monarque et favori de Mars,
  Et parfois tous les deux objets d'un peu d'envie.

Il rendit plus d'un roi de ces exploits jaloux;
  Moi, je fus' harcelé des gredins de Parnasse.
Il eut des ennemis, il les dissipe tous;
  Et la troupe des miens dans la fange coasse.

Les cagots m'ont persécuté;
  Les cagots à ses pieds frémissaient en silence.
Lui sur le trône assis, moi dans l'obscurité,
  Nous préchâmes la tolérance.

Nous adorions tous deux le Dieu de l'univers,
  (Car il en est un, quoiqu'on dise),
Mais n'avions pas le sottise
  De le déshonorer par des cultes pervers.

Nous irons tous les deux dans la céleste sphère,
  Lui fort tard, moi bientôt. Il obtiendra, je crois,
Un trône auprès d'Achille et même auprès d'Homère;
  Et j'y vais demander un tabouret pour moi.[1]

[1] On his death-bed Epictetus
    Receives this gift from Mark Aurelius' hands.
  My lot is fair, is his reply;
    I shall have lived for him, faithful I die. . . .

  More than one king was jealous of his deeds;
    I was tormented by Parnassus' knaves.
  He had his enemies and got rid of them,
    While mine continue croaking in the mud.

  Bigots have harassed me throughout my course;
    His bigots merely fret in silent rage.

The last two surviving letters might almost have been written in the knowledge that the long correspondence was nearing its end. After thanking "Epictetus" for his most recent brochure, "Marcus Aurelius" refers to the latest breeze on the stormy ocean of European politics. "The death of the Elector of Bavaria," he wrote on January 25, 1778, "may involve violent convulsions. Never has the Treaty of Westphalia been so attentively studied and discussed. A fog thicker than that of our hoarfrosts hides the future, and the uncertainty of events redoubles public curiosity. These major distractions have not prevented me from trembling for the life of the Patriarch of Ferney. Heartless journalists have announced your death. The whole confraternity of letters, including my unworthy self, has been aghast. But you have surpassed the hero of Christianity: he came back to life on the third day, but you are not dead. Live to continue your brilliant career for my satisfaction and for that of all thinking men. These are the hopes of the hermit of Sans Souci. *Vale.*"

Voltaire's reply, dated April 1, 1778, was written from Paris, which he had not visited for twenty-eight years, where he received the final ovation, and where he was about to die. His recent silence, he explained, was due to the fact that he had been trying to avoid both hisses and death. "It is pleasant at eighty-four to have escaped two deadly maladies. That comes of being consecrated to you; I have been reappointed by you and I have been saved. It has been a surprise and satisfaction, when a new tragedy [*Irène*] was played, that the public, which thirty years ago regarded Constantine and Theodosius as model princes and even saints, has frantically applauded verses describing them as superstitious tyrants. I have a score of similar proofs of the progress of

---

He, seated on his throne, I in the shades,
Preach toleration.

Both of us worship the universal God
(For one there is, whatever men may say),
But never have we been unwise enough
Him to dishonor by unworthy cults.

Both of us move towards celestial spheres,
He later on, I soon. For him there waits
A throne close to Achilles, at Homer's side;
And I shall ask a footstool for myself.

213

philosophy in all directions. I should not despair of pronouncing a panegyric on the Emperor Julian within a month; and assuredly, if the Parisians recall that he administered justice like Cato and waged war like Cæsar, they owe him eternal gratitude. So it is true, Sire, that in the long run men see the light, and that those who believe themselves paid to blind them cannot always gouge out their eyes. All thanks to Your Majesty! You have vanquished prejudices like your other enemies. You rejoice in your creations. You are the conqueror of superstition as well as the bulwark of Germanic liberty. Outlive me in order to strengthen all your spheres of rule. May Frederick the Great be Frederick the Immortal." Two months later the old skeleton with the piercing eyes was at rest. Shortly before his death he had written a laudatory notice of the King for the forthcoming Kehl edition of his works. "He deigned to admit men of letters to his intimacy," runs the conclusion. "If in this familiar relationship clouds sometimes arose they were followed by the most serene and gentle weather." Forty years of sunshine and storm had ended in an Indian summer.

"What an irreparable loss to literature!" wrote Frederick to d'Alembert. "Perhaps centuries will pass before such a genius reappears. He will live forever by his genius and his works, but I wish he could have witnessed his glory some time longer. The Berlin Academy and I intend to pay the great man the tribute due to his ashes." The first sketch was composed in camp, far from books, during the War of the Bavarian Succession. The finished *Éloge* was read by Thiébault in a special session of the Academy on November 26, 1778, and immediately published. It is a considered utterance, worthy of the occasion and without a jarring note. Of the angry quarrel in 1753 there is no trace: the failings of a great man were buried in his grave and only his glory remained. The *Éloge* is a hymn of praise from beginning to end, the more impressive owing to its mellow and dignified tone. The author records the appearance of the tragedies, the *Henriade,* commenced in the Bastille and finished in London, the election to the Académie Française, the appointment as Historiographer of France, "that beautiful union" with the illustrious Marquise du Châtelet. The King, who had seen him in 1740, desired to possess this eminent genius, who settled in Berlin in 1750. "His knowledge was encyclopedic, his conversation no less instructive than agreeable, his imagination as brilliant as it was varied, his mind quick and ever on the spot. He was the delight of every society. An unfortunate dispute between him and Maupertuis estranged these scholars, who were made to love and not to hate each other."

Passing from biography to criticism, Frederick places the *Henriade* above the *Æneid* and in certain respects above Racine. The latter was more natural, his plots were more probable, and his verses were of an elegance and fluency since unapproached, but the tragedies of Voltaire contained some splendid passages. In *La Pucelle,* the flowering of a brilliant imagination, he measures himself against Ariosto; *Charles XII* was an epic; the *Siècle de Louis XIV* was unique; the *Essai sur l'histoire universelle* showed a fine sense of proportion. Even his novels were original, for behind their apparent frivolity lay moral allegories or criticisms of modern systems where the useful and the agreeable are intertwined. So many talents and so many kinds of learning combined in a single person aroused astonishment: only Cicero could be compared with him. He was worth a whole Academy. "Some of his pieces recall the dialectic of Bayle, others Thucydides; here we meet the physicist discovering the secrets of nature, there the metaphysician grounded on analogy and experience and following in the footsteps of Locke. In other works you find the rival of Sophocles. Here you see him scatter flowers in his path; there he dons the comedian's buskin. But it seems that his soaring spirit is not content to equal Terence or Molière; soon you watch him mount on Pegasus, who, spreading his wings, bears him to the summit of Helicon, where the gods assign him his place between Homer and Virgil." If the panegyrist was mistaken in placing his old friend among the immortals of literature, if in particular he exaggerated the merit of the *Henriade,* he erred in company with most of his contemporaries, for whom Shakespeare was an outsider and the three unities were the last word of classical drama.

The *Éloge* concludes with a tribute to the incomparable standard-bearer of the *Aufklärung,* the enduring significance of whose work even Frederick could not overestimate. "He was equally sensitive to applause and to the stings of literary insects. Far from punishing them, he immortalized them by mentioning their obscure names in his works. But this mud-slinging was a trifle compared with the more violent persecution by ecclesiastics, who, blinded by false zeal and brutalized by fanaticism, desired to destroy him by calumny—for instance, by the charge that he who had employed all the resources of his genius to prove the existence of a God heard himself to his great surprise accused of atheism. His real crime was that he had not concealed the vices of many popes, had denounced abominable massacres, and expressed contempt for the unintelligible and frivolous quarrels to which theologians of all sects attach so much significance. He always distinguished religion from those who dishonor it. He meted out justice to the ecclesiastics whose virtues were the true ornament of the Church, and censures only those whose perverted morals rendered them a public abomination. Had he done nothing more than champion the cause of justice and toleration in the Calas, Sirven, and La Barre cases, he would deserve a place among the small number of the veritable benefactors of mankind." On this occasion the Public Orator meant every word he said, and the warmth of his final tribute was the measure of his irreparable loss. The two most conspicuous figures in the life of Europe had parted in peace.

Chapter X

WILHELMINA

O F Frederick's three brothers and six sisters only Wilhelmina really counted in his life.[1] Had he had no heart he could never have loved her as he did, and had she had no brains there would have been no intellectual *camaraderie*. If he was unlucky in his father, he was singularly fortunate in possessing a sister so unlike other eighteenth-century princesses, so keenly sensitive to the things of the mind. After the death of Jordan she had no competitor for the first place in his affections, and she was the only woman he ever loved. A regrettable estrangement for which she was mainly responsible during the early years of his reign was followed by a complete restoration of harmony and understanding which lasted till her death at the age of forty-nine. Just as Charles II is at his best in his letters to his sister Henrietta, Frederick's softer side is displayed most clearly in the lively correspondence with the Margravine of Bayreuth.

In attempting to visualize this relationship we must not be led astray by her celebrated *Memoirs,* written as they were during the years of misunderstanding, which were also a period of agonizing domestic grief. Their factual unreliability was demonstrated by Ranke a century ago, and a few years later, after the most exhaustive critical analysis to which they have ever been subjected, Droysen contemptuously dismissed them as destitute of historical value. This verdict is too sweeping, for their pres-

[1] A critical edition of the *Memoirs,* which end in 1742, is badly needed. Their historical authority was investigated for the first time by Ranke in an address to the Prussian Academy in 1849, reprinted in *Zwölf Bücher preussischer Geschichte,* Vol. III (in the Academy edition), and in more detail by Droysen (*Geschichte der preussischen Politik*), who denied them all historical value. For appreciations see Sainte-Beuve: *Causeries du Lundi,* Vol. XII, and Gooch: *Courts and Cabinets,* chapters ix and x. The correspondence with Frederick was published in his Œuvres, Vol. XXVII. A German translation, with nearly two hundred additional letters, was edited by Volz and Oppeln-Bronikowski in 2 vols. (1924). The correspondence with Voltaire was published by Horn in *Voltaire und die Markgräfin von Baireuth* (1865). There are good biographies by Edith Cuthell, 2 vols., and Fester: *Die bayreuther Schwester Friedrichs des Grossen.*

entation of the clash of temperaments and generations at the court of Frederick William I is true enough, and there is no reason to reject the picture of happy comradeship of the Crown Prince and his favorite sister at work and at play. We are on much firmer ground, however, in the correspondence published by Preuss in 1856, which contained 347 items, to which 181 were added in a German translation in 1924. All are in French, and almost all are autographs.

The first surviving letter of the Crown Prince, signed *Frederic le Philosophe,* written during the official visit to Dresden with his father in January 1728, just after his sixteenth birthday, describes his amusements and impressions at the most sumptuous of German courts. The second, signed *Le Prisonnier* and written in pencil from Küstrin, is dated November 1, 1730, towards the end of his eighteenth year, when the failure of the plan to escape from Prussia and the brutal execution of his friend Katte changed the boy into the man. "They are going to make a heretic of me after the Council of War, for to qualify as such nothing more is needed than to fail to conform in every particular to the master's sentiments. I care nothing for their anathemas so long as I know that my dear sister ignores them. What a joy that neither bolts nor bars can prevent me expressing my perfect friendship! Yes, my dear sister, there are still decent people in this almost wholly corrupt century who enable me to reach you. Provided I know you are happy, prison will be a time of happiness and content. *Chi a tempo ha vita!* Let that be our consolation. I wish with all my heart to be able to talk to you without an interpreter and to recover those happy days when your *principe* and my *principessa* will kiss again." Wilhelmina published part of this letter in her *Memoirs,* explaining that these were their names for her brother's flute and her own lute.

Emerging from Küstrin at the opening of 1732, Frederick reported to his sister on the blameless but unprepossessing Brunswick girl selected for him by the formidable King. "She is neither pretty nor ugly; not stupid but ill-educated, timid and awkward in society; there is a true portrait of this Princess, and you can judge if I am pleased or not. Her greatest merit is that she procures for me the liberty to write to you, my only consolation in your absence. You cannot imagine, my adorable sister, how often I form wishes for your happiness, and you can see that I always retain that sincere friendship which has bound our hearts to-gether since our tender years. In any case recognize that you have enraged me in accusing me of levity towards you and in believing false reports of my credulity, I who love you alone and whom neither vague nor false reports can change. Do not mistrust me again unless you have positive proofs that *le bon Dieu* has abandoned me and that my head is turned." A fortnight later he reverted to the distressing topic of his fiancée. In answer to Wilhelmina's inquiries, he reported the order of the Queen that she should not be addressed as Highness and should be written to like an ordinary princess. "As for the kissing of hands, I assure you that I have not kissed them and will not do so, for they are not pretty enough to be appetizing. Believe me, no brother ever loved so tenderly a sister as charming as mine."

Wilhelmina's request to Frederick to be godfather to her first and only child was accepted with pleasure. "You could not choose anyone with more respect and attachment for the mother or more friendship for the daughter, everything coming from and belonging to you being precious to me." The twenty-year-old writer then proceeds to pour out his troubles. "I have suffered all that man can suffer for fifteen years, always alternating between the fear and the hope of losing or keeping all that I most love. You ask for news of my affairs, and as I have no better friend than you I open my heart as if before God. The King persecutes me about my marriage. I have no love for the Princess; on the contrary I feel repugnance and there can be neither friendship nor union between us. Apart from that he does not treat me ill, but he distrusts me, and this accursed marriage is my only cause of complaint. I am on excellent terms with the Queen, who loves you tenderly. I live here [Ruppin] in peace with my regiment, and I should be perfectly happy if I could see you every day and if I never married. The King sings your praises and loves you dearly. Grumbkow and Seckendorff are very friendly; I am rarely at Berlin, Potsdam, or Wusterhausen. The King tries to force me to love my beauty, but I fear he will not succeed. My heart cannot be dragooned. If it loves, it loves sincerely."

Frederick William I hung like a dark shadow over his son's life. While marriage had delivered Wilhelmina from her father's yoke, Frederick continued to revolve in the paternal orbit. The anticipation of a royal visit to Ruppin in November 1733 is vividly described. "You know, my dear sister, that the reception of such a guest causes me no small embarrassment. My head is so full of preparations that I do not know what I am writing." In the following year a visit to Bayreuth on his way to a campaign in the Rhineland was frustrated by his father's impatience to reach the front, though he received permission to stop on the way back. "Never have I so much regretted not to be my own master," he wrote en route, "and though I would do anything to pay you my respects, I cannot manage it this time. Since he is only soursweet with me I cannot run the slightest risk, all the more because in a week he will be with the army, where, as you can guess, I should have a fine time if I disobeyed his orders." The Queen, he added, sent a thousand greetings. "She seemed greatly concerned about your illness, but I cannot guarantee her sincerity, for she is totally changed and I no longer know her. So far has this gone that she has done her best to injure me with the King, though it is now made up. Sophie is also changed, for she approves all the Queen says and does, and she is charmed with her big booby [her cousin and husband, the Margrave of Schwedt]. The King is more difficult than ever. There is no pleasing him, and he has ceased to show gratitude for one's attentions. As for his health it is better one day and worse the next, but his legs are always swollen. So you can imagine my joy in escaping from this bondage, for he will only be a fortnight in camp."

The brightest spot in a dark sky was the failing strength of the family tyrant. "Our news is very bad and he is not expected to live long. Well, I can face whatever comes, for I know that so long as he is alive I shall have a bad time. I shall soon forget him. If you are touched, my dear sister, it is because you have not seen him for a long time; if you were to meet again, I think you would let him rest in peace without regret." The next letter, at the end of September 1734, brought news that he could hardly outlive the year, having water on the chest, breathing and sleep a difficulty, no appetite, his legs swollen to above the knee, all red and without feeling. "We must be prepared, my dearest sister, and though my heart suffers in a certain degree, on the other hand I shall be glad to do you service. My happiness and my life are in your hands, so let me beg you on my knees to come to me if it happens. You will be with a brother who loves you more than anything in the world; I will carry you on my hands and guarantee you against all troubles. If you refuse I should die of grief. You would arrange everything and would receive the same respect as though you were the Queen." In all these affectionate letters there is scarcely a reference to his wife, who is described as "the Princess."

A lengthy reply shows that Wilhelmina's devotion was equal to his own. "Your friendship is the only thing to which I aspire. Mine for you is not a matter of interest, but rests on much higher foundations; that is to say, on the strongest attraction and the recognition of your rare gifts. So your proposal that in the event of a change I might be with you is most welcome." The latest news of the King, she added, was better, and she warned her brother to drop such speculations. "I dread his resentment, not believing his death to be so near." The Queen, she added, must be in despair. It would be a terrible blow for her, though, to be frank, she would be all the happier for it. A week later Frederick paid a happy visit of four days to Bayreuth. How treacherous was Wilhelmina's memory may be seen by comparing the unflattering description in her *Memoirs* with her letter written the day after his departure. "Having spent the happiest time in my life I am left with my regrets at your absence and at the brief span of my happiness. But as there is never a misfortune, however great, without some consolation, mine is the memory of all the kindnesses you have showered on me during the visit, which I shall remember as long as I live. My heart is so full of gratitude and so deeply touched that I cannot find words to express my feelings. Everyone is talking of the dear brother and the charming Crown Prince."

On returning home Frederick reported that the King's dropsy was worse and the doctors only gave him a fortnight. "I try to prepare myself for this fatal event, for I am deeply touched." Three months later, at the opening of 1735, he reported that the invalid at Potsdam had completely recovered and was beginning to walk. "I dined with him yesterday and I assure you he eats and drinks for four. In a week he will be in Berlin, in a fortnight on horseback. It is a miracle. After more than three accidents and mortal maladies at the same time it is more than human to be perfectly well again, and one must believe that *le bon Dieu* has very good reasons for keeping him alive." The recovery was less complete than it seemed, though Frederick believed that the semi-invalid was merely playing a game. "The King's malady is purely political," he reported in June 1735. "He is all right when he likes and is ill when it suits him. At first I was surprised, but now I have solved the mystery. You may rely on it, dear sister, thank God he is strong as a Turk and will survive his descendants if he takes care of himself. As for the Queen, you know her good heart; and even when it seems that meddling friends influence her for a time, her goodness and devotion to her children set her right again. I have no reason to complain of her; indeed, I should be ungrateful if I did not sing her praises."

Frederick's mood changed as rapidly as his father's health. "Disgusted as I am with the world, I take refuge in my reflections and conclude that no stable happiness is to be found, that the more one knows the world the less one likes it, since there are more troubles and misfortunes than joy and happiness." A month later he wrote that he was summoned to Wusterhausen, the scene of bitter memories. "Pray for the escape of a soul in purgatory." "I pity you with all my heart," replied Wilhelmina; "for my affection for you is so great that I should like to be at that charming place just to have the pleasure of seeing you." The next parental command was only a trifle less disagreeable. "He wants me to go to [East] Prussia: that is just a little better than Siberia, though only just." Frederick's spirits always rose on returning to his beloved Rheinsberg. "We are quite a big party," he reported in February 1737; "usually we sit down to table twenty-two or twenty-four. We amuse ourselves with trifles and forget unpleasant things. We produce tragedy and comedy, have balls, masquerades, and music. Philosophy, the most unfailing source of our happiness, is not forgotten." Among the trials of his rare visits to Potsdam were the Sunday sermons. When Wilhelmina complained of her boredom in the Easter discourses at Bayreuth, he replied that she was not the only sufferer. "I have sat through ten or twelve of them at Potsdam. In truth I was not so attentive as you, and to save my life I could not tell you what they were about. Ministers are paid to preach an hour or two every Sunday, and when they have filled up the time at the risk of getting consumption, they think their duty is done. I don't trouble these gentlemen; I know all they have to tell me and I believe one can be virtuous without their aid."

The relations of father and son varied from month to month,

but never approached cordiality. "For six weeks," reported Frederick from Berlin in January 1739, "I have been the object of the King's bitter jests and the butt of his anger. It is really inhuman to go for people who have too much fear or respect to defend themselves or complain." Six months later he reported that since the death of Grumbkow relations were of the best. In the spring of 1740, when there was no longer any doubt that the King's days were numbered, Wilhelmina's heart was touched. "Nature speaks and recently he has been very good to me. I should greatly have liked to see him once more, but I must resign myself. It is consolation that he thought of me in his sufferings. Whatever the philosophers may say, to leave the world is a wrench. May God help him and shorten his sufferings and strengthen the Queen, who despite her firmness will be badly shaken." Frederick's reply shows that he was very far from breaking his heart. "I cannot imagine how you are so anxious to come here under present circumstances. The King, it is true, is very ill, but, my dearest sister, the life in Berlin is not for you. Do as you like, but if you regret your choice do not blame me. I will keep you informed. You have not been here for eight years, and that is perhaps why you have forgotten the hundred thousand trifles of which two days in Berlin would remind you. Moreover the illness seems likely to be a long one and you could come later. Have no fears either for the fortitude of the Queen or for my stoicism." A month later he reported that the King was worse and that the end was a matter of weeks, not months.

A brief note on June 1, 1740 reported the end of the drama. "He died with the fortitude of an angel and without much suffering. I can only make up for your loss by my friendship." According to Wilhelmina's *Memoirs* this promise was broken as soon as made. "I wrote to him by every post and always from my heart. Six weeks passed without a reply. Then the first letter was only signed by the King and was very cold. His silence continued. I did not know what to think, and I was worried by this marked indifference. At last, after three months, I was secretly informed from Berlin that he was about to pay me a surprise visit at the Hermitage." Unfortunately for her veracity, we possess half a dozen letters written in his own hand during the imaginary period of silence and breathing the same affection as before. Her first letter to the new monarch, beginning with *Sire,* instead of

223

Mon très cher frère, and concluding with *De votre Majèsté la très-humble et très-obeissante sœur et servante Wilhelmina,* was not at all to his taste. "The title of your brother," he rejoined, "is more glorious than all the *très chrétiens, très catholiques,* or *défenseurs de la foi,* and your friendship is more precious than all the slavish subservience of any subjects. I beg you, my dearest sister, to regard me always as your brother and nothing more." That his letters at this moment were short, he explained, was due to pressure of work, not to lack of affection. Wilhelmina dropped the ceremonious approach and returned to the customary *Mon très cher frère.*

Her memory was equally at fault in the account of his behavior during a visit in August. Two days after his departure she wrote that she could not find words to express her feelings. "Since you left I feel quite forlorn. I seem to be in a desert; my only pleasure is to recall all your kindnesses and the happy moments I spent with such a dear brother, whose image is deeply graven in my heart." Frederick replied with an invitation to Berlin at the beginning of October and promised to pay the expenses of the journey. "You will find a table, the best accommodation I can provide, and all tenderness and friendship to welcome you. Adieu, my adorable sister, love me always." Their mother, he added, would receive her with open arms. "The dear Margrave" was included in the invitation to Rheinsberg. "Tell him that I love him with all my heart and that it will be a pleasure to make his stay as agreeable as I can." There is no evidence for the statement in the *Memoirs* that the welcome was cool, though a feverish attack kept the host in bed for part of the time. Her letter of thanks is lost, but his reply shows no loss of affection. "You possess the art of conversation and letter-writing. You exaggerate so obligingly the little I did to please you that you almost persuade me that I fulfilled the duties of a brother and a host. Despite your indulgence, I know I fell short; but you must put it down to my illness, not in any way to my heart." For her the visit was also memorable as the beginning of a valued friendship with Voltaire, which lasted till the end of her life. Three years later he paid his first and last visit to Bayreuth, where he spent a happy fortnight.

While Wilhelmina stayed in Berlin over Christmas the King wrote cheerful letters from his first campaign. "We shall soon advance on Breslau," he reported from near Glogau on December 23. "I expect to be there about January 10. The gates will open to me and we shall find too little resistance to claim real glory. The troops and the whole organization are first-rate; unless the mountains of Moravia stop us I think we shall soon stand before Vienna." She congratulated him on the excellent news. "You have profited marvelously from the lessons of Maupertuis: he rounded off the earth, you your country." The capture of Glogau with the loss of a lieutenant and about thirty men was reported with delight. "The valor of our troops is beyond description, and I am convinced that they have never been equaled. I have no doubt things are going splendidly." A month later, on April 12, 1741, he announced his victory at Mollwitz, described as one of the fiercest battles in living memory, in which his troops did marvels. A year later he reported a second victory and the withdrawal of Prussia from the fray. "The slackness of the French, the bad faith of the Saxons, and an infinity of reasons compelled me." He had secured the treaty cession of Silesia, but he knew it was merely a truce. For the next two years the correspondence is of little interest. The King writes of his journeys, family news, Italian singers for the opera, while the Margravine dilates on the betrothal of her daughter to the heir of Württemberg. There is no indication of the principal subjects that at this time fill their respective thoughts—his decision to re-enter the War of the Austrian Succession and the shipwreck of her domestic happiness.

Wilhelmina's marriage had turned out better at first than she had dared to expect; but there was not much in the young prince, who lacked intellectual interests, and the sunshine only lasted a few years. The cause of the trouble was the pretty face of one of her ladies, a daughter of General Marwitz; and the infidelity of her husband and the disloyalty of her dearest woman friend broke her heart. In addition to losing her partner's love her attempt to remove the temptress led to a serious and prolonged estrangement from her brother. Since appeals to the guilty pair proved fruitless, the only solution was to find her a husband far away from the court. Unfortunately the choice fell on a man in the service of Austria just when Frederick was about to re-enter the war against the Austrian foe. His reaction was violent, for she had told him nothing of the anguish through which she had passed and he scented political disloyalty in a quarter where he had least expected to find it.

"It is with extreme surprise," wrote Frederick from Potsdam on April 6, 1744, "that I have heard from General Marwitz that you are arranging a marriage between his eldest daughter and Count Burghauss and requesting her father's consent. I am all the more astonished because you doubtless remember the declared wish of the late King, who, in giving you the Marwitz girls, expressly desired that they should not marry outside the country and should return here in due course. So I hope that your reason and your friendship for me will prevent you from going farther in this matter, and that you will openly oppose this marriage, which is infinitely displeasing to me. It could never be sanctioned by General Marwitz, who would suffer beyond expression—indeed, it might kill this brave and worthy General. These are the reasons which make me believe that you have too much goodness of heart and affection for me to pursue this fatal enterprise, which I shall always disapprove. If she could blind him to such a degree that, contrary to my declared will, she wished to marry Count Burghauss, she must expect that I shall declare her incapable of sharing in the considerable heritage of her father as has already happened with the younger daughter for the same reason. I should be inconsolable if this unhappy affair should cause disharmony between us, bound as we are by blood and affection, but please remember that I cannot accept these foreign marriages. So I beg you to tell her in my name that she must not dream of this match, which would expose her to my displeasure and to the execration of her father. In any case please send this lady here, where I will provide for her." Hitherto he had written as the affectionate brother: now he spoke as the King. Three days later he wrote again, enclosing a letter from General Marwitz. "You will find it a faithful reflection of his sorrow and his wishes. I feel sure that your good heart will be deeply touched and that you will take effective action to end his troubles. You know that the first and principal duty of children is to obey their parents, whose right it is to decide their fate. Now you know the anxiety of this brave father to see his daughters again, I hope you will not refuse him but will rescue him on the verge of the grave by their prompt dispatch."

On April 9, 1744, the date of her brother's second letter, Wilhelmina replied to the first in no penitent mood. "I see that General Marwitz has told you of the marriage I was meditating for his eldest daughter. I am surprised, my dearest brother, that you should remind me of the wishes of the late King. I kept my word to him about the Marwitz girls; they did not marry during his lifetime. But his death relieves me of all my promises to him, so you cannot blame me for that. You have never written or spoken to me on the subject. So I have done no wrong, all the more since, after my pressing requests to leave me the eldest, who had renounced the idea of marriage, you did not even do me the honor to reply though it was the only favor I had asked since your accession. I did not think, my dearest brother, that you were so interested in the fate of this girl. We look at things in the same way and I have shed many prejudices, particularly the opinion that a woman of twenty-seven, in order to please her father, should make herself miserable in marrying somebody she does not know. As the courier I had sent was delayed, I persuaded her to marry yesterday. Your envoy arrived too late. So I have only to implore your clemency for this poor creature whose attachment to me is the sole reason for what she has done. I cannot imagine you so hard-hearted as to deprive her of her money or to be angry with a sister who has given you so many signs of friendship, and I beseech you not to drive me to despair by withdrawing it. Surely it will not vanish for such a trifle. I shall look forward to a favorable reply, all the more since it would not have happened if I had known your wishes sooner."

The appeal was in vain, for Frederick was thoroughly roused. The reply was short and sharp. "An old proverb says that we judge people by their actions, not their words. If this is so, you can guess what I think of yours. I will not go into details." The following letters are of the same disdainful brevity. "My health is too unimportant for your notice. I am much obliged that you are good enough to interrupt your amusements to remember me." Not for four months did he revert to the marriage that had excited his wrath, and this time in gentler vein. "Though I have serious reasons for complaint, and though our dear ones can hurt us more than strangers, I am willing to clean the slate and not to discuss in detail the offensive way you treated me, the hard things you wrote to General Marwitz, and your marrying this girl to an Austrian. I wish to think I am your brother and to forget the rest." Here was the olive branch for which she had been pining. Her reply is lost, but his next letter, written from camp in October 1744, at the beginning of the Second Silesian War, returns to the old affectionate method of address: *Ma très chère sœur*.

The wound had been plastered over but by no means healed. There were complaints, for instance, of the appearance of an "odious article" on Prussia in a paper published in Erlangen, the second town in the little principality of Bayreuth. Moreover his belief that his sister had a soft place in her heart for Maria Theresa was confirmed when she paid her respects to that lady on the occasion of her visit to Frankfurt for the coronation of her husband as Emperor, as he pointedly indicated in announcing the conclusion of the Second Silesian War at the end of 1745. "Your interest in all that concerns the Queen of Hungary prompts me to inform you that we have made peace. I flatter myself that this will be the more agreeable to you since your predilection for this princess will no longer be embarrassed by the old friendship which you perhaps retain for me." The charge was stoutly denied by Wilhelmina. "The peace is joyful news, and I doubt if all your victories do you more honor than your moderation when you could dictate terms. As for Her Hungarian Majesty I have never had any predilection nor particular attachment to her interests. I do justice to her merits and I think one may esteem people who possess them; my friendship and attachment for you, my dearest brother, are not less real. Though you make me feel how little you believe in them, I shall anyhow have the consolation of knowing that I have done my best to satisfy you."

In his rejoinder Frederick referred for the first time to the matrimonial distress of his sister, of which, to judge by her published correspondence, she had never told him a word but of which, like everyone else, he was now well aware. "I never suspected your heart of being the accomplice of all the mortifications you have caused me the last three years. I know you too well for that, and I place all the blame on the wretches who abuse your confidence and take a malicious delight in estranging you from people who have always loved you tenderly. I pity you with all my heart for bestowing your friendship so unwisely. Everybody knows the unworthy character of this creature whom I will not name for fear of soiling my pen. You were the only person whose eyes were blind. You remind me of the cuckolds who are always the last to know what is going on under their own roof while the whole town is buzzing with the news. Forgive me if I offend you, but after your last letter I could remain silent no longer."

Wilhelmina welcomed the assurance that her brother had never doubted her affection, but there was little else in the letter to assuage her sorrow. "You have been dearer to me than life," she rejoined, "and the more I have loved you, the more I have felt the estrangement. Forgive me for saying what I feel: for some years I have not found in you the brother I adored and loved so tenderly. I thought his friendship entirely dead: I fretted under it and vainly strove to regain his heart. Perhaps my distress led me to make mistakes, but I always knew that I had not changed, that I was warmly interested in your doings and above all in your immortal glory. I excuse you, my dearest brother, in many things. I am aware of all the rumors about myself and our court, and I have long been indifferent to the calumnies. Some years ago Superville was supposed to run everything here, then du Châtelet, now the Burghauss, and if she left me it would be somebody else. As many of my friends tell me what people are saying, I should be a simpleton not to have learned the truth. I know I am charged with weakness, arrogance, intrigue, pleasure-seeking. People talked like that in Berlin when I was there, and I am not surprised that such a nice portrait has turned you against me. Those who know me can judge if it in the least resembles the original. So I will explain my manner of life and thought. I am now at an age when one no longer cares about boisterous pleasures; my health, which grows worse from day to day, does not allow me to enjoy them much. I prefer the society of intellectuals to this tumult of diversions. Rulers and intrigues are not among our topics. The fools who are not admitted, jealous of talent, perhaps desire to revenge themselves on our little society by malicious talk. I hope this letter will clear away all your misconceptions."

The apologia fell on deaf ears, and Frederick's reply was a fresh rebuke. "If there has been an estrangement between us, I did not begin it. It was the scandalous marriage of these unworthy creatures that cast the apple of discord between loving relatives. Since then you let a rascally Erlangen journalist tear me to pieces twice a week, and instead of punishing him you let him escape. The Margrave has had a marked partiality for everything Austrian, and you have given way again and again to my most cruel enemy, the Queen of Hungary, at a time when she was bent on my destruction. That creature whom I cannot name without my blood curdling, that Medea, was preferred to everything, and since she breathed vengeance she converted you to her views. If you were impartial you would not wonder that so many monstrous proceedings have chilled my heart. Anyone but myself might have made a row, but I have never forgotten that you are my sister and that I have loved you tenderly. I never complained to anyone about you. All Germany has witnessed both the injuries you inflicted on me and my studied moderation. Anyone who spoke to me disrespectfully of you would get more than he bargained for. No one condemns your pleasures; on the contrary we wish you all the amenities you can desire, such as intellectuals worthy of your society. But we also wish you to send to the devil all the accursed pests who set you at variance with all your relatives and whom I would flay without scruple, though I am not a cruel man. You are not regarded as ambitious or intriguing, but when you show me neither friendship nor the slightest consideration, no wonder one cools off. We can only love those who love us, and we feel most keenly the pain inflicted by dear relatives. I have not offended you, I have nothing to reproach myself with, and despite everything that has happened I love you still."

A lost reply from Wilhelmina led to a lull in the painful polemics. "I find that one is easily persuaded when one so wishes," wrote Frederick, "and my heart, which pleads for you, would find you innocent even should my reason pronounce you guilty. Your efforts to exculpate yourself are enough for me, and I am delighted to recover a sister in place of an enemy. This will be the last time I shall write to you on a matter so distasteful to me that I am glad to forget it." The harmony of brother and sister was never again disturbed. Looking back over the era of discord we may say that Wilhelmina erred gravely in marrying the guilty girl to an Austrian without consulting the King, and that Frederick's charge of Austrian sympathies was utterly unjust.

For the next two years the letters are filled with family affairs, the exchange of presents, news of the opera and the stage, the purchase of art treasures, inquiries about health—indeed, everything except politics. "We are emerging from barbarism," wrote Frederick, "and we are still in the cradle. The French have made some progress and are more than a century ahead of us." Wilhelmina, like his other correspondents, was treated to disquisitions on the art of life. "The history of humanity is a tissue of blessings and evils; exposed to thousands of maladies, accidents, and misfortunes, it is a marvel we are no worse off. A moment of pleasure, a faint breeze of gaiety, is enough to pass the sponge over a misfortune; our inconstancy and levity make our happiness possible. We are what the author of nature has made us. The technique of happiness demands that we should be satisfied with our state and that we should enjoy the present without prying into the future, all the more since grief does not mend our ills and the impossibility of changing them should teach us patience and resignation. We should congratulate ourselves on all the misfortunes we escape, enjoy the good things that come our way, and resist the melancholy that spoils our pleasures. Montaigne said that everything has two handles, one good and one bad; so we must take hold of things by the good side and restrain the mood of sadness, which poisons the best in life."

At the opening of 1748 Wilhelmina returned to the subject of their past estrangement and, with a definite purpose in view, confessed that the fault had been entirely on her side. "All your kindnesses encourage me, dearest brother, to enter into details that I have always hoped to be able to avoid. Allow me to open my heart on a subject that has caused me the most terrible grief for several years. How often have I reproached myself with the irregularity of my conduct towards you! My last illness and the nearness of death have stimulated my reflections. Mature self-examination has convinced me that in the whole course of my life I have erred only in regard to a brother whom a thousand reasons endear to me and to whom my heart had been bound in the most perfect and indissoluble friendship since my tender years. Your generosity has made you forget my past faults, but that does not prevent me from thinking of them every hour. An injudicious compassion and an excessive weakness for a person I thought wholly devoted led me astray. I have no other plea to advance, and without implicit confidence in your kindness I should not venture to beg you to extricate me from the labyrinth into which I so foolishly strayed. I had the same experience as many great lords: I thought I had found a true friend, a priceless treasure for princes. I have been repaid with all imaginable ingratitude. My pride groans that I was duped, and my heart grieves to be deprived of the only thing that brings happiness. I made the fatal marriage of the Burghauss, the cause of all the trouble. She has lost all her property and is now in terrible distress, her husband having had nothing from his regiment for two years and no private means. What little I can give her does not nearly keep her and we no longer get on together. Judge if I can abandon her in her present condition and send her into beggary after the commotion I have made. I leave it to your decision as a cherished brother, a true friend, and an enlightened judge, placing my honor and reputation in your hands. Only you can restore peace to my mind and heart in this matter in allowing her what her father left, in which case she is resolved to leave the country forever. I beg you with clasped hands to grant me this favor."

Frederick's anxiously awaited reply proved as kind as she had dared to hope. "My heart responds in the fullest degree. Our differences were so small in their origin that they were not worth a serious quarrel. Your good heart judged others by itself. If you were deceived, perfidy is all the more horrible and you have no cause to reproach yourself. You deserve to find hearts like your own, but they are rare. The more one knows the world, the more one recognizes that virtue is only found in novels, that most people ignore it, and that love, interest, and ambition are the tyrants that rule mankind. But do not regret your generosity. Your life is so pure and you have nothing to reproach yourself in regard to me. You may be sure that I shall not abuse your confidence and that I will do my best to set your mind at ease about this ungrateful person. Think of your health, my dear sister, and banish the painful thoughts that impair it. Despise a person contemptible for her ingratitude, and do not take too much to heart disagreeable matters too insignificant to disturb one's tranquillity." The restoration of trustful comradeship was completed by a happy visit to Sans Souci in 1750. Wilhelmina was even moved to the composition of a poem dictated, as she modestly confessed, not by the gods but by her heart. The letters after the parting glow with affection. "I have kissed your dear letter a thousand times," wrote the grateful guest. "My heart speaks a language that I cannot put into words. It is full of you, owes everything to you, is entirely yours." "I have not told you half what I feel about your departure," rejoined the host; "your cult is re-established in my heart, which is wholly yours." These lonely people sorely needed each other's love.

The outstanding theme of Wilhelmina's correspondence during the next three years is the sojourn of Voltaire at Berlin, where the friends met for the third time in the autumn of 1750 and enjoyed each other's company more than ever. She was one of the few celebrities of his acquaintance whom he was never tempted to despise. Her first letter after her return to her stuffy little capital reveals that she had left her heart behind her. "I promised to write to you and I keep my word. Our correspondence, I hope, will not be as slender as our persons, and you will doubtless often give me some reason to reply. Today I will not speak of my grief, for that would renew it. In imagination I am always in your abbey and you can imagine that the Abbot is constantly in my thoughts. Think of me sometimes during your suppers." Voltaire's reply gallantly regretted that he could not spend the three winter months at Bayreuth, as the King had plenty of society. "I would come from the east, my niece from the west, and then odes and new tragedies! Wouldn't that be much more worth while than a visit to Italy? I would give the palm to you rather than to St. Peter's, the Catacombs, and the Pope. Would it be so utterly impracticable?" He proceeded to describe his new and happy environment. "Day and night I work at the *Siècle de Louis XIV;* perhaps it may entertain your leisure hours. I am writing amidst the beat of drums, the blast of trumpets, and a thousand noises that almost deafen my peaceful ears. That is all right for Frederick the Great, who cultivates armies in the morning and Apollo in the afternoon. Every monk lives peacefully in his cell. I am always poorly, always busy, always the monk, in Berlin as in Potsdam. I know only my cell and the venerable Father Abbot, with whom I wish to live and die and who is my only consolation for being unable to live near you. Your abbey and his are the only ones where a soul like mine can find salvation."

The reply of the Abbess of Bayreuth, as he called her, written on Christmas Day 1750, shows her still under the spell of Berlin. "Sister Wilhelmina sends Brother Voltaire her greetings. These words may prove to you that I still regard myself as one of the lucky inmates of your abbey though no longer there. I greatly hope, if God grants me a long and happy life, to return one day and resume my place. I have received your comforting epistle and I swear to you that it edified me far more than the epistle of the Apostle Paul: that, like opium, made me sleepy, while yours woke me up. If you have abandoned your journey to Paris I hope you will keep your word and visit me here. Apollo used to mingle with mortals and, in order to teach them, deemed it not beneath his dignity to become a shepherd. Follow his excellent example." Voltaire replied that he hoped to visit Bayreuth in a few weeks on his way to Paris, where he had to look after business affairs that he had had to neglect in the service of the King of Prussia. Though she felt herself in some measure his disciple, she had opinions of her own, and she declined to share the enthusiasm of the author of the *Henriade* for Henry IV.

The opening months of Voltaire's sojourn in Berlin had been happy enough, but clouds soon gathered in the sky. That the climate did not suit this delicate valetudinarian was bad enough, but there was something worse. "Brother Voltaire," he wrote on January 30, 1751, "is doing penance. He is engaged in a wretched lawsuit with a Jew, and in accordance with Old Testament law he will have to pay for being robbed." A month later he reported the result. "The Duke of Sully often had lawsuits with Jewish army contractors. So you will pardon me if I have also won a case against a worthless Jew, whom I have handled too gently even after his condemnation. The whole story was horribly painful because, as Your Royal Highness remarks, the task of gentlemen of the pen is to write, not to sell diamonds." That this was not the whole story of this unsavory episode she had already learned from her brother. "All well here," reported Frederick on the last day of 1750. "The Queen holds a court today, my brothers are acting, I am busy with politics, Voltaire is cheating the Jews." On January 27, 1751, in reply to a request for information about the lawsuit with Hirsch, he flagellates the guest whom he had been so eager to attract. "It is a case of a rascal trying to deceive a cheat. The matter is in the hands of justice and we shall learn in a day or two which is the greater rogue. Voltaire got into a passion and went for the Jew. He nearly insulted Cocceji and has behaved like a madman. I am only waiting for the sentence to give him a good dressing and to see whether at the age of fifty-six we cannot make him, if not more reasonable, at any rate less of a rogue." The case, he added on February 2, was not yet finished. "I expect he will wriggle out of it. He will be as clever as before, but his character will be less respected than ever. I shall see him when it is all over. In the long run I would rather live with Maupertuis, who is reliable and who understands conversation better than the poet, who is always pontificating."

The savage and unprovoked attack on Maupertuis completed the estrangement of his patron, which had begun with the Hirsch lawsuit, and Wilhelmina was too loyal to her brother not to edge away from the culprit. When Voltaire had left Berlin forever in March 1753, the exasperated sovereign summarized the lamentable story of the visit. "You ask for news of him and here is the truth. He has behaved like the greatest criminal in the world. He began trying to set everyone at loggerheads by lies and infamous calumnies without a blush. Then he wrote libels on Maupertuis and took the side of König, whom he hated just as much, in order to annoy Maupertuis and make him ridiculous, and to become president of our Academy. All this was accompanied by intrigues that revealed his wickedness and duplicity. He published his *Akakia* here in Potsdam, abusing a permit I had given him to publish the *Defense of Lord Bolingbroke*. Hearing of it, I seized the edition, burned it, and forbade him to print this libel elsewhere. Hardly had I reached Berlin when the *Akakia* appeared on sale, on which I had it burned by the executioner. Instead of stopping there, he doubled or trebled the dose and attacked everyone. It was good of me to let him go. He is now in Leipzig, where he is distilling new poisons and pretends to be ill in order to revise a terrible work he is writing. So you see that, far from ever wishing to see the wretch again, I shall break with him entirely. I should not mind if he went to Bayreuth, for with your consent I would dispatch someone to recover the key and the cross he has with him, and above all an edition of my poems which he has sent to Frankfurt, and which I cannot possibly let him keep in view of the use he might make of them. I advise you not to write to him in your own hand: that is how I was caught. He is the most treacherous villain who ever lived. You would be astonished at all his shady tricks, duplicities, and malignities. Plenty of criminals who are broken on the wheel deserve their fate less than he. Forgive this wearisome detail, but it is good that this evil character should be unmasked."

Wilhelmina had never thought so badly of Voltaire as her brother, but she had never known him so well. "His letters to his friends here speak very respectfully about you. He gives you the well-deserved title of great man. He complains of your preference for Maupertuis and your prejudice against himself. He is most amusing on Maupertuis, and I confess I could not help laughing in reading his article. I will tell you all I hear about him." Frederick, exasperated by his latest encounters, returned to the charge. "Do not imagine that I have told you the hundredth part of his rogueries: they would fill a volume of Bayle's *Dictionary*. It is a pity that his great talents are tarnished by the blackest and most perfidious soul, which turns his mind sour." Mme du Deffand, added Frederick, never wished to see him; for, as she said, she could buy him for two florins and enjoy his works without exposing herself to his naughtiness.

Even in the hour of disgrace Voltaire guessed rightly that the Margravine, starving for intellectual companionship, kept a soft place for him in her heart; she alone, he felt, might plead for him with hope of success. "I venture to beg Your Royal Highness to forward the enclosed petition to His Majesty," he wrote from his quasi-imprisonment at Frankfurt on June 29, 1753. "Our only hope lies in your intervention. My terrible situation must excuse these few lines, written with my tears. I throw myself at your feet." The commission was executed in a carefully phrased covering letter to the angry King. "I have just got quite a bundle from Voltaire and Mme Denis," she reported. "I am sorry they write to me, but, fearing to be mixed up in this nasty business, I send it on. Her letter is tactful and clever; evidently she does not know why you held up her uncle. If he had followed her advice he would have acted more sensibly. I consider him as the most unworthy and miserable of men if he has failed in respect to you by pen or tongue: such conduct can only bring him the contempt of decent folk. A man so hasty and passionate goes from one folly to another when once he starts. Yet his infirmities and his reputation, which is smirched by this catastrophe, inspire me with a certain compassion. A man reduced to despair is capable of anything. Perhaps, dearest brother, you will feel that I am too lenient, in view of his intellect; but you will not disapprove my having for him the pity we owe even to the guilty when they are unfortunate and even when they deserve punishment. His fate is like that of Tasso and Milton, who ended their days in obscurity, as he may well do." In returning the letters of Voltaire and his niece Frederick remarked that they were both liars, that their accusations were unjust, and that their adventure was very different from their version. "Yet despite all their offenses I gave orders a fortnight ago to let them proceed. You could not believe the extent to which these people are comedians: all these convulsions, maladies, and despair are only a trick. I was taken in, but only at first. Voltaire does not dare to return to France; he will go to Switzerland to wander from country to country. I do not mind his attempt to damage me, but I have prevented him from doing it again; that is why I made him return my verses and my letters."

At the end of the fatal year 1753 Voltaire implored Wilhelmina to save what she could from the wreck. "The misfortune has occurred, but cannot it be made good? Can the King's philosophy, your humanity, your counsels, your appeals, be without result? Who will tell the great man the truth, madame, if not you? I have told him by tongue and pen, and I shall always regret that my conduct was wrong." After this brief apology, however, the writer passes to the offensive. "I ask you, madame, is it then such a great state affair? No, it is nothing but literary childishness, an algebraical contest, a bagatelle, and for this I was kept prisoner in Frankfurt for six weeks, lost the whole season and the use of the baths for a stubborn complaint; for this my niece had to be dragged through the streets of Frankfurt by soldiers; for this a rascal who was alone with her at night and had removed her attendant tried to insult her. These monstrosities were carried out by a certain Freytag, who functions as Minister of the King. Doubtless the King is the only person who is unaware that this creature had been in prison in Dresden. And what is my situation, madame? I am old and delicate, I sacrificed the last years of my life, for three years I have lived for him, all my time was divided between him and my work, as he knows. So should he not forget an unfortunate literary controversy? The whole trouble arises from a letter that your royal brother published against König and myself at a time when he was not fully acquainted with the details. I do not say so to disclaim all guilt, for I confess I was very wrong not to hold my tongue. But fifteen years of the tenderest affection surely deserve forgiveness for a momentary caprice. That is for Your Royal Highness to decide, but I ask you if it is not also praiseworthy in so great a man to forget a mistake and remember services? Must our whole memorable correspondence and the boundless respect I have always shown him be brought to a stop so that posterity has to say: All this ended with prison and with insult to an innocent woman? Oh, madame, is the possession of a good army the only title to fame? Your royal brother loves and deserves true fame. He loves you too and must believe you. Madame, show your magnanimity and try to touch his heart; do everything you think of use. I place my fate in your respected hands. I am not talking of what people say about it in Versailles, Vienna, Paris, and London. The King must listen to your heart; appeal to his and you will surely touch it, for you understand it." Such a letter could only have been written to one whom he regarded as a faithful friend.

Voltaire's assertion that his attack on Maupertuis was the sole cause of the trouble was grotesque; it was rather the last straw, for Frederick had already lost all respect for his character. Wilhelmina appears to have done her best, but her efforts were in vain. Frederick was not heartless, but he could be hard as steel. Following his warning, which resembled a command, she abstained from correspondence for the next three years, but something better than letters was at hand. On her way to spend the winter of 1754 in Italy for her health, she met her old friend at Colmar, where they talked for eight hours at a stretch. It was balm to his wounded pride, for she brought him a present and asked to be introduced to Mme Denis, in whom the King refused to take the slightest interest. "It seemed like a dream," he reported; "women are better than men." Another happy meeting took place at Lyon, and the old friendship, so precious to both, was fully restored. "You belong to the higher beings," he wrote, "who are only here to diffuse happiness and joy." He was a master of compliments no less than of satire, but on this occasion the tone rings true. She resumed the delightful correspondence in the last year of her life, pouring out her heart over the tragedies of the Seven Years' War and her own rapidly declining health. "More than ever your friend," she wrote in her first letter. "When I give my friendship, I do not give it by half," she added in the second. Voltaire had grave faults, Wilhelmina a few failings, but in their contacts of eighteen years there is nothing that we should wish away.

When Voltaire had passed out of his life, love of his sister warmed Frederick's heart more and more. "I leave you, overwhelmed by your kindnesses," he wrote after a visit to Bayreuth in June 1754. "I exchange peace and friendship for trouble and cares. Take care of your health, on which the happiness of my life depends. I shall never forget these happy days with you, in which nothing was lacking but to see you in perfect health." "You have carried away with you my heart, my joy, and my health," replied the hostess. "I only seem to languish since my good star has disappeared. I am in the depth of depression. Can one get used to your absence when one knows you and loves you as tenderly as I do? No, I feel it impossible. My only consolation is to hear praises of my hero all day long and to find that even in our savage clime hearts are devoted to him." When she found distraction in a prolonged visit to France and Italy, he described himself as living like a Carthusian in his cell. He had other affectionate sisters, but there was only one Wilhelmina.

In September 1755 Frederick attempted to relieve anxiety about the European situation. "You say you are afraid of war, but, my dear sister, it is a far cry from the Ohio river to the banks of the Spree. Moreover there are so many hazards in life that war is only one little item more." At the opening of the fateful year 1756, however, he threw off the mask of nonchalance. "You can guess if I am busy or not. Having to mix myself up in an infinity of matters that really do not concern me, I am plunged in very delicate and thorny negotiations; I fear I should weary you if I entered into details." Five months later, on July 12, he was a little more precise; he was preparing for all eventualities without giving offense to those who wished to take it. On July 28 he confessed that war was very near. "Surrounded by shipwrecks of ambition, I try to shape my conduct by the maxims of my age: far from following my first emotions, I take a safer path.

I have started negotiations with my enemies in the hope that they will declare their intentions and that my conduct may thereby be justified in the eyes of the world. If after these attempts they show themselves intractable, if in their intoxication they are deaf to the voice of reason, I shall act like anyone else in my shoes, with a good conscience and entire confidence in the justice of my cause. Do not worry about the future: happily it is veiled from our eyes. Neither our hopes nor our fears will shape events; born as we are for happiness and sorrow, we must prepare ourselves to receive with equal composure whatever brew Jupiter chooses to empty over us from his two urns. So it is a mistake to expect only disasters; our fortunes are mixed and we can count on more good than evil." The last letter before the plunge, dated August 23, reported that he was awaiting the reply of the Queen of Hungary, which would decide on war or peace. "I wish it had come so that I knew where I stand, for nothing is more upsetting than uncertainty." As a matter of fact there was no uncertainty. He knew that the Grand Coalition was aiming not only at the recovery of Silesia but at the virtual destruction of the Prussian state, and he was resolved to get his blow in first.

During the two last years of Wilhelmina's suffering life the correspondence is almost exclusively concerned with the desperate struggle, and the letters are at once more frequent and more intimate. The campaign opened auspiciously on August 26, 1756, with the almost unresisted invasion of Saxony and the defeat of the Austrians at Lobositz. "May heaven grant that the valor of my army may win for us a stable peace," wrote the King on October 4; "that should be the object of the war." The opening of 1757 found him in good spirits. "I am not a bit afraid of all the great projects of my enemies," he announced from Dresden on February 3; "I flatter myself that when the campaign begins I shall give these people who are now talking so loudly something to do. I laugh at the Diet and its Resolutions; perhaps I shall make them swallow some that at the moment they do not contemplate. In the spring people will see what Prussia is like, and that by our strength and, above all, our discipline we shall overcome the numbers of the Austrians, the impetuosity of the French, the ferocity of the Russians, the masses of Hungarians and all our opponents. When they show their hand we will silence the impertinent cackle of all this canaille, French as well as Russian. Pardon me this phrase; at times I lose patience, and I expect that at Schönbrunn they speak even less flatteringly of myself." The buoyant mood did not last long, for Frederick was forced to raise the siege of Prague and suffered the first military disaster of his life at Kolin. The whole landscape changed overnight. His first thought was that, since he had not yet crossed swords with the French, perhaps a clash with them might be avoided. "If only you could get them to tell you their conditions of peace," he wrote on June 28, "so that one could judge of their intentions and see if anything could be done with them, and you could promise them good dispositions on my side; perhaps we might discover if their treaty with the Austrians that is talked about has really been made. In any case we should learn from their proposals what to expect. If peace came to me through your hands it would be doubly precious, and you would have the honor of having pacified Germany."

Wilhelmina's anxiety for her brother's safety evoked the reply that it was useless to worry. "You have nothing to fear for me; we are always in the hands of what is called destiny. Plenty of people have accidents in their walks, in their homes, in their beds; many survive the dangers of war, which are less frequent for a commanding general than for his officers. I shall be busy, but of that I am not afraid; I shall have hardships, but the doctors say exercise is good for health. So it will all go as heaven pleases. Germany is now in a terrible crisis. I have to defend her liberties, her privileges, her religion, all alone; if I succumb they will be lost. But I have good hopes, and however numerous my enemies, I trust to my good cause, to the admirable valor of the troops, to their spirit from Field-Marshal to private."

On July 7, ten days after the appeal to Wilhelmina to wave an olive branch towards Paris, he returned to his plan. "Since you are willing to undertake the great task of peace, I beg you to send this M. de Mirabeau to France. I will pay his expenses. He may offer the favorite [Mme de Pompadour] anything up to half a million crowns for peace, and more if other advantages can be secured. You will understand the precautions I must take and how little I must appear in the picture; the least rumor of it in England would spoil everything. I think your emissary could also approach his relative who has become a Minister and whose credit increases from day to day. I leave it to you. To whom could I better entrust the interests of a country I have to make happy than to a sister whom I adore, and who, though much more accomplished, is my other self?"

The warrior who in the first two Silesian Wars had told his sister nothing now told her everything. "I am getting so many blows," he wrote on July 13, "that I am almost stunned. The French have seized Friesland and wish to cross the Weser; the Swedes, whom they have set against me, are putting 17,000 men into Pomerania; the Russians are besieging Memel; the troops of the Empire are ready to march. All this will compel me to evacuate Bohemia when all these enemies begin to move. I shall do my utmost to save my country; we shall see if fortune changes her mind or turns her back on me entirely. Here are contingencies beyond the range of human foresight. Happy the moment when I made acquaintance with philosophy, which alone can steel the heart in a situation as mine. If it only concerned myself I should not worry, but I must watch over the safety and happiness of my people. I should have to reproach myself for the smallest error if by tardiness or haste I caused the smallest incident, all the more since just now all errors are mortal. The liberty of Germany and the Protestant cause, for which so much blood has been shed, are two great interests at stake. The crisis is so acute that an unlucky quarter of an hour could rivet the tyrannical yoke of the house of Austria on the Empire forever. I am like a traveler surrounded and about to be assassinated by a band of criminals who are out to divide the spoils. Since the League of Cambrai there has been no such conspiracy as the infamous triumvirate. It is horrible, a disgrace to humanity and morals. Have we ever seen three great princes plotting to destroy a fourth who has done them no harm? I have had no quarrel with France or Russia, still less with Sweden. If in civil society three citizens decided to despoil their dear neighbor, they would be rightly broken on the wheel. What a shocking example to their subjects these sovereigns are! Those who ought to be the lawgivers of the world are teachers of crime. One might as well live with tigers, leopards, lynxes as in a century supposed to be civilized among these assassins, these brigands, these perfidious people who govern this poor world. Happy, my dear sister, the unknown person who has from his early years renounced all sorts of glory, who excites no envy because he is obscure, whose fortune does not excite the cupidity of scoundrels. But my reflections are useless. The accident of birth decides. I felt that being King it was my task to think as a sovereign, and my principle has been that a prince's reputation should be to him dearer than life. They have plotted against me and my honor forbids me to suffer it. The remedy is difficult; in violent illnesses only desperate expedients are of use." This shrill invective would be more impressive if we could forget that the writer had started the avalanche himself by his fateful action in 1740.

The letter of July 22 was equally bitter and depressed. "The bad conduct of my brother [August Wilhelm] has forced me to leave Leitmeritz, but I hope to repair his follies if humanly possible. As I have no control over secondary causes I do not pretend to shape my destiny. I content myself with prudence and the seizing of opportunities, and I am resolved to present a face of brass to every blow. When a horse takes the bit in his teeth he sees no danger. I despise the troops of the Empire, the French, the Swedes, the Austrians, if they come on in turn; but if I had as many arms as Briareus I could not hold off the hydra which grows from day to day and assails me from every side. When I am assassinated it will matter little that two Empresses, a *Roi Très Chrétien,* and I know not how many great princes, all very just and very religious, have done me that honor. I wager that France will sooner or later repent her folly, but that is no consolation. Madame Justice is sometimes led astray. Men have been hanged in haste whose innocence has been subsequently recognized, and polite excuses have been made to the widow and children; but that did not restore the dead to life, and the victim lacks even the consolation of learning about the regrets."

It was a comfort to the distracted monarch to pour out his heart. "All I can do," he wrote on September 9, "is to fortify myself with philosophy. Hitherto misfortune has steeled me rather than cast me down. My experiences have been hard, but I am only affected by the troubles of a people whom it is my task to make happy. One must be patient and swim against the stream as long as one can. I beg you to calm yourself. I appreciate your anxieties and I regard you as the only example of perfect friendship in this corrupt century; but worrying cannot alter destiny

243

and we must be prepared for anything. That is, if you like, deriving consolation from the necessity of evil and the absence of remedy, but there is nothing else to be done. My heart is full of tenderness and gratitude; the memory of so much virtue will remain as long as I live. I cannot express all I feel, but if I did not love you passionately as a brother I should adore you as the miracle of our times." Wilhelmina's reply on September 15 was even more emotional. "Oh, my dear brother, you say you love me, yet you plunge a dagger in my heart. Your *Épître*[1] made me shed a torrent of tears; I am ashamed of such weakness. Your fate will decide mine; I shall not survive your misfortunes nor those of my house. That is my firm resolution. Yet fortune can change once more. A great genius like yours discovers resources when all is lost and this frenzy cannot endure. My heart bleeds when I think of the unhappy Prussians. What savage cruelties are being committed! I suffer a thousand times more than I can say, but I am not without hope."

Frederick's letter of September 17, the longest of the whole correspondence, confessed that the situation had grown worse. "Destiny, it seems, wishes to vent all its fury against my poor state. The Swedes have entered Pomerania; the French are marching on Halberstadt and Magdeburg; from [East] Prussia, where the opposing forces are 25,000 against 80,000, I expect news of a battle any day; the Austrians are in Silesia. I shall fall on any of my enemies who approaches me, whatever the odds, and I shall bless heaven if it grants me the favor to perish sword in hand. If this hope is denied me you will agree that it would be too hard to grovel before a gang of traitors whose lucky crimes allow them to impose their will. How, my incomparable sister, could I repress the sentiment of vengeance against all my neighbors, each of whom would have hastened my fall and shared in the spoils? How could a prince survive his state, the glory of a nation, his own reputation? Had I followed my inclination I should have dispatched myself after the lost battle [Kolin], but I

[1] The *Épître* ended thus:

> *Ainsi mon seul asile et mon unique port*
> *Se trouve, chère sœur, dans les bras de la mort.*

> *And thus my refuge and my only port*
> *Is found, dear sister, in the arms of death.*

felt that would be weakness and that my duty was to retrieve the situation. For the moment I can achieve nothing; there are too many enemies. Even if I defeated two armies I should be crushed by the third. I shall strive on against misfortune, but I will never sign a disgraceful peace. You are the only person left who is attached to me; my friends are dead; I have lost everything. If you have formed the same resolutions as myself, we will end our misfortunes together. These are sad reflections, but no one will be able to say I survived the liberty of my country and the greatness of my house. My death will inaugurate the tyranny of the house of Austria, but my memory will not be burdened with the misfortunes that occur after my death. It will be recognized too late that I opposed to the end the oppression and slavery of my country, and that I only succumbed to the cowardice of those who, instead of joining their defenders, rallied to the cause of their tyrants."

The late autumn of 1757 witnessed a dramatic change that rescued brother and sister from black despair. "After so many anxieties," reported the victor of Rossbach, "here, thank heaven, is a favorable event, and it will be recorded that 20,000 Prussians defeated 50,000 French and Germans. Now I can die in peace since the reputation and honor of my nation is saved. We may be unlucky, but we shall not be dishonored. You, my dear sister, my good, divine, and tender sister, who are kind enough to interest yourself in the lot of a brother who adores her, deign to share my joy." A month later came the triumph at Leuthen. "We have just routed the Austrians. Tomorrow I re-enter Breslau. We have lost only 2,000 killed and wounded, the enemy, I estimate, over 10,000." Things had gone far better than expected, he added, but they would hardly secure a good peace.

Wilhelmina's health had never been good, and by the summer of 1758 it was clear that the end was in sight. Writing on July 20, after the death of their brother August Wilhelm, the anxious ruler besought his sister to live. "You, the dearest of my family, the dearest person in the world, keep alive so that I may at any rate have the consolation of being able to shed my tears on your bosom. Have no fears for us: you will see we shall pull through. As I have had no news for a very long time, I tremble for your life. For God's sake tell someone to write: 'the Margravine is all right,' or 'the Margravine is unwell.' That would be better than my cruel uncertainty. Rescue me by a single word and believe that my life is inseparable from yours." "What you tell me about my Bayreuth sister makes me tremble," he wrote to Henry on August 3. "After our good mother she is the person I loved most tenderly, a sister who possesses all my heart and all my confidence, and whose character is beyond the price of all crowns in the world."

The last letter in her own hand, dated July 18, was almost illegible and filled her brother with foreboding. "I was more dead than alive when I got it," he replied on August 9. "My God, what handwriting! You must have returned from the tomb, for you must have been worse than I was aware. I thank heaven for my ignorance, and beg you to find somebody to write. Without you there is no pleasure for me in a life that it depends on you to shorten or prolong." A dictated letter of August 10 from the dying woman, which crossed this appeal, left little hope. "I have been in hell—more in mind than in body. To hide our loss [the death of August Wilhelm] the Margrave held back all your letters and I thought all was lost; now I have received them. I have been in bed for six months. I have a bad dry cough, my legs, hands, and face are swollen. I am quite resigned; I shall live or die content so long as you are happy. My heart tells me that heaven will work further miracles in your favor. Your enemies are near their ruin; when they score some little advantage, their pride puffs them up and makes them commit the greatest follies. My chest is so weak that I can hardly speak."

On August 30 Frederick reported the dearly bought victory over the Russians at Zorndorf, but nothing could bring him joy while his sister hung between life and death. "If you love me, give me some hope of your recovery. Life would be unbearable without you. These are not phrases but the truth. Think what would become of me if I lost you. Oh, my dear, my divine sister, do the impossible and recover. My life, my happiness, my existence, is in your hands." Her last letter, dated September 25, congratulated him on his victory and predicted further triumphs. His last, dated October 12, brought a poem and fresh assurances of his love. "I am so full of you, of your dangers and my gratitude, that, awake or in my dreams, in prose as in poetry, your image reigns in my heart and shapes all my thought. May heaven hear my appeals for your recovery! Cothenius [his doctor] is en route. I will make him into a god if he saves the person I love best in the world." Two days later, on October 14, the day of the disaster at Hochkirch, the suffering and unhappy woman died at the age of forty-nine, and the last touch of romance vanished from her brother's stormy life.

Chapter XI

PRINCE HENRY

O F Frederick's three brothers Henry alone counts.[1] August Wilhelm, the eldest, died at the age of thirty-six, but a longer life or even succession to the throne would scarcely have increased his stature. Ferdinand, the youngest, was a good-natured mediocrity: no portion of the King's family correspondence is less interesting than that with this dull and blameless man who lived quietly in the palace of Bellevue in Berlin and whose sole significance lies in the fact that he was the father of Prince Louis Ferdinand, the hero of the Jena campaign. Henry, on the other hand, would have made his name even had he not been a prince of the blood. So good a judge as Catherine the Great described him as one of the outstanding personalities of the century; Wraxall, the English traveler, discovered that some people in Berlin thought him an abler man than his brother; and Mirabeau flatteringly declared that he possessed the genius of a hero, the mind of a sage, and the confidence of Europe. Though his caution in the field might have missed opportunities had he been in supreme command, he never sustained a serious defeat; he ranks among Prussia's greatest soldiers and earned the praise of Napoleon. His talent for diplomacy was displayed in important missions

[1] The best biography is by Chester V. Easum (1942), which contains a full bibliography. Krauel: *Prinz Heinrich von Preussen als Politiker*, is most useful on his later years. *Rococo: The Life and Times of Prince Henry of Prussia*, by A. E. Grantham, is a lively sketch. The military correspondence with Frederick appeared in 4 vols. (1851-4), a selection from the personal and political letters in *Œuvres de Frédéric le Grand*, Vol. XXV, and the *Politische Correspondenz, passim*. The Diary of Princess Henry is published in *Quellen und Untersuchungen zur Geschichte des Hauses Hohenzollern*, Vol. IX. The correspondence wtih Catherine the Great is printed in Krauel: *Briefwechsel zwischen Heinrich Prinz von Preussen und Katherina II von Russland*. There are appreciative snapshots in Lehndorff's diaries and in *Forty-five Years of My Life* by his niece Princess Louise of Prussia. The article in the *Allgemeine deutsche Biographie* is too laudatory. A selection from his extensive correspondence with his brother Ferdinand, to whom he always poured out his heart, would be welcome. His life in his beloved country home is described in Krauel: *Prinz Heinrich von Preussen in Rheinsberg*, in *Hohenzollern Jahrbuch*, Vol. VI.

to Russia, and indeed politics attracted him more than war. Loving literature and the arts, French culture appealed to him no less than to Frederick himself, and, like the King, he enjoyed the classics in French translations. He loved his violin almost as much as his brother his flute. He could be charming if he liked, and Voltaire reported to Wilhelmina, after seeing him act, that he was graceful in all he said and did. A man of such outstanding abilities could hardly be expected to content himself with the strictly limited influence which was all that a prince or even an heir could exercise in a state ruled by a superman. Alone of the royal family, he refused to admit the immeasurable superiority of its head and regarded himself as the better soldier of the two. A morbid touchiness and a chronic sense of frustration poisoned relations between the brothers, and there was no real affection behind their conventional salutations. He fretted at his impotence, and the tragedy of his life was the knowledge that he would figure in history merely as "the brother of Frederick the Great." His extravagance and resulting embarrassments were an additional source of friction. Yet their correspondence, extending over half a century and filling fifty manuscript volumes, is as historically valuable for the later decades of Frederick's life as that with Wilhelmina for the earlier, for we meet him at almost every turn.

Though Henry, the thirteenth child of his parents, was only fourteen at the death of his father, he was promptly made a colonel, for he was destined for a military career. The first letters of the new ruler are those of a big brother guiding the footsteps of an inexperienced boy. On receiving a favorable report from the officer to whom he had entrusted his education, Frederick expresses his satisfaction; but a few weeks later, writing from headquarters during the first Silesian campaign, he regrets that the lad is beginning to prefer pleasure to study. "If you wish to please me you will devote more attention to belles-lettres, which will be infinitely more useful to you than anything else. If you wish to make something of your life you must learn to distinguish the useful from the agreeable, the solid from the frivolous, and you must see that pleasure does not divert you from essential things." A submissive reply earned the compliment that it was worthy of a prince of the blood. In the First Silesian War Henry was present at the storming of Glogau and the Battle of Mollwitz, and at the age of sixteen he received his baptism of fire at Chotusitz. In the Second Silesian War he won golden opinions by his bravery at Hohenfriedberg and became a major-general at the age of nineteen. "My brother Henry," wrote the King on October 24, 1745, "greatly distinguished himself in our march on the 16th, and the army is becoming aware of his talents." At eighteen he was presented with Rheinsberg, his beloved country home for the rest of his life.

Henry, aware of his abilities, no longer fed out of the King's hand. Undated letters during 1746 show that the brothers were seriously out of tune. "The scanty friendship you display towards me on all occasions," wrote Frederick, "does not encourage new approaches towards a brother who gives so little in return." A lost reply brought no improvement. "If you love me, your love must be metaphysical, for I have never seen people love in that way—without a look, without a word, without giving the least sign of affection. Happy are those whom you love—that I can well believe. If I am one of them I confess that I live in profound ignorance of your sentiments. I know only your aloofness, your lukewarmness, your utter indifference." A second letter from Henry requested and obtained an explanation of the royal displeasure. "You know what pains I have taken to win your friendship; I have stinted neither caresses nor advances to gain your heart; I have done my best for your establishment. Yet, despite this cordiality and all my proofs of affection, I have failed to gain your friendship. You had confidence in me only when your amours required my help. I have found only extreme coldness, and you have lived with me not as a brother but as a stranger. At last I have lost patience and have modeled my conduct on yours. How can you expect me to be warm when you are cold as ice? I have felt it all the more because I am drawn to you by liking as much as by ties of blood. You cannot condemn my conduct without condemning your own; it is a mirror which reflects your extreme coldness. It depends entirely on you to make a change. To show that I ask nothing beyond your friendship and your confidence I gladly make a step forward and forward the plans for which you ask, assuring you that, despite your reserve, I feel that I am your brother and that you occupy an infinitely greater place in my heart than I in yours."

We cannot tell what produced this encounter, but the last

letter of 1746 shows that the estrangement persisted, and that it was increased by a veto on the plan of studying foreign armies. "I was certainly not expecting a letter. For six whole months you have thought fit to sulk, living in the same house without seeing me, only speaking when compelled by appearances; so nothing can surprise me. Still less was I prepared for the project you have in mind. I do not condemn your desire to inform yourself, but the little attention you give to our army does not point to prowess in the field. Foreign armies are so different from ours that you would learn nothing. Moreover, in the present European situation I cannot send you to either of the two armies [French and Austrian] without exhibiting an undesirable favoritism. To all these reasons I should like to add another, perhaps the strongest of all: namely, that I always remember I am your brother despite your extreme coldness towards me, and that I feel your life should not be jeopardized except for the safety of our country. Though I cannot consent to your project I beg you to restore your friendship."

The next published letter, three years later, shows that the royal brothers were still far apart. The King's instruction to a colonel to restore order in Henry's regiment was bitterly resented, as August Wilhelm reported to the King. His cold and cutting reply is brief enough to be given in full. "Monsieur, I thought it right to restore discipline in your regiment as it was going to pieces, and I am not responsible to you for my actions. If I have made changes it is because they were necessary. You will also need to make plenty of changes in your conduct, but I will deal with that another time. That is all I have to say at the moment." The next letter, a few weeks later, is almost equally sharp. "Since your latest escapades I should be unwise to take my eye off you; I tell you frankly that I shall not leave you to yourself until you find your feet. Is it for you to complain of your regiment? Do you not see that I am drafting a number of people into it and that the discipline of a garrison will become just as good as that of an old regiment? If you love the service, you will make it a matter of honor to bring it up to standard; but so far as I can judge, you only use the name of officer to further your own little plans. As for the house in Berlin I am building for you, it will not be ready just yet, and you will only take possession when you can enjoy it wisely. I fear my letter will annoy you, but I prefer frankness to pretense. I do not love you any the less for this, but there must be no more of such scenes. If you wish for my confidence, I must be sure you know how to behave yourself." Since Henry was sensitive and vain and had yielded to the temptations that beset young princes, such admonitions left scars.

When the curtain rises again, in 1752, after a long gap. in the correspondence, Henry, now a man of twenty-six, is about to marry a Hessian Princess with a good dowry. The King, who had made the choice, was disagreeably surprised by the project of using part of the windfall to pay his debts. "I thought that as they were all paid quite recently there was nothing more to do. My sincere friendship for you prompts me to suggest that you should keep the sum intact and try to live within your means; if you begin touching this money it will soon be gone. You should invest it and avoid new debts, as is quite practicable with your income." The letter was dictated, but the King added a brief postscript in his own hand: "You will soon be in hospital, my dear brother, if you continue to spend your capital and run into debt. After meeting your expenses I calculate that you have 27,000 crowns that you can use for extraordinary expenses." Frederick never possessed a light hand and he became increasingly censorious with advancing years. The Prince, however, also had his faults. He complained that the King loved nobody, but his own nature was even less affectionate.

Though Henry had not the slightest desire to marry and there was little chance of a love match in the eighteenth century, Princess Wilhelmina of Hesse-Cassel might have been expected to win and keep a husband's heart. He grudgingly accepted his brother's choice as Frederick had accepted that of his father, firstly because opposition to the royal will in such a matter was unthinkable, and secondly because it gave him the increased independence for which he longed by possessing a home of his own. He never loved her and apparently never even liked her as much as his elder brother had liked his far less attractive Brunswick Princess during the Rheinsberg years. Yet the King described her to Wilhelmina as the most charming person in the world, and August Wilhelm poured out his heart in letters to his sister-in-law when the King deprived him of his command in 1757. Most people, including the Queen Mother, liked the pretty and cultivated girl. The opening years were not unhappy, but there were no children and the long separation during the Seven Years' War killed any lingering sentiment on Henry's part. Her sorrows are recorded in her diary covering the years 1756–62, published in 1908.[1] She was hurt by his coldness on a brief visit to Berlin after an absence of two years, and a definite breach occurred in 1761 when she appealed to him in regard to financial difficulties. "I have had a most disobliging and disagreeable reply from the Prince," she wrote in her diary. "I have felt it deeply, and try to hide my troubles so as not to be unbearable to others. I spent the whole night in the saddest reflections on my lot. My conscience is clear, yet I am hurt by the Prince's conduct towards me, all the more because unfortunately I love him so sincerely." Yet the fault was not all on his side. "We are all united in the family," reported the good-natured Queen to her brother in 1760; "it is only Princess Henry who cannot get on with anybody and is always discontented without reason. Her pride is unbearable. She began to give herself airs after the death of the late Queen, but it has increased since that of the Prince of Prussia. Far from making friends, she makes enemies. I do not think Prince Henry would approve, and I hope for her own sake she will change; otherwise she will have trouble, she who could be so happy, for we have all shown our goodwill to her while she has shown none to me."

Henry, like his brothers, disapproved the King's policy in the decisive year 1756, and believed that he had been talked into it by Winterfeldt, but he had been told so little of what was going on behind the scenes that their judgment carried no great weight. His fondness for the French language and literature, which was noted and reported by successive French ambassadors, broadened into a conviction that France was Prussia's natural ally. Believing that the alliance of 1744, which was about to expire, could and should have been renewed, he regarded the Convention of Westminster as a needless provocation to a loyal friend. That the court of Versailles was moving steadily towards "the overthrow of the alliances," and that the King hoped to avert Russia's co-operation with Austria and France through the good offices of England, he was aware; but these facts failed to modify his attitude. His advice to beg France to guarantee the continuance

[1] *Aus der Zeit des Siebenjährigen Krieges: Tagebuchblätter und Briefe der Prinzessin Heinrich und des Königlichen Hauses.*

of peace was Utopian, and his conviction that the invasion of Saxony was born of a desire for personal glory was radically unjust. The advice of the royal brothers was never sought, and they angrily resented the influence of Winterfeldt, the only soldier who was allowed a say in *la haute politique*.

When the King had taken the plunge a cautiously phrased letter announced that Henry would obey the summons to Potsdam. "I believe in your foresight, and experience teaches me, that you will be ready for all eventualities. Forgive me this reflection, my very dear brother. I do not presume to penetrate your designs, but I beg to assure you that, whatever they be, no one can take such a lively interest in their success as myself." The writer was now thirty, and the outbreak of the Seven Years' War gave him his chance. He was made Lieutenant-General and his military talents were quickly revealed. "Henry has done wonders," wrote the King to Lord Marshal Keith after the Battle of Prague, in May 1757, the first victory over the Austrians, in which the Prince displayed conspicuous bravery. "I tremble for my worthy brothers; they are too brave." "My brother Henry," ran the report to Wilhelmina, "has won very high praise. As a soldier he has behaved like an angel, and he has been an excellent brother as well." In the dark days after Kolin, where Henry was not present, Frederick expressed gratitude and confidence in a lengthy poem.

> *Vous que notre jeunesse avec plaisir contemple,*
> *De ses futurs exploits le modèle et l'exemple,*
> *L'ornement et l'appui,*
> *Soutenez cet État, dont la gloire passée,*
> *Mon frère, sur le point de se voir éclipsée,*
> *S'obscurcit aujourd'hui.*[1]

Though the King admired Henry's military talents he had no use for his political counsels, and the advice to throw himself into the arms of France was contemptuously ignored. Henry was as good a Prussian patriot as Frederick, but he lacked his nerves of

[1] *You whom our youth delight to contemplate,*
   Model and mirror of their future deeds,
   Ornament and prop,
   Sustain this state whose glory of past days
   Is now in dire danger of eclipse.

steel. Though Mitchell, the British Ambassador, described him as "absolutely French in feeling," the experienced diplomatist shared the conviction that Prussia could only be rescued with the aid of France—in other words, at the cost of territorial sacrifices that the King declined to contemplate.

The King's letters were now long and cordial; Henry is treated as a trusted colleague at last. *"Mon cher cœur,"* he wrote on December 5, 1757, on the evening after his victory at Leuthen, "today, a month after the day of your glory [at Rossbach, where he was wounded in the arm], I have had the pleasure of beating the Austrians in similar fashion. Tomorrow I march on Breslau. *Adieu, mon cœur; je vous embrasse."* Never before had he employed such terms, and his exuberance must be partially attributed to the excitement of victory. *"Mon très cher frère,"* replied Henry, "you have defeated our proudest enemies. You can imagine the excess of my delight. The honor of the troops, the welfare of the state, your glory—that is what I care about most." Though he was coming into his own at last, bitter memories continued to rankle. "I have had some suspicion," reported Sir Andrew Mitchell to London on December 19, 1757, "that Prince Henry is paving the way to a negotiation with France without the knowledge of the King. He is very vain and hates his brother, of whose greatness he is jealous; at the same time he has talents, but more cunning than real parts and is French to the bone. I live well with him, but have carefully watched him; I know his way of thinking; ambition is his only principle. He imagined (looking on the state of affairs as desperate) that he should have the chance of making peace." Henry had indeed sent Count Mailly, a French officer captured at Rossbach, to take soundings; but Frederick was equally anxious to detach France, though less optimistic as to the result. In 1758 Henry was appointed to the command of the army in Saxony and became General of Infantry, but he regarded his growing prominence as nothing more than his right. The disgrace of August Wilhelm, to whom he was tenderly attached, was passionately resented and never forgiven, for he believed it to have been undeserved. His new position as the second personage in the state was registered by his appointment as tutor to his nephew Frederick William, a boy of fifteen, heir to the throne, and during the remainder of the war the King looked to him to take the helm in the event of his death in battle; but he belonged to the unfortunate class of human beings who are never fully satisfied.

Frederick was partially aware of Henry's hostility, and on the death of August Wilhelm in June 1758 he attempted to put himself right. "I have received sad and entirely unexpected news from Berlin—the death of my brother. I feel it all the more because I always loved him tenderly, and I attributed all the trouble he caused me to bad advice and the choleric temperament he could not always control. Remembering his goodness of heart and other qualities I bore gently many things that were highly irregular. I know your affection for him. I hope that after the first pangs you will do all that a strong spirit can, not to forget a brother who will always have a place in our hearts, but to moderate the excess of grief that might be fatal to you. Think, I beg you, that in less than a year I have lost a mother whom I adored and a brother whom I always tenderly loved. In view of my critical situation, do not cause me fresh afflictions by giving way to grief. Use your reason and philosophy as the only means of bearing evils for which there is no remedy. Think of the state and our country, which will perhaps be exposed to the greatest misfortunes. Remember also that men are mortal, that our tenderest ties are not exempt from the common lot of our species, that in any case our life is so short that it gives us no time to grieve, and that in weeping for others we know that others will soon be weeping for us. I will say no more on the sad subject of this letter. I am anxious about you. I wish you long life and good health, and I hope that the multitude of your occupations and the glory you are winning will serve as a distraction from objects that can only break your heart and crush you."

Henry's reply shows how deeply he had been shaken. "My emotions are stronger than my reason. The sad object of a tenderly loved brother, his last days, his death, is continually before my eyes. Though life is full of troubles, and I have had my share, this is the cruelest blow of all." Hermits, he added, were happier than princes, and his only consolation would be the performance of the duties entrusted to him. Frederick's rejoinder was a further appeal to pull himself together. "You have lost a brother, but there is still a family that loves you, and you must preserve yourself for their sake. I am quite alarmed about you and I fear this grief may destroy your feeble health."

Such exhortations did more harm than good, and in writing about his brother's will Henry for the first time referred to the subject that was gnawing at his heart. "I grieve over the discord that existed between you and my brother, but respect and sorrow impose silence on this subject. I must continue to suffer while my brother is beyond the reach of misfortune. If he were still alive I would gladly shorten my days to cancel your displeasure. That is impossible and I will bear my trouble patiently." Frederick briefly replied that they had enough enemies without indulging in family quarrels. "I hope you will do me justice and not regard me as an unnatural brother and relative. The task of the moment is to preserve the state and to employ all our resources to defend ourselves against our enemies."

On the eve of the great encounter with the Russians, which had been hanging over him throughout the summer of 1758, Frederick wrote a letter on August 10 which recognized Henry's position in the state as ungrudgingly as any young prince could desire. "Keep what I tell you an absolute secret. Tomorrow I march against the Russians. Since war is full of accidents and I can easily be killed, I feel it my duty to explain my measures, all the more since you are the tutor of my nephew, with unlimited authority. If I perish, all the armies must at once swear fidelity to him, and the enemy must not detect any change in the command." He proceeded to explain the plan of the campaign against the Russians and the Swedes. "As regards finance I must inform you that our difficulties, actual and prospective, have compelled me to accept English subsidies, which will only be payable in October. As regards politics, it is certain that if this campaign goes well the enemy, exhausted by the war, will be the first to desire peace, probably during the coming winter. That is all I can tell you; for details you must immediately get in touch with the whole situation. If, directly after my death, an excessive impatience for peace is displayed, that is the way to get a bad one and to receive orders from those we shall have defeated."

The clash of arms took place on August 25 at Zorndorf, and the victor briefly reported this success the same evening before he knew the losses on either side. "Adieu, dear brother," he concluded, "I am done up; I embrace you with all my heart." A few days later he added that the advantages of the victory were much greater than he had thought. "You must have *Te Deum* in your army." The Russians had 80,000 men to his own 37,000, and had left 26,000 dead on the field. "In a few days there will be no more Russians in the country. Of all our enemies the Austrians are those who understand war best, the Russians are the fiercest fighters, the French the lightest weights. You cannot imagine all the barbarities these devils commit; they make my hair stand on end. They slaughter women and children, mutilate the prisoners, pillage and burn. But for the difficulties of the terrain in those countries I could quickly have stopped these calamities; but I have my reasons, and I flatter myself that our misfortunes are near an end."

A meeting of the brothers was followed by a note of unwonted cordiality from the King. "A thousand thanks for an agreeable day. Except for the moment when I saw my sister Amelia nothing has given me so much pleasure for the last six months." The slight *détente* was a partial compensation for the twin disasters of the autumn of 1758, the defeat at Hochkirch and the death of Wilhelmina. If Henry was jealous of his elder brother, Frederick never stinted praise when it was due. "Congratulations on your successes," he wrote in May 1759. "Europe will learn to know you not only as an amiable prince but as a master of war. Despite all my anxieties this gives me genuine pleasure, and it is also much to the advantage of the poor orphans [the sons of August Wilhelm] who are confided to me. Continue, my dear brother, as you have begun. You can only increase the esteem and friendship I feel for you. Even were I merely a simple citizen I should wish to express my gratitude for your distinguished services to the fatherland."

Frederick's first letter announcing the catastrophe at Kunersdorf in August 1759 is lost, but the second reveals his sorry plight. "When I told you of our misfortune everything seemed desperate. The danger is still great, but you know that I shall keep the flag flying as long as I live. A case in my pocket saved my leg. We are all in rags. Hardly anyone got off without two or three bullets in his clothes and hat. Imagine all my sufferings in this cruel crisis, and you will realize that they exceed the tortures of the damned." Henry's letters during the autumn of 1759 continue to be respectful and reserved; but there was anger in his heart, and the humiliating capitulation of a Prussian corps at Maxen, which he attributed to Frederick's rash strategy, drove him to

thoughts of resigning his command on the plea of bad health unless the King was prepared to make peace with one or other of
his enemies. An annotation on a letter dated December 1759
shows that he was as critical of his generalship and statesmanship
as ever. "I am very doubtful about this news. It is always as con-
tradictory and uncertain as his character. He plunged us into this
cruel war, from which only the valor of our generals and soldiers
can extricate us. Since he joined my army he has brought disorder
and misfortune. All my efforts in this campaign, and the luck
which helped me—he has ruined it all." "As for the state," he
complained to his brother Ferdinand on December 20, "it is a
word that is employed to amuse the public." The King's resolve
to continue the desperate struggle he attributed to obstinacy and
bellicosity.

At the opening of 1760 Henry received well-deserved promotion. "I am glad he is to have the command of a separate and
independent army on the Russian front, to which he is in every
way equal," wrote the British Ambassador. "But I must own that
I never wish to see the two brothers in the same army. My reason
is that there cannot be two suns in the same firmament." The
King's reiterated exhortations to act incensed the cautious Prince
who regarded himself as a far better strategist, and the relations
of the brothers were strained almost to breaking-point. Henry
took no part in the victory at Liegnitz in August or in the murderous encounter at Torgau in November, neither of which
brought peace any nearer. Convinced that a cautious defensive
was the only course for the weaker side, he frowned on the
King's method of gambling for high stakes. His letters to his
brother Ferdinand are filled with complaints both of Frederick's
strategy and of the treatment of himself. As the conflict length-
ened, the gulf between the two commanders narrowed, for the
King realized the danger of attack with his diminished and inferior troops. That 1761 passed without further disasters was
partly due to the skill and caution of the Prince. He surpassed
himself, wrote Frederick to Amelia. "I can say I really love him
and am grateful for his goodwill. I lean on him. He is clever
and capable, two qualities precious in such times."

When 1762 opened there was no sign of a break in the clouds,
and Henry asked to be informed of the plans for the coming
campaign. If no help was forthcoming, replied Frederick, he

saw nothing to save him. "However, since you wish to know what I should do for the best in such a predicament, it would be to unite all our forces and to throw the whole mass against the enemy. That is not enough, and I hear your criticism in advance. But just ask yourself: What is the difference between dying *en masse* or *en détail*? Besides, if with our massed strength we could smash one of the three armies we should be better able to cope with the other two and separate our own forces. Turn it over in your mind. That is the only way I can see, and it is for your ears alone." For once Henry took his courage in both hands and confessed what he thought of the plan. "It seems to me a counsel of despair. If you unite all your forces you cannot survive. The undefended provinces will be occupied by the enemy and the stores will be divided up. If, even after some successes, we return to this or that province, the misery of the whole country would render aid impossible, the stores would be gone, and we should have to clear out again. Moreover, experience has taught us that an enemy is not destroyed at one blow. Again, the army singled out for attack will withdraw into one of the places of which there are so many in the theater of war. I admit the difficulties of confronting all enemy forces, but if we are to perish we must choose the slowest death; if it takes a long time there is a chance of something turning up. I firmly believe that we can hold off our enemies by offering some opposition rather than by leaving them freedom of action." Frederick replied briefly, but without showing signs of annoyance. "I have a violent fever case to treat; in an extreme case I prescribe an emetic, you alleviations. But we are not yet at the last gasp." When this doleful exchange took place the Tsarina was already dead, though the news took a fortnight to reach Breslau, where Frederick was spending the winter. In a moment the whole situation was transformed and the harassed ruler could smile again. "I send you the good news that Czernichev is going back to Poland with his Russians. For the moment there is nothing more to fear from these gentry. Now, thank heaven, our flank is free. So all the corps watching Berlin can be used elsewhere if you need them. This great event will also take the Swedes out of the war, so all the troops of Pomerania and Mecklenburg will be at my disposal. Let us bless heaven for this event, which promises even better results."

At this moment, when Prussia was unexpectedly rescued from

the edge of the abyss, Henry revealed the morbid irritability which made him throughout life a *mauvais coucheur*. So angrily did he resent instructions that appeared to reflect on his military dispositions that on March 29 he wrote to the King's Political Secretary, good old Eichel, as his master called him, to announce that he would be compelled to resign his post. "My ruined health, my troubles, the hardships of war, do not make me in love with the task entrusted to me by the King. If I write to inform him I count on you to secure the honorable treatment that other states extend to those who have rendered services. Of these I have no high opinion, but it would damage the King more than myself if he treated me ill in my retirement." Four days later a brief note to Frederick revealed the bitterness that filled his soul. "Your previous letters, on which I desire to keep silence, and this last failure of affection bring home to me what I have sacrificed during these six years of war." The King's reply was equally curt. "Spare your wrath, monseigneur. You who preach indulgence, keep some of it for those who have no intention to give offense or to withhold respect, and deign to receive with greater benignity the humble representations that circumstances sometimes compel me to make."

A further letter from Henry on April 11 provoked an exercise of the royal authority. "The only reply you can expect is that I will never consent to your plan, from which your honor, your reputation, and your duty to the state should deter you, all the more since the present situation does not admit of your quitting the army entrusted to your care. So I shall continue to tell you my news but shall not touch on other topics." This was plain speaking, but the exasperated Prince returned to the charge. "I am too sensitive to forget your friendship without emotion at a time when I need it so much. Do you imagine one renounces an army command without good reason? What better could I hope for during the rest of my life? What career can I look forward to, what pleasure, what happiness? None. Mediocrity will be my lot. It will be for you to soften my fate by your favors and to remember that I have done my best to deserve them. That is at any rate all that remains to me and the source of my glory in the eyes of the world." Once again and at greater length Frederick explained why his wish could not be granted. "Your letter grieves me. No one knows my situation better than yourself. At other moments

I should not oppose your desires, but in present circumstances, so full of difficulties for me, you increase them. Consider, I beg you, if I acted on your request to give General Seydlitz the command of your army, what harmony there could be among the generals, some of whom are his seniors, not to mention other inconveniences. Moreover, I do not see how the fatigues of the campaign can have enfeebled your health to such an extent that you wish to abandon your army, bearing in mind that things have been fairly quiet on your front. I should hope rather that your troops may find the opportunity to play an active part in the coming campaign. It looks as if you will have a better chance of distinguishing yourself than at any previous period of the war."

The murder of the Prussophil Tsar sent the wheel of fortune spinning back in the wrong direction. "You can imagine my cruel embarrassment," wrote Frederick, "just as my operations seemed to be taking a happy turn." The attitude of Catherine was unpredictable, but a few days later he could report better news. "Thank God, the menace is removed. The Empress assures me that the change will in no way affect the peace recently concluded, but that the troops have been ordered to withdraw. You may count on the maintenance of peace and the permanence of good relations with that court. Berlin will have nothing to fear." A week later he reported that a treaty had been signed with the Turks, who would carry the war into Hungary, and that, he hoped, would make a strong impression in Vienna. Henry would surely be able to take Dresden and perhaps Prague. "That will bring peace, my dear brother, but not before the spring." The Turkish intervention failed to materialize, as the Prince had always believed it would, but in October he reported his victory over the Austrians and troops of the Empire at Freiberg, which proved to be the last pitched battle of the war. Even Maria Theresa was convinced that it was useless to continue the struggle, and on November 24 an armistice was signed. The joyful tidings moved the King to terms of unusual warmth. "Your letter, my dear brother, has made me twenty years younger. Yesterday I was sixty, today I am forty. I bless heaven for preserving your health and for these happy events. You were quite right to anticipate the attack, and by your sound tactics you overcame all the difficulties of a strong position and a vigorous resistance.

It is a service of such importance to the state that I cannot sufficiently convey my gratitude, which I hope to express in person. That your losses were small is the greatest satisfaction. That is doing things in fine style, and your laurels are not moistened by your tears." It was now that the King is believed to have described him as the General who never made a mistake. After visiting the battlefield at Freiberg the grateful King presented his brother with some property in the principality of Halberstadt. "If I consulted my feelings," replied Henry, "I should at once come and thank you by word of mouth. It is a most substantial gift. I do not deny that my needs make it most acceptable, but my greatest pleasure consists in having clear proof of your satisfaction."

At the opening of 1763 the end, as Frederick had foretold, was at last in sight. "We shall have peace at the close of February or the beginning of March," he wrote on January 14, "and at the beginning of April we shall be as we all were in 1756. Adieu, my dear brother, and do not forget your old brother whom war, politics, and finance are sending to the devil." In announcing the fall of the curtain he added: "You know me too well to believe that I have signed anything disadvantageous to those who come after us. I believe we have made the best peace possible under the circumstances. Our currency will be put straight by June, and I shall pay off all public debts before then. After that I can die when I like. I have taken an infinity of measures for the welfare of the provinces and hope that in two years there will be no visible traces of the war. I feel no regret that the peace is what it is. If we had acquired a province it would of course have been a benefit; but as that depended on fortune, not on me, it does not worry me in the least. If I repair the misfortunes of war I shall have done something, and that is the limit of my ambition. I cannot foretell the future, but I guess that this peace will last the brief remainder of my life. Kaunitz and his sovereign are weary of the war. So far as I can judge, I believe that, at any rate for the present, they wish to live on good terms with us. Yet we must not forget the fable of the cat and mice; the cat remains a cat whatever it does." Though the King was satisfied with the settlement, Henry regarded the restoration of the territorial *status quo* as confirmation of his opinion that the war had been waged in vain.

On the return of peace Henry retired to his tranquil Rheinsberg, worn out by the hardships and anxieties of the long struggle. In the following year, at a big review in Berlin where he
commanded the troops, his military career was publicly com-
mended by the King, but he realized that his services were no
longer required. Frederick built for him the stately palace in the
Linden, afterwards used for the University of Berlin, where,
though he never loved the capital, he usually spent the winter
months. Presents of fruit were exchanged and the Prince supplied information for Frederick's record of the war. The latter's
will, drawn up in 1769, provided a legacy of money, wine, glass,
"the green diamond I wear," horses, and a carriage. The correspondence is friendly enough, but the brothers rarely met. When
certain Polish circles suggested that Henry might be a candidate
for the Polish throne on the death of Augustus III in 1763, the
plan was rejected by the King on the ground that it would be
equally distasteful to Vienna and St. Petersburg.

Henry was not a happy temperament, and his childless marriage had turned out badly. Three years after the end of the war
he appears to have believed that his wife had been unfaithful,
and it was widely held that only the intervention of the King
prevented a divorce. Her last visit to Rheinsberg was in 1765.
Henceforth they occupied separate wings in his great palace at
Berlin and only met at an occasional court function without
speaking to each other. Attempts at reconciliation made by
various members of the royal family were in vain, for, as one of
them remarked, "he is a great Prince but he does not forgive."
Whether there was anything for him to forgive we cannot be
sure, and in any case the source of the trouble lay in his osten-
tatious indifference to a woman who was made to be loved. "For
the last three years," he wrote in 1769, "I have entirely broken
with her; there is no one whom I so greatly mistrust. She would
never miss an opportunity of injuring me. Her intimate friends
cannot be mine."

Henry's sympathy with the King's passionate grief at the
death of his favorite nephew, Prince Henry, younger brother of
the heir, in 1767, was deeply appreciated. "I thank you with all
my heart. This news has fallen on me like a thunderclap. I loved
this child as my own son. He is a great loss to the state. Such is
life—the sorrow of burying one's dearest relatives. I embrace

you, my dear brother. Heaven grant that he is the last for whom I must perform this sad duty." The final lines of this letter are blotted with the writer's tears. The death of the promising lad was his greatest grief since the loss of Wilhelmina. "I have striven to find distraction in occupations of duty and necessity, but it is very difficult to efface these profound emotions. My child has stolen my heart by a number of good qualities without a single fault. I rejoiced in the hopes he aroused. He combined the wisdom of maturity with the fire of youth. His heart was noble and full of zeal. He needed no pushing and learned with passion. His cultivation was above the average. In a word, my dear brother, I saw in him a prince who would sustain the glory of our family. I had planned to marry him to help in assuring the succession. When I think this child had the best heart in the world, that he was born kind, that he was attached to me, I cannot restrain my tears. I have never been a father, but I feel sure that no father regrets an only son more than I this lovable child." Never before and never again did the lonely monarch open his heart in such a manner to any of his brothers. When the Emperor Joseph visited Frederick at Neisse in 1769 he noted not merely Prince Henry's powers as a conversationalist but his silence in the presence of the King.

The main lesson learned by Frederick from the Seven Years' War was that he must keep on good terms with Russia, not only in order to prevent a new coalition but as a makeweight against Hapsburg ambitions. The treaty of mutual assistance concluded in 1764 seemed to favor the Empress, bent on expansion at the expense of the Turks and on placing her old lover Stanislas Poniatowski on the Polish throne, rather than the King, who had had his fill of war; yet to be free from apprehension on his eastern frontier was an immeasurable relief. "At the moment, my dear brother," he wrote in 1769, "the Russians are in full agreement with me, and they feel it more to their advantage to take our money than our soldiers. Heaven keep them in this happy mood which saves us from war. They are increasing their army by fifty thousand men whom they wish to have ready in war or in peace. It is a terrible power, which in half a century will make all Europe tremble. Sprung from the Huns and Gepidæ, who destroyed the Eastern Empire, they will soon encroach on the west and give headaches to the Austrians, who by their short-sighted policy summoned this barbarian nation to Germany and taught it the art of war. But the venomous hatred felt for us by the Austrians blinded them to the consequences of their action, and the only remedy I can see is the eventual formation of a league of the great sovereigns to oppose this dangerous torrent." Despite his contempt for a lower type of civilization the King had no intention of challenging the Russian steam-roller or giving the Tsarina any cause of complaint. Some Russophobe Poles would have liked Henry to succeed Augustus III, and he would have welcomed a crown, but the matter was never officially discussed since Catherine's assent could never be obtained. When Count Guines arrived from Paris in 1767 to renew diplomatic relations and to loosen the tie between Berlin and St. Petersburg, he was coolly received by Frederick, and Henry seemed to be France's only prominent friend. While warmly welcoming the envoy, the Prince regretted that owing to his brother's orders he could not see more of him. "His penchant for the French," the diplomatist reported, "leads me to believe that he is the only person from whom one could obtain information if he were allowed to speak." Henry's views counted for nothing, and when he proposed that Frederick and Joseph should use Russia's absorption with Poland and Turkey to divide Germany between them like Octavius and Antony, the King replied that he was too old for great enterprises.

However much Frederick disliked and distrusted Russia, he was quite ready to utilize her strength for his own purposes. He had always coveted West Prussia though he had no intention of fighting for it and little hope of its early acquisition; but he was eager for the termination of the Russo-Turkish War, which broke out in 1768, carrying with it the payment of "those accursed subsidies" and the deadly risk of being involved in an Austro-Russian conflict.

In the summer of 1770 Catherine begged Frederick to allow Prince Henry to combine a visit to his sister the Queen of Sweden with a call at St. Peterburg. The cause of the invitation was her desire to find out what was going on between Prussia and Austria and what advice he was giving at Stockholm. "Herewith a copy of a letter just received from the Empress of Russia," wrote Frederick in August. "She asks for you with so much eagerness that I do not think you can refuse. It may not greatly appeal to

you, but you must make a virtue of necessity. If you need money
I could put eight thousand crowns at your disposal at St. Petersburg. You realize, my dear brother, how careful we must be in
dealing with this woman. If you can reconcile her with my sister
in Sweden I shall be delighted. In general you will have to consider all matters that concern our interests. You will meet a lot
of people of whom we have need. Please convey my most flattering compliments to the Empress, and tell her all you can of the
universal admiration she excites. During your journey you will
be able to collect a store of eulogies which you can produce at
the fitting moment. I rely on your skill to seize occasions when
they come." He would be fully repaid for the hardships of the
journey by the sight of one of the greatest princesses in the world.
"You will find many things in St. Petersburg to admire, but what
are mansions and a pompous court in comparison with the
princess who rules this country with so much glory? That is the
only experience I envy you—to get to know this powerful genius
who almost surpasses Peter the Great. To congratulate the Empress on every success of her arms would become wearisome to
her, and so in sharing in her victories in Bessarabia, on the Pruth,
and at Bender I admire in silence. The reigning Empress puts
the coping-stone on the labors of her predecessors." Other letters
described her genius as far surpassing that of Peter the Great,
and foretold that if all her grandiose projects were carried out,
Russia would soon be the first nation in the world. Such fragrant
bouquets were clearly intended to reach the lady's eyes.

After receiving the King's consent Catherine dispatched a
flattering invitation to his brother in Stockholm and received
a cordial reply. The initiative had been taken by Henry himself
in the spring when he sent a confidential message to St. Petersburg that he would welcome an invitation if Frederick were not
informed of this step, his undeclared object being to prepare the
way for the acquisition of West Prussia at Poland's expense.
Accompanied by a large suite, Henry reached St. Petersburg via
Finland on October 12, 1770 and paid his first visit to the Empress
on the following day. They had known each other as children
and might perhaps have married had she not been selected for
the Russian heir. They had not met for twenty-six years, but his
stiffness quickly wore off. He was only outwardly cold, she wrote
to a friend, but it was soon obvious that he was very clever and

267

an accomplished conversationalist. After a few days they were on such friendly terms that he was invited to visit her in her leisure hours and to share her meals whenever he chose. Thus they met almost every day, discussing not only politics but literature, science, and art, for both were intellectuals and children of the *Aufklärung*. "This hero," wrote the hostess a week after his arrival, "is at the height of his fame and is a man of the first rank quite apart from his birth." Her admiration grew steadily, and after three months of his society she wrote to a friend that she had never seen anyone with whose ideas she so fully agreed. "Often we open our mouths at the same moment to say the same thing. Perhaps that explains why he likes my society. I confess that no princely visitor could be more welcome. Nothing escapes him and one must really admire him very much. He is always gay, his character is upright and humane, his mind lofty and noble; in a word, he is a hero who has given me abundant friendship." He was no less impressed by the vivacity and versatility of his hostess and by the pageantry of her sumptuous court.

While Henry's bulletins were on their long journey to Berlin, Frederick wrote in cordial terms to his brother in January 1771. "I regard you as Pythagoras or Plato, who journeyed among the Scythians and the most barbarous peoples in order to learn the secrets of nature and collect information. I am ready to admire all you have seen that is worthy of admiration, but for all the treasures in the world I could not go where you have been. I thank you a thousand times for remembering my old birthday. I confess, my dear brother, that I would far rather have you here than among the barbarians. Even the tamest lions often show signs of their native ferocity, and I believe it is the same with the Russians. You must be ready to answer plenty of questions—that is a tribute that every traveler has to pay to his countryman on his return. I dined this evening with my sister Amelia and we talked much about you; but you were in good hands, so you need not be afraid of your reputation." When Henry said good-by to his hostess on January 30, 1771, after a visit of three and a half months, he knew that he had won her confidence and had rendered useful service to Prussia. The attempt to terminate the Russo-Turkish War had failed, but an important advance was made towards the acquisition of West Prussia, a project on which he had set his heart. The Prussian Minister at St. Petersburg reported that he had made himself generally beloved and that the Empress spoke of him in most flattering terms, adding that his departure left a vacuum she could not fill. To Frederick she wrote as she had never written before and was never to write again. Everyone who had met him missed him: "We are left only with the imperishable memory of a beautiful dream."

On his return in the middle of February 1771, Henry spent a week at Potsdam reporting on his visit and discussing further action. Frederick was no less eager to secure West Prussia, but the Seven Years' War had taught him caution, and no one but his brother could have removed his scruples. Henry collaborated in drafting a letter from the King to the Empress and a memorandum instructing the Prussian Minister at St. Petersburg to go ahead, and he was asked to revise Frederick's reply to the note from the Empress which he had brought. Never before or after did his political advice receive so much consideration. It was indeed the high-water mark of his career, for he felt that he was making history. After thus agreeing in principle, however, the brothers proceeded to disagree in tactics. Henry advised an agreement with Austria, which the two powers would then press Russia to accept, while Frederick preferred an agreement with Russia, convinced that in such case Austria would automatically come in. When the Prince had left Berlin in the summer of 1770 the King had been anxious for the termination of the Russo-Turkish War; now he desired it to continue till the partition of Poland was arranged.

After reporting to the King, Henry wrote to thank his hostess for the visit. "My heart is filled with gratitude in recalling the friendship with which you have honored me. I am always thinking of the time which passed so rapidly and in which I received every day new proofs of your attention." Catherine replied that her friendship was assured and that the memory of his visit would never fade. "Birth is an advantage in the eyes of the world, but merit and mind surpass it and set it off. If all the kings of the earth except your brother had come to see me I should have suffered from boredom and not have felt the satisfaction derived from your short visit. Your friendship is most precious, for among your fine qualities is that of sincerity." When a secret Russo-Prussian treaty for the partition of Poland was signed on February 17, 1772, she expressed her gratitude for his share in

"the great matter now concluded between your brother and myself. Here are a number of peoples who, thanks to your efforts,
will enjoy sweet repose for a very long time." After taking possession of the territory in White Russia that fell to her share, she
renewed her thanks for his help "in this great affair of which
you may be regarded as prime mover." He was always proud of
his share in the partition on the ground that the Poles in the
Prussian zone fared far better under the new regime than under
the old. But there was a much more important reason for satisfaction. "I want to see you Lord of the Baltic," he had written
to Frederick in the spring of 1770, and he had helped to make
him so.

No sooner was the partition treaty signed than a new storm
blew up. On August 19, 1772 Frederick's nephew Gustavus III
restored the absolute authority of the crown in Sweden, a decision attributed by Catherine to the influence of France and
Russophobe circles at Stockholm. For a moment the angry
Tsarina thought of war, and Henry at his brother's suggestion
pleaded for moderation at both St. Petersburg and Stockholm,
not only for the sake of his widowed sister but because if hostilities occurred Prussia was pledged to supply troops for her Russian ally. His intervention aroused no resentment at St. Petersburg, though it was the continuance of the Turkish war rather
than appeals from her friend at Rheinsberg that induced her to
stay her hand.

A few months later, at the opening of 1773, Henry once again
served the cause of Russo-Prussian friendship by supporting
Frederick's plan for the marriage of the Grand Duke Paul to a
Princess of Hesse-Darmstadt, a relative of the Prussian house.
He was still in high favor, and early in 1774 an invitation to pay
Catherine another visit was accepted with effusive gratitude.
For various reasons enumerated by the Empress the meeting was
postponed for two years. "I thought I was approaching a time
of life when the sentiments of pleasure are more moderate," he
wrote in November 1775, "but Your Majesty's letter has made
me feel such joy and satisfaction that I begin to believe that I am
still an adolescent. I cannot describe my contentment when I
read you have fixed the hour of my happiness." The following
Easter would suit him excellently. There was policy in all these
gushing compliments, for so long as Austria was hostile the

goodwill of the autocrat of Russia was indispensable. Frederick's reaction to the invitation was expressed in less flattering terms. "She treats you as a friend. To decline is to break with her, and you know the Indians say they must worship the devil to prevent him from harming them."

The visit in the spring of 1776 was overshadowed by the death of the wife of the Grand Duke Paul, the only child of the Empress, who apologized for the consequential interruption of the usual festivities. "Prince Henry, I think, is dying of boredom," wrote his hostess to Grimm, "though he is too polite to confess it. We gossip occasionally, but I do not feel quite up to entertaining him just now. He will tell you he is not bored here, but do not believe it. He loves fetes, and I could not give him any. Everything has been dull on account of the mourning." Though the glamour of 1770 had faded, the visit was not without result, for the friendship of the heir to the throne, however powerless he might be during his mother's lifetime, was worth winning. When the Grand Duchess died in giving birth to a dead son, Catherine begged her visitor to support her request for the hand of a Württemberg princess who was also a relative of the Prussian house. "Your Royal Highness is assuredly a unique negotiator. May this affair perpetuate the contacts that unite our two houses." Henry discharged his commission with zeal, Frederick approved, the match was speedily arranged, and the Grand Duke Paul left with Henry for Berlin to meet the bride chosen for him. "I am more grateful than I can say for all the care and attention you have been good enough to show the Grand Duke during his journey, which my son has described in a letter full of gratitude, and you have increased my debt by informing me of the safe arrival of my Télémaque under the ægis of your Royal Highness. The welcome by the King, the royal family, and the public has been all I could desire. You know that when my feelings are deepest words fail me. At this moment my pen is in the same predicament, but you know I shall always retain the liveliest recollection. I am expecting the success of the project since the affair is in your hands." Paul's letters to Henry breathe no less gratitude for his kindness and counsel in the time of his domestic grief and his new-found happiness. The new Grand Duchess won all hearts at St. Petersburg and formed a new link between the two countries.

Never had the relations of the two courts been more friendly. "I regard this union," wrote the Tsarina to Frederick, "as a strengthening of the ties of friendship between our houses. I cannot help mentioning how grateful I am to the Prince, your brother, who has shared all my feelings and shown me a thousand signs of his friendship." On the other hand, the warm attachment of her son to Henry was not altogether to the taste of the Tsarina, who callously excluded her heir from all political influence and disliked the notion that he possessed direct means of approach to the Prussian court. As a result of the growing estrangement from her son her attitude to Prince Henry became more reserved, and after 1780, when she turned from Berlin to Vienna, the correspondence ceased. In 1781 Henry attempted through Grimm to resume contact, and a present was coldly acknowledged through the same intermediary. Any lingering sentiment on her part vanished when in his closing years Henry's love of France and sympathy with certain aspects of the French Revolution provoked her to angry denunciations of *"le citoyen Henri de Rheinsberg"* and *"l'oncle Jacobin."*

Frederick was well aware of the value of his brother's services and of the fact that they could have been rendered by no one else. The alliance concluded in 1764 and renewed in 1769 was again extended in 1777 for eight years. To keep the friendship in repair was all the more vital since he was beginning to worry about the ambitions of the Emperor Joseph in a new quarter. "He may force every prince who loves German independence and liberty to unite against him. He is probably preparing a cruel war, perhaps as bitter as the last. If the Elector of Bavaria dies before me, if the bugle sounds, we must mount our horses once again. That will doubtless be a matter for my successors, just as my father often said that I should have to vindicate his rights in Jülich and Berg. Great events demand the flower of one's strength; when body and mind are failing, sensible men should think of the tomb. You may think this moralizing too austere, my dear brother; happily you are not old enough to need it. For a veteran like me it is necessary. Everything separates on, from the world. One loses friends and acquaintances, is lonely, becomes conscious of progressive enfeeblement, and nature warns us to prepare for the journey from which there is no return. That is no great business, and it is best to close down before entire decrepitude sets in and one becomes a burden to oneself and others."

Since Frederick was always haunted by the thought that his father and grandfather had died in middle age, and the heir to the throne, a lazy sensualist, was everything a king of Prussia ought not to be, his thoughts turned increasingly to Henry, soldier and diplomatist. Hearing of military activity in Bohemia early in 1776, Henry asked for information. "What you have heard about the Austrians," replied Frederick, "has some foundation. They think my end is near and are strengthening their troops in Bohemia so as to occupy Saxony and invade this country. So it will be if I die; and my big booby of a nephew will have a bad time unless he exerts himself. But nothing can overcome his indolence, and I must leave the future to your prudence." A few days later he was more precise. "I can tell you things about our affairs which not even the ministers know, and that will make you so indispensable that everyone will have to come to you for information and help." A third letter brought an invitation to Potsdam. "I shall not die tranquil about the state unless I see you in some manner its guardian. I regard you as the only person who can sustain the glory of our house and become the pillar of our fatherland. I can explain my ideas more fully in conversation." The talks seem to have been satisfactory, for Frederick wrote a grateful letter after the visit. "I should make an unpardonable mistake if I did not try to arrange that a person of your wisdom may share in the government, so that your good advice may make up for the negligence, imbecility, and weakness of a creature incapable of governing himself, much less others. Convinced of your friendship for me, I have opened my heart on this matter, which has long occupied me. I thank you a thousand times for your willingness to do as I wish, and if heaven could be moved by our prayers, I should ask that it pour down on you its richest blessings." Later in the same year 1776 he returned to his fears. "The Austrians are trying to embroil us with the Russians in order that, with their hands freed in this quarter by my death, they can fall more effectively on our tall fool [the heir]. What is to happen if the good Lord does not preserve your life and health?" The plan of a virtual regency for his brother consoled him for the time, but was quickly abandoned as the heir grew to manhood, for his own experience on

his accession had taught him that a ruler's authority in an auto-
cratically governed state vanishes at death.

Henry's services were once more in demand when the death
of the childless Elector of Bavaria at the beginning of 1778 set
the Emperor Joseph on the warpath. Like Maria Theresa he
realized that it was useless to attempt the reconquest of Silesia,
but unlike his mother he was determined to seek a satisfactory
equivalent. Bavaria was a tempting morsel, and the extinction
of the Bavarian line of the Wittelsbachs seemed a heaven-sent
opportunity of securing a part if not the whole. Frederick had
had his fill of war, but he had to consider the threat to the long-
range security of Prussia implied in such an aggrandizement of
the house of Austria. His decision to stand up to the Emperor's
challenge was regretted by Henry, who in politics no less than
in war shrank from major risks. Dissociating himself from all
political responsibilities, he accepted the invitation to command
one of the two Prussian armies. He won warm praise from the
King for his skillful maneuvers in a war of limited liability, and
gratitude for his efforts to secure the moral support of Catherine.
His heart, however, was not in his work, for he never believed
that the existence of his country was at stake.

At the close of the almost bloodless campaign of 1778, in which
military differences had emerged, Henry for the second time
begged leave to resign his command. "In my desire to serve you,
my very dear brother," he wrote from Dresden, "I did not think
of my health when I took command of the army you entrusted
to me, believing I could fulfill all its duties. The campaign has
been fatiguing, though not so much as some others, and it did
not last long; yet it is impossible to depict all my sufferings in
mind and body and all the efforts I had to make to carry on. I
have no definite malady, but my constitution is so enfeebled,
my nerves so shattered, that I should not have believed it had I
not experienced it. This prevented me from moving about as
much as I wished. My eyes run; if I am long on horseback I become terribly thirsty and giddy; my digestion is out of order.
Any sort of news produces an excitement such as I never knew,
and this causes low spirits. In this situation, for which I know
of no remedy, I must beg permission to resign when you have
chosen my successor in command of the army. My unhappy
plight is only too well known. I return to obscurity and lose all

the honors of the command. I have always tried to be useful. I am deprived of all these honors and hopes. Forgetfulness of my services is my greatest worry, yet I can do nothing else. It is humiliating to have such feeble health, but it would be dishonest to hide it and to undertake a burden beyond my strength. If eleven campaigns, in which I have received letters and flattering promises from you, and services in time of peace, for which I have also received proofs of your satisfaction and assurances that your favors will be made known some day: if these services, I say, remain in your memory, I shall have the only consolation in my misfortune. Even without that I should still have the consolation of having been disinterested in all my tasks and of having discharged them, if not with all the virtuosity of others, at least with complete integrity, and of having earned at any rate on some occasions your approval and that of the public. In my complete retirement I shall await death without desire or fear."

Frederick expressed his sympathy, but pointed out that his retirement would prove very embarrassing, since commanders of his stature were not easily found. The Duke of Brunswick alone was up to the task, but he could not be spared from Upper Silesia. "The war may or may not continue, so I beg you to postpone your plan till we know where we stand. What you say about being forgotten would make sense in the mouth of a man who never distinguished himself. In your case such language is inapplicable, unless you believe that the public is unjust and that I am the most ungrateful of men, and I hope you do not think that." This gracious letter, replied Henry, was a real consolation. "The happiness of serving you, of which you so kindly speak, makes me regret that I cannot do as I should wish; but I shall never lose the desire, even in the smallest matters. I have explained my sad situation; I had to do so, regardless of peace or war. I place all my interests in your hands: you will decide. If I could be of use to you in the slightest degree I should congratulate myself, for it would show the public not only that I am attached to you but also that I have not deserved to lose your confidence." His wish was granted, and Brunswick took command of the army on December 3. "It is true," wrote Frederick, "that the war demands a robust constitution and that infirmities go ill with the blows to body and mind to which one is constantly exposed. Good will is not enough: the machine must work. The present war will certainly be my last; I only hope the end may be as happy for our country and for Germany as I desire." Henry's retirement made no practical difference, for peace discussions through the mediation of France and Russia, the allies of the two belligerents, were in sight.

Frederick's strictly limited aim in the War of the Bavarian Succession was attained with a minimum of bloodshed and he was glad to stop. Henry had strongly disapproved the resort to arms on the ground that an acceptable arrangement with Austria might have been secured by negotiation, but since fighting had taken place he thought Prussia entitled to some territorial reward. These complaints produced an explanation from the realistic ruler. "You will remember, my dear brother," he wrote on March 4, 1779, "that I told you in Berlin we could desire nothing better than to make the Austrians disgorge. That is important, because if this act of violence had come off they would have established a despotic authority in the Empire of which we should sooner or later have felt the fatal effects. Though this restitution is not as complete as could be desired, the first objective of the Emperor's mad ambition has failed, and we gain the great advantage that we are regarded in the Empire as a useful makeweight against Austrian despotism. I am so angered by all this Austrian breed that I would gladly sacrifice my life for revenge. It is lack of money which compels these wretches to make peace, but it will only be a truce." In April he announced that peace was as good as made—"not by sacrificing our allies, but a peace conformable to the honor and dignity of Prussia. The Elector of Saxony will have four millions in cash, the Prince of Zweibrücken will get his rights, and Bavaria will be saved from dismemberment by Austria." All that the aggressor had gained was the so-called Innviertel.

Frederick's apologia fell on deaf ears, for Henry was thoroughly disgruntled. "I will never draw the sword for him again in peace or war," he wrote to his brother Ferdinand on March 9, when the end of the war was in sight; "my career is over and I am nearing the goal that liberates us from all human ills." He had experienced so much injustice in the past thirty-nine years, he confided to Grimm, that he should have learned to bear it without indignation, but he had not. So long as Frederick was alive he could hope for nothing but *otium cum dignitate,* and only a grave crisis could have drawn him from his retreat. In the autumn of 1779 he declined an invitation to Stockholm, where his sister, the widowed Ulrike, desired his good offices with her temperamental son Gustavus III. He had no wish to get mixed up with his nephew, he replied, or to be subjected to the new ceremonial established at the Swedish court. When an envoy to Russia was required in the following year, the King's choice fell on the Prince of Prussia, who armed himself with letters from Henry to Catherine and the Grand Duke Paul. The heir to the Prussian throne struck the Tsarina, as she informed Grimm, as thoroughly unattractive. "How different from his uncles!" Yet Henry himself could hardly have succeeded in counterworking the Austro-Russian rapprochement that it was the main purpose of the mission to avert.

After the signing of the Treaty of Teschen on May 13, 1779, the correspondence between the brothers, which had flowed almost as freely during the crisis of the Bavarian Succession as during the Seven Years' War, became a trickle, and Henry's dislike of the King was paraded in conversation with strangers. Polite inquiries are exchanged about each other's health, and occasionally deeper notes are struck. Their ideology was much the same, for both were children of the Age of Reason. "It has always seemed very easy to combat religious dogmas," wrote Henry on the eve of the King's seventieth birthday; "most of them being merely the work of man, it is naturally easy to prove their nullity. Every reasonable man must regard religion from two points of view, truth and social utility. It is right to combat all dogmas dangerous to society, the authority of priests, the absurdity of eating a God, etc. But the true philosopher, for the good of society, will halt where religion impinges on the laws of the state and where dogma, no longer harmful, may be an error though it is useful to society. Such, for example, is the opinion in regard to another life; whoever believes in it, whether truth or error, has certainly an extra motive to be a good citizen. Such are also most of the axioms of morality, which count more in the eyes of people who believe in some religion. In a word, it is an extra brake, which, if it is ever totally relaxed, will have results perhaps as fatal as were the horrible wars of religion. That time is still far away, for the peoples are not yet influenced by reasoning; but I believe that an observant eye can detect the germ that these novelties are preparing."

Frederick's reply reminds us of the philosophic dissertations he used to address to Voltaire and d'Alembert. "In regard to religions I share the view of Fontenelle, who said that, if his hand were full of truths, he would not open it since the people did not deserve enlightenment. If I had the choice of all the Christian sects I would choose the Protestant because it is the least harmful. I am convinced that everyone should have liberty to believe what he can; if that includes immortality I raise no objection so long as there is no persecution. As for morals, we have only to examine the annals of all ages, nations, and religions to find an equal corruption, for opinions cannot change people, and passions are the same in all countries and sects. Look where you will, you find no curb on evil actions except in penalties and disgrace. That is what holds some people in check and prevents them harming society. Momentary advantages of interest, ambition, or self-indulgence will always count for more than punishment in another life, because the present weighs more than any risks after a death which they believe to be far away. So religions and philosophies will always fail unless they are buttressed by the fear of the gallows and public contempt. Religion helps the ambitious only in moments of enthusiasm as in the reign of Constantine, the Crusades, the reforms of Luther and Calvin; when the effervescence passes, lukewarmness succeeds to fanaticism. Invent what you will, renew the principles of stoicism, the disinterestedness and humility of the early Christians: the people will hear these fine discourses without understanding them, man will revenge himself if he is offended, flare up if he has too much bile. Such is our species. I would gladly have ennobled it if I could, and it would have flattered my vanity. But when one looks carefully into things, and especially when one reviews bad cases from the courts in order to confirm sentences, one is obliged, as I am, to recognize that so long as the world is inhabited by human beings morals will no more restrain them than they do today. Perhaps some unknown globe may be inhabited by angels, or by sages imagined by the Stoics, or by some species superior to ourselves, and there perhaps religion and morality may produce more effect than here."

Though his strained relations with the King were known to all the courts and cabinets, Henry remained a prominent figure on the European chessboard. In 1781, on the occasion of a journey to the Austrian Netherlands, the Emperor visited him at Spa, where he often took the waters. The Prince, reported Joseph to Kaunitz, made no secret of his differences with the King: he hoped that the reign would not last much longer and that relations with Austria would improve under his successor, whom he believed he could influence in that direction. The Emperor was not impressed, suspecting that the disagreements between the brothers were staged and that Henry's indiscretions might have the purpose of provoking him to follow suit. The meeting bore no fruit, for the visitor realized that Henry was too good a Prussian to be sincerely Austrophil, while the Prince told his brother that he doubted the value of Joseph's friendly assurances.

Henry's unofficial visit to Paris in 1784 was the fulfillment of a lifelong desire to see *la ville lumière*.[1] On his way he met Goethe at Weimar, Necker at Geneva, and Gibbon at Lausanne. After crossing the frontier from Switzerland Count Oels, as he called himself, received an invitation from Louis XVI to the capital, where he spent two crowded months, all arrangements being made by Grimm. Frederick willingly gave permission and took the liveliest interest in the journey, which in old days he had longed to make himself, but there was also a political motive for his satisfaction. Here, it seemed, was an opportunity to win France for the project of resisting the ambitions of the Emperor. Despite the memory of Rossbach, Henry was treated with the highest consideration by the King as well as the intellectuals, for his affection for France was notorious. He attended sessions of the Academies, patronized the Opéra and Comédie Française, met Beaumarchais, Mme Lebrun, Condorcet, Boufflers, Mme de Sabran, and other celebrities, and thoroughly enjoyed himself. "You cannot imagine what the French are like," he wrote to his brother Ferdinand. "You know I always loved them, and now I would be ready to die for them. Everything here is delightful and lovely." France, he declared ecstatically, was a land of the gods. Dining occasionally at Versailles, he was impressed by the goodness of the King and the beauty of the Queen, but his contacts with the court were perfunctory. "They send the King out

[1] See Krauel: *Prinz Heinrich von Preussen in Paris.*

hunting," wrote Frederick, "to shield him from your influence and out of deference for the court of Vienna." After all, Marie Antoinette was the sister of the Emperor and the visitor was no friend of Austria.

Frederick wished to discover whether France, whose relations with Austria had cooled since the end of the Seven Years' War and had become little more than a memory since the War of the Bavarian Succession, was inclined to a rapprochement with Berlin. Prussia was no longer tied to Russia, and the French Government disapproved the Emperor's attempt to coerce the Dutch into opening the Scheldt. Calonne, the Finance Minister, informed Henry that the French Government would not tolerate the oppression of the Dutch and would be prepared to concert measures with the King of Prussia. The threat of Franco-Prussian co-operation sufficed and Joseph abandoned his designs against the Dutch. Henry was flattered by these marks of confidence, which pointed to the rapprochement on which he had set his heart ever since the Seven Years' War. Frederick, whose suggestion of a defensive alliance had been courteously declined in the previous year, warned him not to take the friendly words of his hosts too seriously, since Marie Antoinette's influence was intact and France would be a weak and unreliable ally. Moreover he still hoped for a change of policy in Russia when Paul should succeed his mother, a possibility that the traveler declined to consider. Henry found no disposition to general commitments, and Frederick, having no great expectations, was not disappointed. "There will be nothing doing unless the Emperor breaks the windows or attacks the Turks or some ally of France, and the credit of the Queen will be strong enough to affect the nerves of ministers even if one of them might chance to have the right ideas. So we must limit ourselves to keeping the court in good humor with the Prussians; to count on them would be a mistake." Since Frederick's health was known to be failing, Henry's potential influence over his heir was rated so highly that Louis XVI sponsored a substantial loan from a French bank to the distinguished visitor.

Politics apart, the old monarch took the liveliest interest in his brother's visit. "To know Paris well is to know the whole kingdom. It is the headquarters of all the higher nobility, the home of the sciences, the center of government, I might say the pineal gland of this great empire. For myself the only suitable journey is to the Elysian Fields; but as the couriers are not so well organized between that unknown country and ours as between Paris and Berlin, any reports I might make would not reach their address. What a come-down to exchange Paris for Potsdam, where you will find an old dotard who has already sent part of his heavy luggage ahead! There you have seen statuary, heard operas, listened to famous academicians. Here you will see a worn-out body whose memory is nearly gone and who will bore you with his prattle. But do not forget that this old fellow cares more for you than do all the *beaux esprits* at Paris." Yet Henry had immensely enjoyed the change from his hermit life at Rheinsberg. "I have spent half my life wishing to see France," he wrote to an old French friend, "and now I shall spend the other half regretfully looking back." The traveler presented his brothers with copies of the fine bronze bust made by Houdon during his sojourn in the capital.

The last year of the reign was disturbed by the Emperor's renewed attempt to add Bavaria to his dominions in return for the cession to the Elector of the Austrian Netherlands with the title of King of Burgundy. At the first attempt the Tsarina, still the ally of Prussia, had resisted his ambitions; now the alliance with Potsdam was a memory and she favored the plans of Vienna. When Frederick complained that France, a guarantor of the Treaty of Westphalia, was neglecting her duties, Henry displayed his usual dislike of risks. Joseph, he declared, would not go to war for Bavaria; France would not accept the exchange unless the Prince of Zweibrücken received a satisfactory equivalent and unless Prussia and the other princes of the Empire agreed. Since Prussia was too weak to challenge Austria and Russia, it was vital to win over France. The French court, he admitted, was lukewarm, but it had to recognize the situation. "One must handle her with consideration as the doctor handles a patient whose weak nerves he spares till suitable remedies have restored his strength." He criticized the League of Princes on the ground that it was unnecessary, that it would be displeasing to France, that a French alliance would be much more useful, that Prussia was no longer tied to Russia, and that the French Government disapproved the Emperor's attitude to the Dutch and the Turks. There was another reason at the back of his mind. He hoped that sooner or later Prussia might possess not only the southern shore of the Baltic from the Elbe to the Vistula but the German states through which the Elbe flowed, and for that reason he disapproved the idea of a permanent League of Princes, including some that he hoped would fall to his house.

The letters of the brothers during the King's last two years are largely concerned with his physical infirmities. The tone is friendly enough but there is little warmth in the autumn air. Henry can hardly be blamed for not loving the man or not desiring his life to be prolonged, but a nobler nature would have displayed more magnanimity. His hostile annotations on the *Histoire de la Guerre de Sept Ans* were not for the public eye; but in 1791, five years after the death of the King, he erected a War Memorial at Rheinsberg in honor of his brother August Wilhelm and the officers who distinguished themselves in the three Silesian wars which tells its own tale. For the name of the principal hero of that epic struggle we look in vain, and his friends Winterfeldt and La Motte Fouqué are also conspicuous by their absence. "I have recalled the names of those unmentioned by the great Frederick in his lying memoirs," he explained. Of his Francophil activities during the reigns of Frederick William II and Frederick William III and of his fruitless efforts to secure the political influence denied him by his brother this is not the place to speak. He died in 1802 at the age of seventy-six and is buried at Rheinsberg, ever dearer to his heart than Potsdam or Berlin. Despite the gifts of birth and fortune, he had been throughout life too thin-skinned, too self-centered, too jealous of his elder brother, too dissatisfied with his opportunities and rewards, to be accounted an enviable or even a happy man.

Chapter XII

THE *ANTIMACHIAVEL*

During his crowded life Frederick found time to produce not merely elaborate histories, essays, and poems, but solid treatises on the problems of government. His earliest political confession of faith, the remarkable "letter" of February 1731 to Natzmer, his Gentleman of the Chamber, reveals the precocity no less than the ambition of the nineteen-year-old prisoner of Küstrin. His system, he explains, envisages peace and friendly relations between the King of Prussia and his neighbors. Since his territories sprawl across Europe he must naturally keep on good terms with all kings, the Emperor and the principal electors. War could bring him no advantage; he is too much shut in, his possessions are too scattered, he could be attacked from more than one quarter, and his efforts to defend himself everywhere would leave him no forces to take the offensive. This consideration, however, in no way rules out aggrandizement; on the contrary, fragmentation suggests consolidation. The recovery of Prussian Poland, formerly in possession of the Teutonic Knights, would connect Pomerania with East Prussia and establish a hold over the Poles by controlling their exports to the Baltic. Next on the list comes Hither Pomerania, which would be a most welcome acquisition. When combined with the portion of Pomerania already in Prussian hands, it would bring a large increase of revenue, form a bulwark against Swedish insults, liberate a considerable force now needed to defend the Peene frontier, and open the way to the occupation of Mecklenburg when the ducal line became extinct. "I always advance from country to country, from conquest to conquest, selecting, like Alexander, new worlds to conquer." The next item is Jülich and Berg, so necessary to terminate the isolation of Cleves and Mark. The combination of these little western states would allow of a garrison of thirty thousand men, and enable their ruler to defy the insults to Cleves, which might be said to belong to Prussia only while France allowed it. After unification the countries would be able to de-

283

fend themselves. Silesia, it is interesting to note, is not mentioned in this juvenile program.

In setting forth his projects, adds the Crown Prince, he made no reference either to the legal rights of the house of Brandenburg to these provinces or to the means of securing them. He only desired to prove the political necessity and duty of every wise minister to pursue these aims. "I hope too that all I have said will seem reasonable, for in due time the King of Prussia could cut a fine figure among the great ones of the earth, giving or preserving peace only from love of justice, not from fear, and, if the honor of the house and country demand war, being able to wage it with vigor, fearing no enemy except the anger of heaven, which need not be apprehended while piety and the love of justice prevail in the country over irreligion and faction, avarice and interest. I hope that this house of Prussia will raise itself high above the dust in which it has lain, so that it may cause the Protestant religion to flourish in Europe and the Empire, that it may be the resource of the afflicted, the support of widows and orphans, the friend of the poor, the enemy of the unjust. If it were changed, if injustice, religious indifference, partiality, or vice should prevail over virtue, which God forbid, I wish its fall to be quicker than its rise."

Frederick's first political treatise, *Considérations sur l'état présent du corps politique de l'Europe,* written in 1738 at the age of twenty-six but not published till after his death, assumes that princes aggrandize themselves up to the limit of their power. His reading of human nature is not flattering. Men are the same in all times and countries, the same passions and inclinations leading inevitably to the same results. Princes have two common weaknesses: ambition and laziness. "The policy of great monarchies has never varied. Their fundamental principle has been ceaseless aggrandizement; their wisdom has consisted in anticipating the stratagems of their enemies and in winning the contest of wits." The peace of Europe, which depends on a just equilibrium of the leading powers, is continually threatened by these vaulting ambitions. Most princes believe that their subjects are expressly created for their grandeur and their pride, mere instruments of their unruly passions. Hence the cult of false glory, the instinct of aggression, the severity of taxation, the idleness, pride, injustice, inhumanity, tyranny of the ruler. If he would trace the authority of his house back to its source he would see that the elevation of its first member was the work of the people, and that the thousands committed to his charge did not enslave themselves to an individual in order to increase his power or to become the victims of his caprice. On the contrary they chose the man whom they thought the most just, the most paternal, the most humane, the most capable of defending them against their enemies, the most prudent in avoiding ruinous wars. If this principle were accepted, princes would avoid the two shoals that have at all times caused the shipwreck of empires—measureless ambition and cowardly neglect of their duties. Here is the gospel of the Social Contract, though neither this nor any other of Frederick's political dissertations admits the right of the people to resist their ruler if he becomes the scourge instead of the father of his people. The moral obligation to do his duty is explicitly recognized, but it is left in the air since no sanction is supplied. The omission is the more significant since he is a merciless critic of the performances of princes past and present.

In addition to these academic reflections and platitudes the essay deals with concrete issues in a practical spirit, and it is here that its *raison d'être* is to be sought.[1] A letter to Voltaire in April 1738 explains that Frederick had once intended to print it anonymously in England as the work of an Englishman in order to mobilize British opinion against France; for France is the villain of the piece. Her land hunger at the expense of Germany and the Netherlands is hotly denounced, and she is charged with aiming at universal monarchy. This ambition was the more dangerous to Germany since Austria was striving to rob the Empire of its freedom of election by making the Imperial crown hereditary in the house of Hapsburg. Whereas the ambition of Louis XIV was so blatant that it aroused widespread antagonism, Fleury lulled suspicion by a veneer of gentleness. Yet he had taken Lorraine and would soon get more. France, like ancient Rome, interfered in everything, and the disunion of her possible opponents, including the princes of the Reich, made her the arbiter of European disputes. To whom, then, could one look for the maintenance of the European equilibrium by resisting her power? To England and Holland, is the reply, aided where

[1] See *"Eine Flugschrift des Kronprinzen Friedrich,"* in Duncker: *Aus der Zeit Friedrichs des Grossen und Friedrich Wilhelms III.*

possible by the states of northern Germany. There is no direct criticism of his father's policy, but the author clearly disapproves the co-operation with and subordination to Austria practiced by the first two Prussian Kings. Prussia had been looking forward to the reversion of the duchies of Jülich and Berg, but Austria had broken her word. Having promised support of her claims as a reward for recognizing the Pragmatic Sanction, the Emperor proceeded to whittle down his obligations not only by eliminating first the Duchy of Jülich and then Düsseldorf, the capital of the Duchy of Berg, but also by championing the rival claims of the Sulzbach branch of the family of the Elector Palatine to both duchies. The truth of the matter, as the author saw it, was that neither France nor Austria desired the strengthening of a Protestant state. For this very reason, he argues, Protestant England and Holland should support the claims of Prussia. Yet here again there were difficulties, for the Elector of Hanover was jealous of the Elector of Brandenburg, and Holland disliked the prospect of seeing East Frisia and its port at Emden in Prussian hands. Despite such local rivalries the author appealed to the larger interests at stake, and his appeal for Anglo-Prussian co-operation against the designs of France and Austria anticipates the grouping of the Seven Years' War.

A year later, in 1739, Frederick informed Voltaire that he was meditating a treatise on *The Prince*. *L'Antimachiavel* was completed in 1740, sent to Voltaire for revision, and published anonymously at The Hague in September 1740, soon after his accession and shortly before he marched into Silesia.[1] The original version, which differs in many details, was included a century later in the eighth volume of the *Œuvres*. The preface strikes the lofty moral note that is sustained throughout. Machiavelli, the corrupter of politics and the enemy of sound morality, had been denounced by certain moralists, but his authority remained unimpaired. "I venture to undertake the defense of humanity against this monster who desires to destroy it, to oppose reason and justice to sophistry and crime. I have always regarded *The Prince* as one of the most dangerous books in the world, for an ambitious young

[1] Frederick's views on the relations between politics and morals are fully analyzed in Meinecke's classical work: *Die Idee der Staatsräson*. His theory and practice are also illustrated in Paul Dubois: *Frédéric le Grand d'après sa correspondance politique*.

man, too immature to distinguish good from evil, may only too easily be led astray by maxims that flatter his passions. That is bad enough in a private individual; it is far worse in reigning princes, who should set an example to their subjects, and by their goodness, magnanimity, and mercy, be the living images of deity. The passions of kings are worse than flood, pestilence, and fire, for their consequences are more lasting." To the plea that the Florentine tempter described what princes do, not what they ought to do, he rejoins that there have been plenty of good ones.

The critic begins by recalling the objects for which rulers were instituted—namely, the protection and well-being of the community. In view of this contract the sovereign, far from being the absolute master, is merely the first servant—*le premier domestique*—of the people. In recognizing his specific obligations to his subjects, Frederick sides with Locke against Hobbes, but he differs from the former on a much more vital issue. The philosopher of the Glorious Revolution approved resistance when the breach of contract was deliberate and notorious. Hobbes forbade it, however grievous the provocation. Frederick, with the long tradition of Continental absolutism in his bones, preaches neither resistance nor passive obedience but tacitly assumes compliance with the ruler's will. Prussia lacked representative institutions and political experience, and the press never raised fundamental issues. No German publicist in the first half of the eighteenth century hoisted the banner of self-determination, and had he done so, no one would have rallied to his call. There are three legitimate ways of becoming master of a country, declares Frederick—succession, election, or as the result of a just war. Usurpers are criminals and have no rights. Hereditary monarchy is the easiest system to work, for the ties between ruler and people are most numerous. "A contented people will not think of revolt, for its prince is its benefactor, and the sovereign fears no diminution of his power. The Dutch would never have risen against the Spaniards if their tyranny had not been so flagrant." That there are limits to human endurance is recognized in this and other passages, but the logical consequences of the admission are ignored.

Machiavelli, we are reminded, lived in a semi-barbarous age when conquests were held to be glorious, but in his advice on the methods of preserving them he was worse than his contemporaries: he even recommended the extermination of the defeated dynasty. Since then there had been some improvement. If among Christian peoples there were now fewer revolutions it was because the principles of sound morality were beginning to spread. Men had grown more cultivated and less ferocious, perhaps owing to the writers who gave Europe polish. National temperament, of course, differs widely, and the restless frivolity of the French makes them peculiarly liable to revolutions. The size of a state is of far less importance than the number and enterprise of its inhabitants, as is shown by the contrast between Russia and Holland. Cæsar Borgia, the model of Machiavelli, was not only a conqueror but an assassin and a poisoner, "the most abominable monster ever vomited out of hell." Though the rule of such devils in human form is the worst of all political systems, republics suffer from different yet deadly faults. The republican, inordinately jealous of his liberty, resents all limitations and revolts against the very idea of a master. Many republics have fallen back into despotism, and such appears to be the fate of them all. "For how can a republic forever resist all the causes that sap its liberty? How can it always repress the ambition of the grandees within its bosom? How can it in the long run control the intrigues of its neighbors and the corruption of its members while interest alone counts among men? Republics are formed, flourish for a few centuries, and perish by the audacity of a citizen or the arms of their enemies." Empires and great monarchies also have their day; but republics can never be unmindful of their fragility, and they regard every powerful family as the germ of the malady that will bring them down.

Frederick's estimate of human nature, though never flattering, was somewhat higher in his youth than in his riper years. To Machiavelli's argument that goodness in this wicked world spells catastrophe he rejoins that to avoid disaster one must be good and prudent. Accepting the paramountcy of interest, he gives it a different interpretation. Men are as a rule neither all good nor all bad, but they will all accept a powerful, just, and skillful prince. "The good king will be well served." No good ruler had been dethroned in England by large armies, and the bad ones had succumbed to rivals who started out with a limited force. "Do not be wicked with the wicked, then, but be virtuous and intrepid with them. You will make your people virtuous like yourself, your neighbors will imitate you, and the wicked will tremble." Discipline is needed for the army, but severity should never sink into cruelty. "I should rather, on the day of battle, be loved than feared by my soldiers." The fashion of revolutions seemed to have died out. In England alone had the King any ground for apprehension, and even there he had nothing to fear unless he himself raised the storm. A cruel prince is most likely to be betrayed, for cruelty is insupportable. Perfidy, another instrument recommended by the oracle of tyrants, is equally unwise, for people cannot be duped more than once.

At this point the preacher leaves the pulpit. There are painful necessities, he admits, when a prince cannot avoid breaking treaties and alliances. Even in such regrettable emergencies he must act *"en honnête homme,"* giving his allies notice and above all never proceeding to such extremities unless compelled by the safety of his peoples and dire necessity. These elastic conditions would have satisfied the author of the *Prince,* who proclaimed the gospel of *raison d'état,* not as a cynic mocking at virtue, but as a historian and publicist deeply convinced that it was the only chance for a state to survive. After this damaging admission of exceptions the reader may well feel that the author of *L'Antimachiavel,* despite his loud professions of superior morality, is engaged in a sham fight.

The final chapter, which deals with the problem of just and unjust wars, carries us still further away from the maxims of the Sunday school. "War is a resource in emergency, only to be employed in desperate cases and after careful consideration whether one is motived by pride or by a solid reason." There are wars of defense, wars of interest, and wars of precaution. The first are naturally the most just. The second must be waged when kings have to preserve contested rights; they plead with arms in their hands and battles decide. Wars of precaution are offensive but are not the least just. "When the excessive greatness of a power seems ready to overflow and threatens to engulf the universe, it is the path of prudence to make dikes and to arrest the violent course of a torrent while still under control. One sees the gathering clouds and the lightning that heralds the storm. The sovereign whom it menaces, unable to avert it alone, should unite all threatened by a common peril. Since the lesser evil is to be preferred, it is better for a prince to enter on an offensive war while he can choose between war and peace rather than to wait till the situation is desperate and a declaration of war could only postpone enslavement and ruin by a few moments. Thus all wars are just that aim at resisting usurpers, maintaining legitimate rights, safe-guarding the liberty of the universe, and warding off the oppression and violence of ambitious men. Sovereigns who wage such wars need not reproach themselves for the shedding of blood. Necessity compels them to act, and in such circumstances war is a lesser evil than peace." Not a word of this justification of the hypothetical right and duty of rulers to launch an offensive would have needed alteration had the King desired to justify the seizure of Silesia in 1740 or the decision in 1756 to open the Seven Years' War by getting his blow in first.

The ideological difference between the monarch and the publicist was that, while the former proclaimed the right to do everything for the sake of his state, the latter encouraged the prince to think first of himself. Yet Frederick was unjust to Machiavelli, who was not a monster delighting in iniquity but a thoughtful patriot. His political doctrine ripened in an Italy divided into fragile little states in which many of the princes, like the priests of Nemi, had snatched power from wily competitors and were compelled to trust to their wits. Their life was a constant struggle not only against envious rivals without but against foes within. Inheriting an uncontested title and an obedient, illiterate, and mainly agricultural people, the author of *L'Antimachiavel* failed to visualize the feverish atmosphere of the city states of Renaissance Italy. Since there was no tradition of revolution in his territories and no one ever dreamed of revolt, the ruler, fortified by his sense of personal safety, could devote his whole energies to the welfare of his people. The shrill invective loses its effect when we realize that it rests to a large extent on a misunderstanding. Moreover, in the sphere of foreign affairs there is little difference between the two, for the Crown Prince, who begins his treatise as a strait-laced moralist, ends by encouraging the ruler to make war whenever he thinks fit.

Chapter XIII

THE POLITICAL TESTAMENTS

THE two Political Testaments, the first written in 1752, the second in 1768, were first published in full by Volz in 1920, when at last dynastic secrets could be safely revealed. The title was probably taken from that of a similar exposition attributed to Richelieu, a copy of which was in the library at Sans Souci. They contain a comprehensive survey of the machinery and duties of government based on Frederick's experience as the ruler of a small, poor, and scattered state. They would have been read with satisfaction by his father, whose own Political Testament, published in the third volume of the *Acta Borussica,* anticipates them not only in spirit but often in phraseology. Though a man of great physical strength and an indefatigable worker, Frederick William I was subject to serious illnesses, and in 1722, at the age of thirty-three, the thought of death impelled him to draft a striking exhortation to his successor, a delicate child of ten. The Puritan monarch begins with a confession of faith. "I am at peace with Almighty God. Since my twentieth year I have put my whole trust in God. I have continually besought Him mercifully to hear me, and He has heard my prayer." Rulers who have God before their eyes and do not keep mistresses will receive abundant blessing. Plays and operas, ballets and fancy balls, gluttony and drunkenness are frowned on, though here the King, who loved comedies and liquor, often failed to live up to his precepts.

The royal author deals first with the army, and threatens the loss of his blessing if his son should reduce military expenditure. Having made it equal in effective strength to the forces of much larger powers, he exhorts him to maintain its well-being and discipline unimpaired. For this purpose he must devote equal attention to the finances of the state. "You alone must superintend the revenue and keep the supreme command of the army firmly in your hands. Officers and officials must know that you hold the purse-strings." On coming to the throne the heir should reduce all official salaries by about twenty-five per cent, but not the sum allotted to the army; after a year he may restore the salaries of those who are doing their duty. More important than anything else is the example of the monarch himself. "You must work as I have always done. A ruler who wishes to rule honorably must attend to all his affairs himself, for rulers are ordained for work, not for idle, effeminate lives such as, alas, are led by most great people." In the economic field Frederick William I is naturally a mercantilist. Population is wealth. Towns must be founded, textile and other industries established. "A country without industries is a body without life, always poor and wretched. Therefore I beg you, my dear successor, maintain the industries, establishing them wherever possible throughout the country."

The heir is urged not to raise loans but to save a fixed annual sum. He should travel through every province once a year to see that everything is in order. Churches and schools should be built. Calvinists and Lutherans must not be allowed to quarrel, and Catholics, excepting the Jesuits, should be tolerated, but foreign Jews should not be allowed to enter the country as settlers. The document ends with a proud survey of the work achieved. "When my father died in 1713, I found the province of Prussia almost at its last gasp with plague and murrain, most of the domains mortgaged, all of which I have redeemed, and the finances in such a plight that bankruptcy was imminent, the army in so bad a way and so low in numbers that its shortcomings baffle description. It is surely a masterly feat to have restored order once more in all affairs of state in nine years. Your task, my dear successor, is to keep what your forefathers have begun and to win the territories claimed by us which belong to our house by the laws of God and men. Pray to God and never begin an unjust war, but never relinquish what is justly yours." At what date these maxims came into his son's hands we cannot tell, but we may safely assume that they were carefully studied and taken to heart.

The primary duty of a citizen, explains Frederick in the Introduction to the Political Testament of 1752, is to serve his country. He had tried to do so, and as the first magistrate he had the opportunity and the means of being useful to his fellow citizens. His love for them made him wish to render them service even after his death. He did not dream of assuming that his precepts or example would bind his successors; death destroyed man and his projects, and everything was subject to the laws of change. His only intention was to inform posterity what he had learned as a pilot in stormy seas, to indicate the shoals they should avoid and the harbors in which refuge could be found. Government turned on four principal points—justice, finance, the army, and policy. In the administration of justice he had found much to reform, and in Cocceji, his Grand Chancellor, he possessed an admirable colleague, convinced like himself that all laws should rest on natural equity. Injustice had in consequence become more rare, the judges were of higher character, the cases shorter, arrears few. Rulers should take the utmost care to appoint men like Cocceji to supervise, for they were entrusted with a portion of the sovereign's authority and held the fortunes of their fellow citizens in their hands. The author proclaims his resolve never to interfere in legal cases: "in the tribunals the laws must speak and the sovereign be silent." Silence, however, does not exempt him from the duty of watching the conduct of judges and denouncing them if they fail in their duty. Such cases should be sternly treated, for the sovereign becomes in some degree the accomplice in crimes that he fails to punish.

The discussion of finance is much more detailed, for here the ruler's duty is not merely to watch but to act. If a country is to be happy and a prince to inspire respect, he must keep his house in order. Poor governments never receive consideration. The Emperor Maximilian, whom the Italians called *Massimiliano senza denari,* was the laughing-stock of Europe. More recently the Emperor Charles VI left his state in such disorder that Maria Theresa was compelled to accept English subsidies, which made her the slave of King George and cost her the loss of fine provinces to Prussia and the King of Sardinia. This wise princess in consequence was now busily engaged in the work of repair. If France continued her unwise practices she too would be abased and despised by her rivals. What was true of other countries was particularly applicable to Prussia, which possessed neither colonies, nor rich companies, nor a bank, nor many other resources at the disposal of France, England, and Spain. Even in an emergency only a small internal loan could be raised. The prince could increase his revenues, not by imposing new taxes, but by stimulating the productivity of the soil and developing industry. The whole of the year's revenue should not be spent, and the treasury should be ready to at any time to support a four years' war and to confront any calamity. The discussion closes with reflections on the duty of the sovereign. He must show his love and care for his people by remissions, by lightening burdensome taxes, by sustaining the privileges of the nobility and the towns, by punishing functionaries who abuse their position. He must be on guard against plausible planners. There was not a ruler in Europe who had not been duped by these rascals, the King of Poland most of all.

The discussion of policy, the third of the four departments of state, opens with the declaration that the ruler must know his people—whether gentleness or severity is needed, whether they are inclined to revolts and intrigues, what talents they possess. "Speaking broadly, the inhabitants of [East] Prussia are intelligent and supple. They are accused of being false, but I do not believe they are falser than others. Many have served and are serving with distinction in military and civil duties, but I cannot accuse anyone I know of falsity." The Pomeranians are the best subjects for war or peace, but they are too outspoken for delicate negotiations. The nobility of the Electorate [Brandenburg] is pleasure-loving, lacking the intelligence of the Prussians and the solidity of the Pomeranians. The Silesians are backward, disinclined to work, and unfriendly to the government, since they are Catholics and most of their relatives are under Austrian rule. The inhabitants of Cleves are placed at the bottom of the list— "muddle-headed fools, conceived when their fathers are drunk, without either natural or acquired talents." On the whole the nobility have a good record of service; their fidelity and merit deserve protection. "In this state there are no factions or risings to fear. Gentle treatment suffices, and it is only certain gentlemen and ecclesiastics in Silesia who work for the enemy as spies. Severity is rarely needed if care is taken in the choice of men. Few are born without talents."

One of the most serious problems for the ruler is that of the Churches. Frederick notes with satisfaction that Catholics, Lutherans, Calvinists, Jews, and other sects live peaceably together in his dominions. Excessive zeal on his part for one or other of them would speedily provoke controversies, persecutions, and the emigration of useful citizens. It is all the same whether a ruler is himself religious. "All religions, when one looks into them, rest on a system of fable more or less absurd." No one of good sense who studies the matter can fail to see the errors, yet these errors and prejudices must be treated with respect so as not to shock believers. Jews are the most dangerous sect because they injure the business of Christians and are useless to the state. They are needed for a certain class of commerce in Poland, but their numbers must not be allowed to increase and they must not meddle in big business. The Catholics in Silesia enjoy religious freedom, but to prevent the convents from endangering the increase of population, no vows must be taken before the citizen comes of age. The curés are fairly good folk, and the monks are less Austrophil. They have to pay thirty per cent of their revenues, so that they are of some use. The Silesian Jesuits, the most dangerous of priests, are fanatically Austrophil. "I am in a way the pope of the Lutherans and the head of the reformed churches. The other Christian sects are all tolerated here. One shuts the mouth of the first that wishes to stir up civil war. I am neutral between Rome and Geneva. In this way I can diminish religious hatreds by preaching moderation to all parties, and I try to unite them by reminding them that they are all citizens." While striving to keep on good terms with the Pope, he advised his successors not to trust the Catholic clergy without proofs of their fidelity.

Princes of the blood—"a sort of amphibious species neither sovereign nor subject and sometimes difficult to manage"—are dismissed with contempt. Their lofty birth generates a pride that renders obedience insupportable and restrictions odious. If there is some intrigue on foot, it is probably due to them. In Prussia they can do less than anywhere else. But the best plan is promptly to suppress the first who raises the standard of independence, to treat them with all the distinction due to their birth, to load them with external honors, but to exclude them from public affairs and only to entrust them with command of troops when they are talented and trustworthy. "What I say of princes applies equally to princesses, who should never, under any pretext, mix themselves up in government." Frederick never thought very much of any woman except Wilhelmina.

The survey of domestic policy closes with a plea for enlightened autocracy. In a state like Prussia the prince must be the actual ruler. If he is wise he will pursue exclusively the public interest, which is also his own. While a minister is liable to be swayed by selfish considerations and to promote his protégés, the sovereign will support the nobility, keep the clergy in their place, prevent the princes of the blood from intriguing, and reward genuine merit. Even more essential is it that he should control foreign policy, making alliances when necessary, forming designs and making decisions in delicate situations as they arise. Finance, administration, policy, and the army are so indissolubly connected that one cannot be handled without the rest. If this is forgotten the ruler suffers. In France, for instance, four ministers run the kingdom—those of finance, the army, the navy, foreign affairs. These four kings never co-operate, hence all the contradictions we observe. "One upsets out of jealousy what another has cleverly constructed; no system, no plan; chance rules. Everything is decided by court intrigues; the English know everything that is being discussed at Versailles; no secrecy and therefore no policy. A well-conducted government must have a system as coherent as a system of philosophy, so that finance, policy, and the army are co-ordinated to the same end: namely, the consolidation of the state and the increase of its power. Such a system can only emanate from a single brain, that of the sovereign. Idleness, pleasure-seeking, and imbecility are the causes that keep princes from the noble task of securing the happiness of their people. The sovereign is the first servant of the state."

The impressive discussion of foreign policy, which had been omitted when the rest of the work was published in the *Acta Borussica* in 1907, opens with a reminder that the Prussian Kingdom is not a compact whole. The core of the state and the source of its strength is the Electorate, Pomerania, Magdeburg, Halberstadt, and Silesia. [East] Prussia, which is separated from Pomerania by Polish territory, is the neighbor of Poland and Russia. The Duchy of Cleves and Frisia touch Holland. Silesia adjoins Bohemia, Moravia, and Hungary. The Electorate and Magdeburg partially surround Saxony. Pomerania borders on Swedish Germany. Prussia is the neighbor of Europe's greatest princes, all of them jealous or secret enemies. Writing shortly after the War of the Austrian Succession, Frederick pronounces the house of Austria the most ambitious of them all. "The pride of the Emperor descends from father to son in this Imperial race. The longing to enslave Germany, to extend the limits of its domination, and to establish its family is the basis of all its plans. Of all powers it is the one to which we have given the greatest offense, and which will never forgive the loss of Silesia and of portions of its authority in Germany." For the moment its policy was to reconstitute the army and the finances, to procure allies, and to keep the peace till all arrangements for another round were complete. Austria was to Frederick what France was to Bismarck and Bülow—the irreconcilable foe.

Other powers are judged with slightly less severity. The King of England envisages Europe from the standpoint of his Electorate. His hatred of Prussia arose partly from old quarrels between the Ministries of Hanover and Berlin, partly from jealousy of his neighbor's growing strength. These animosities between two dynasties, however, would end with the death of George II; for his grandson, born and educated in England, would care less for his German heritage and would probably prefer the advice of English counselors. Russia should not be reckoned among Prussia's real foes: she was an accidental enemy, for there had been no disputes between them. Her policy was to retain her influence over Poland, to preserve tolerable relations with the house of Austria in order to secure its aid against a sudden Turkish attack, and so far as possible to influence affairs in northern Europe. France, on the other hand, was one of Prussia's most powerful allies. A feeble monarch believed himself to be her ruler, whereas his ministers left him power only in name. A greedy mistress (the Pompadour) and thieving officials piled up the debt. Business was neglected in the country whose god was pleasure. The vivacious French only acted by fits and starts. When they wished for something they wished intensely, but they quickly cooled and swung over to the opposite view. Yet despite all these abuses France was the most powerful kingdom in Europe. Her permanent interest was to abase the house of Austria, to uphold the prerogatives of the princes of the Empire, to diminish English commerce, to support the interests of Spain. She dreamed of extending her frontiers to the Rhine. In negotiating with her one must be on one's guard, for she strove to place the heaviest burdens on her allies, the lightest on herself. Poland retained the old feudal government that the other powers had abolished. Her neighbors, whose interest it was to keep this republican monarchy in its anemic state, supported the independence of the grandees against the ambition of their kings. Divided internally between two powerful parties, she was a danger to nobody, and her neighbors were practically safe from attack since nothing was easier than to split the Diet.

The Holy Roman Empire, continues Frederick, was less united than ever. The Emperor's authority was very limited. The ecclesiastical princes were attached to the house of Austria, to whom they owed their elevation, but the secular princes looked to France. "To the shame of my nation I must confess that the public interest has never been more sacrificed to personal interest than today. A King of England crosses the sea with a bag of guineas, and modest sums suffice to corrupt the most powerful princes of the Empire. They have become merchants, trafficking in the blood of their subjects, selling their votes. I believe they would sell their persons if they found a buyer." Prussia had never been base enough to receive subsidies except under Frederick I. "The power that accepts wages from another binds its hands and plays only a secondary part, for it is always dependent on its paymaster and is obliged at the peace to follow his lead." Among the smaller powers which receive brief notice, the Papacy is treated with least respect. "The Pope is an old neglected idol in his niche. He is at present the chief almoner of kings. His thunderbolts are no more. His policy is known. Instead of laying peoples under an interdict and deposing sovereigns as of old, he is content if no one deposes him and lets him say Mass quietly in St. Peter's."

In a Europe thus deeply divided, Prussia could always find allies, and in choosing them she should ignore likes and dislikes: state interest alone must decide. Her present interest, particularly since the acquisition of Silesia, was to co-operate with France and other enemies of the house of Austria. She must support her retention of Alsace and Lorraine, while France could not allow Austria to recover Silesia, which would weaken a valuable ally. This Franco-Prussian alliance was natural, for the policy of both powers had always been to oppose the aggrandizement of the emperors. Yet even if Sweden and many German princes were added to this partnership, he did not count on them, but on his own forces alone. "Whatever we may expect from war, my present system is to prolong peace so far as possible without sacrificing the dignity of the state, above all because France is in a total lethargy and her finances are too disordered to embark on hostilities." Moreover, there was no reason to renew the war. A coup such as the conquest of Silesia was like certain books—the originals were a success, the imitations a failure. "We have aroused the envy of Europe by the acquisition of that fine duchy, which has made all our neighbors prick up their ears. There is not one of them who does not distrust us." Further, would war suit Prussia while Russia stood in armed strength on her frontier, awaiting the moment to act though that would require English subsidies? It would be time for Prussia to move when the European landscape was more favorable, though even then it would be best to wait till the others were exhausted. Her finances could only stand three or four years of war. Cardinal Fleury's maxim that the winner is he who has the last crown in his pocket should be kept in mind.

An experienced statesman should pursue an elastic policy. If a ruler's conduct is uniform his enemies can predict his course; if he varies it they have to guess. The great art is to conceal one's designs. If one has many enemies one must divide them, concentrate on the most irreconcilable, negotiate with the others, lull them to sleep, make peace separately even at a disadvantage; when the chief foe is destroyed, there is always time to return and fall on the others on the pretext that they have broken their engagements. In addition to spies the ruler employs ambassadors to lull suspicions, to corrupt enemies, to discover the plans of neighbors, to make insinuations, to negotiate treaties and alliances. For this he needs supple, discreet, incorruptible men, capable of the most profound dissimulation. Different types of diplomat must be chosen for different capitals. For instance, "if we are on bad terms with the court of London a spy is enough; if on good terms, an agreeable debauchee should be sent who carries his wine better than the English and can hold his tongue."

Turning to what he calls *Rêveries Politiques* Frederick discusses possible increases of territory. The little states of Bayreuth and Anspach, ruled by branches of the Hohenzollern dynasty, would fall to Prussia if there were no heirs.[1] More important would be Saxony, Polish Prussia, and Swedish Pomerania. The first would be the most useful, and even a portion would be very welcome. "You may think that it is not enough to indicate our

[1] They did so in 1791.

desires, and that we must also suggest the means. Here they are. One must conceal the project, exploit favorable situations, and when they come, act with vigor." The conquest of Saxony would be facilitated if she were allied to the Queen of Hungary and broke with Russia. This would serve as a pretext to invade her and disarm her troops. France would be reassured by explaining the unwisdom of leaving such a powerful enemy on the flank. If Prussia were to wage war successfully with Austria and Saxony, Russia would have to be at war with Turkey, and it would be necessary to mobilize as many enemies of Vienna as possible so that Prussia would not have to meet the whole of the Austrian forces. When Saxony was subdued Moravia should be occupied. In the subsequent campaign a rising in Hungary should be encouraged, and then Bohemia could be conquered with ease. If England proved troublesome, French troops could keep Hanover quiet. At the ensuing peace France would secure Flanders, while Prussia would restore Moravia to the Queen of Hungary and exchange Bohemia for Saxony with the King of Poland. "I admit that this plan is impracticable without plenty of luck. But if it fails, so long as the secret is not divulged, there would be no disgrace, and it would be quite possible to detach a portion of Saxony." The chief point was that Russia and the Queen of Hungary should have war with Turkey, France, and the King of Sardinia on their hands. Here was an interesting anticipation of the campaign of 1756. Austria was enemy number one, Saxony the glittering prize, France the natural ally. That the last might change her tune and thereby place the owner of Silesia in mortal danger was beyond his range of vision in 1752.

Next to Saxony, Polish Prussia would be the chief prize, for if [East] Prussia were attacked by Russia, it could not be saved. "I do not think that arms are the best road to this acquisition, and I am tempted to quote the King of Sardinia: 'My son, the Milanese must be eaten like an artichoke, leaf by leaf.' " Poland was an elective kingdom, and when a king died the factions saw their chance: here was Prussia's opportunity. Her coveted neutrality might gain now a town, now a district, till it was all gobbled up. Forts on the Vistula would keep Russia at bay. Acquisitions by the pen were always preferable to those by the sword. They were less hazardous, and neither the finances nor the troops were ruined. In making this pacific conquest Danzig would have to be the last morsel, for it would shock the Poles, who exported their corn through it and would rightly fear the loss of economic independence through tariffs on her exports. Swedish Pomerania, a more difficult problem, could only be secured by diplomacy, perhaps by obliging Sweden in a war with Russia. These *rêveries politiques* were more than dreams, for within a generation after the author's death all three goals had been reached. "If this house produces great princes, if the army is kept up to the present standard, if the sovereigns economize in time of peace in order to finance war, if they know how to profit from events, I do not doubt that the state will continue to expand and that in time Prussia will become one of the most considerable powers of Europe." To the suggestion that the King of Prussia might one day become the Holy Roman Emperor the author rejoins that to acquire a province is more important than to decorate oneself with a vain title.

After a technical discussion of the organization of the army Frederick ends with a section on the Education of a Prince, which is colored by his own unhappy experience. The heir to the throne, he complains, is as a rule badly trained, partly because the ministers desire to keep him under their thumb. He is taught to consider himself a sort of divinity whose will is law and whose lofty station forbids him to descend to the level of ordinary mortals. Details, he is assured, are unworthy of his attention: *un fainéant heureux,* he is encouraged to live in timeless tranquillity, like the gods of Epicurus. He is tightly bound by etiquette and is taught to ask the advice of his governor about every trifle. Thus he grows up embarrassed in an unfamiliar world, distrustful of himself, timid, bored by work—in a word, a slave instead of a master. Ecclesiastics try to turn him into a superstitious bigot, treating his least action as a crime in order that his conscience, in perpetual fear of eternal flames, should be docile to their lead. A profound veneration for the priesthood is inculcated, a holy hatred against every religion except that in which they have brought him up. To interested ambitions of ministers and ecclesiastics are added the good intentions of his parents. "They wish their son to become a perfect mortal, not realizing that without passions he would be an imbecile." They cram him with miscellaneous erudition, either disgusting him with the sciences or making him a pedant. To reform his character they keep guard over his slightest desires. At fifteen they pretend that his mind is formed. They even assume that he falls in love at the moment his father decides and with the person chosen by him. From this education the pupil emerges as a mediocrity, and on his accession he is crushed by the burden of government. "That is what I have seen, and, if I except the Queen of Hungary and the King of Sardinia, all the other princes of Europe are merely illustrious imbeciles."

After these bitter reflections Frederick indicates the better way. Assuming the child to be normal, a governor must be chosen, both firm and gentle, who faithfully carries out the prescribed plan. All the other members of his entourage must be chosen with equal care in order that he receive the right impressions. Between six and twelve he should be taught the elements of ancient history and of the modern world since Charles V. In addition to storing his memory the teacher must appeal to his mind, inspiring him with the noble ambition to emulate great men and with indignation for lazy and criminal princes. Since the army is the foundation of the state, the child must be taught to love the profession of arms. In his presence it should be spoken of with the holy respect with which priests speak of their imagined revelation.

Since every mortal seems bound to commit follies, let the child pay his tribute and receive his punishment before he mounts the throne, when he owes an example of wisdom to his people. "Accordingly I desire that he should do what he likes; that his governor should not follow him everywhere, but should reprimand or punish him severely for his escapades so that he learns to control himself." If he loves hunting, music, dancing, cards, let him have his fill and get tired of them. "The principal aim of his entourage should be to form his heart, to render him grateful for services, tender to his friends, sympathetic with misfortune, filled with lofty sentiments and with the noble ambition that impels fine characters to rival their equals in merit. Above all I should like to see him made human, mild, inclined to clemency, and tolerant." Had the author himself enjoyed a gentler upbringing he might perhaps have approximated a little more closely to the ideal so eloquently recommended to his successors.

In the sphere of religion the prince must profess the reformed faith of his fathers and must know enough theology to recognize the Catholic cult as the most ridiculous of all. At thirteen he must receive lessons in ethics, physics, metaphysics, mathematics, fortification. He should pass through all the grades of the army. He should be trained without vanity and pomp like a private citizen, deriving from officers the sentiments of honor and probity particularly associated with the profession of arms. Let him have a little money at his disposal and keep his own accounts. "Men are almost always in little what they will be in full if they are masters." Fluent French is indispensable, Latin and Polish useful, but he should not be overburdened with languages. Let him mix with everybody and learn to know men, but he should be kept from dissolute company. On the other hand, all young people have lively passions and inclinations to debauchery. They should be treated with tolerance and even compassion in view of the violence of the passions that dominate them. "If I had a son I would pardon him a hundred adventures rather than a constant attachment. The former pass away, but those based on sentiment remain when the physical element weakens. All the mistakes of Henry IV were due to his extreme indulgence for his mistresses." At twenty the prince should be his own master, study constitutions, administration, the art of war, the European chessboard, diplomacy, the finances, industry, commerce, justice. The greatest triumph would be to give him a taste for reading, for in good books on politics, philosophy, history, war, literature, he grows and gains the knowledge he needs. In studying historical works he will become conscious of the judgment that posterity will one day pass on himself. He should command a regiment, visit every part of his dominions, and master every detail. He should not marry too young. In premature marriages the prince becomes tired of his wife, and the son, growing up while his father is still young, becomes impatient at having to wait so long for the throne. Twenty-five is early enough. Foreign travel is undesirable, not only because the heir to the throne might bring back prejudices and form extravagant habits, but because observant eyes might note his failings and turn them to account in years to come.

The Second Political Testament, composed in 1768 and covering the same ground as the first, reflects the anxious experiences of the Seven Years' War. In his new survey of the resources of the state Frederick laments the destruction of forests during the recent conflict, but, thanks to her army, Prussia survived. "Prussia is a land power; she needs a good army but not a fleet." Her Baltic ports were unfavorably situated for distant navigation. "If we have no colonies in Africa or America I congratulate my successors, for these distant possessions drain a mother country of population, require a large fleet for their preservation, and provide endless occasions for war, as if we had not plenty of the last already." These words might have been written by Bismarck a century later when the demand for colonies was growing too strong for him to resist.

The second characterization of the different provinces is enriched by the author's latest impressions. The nobility of East Prussia had disappointed him in the war, for they were more Russian than Prussian and were capable of all the baseness often attributed to the Poles. The citizens of Magdeburg, on the other hand, had collected money for the Pomeranians, who had been robbed and ravaged by the Russians. In the little principality of Minden the peasants came forward of their own free will to fight for their country, and what had the ancient Romans to show finer than that? The inhabitants of Silesia are chastised as vigorously in 1768 as in 1752. No reliance could be placed on the nobility, most of whom had family ties in Austria, or on the clergy and monks. At the approach of another war, suspects should be arrested and sent to Magdeburg or Stettin for the duration, in order to prevent treason and avert the need for sterner measures. The Austrians had stationed people in Silesia to serve as spies, and those under suspicion must be watched. The terrible ravages of the Thirty Years' War had not been fully repaired by his predecessors, and the Seven Years' War had brought almost equal desolation; but he had flung himself into the breach and by the utmost efforts everything had been restored.

The section on religion is even more contemptuous than in the First Political Testament. "An old metaphysical romance, filled with marvels, contradictions, and absurdity, born in the ardent imagination of Orientals, has spread into our Europe. Enthusiasts have purveyed it, careerists have pretended to accept it, imbeciles have believed it. The quacks had become sovereigns and Europe was once governed at their word. The theological pride and the despotic spirit then formed survive in all varieties of the priesthood, but the time when it meddled in all affairs of state is gone." The Lutheran and Reformed Churches in Prussia could never harm the state so long as their clergy were kept within the existing limits. They could do good to their hearts' content, but they were reined in if they tried to go beyond their sphere. The Catholics of Silesia and Cleves should be not merely tolerated but protected against all vexations and injustices. The metaphysical opinions of individuals were no concern of the state: it was enough if everyone conducted himself as a good citizen and patriot. These three religions could live in peace so long as none received preferential treatment. The fanaticism of the clergy in Silesia was visibly waning. The survey of domestic policy closes with warm tributes to the Great Elector, "who well deserved the name of Great, not only because he did everything himself, but because he rebuilt the state and laid the solid foundations of its greatness," and to Frederick William I, "who understood that to restore the state it was necessary to descend to the smallest details."

Passing to foreign affairs, the author reiterates the need of precise knowledge. He begins with Russia, the largest Empire in the world, on the morrow of a war in which the scales inclined to the side that received her support. At the moment her population was only nine millions, but she would be the most dangerous power in Europe as she developed her heritage. The Turks had a large army, but they were disinclined to war, and his efforts to unleash them against the Austrians in the recent conflict had failed. They were sunk in ignorance and inertia, while every other European people had progressed. Poland hardly counted, for the population was small, the landowners treated their dependents as slaves, the finances were in disorder, and the army consisted of 13,000 men. All the vices of the old feudal government lived on, the elective monarchy involving civil wars, tumultuous diets, no legislation, no justice; in a word, the reign of anarchy. Poland would have been subjugated long ago but for the jealousies of her neighbors. Torn by faction, she was always weak. The nobility was arrogant in prosperity, cowardly in misfortune, venal, incapable of vigorous action. "In one word, she is, in my view, the lowest nation of Europe." This sweeping denunciation, written on the eve of the First Partition of Poland, shows which way the wind was blowing.

Frederick always spoke of Maria Theresa with marked respect.

The house of Austria had gone downhill since Charles V, but it revived under Charles VI. After his death without male heirs, Europe believed that it was done for. "A woman raised it up again and firmly supported it. She became the idol of a nation hitherto seditious [Hungary], which she induced to fight for her interests." She had brought order into the finances; she possessed a large army and clever ministers; her council was superior to that of all other sovereigns in wisdom and system. She did everything herself. Like all other great princes she doubtless dreamed of extending her domination. The Emperor Joseph, her son and political pupil, had a strong instinct for economy, but some people attributed to him projects of aggrandizement, particularly the conquest of Bavaria when the Electoral house became extinct. "We must wait till he succeeds his mother in order to judge his character and designs."

France was temporarily pacific, since with her disordered finances a fresh campaign would spell bankruptcy. Spain was absolutely dependent on France. England was also on the verge of bankruptcy, for her debt exceeded the value of her Empire. In the recent war she had been mistress of the seas, while her armies won victories wherever they were employed; yet these advantages had been thrown away by concluding a precipitate peace. "Bute, the King's tutor, hitherto unknown in Europe, has become the Minister of his pupil. He flattered himself that he would be the idol of the nation in hurrying on the peace, but in so doing he sacrificed all England's allies and his conduct towards me was infamous." This man threw away all the advantages the English had gained by their valor, and created factions which destroy the consideration that England should enjoy with foreign powers. The real cause of trouble was the King's mother, who supported him and, in the event of his death, would place her first lover at the head of affairs. Though not particularly intelligent she would follow her instinct for intrigue to the day of her death. England had no system, and would have none till the nation forced the Ministry to break with France and Spain. "Yet we must not rashly conclude that England is in decline. If war breaks out, many ministers will be dismissed till a man of genius appears. The Tories, now in power, only care for commercial advantages, avoiding land wars and Continental alliances."

After surveying the other states of Europe, Frederick returns to the position and prospects of his own. France, England, Austria, and Russia were the four great powers. The object of France, in conjunction with Spain, was to undermine England's commerce and to grapple with her at the first opportunity. The house of Austria, after restoring its finances, hoped to renew the struggle for Silesia. Russia had designs on Poland. Since Austria was an irreconcilable foe and France was now her ally, and since England had not only abandoned Prussia but betrayed her, the latter had to ally herself with Russia. "The first concern of a prince is to maintain himself, the second to extend his territory. This demands suppleness and resource. What fails at the first attempt matures with time, and the way to hide secret ambitions is to profess pacific sentiments till the favorable moment arrives. That has been the method of all great statesmen, for any other course would give time to other people to forestall one's plans. The problem is to decide when one should launch what are called great strokes, a euphemism for duping others. Defenders of this procedure argue that in dealing with rascals there is no real choice, while others maintain that rascals discredit themselves. In my view one should depart from probity as little as possible. If one sees that another prince does not play fair it is certainly legitimate to pay him back in his own coin; and if a breach of engagements is ever excusable, it is when necessitated by the safety or the supreme interest of the state." Such disagreeable situations, however, can be avoided by careful consideration of the terms of an alliance before it is made. Even then allies must be carefully watched, and less reliance should be placed on them than on one's own strength. Someone may ask: What then is the good of allies? They are at any rate of negative value, for it is much to know that this or that great power will not make difficulties during a hazardous enterprise. The diplomatic corps must also be kept under the closest observation. "Distrust is the mother of security; it is allowed only to those who do not know men trust them."

A short *Essai sur les formes de gouvernement et sur les devoirs des souverains,* privately printed in 1771 for Voltaire and a few other friends,[1] adds nothing to the doctrine of the Political Testaments, but contains passages of personal interest. The longer he

[1] *Œuvres,* ix, 195–210.

lived the worse Frederick thought of his fellows. "Men are wicked; one must safe-guard oneself especially against surprise. European politics is so fallacious that the best advised can be duped if he is not always alert and on the watch." Once again he stresses the moral responsibility of the ruler. "He must often remind himself that he is a man like the least of his subjects—the first judge, the first general, the first financier, the first minister. He is only the first servant of the state, obliged to act with probity, wisdom, and entire disinterestedness, as if at any moment he had to render an account of his administration to the citizens. Since he is the head of a family, he must always be the last refuge of the unhappy, a father to the orphans, the succor of widows, caring for the meanest unfortunate as for the highest courtier."

If it be objected that such a sovereign never existed, though Marcus Aurelius approached most closely to the ideal, the author replies that he hopes his little essay may help to form such men. Even the hardest worker, he admits, can never reach perfection. "With the best will in the world he can make mistakes in the choice of his agents; he can be misinformed; his orders may not be punctually executed; injustices may never reach his ear; his officials may be too severe; in a word, the ruler of a large country cannot be everywhere. Such is and such will be the destiny of things on earth that man will never attain to the state of perfection required for the happiness of the peoples; and therefore in governing, as in everything else, we must be content with what is least defective." This closing paragraph is notable not only for its frank admission of the inevitable limitations of autocracy, but for its astonishing blindness to the possibility of alternatives such as constitutional monarchy or full self-government. Frederick was the greatest ruler of the age of the *Aufklärung,* but distant horizons were beyond his gaze. He thought of his subjects as Lord Curzon thought of the Indian peoples.

In 1782, four years before his death, the indefatigable monarch wrote a four-page Memorandum entitled *Considérations sur l'état politique de l'Europe,* which reveals a personal anxiety gnawing at his heart as the shadows began to fall. Frederick William, the heir, seemed to him and to everyone else as unfitted for the throne as the author had appeared to his father half a century before. "If, after my death, my nephew goes soft; if he takes no interest in things; if, extravagant as he is, he wastes public money; if he does not rally the spiritual forces of the people, I foretell that Monsieur Joseph will get him down, and that within ten years there will no longer be either a Prussia or a house of Brandenburg; that the Emperor, after having swallowed up everything, will end by dominating Germany, despoiling all the sovereign princes, and forming a monarchy like the French. I frame a thousand prayers that my forecast may be wrong, that my successors may do their duty like sensible beings, and that Fortune may avert the major part of the catastrophes by which we are threatened." No more annihilating criticism of his one-man system has ever been written than this septuagenarian's cry of distress.

The political treatises of Frederick the Great are the classic presentation of the doctrine of Enlightened Autocracy as practiced by the so-called Philosophic Despots. Here in all its clarity and resonance is the gospel of work, proclaimed by a man who scorned delights and lived laborious days. The ruling of a state is exhibited as the grandest and most onerous of human responsibilities. The prince must know everything and supervise everything. There is not only no nonsense about divine right, but no exaggerated dynastic pride. In his *History of the House of Brandenburg* he selects the Great Elector and his own father for special praise, but some of his other ancestors, particularly his grandfather, receive very low marks. Homage is paid not to their birth but to their work. Every ruler must justify himself by his acts. This was the assumption of the Cameralists, whose writings dominated political thought in Germany from the middle of the seventeenth to the end of the eighteenth century. Justi and his school accepted the absolute state as an axiom and discussed how best to satisfy its financial needs. It was the science of administration, not the science of politics or society. Even the sharpest critics of the abuses of feudalism and autocracy such as Schlözer and Moser never looked beyond the reform of the system, which lived on without serious challenge till the War of American Independence and the French Revolution encouraged German publicists to think on bolder lines.

The watchword of the ruler, according to Frederick, must be *L'État c'est moi,* and he must derive inspiration, not complacency, from the thought. His supreme duty is to maintain its vitality by the maximum development of its resources, the most thrifty administration, the maintenance of justice, the increase of its armed strength; for only a virile, disciplined, and so far as possible self-sufficing community can hope to survive in a world where conflict is the law of life. He must be the model citizen, teaching these lessons not by precept but by example. Frederick's system was better than any regime in Europe except where constitutional government prevailed, and it formed a bridge between feudalism and the modern democratic state. His genuine devotion to the welfare of his subjects shines through his pages, and in the conscientious discharge of the duties of administration he towered above his contemporaries. The Frederician monarchy, small though it was, earned something of the prestige that the France of Louis XIV had possessed in the seventeenth century.

The weakness of Enlightened Absolutism, as of all dictatorships dynastic or otherwise, was that its successful operation postulated an unbroken series of supermen; but Frederick II was the first and last of that species in the Hohenzollern family. The bow of Ulysses is useless if no one can stretch it, and what is just practicable in a small state becomes impossible in a large one. He was more of an autocrat than Louis XIV, for he was Commander-in-Chief as well as head of the state and head of the government, and none of his ministers was allowed the power enjoyed by Colbert and Louvois. How rapidly the imposing edifice crumbled away when the hand of the master-builder was withdrawn was revealed on the stricken field of Jena twenty years after his death. That the concentration of power could be pushed too far, that "everything for the people, nothing by the people," was a short-sighted slogan, was realized by Stein, Hardenberg, and Humboldt after the French Revolution liberated the spiritual energies of a great nation. That too much depended on the ruler and that the people might be a partner, even a junior partner, were hidden from his gaze, for he lacked the faith in human nature that enables nations to grow in stature. On one occasion in the last year of his life he spoke of the canaille. "Those who welcomed you yesterday on entering Breslau were not canaille," objected Garve. "Put an old monkey on horseback and drive him through the streets," retorted the King, "and they will come crowding to see it in the same way." He had distant glimpses of the *Rechtsstaat,* but he suggests no means of creating it if it does not exist or of preserving it if it does. Rulers come and go, and even a well-meaning monarch may degenerate. Autocracy and the rule of law are incompatible. Everything depends on the prince, and if he fails there is nothing to be done. "If ever a foolish prince ascends this throne," declared Mirabeau, "we shall see the formidable giant suddenly collapse and Prussia will fall like Sweden." Frederick thought as meanly of most rulers as of their subjects and he sensed the fragility of his edifice, yet he refused to draw the necessary conclusions. The supreme exponent of the theory and practice of benevolent despotism was essentially uncreative. The machine state, in outward appearance so strong, proved in unworthy hands as brittle as glass.

In the sphere of foreign relations Frederick's maxims are unfortunately much less out of date. He would have approved Palmerston's aphorism that England had no eternal enemies and no eternal friends—only eternal interests. A country must always be ready for war, offensive or defensive, and preparedness depends on the condition of the army and the finances. Diplomacy without armaments, he declared, is like music without instruments. The most difficult of the ruler's tasks is to conduct his country's relations with other states, for it is surrounded by jealous and greedy neighbors. The condition of survival is eternal vigilance. Full and up-to-date knowledge is required of the resources of every political unit in Europe, of the characteristics of their people, the temperament of their rulers, the political tradition, and the dominant aims. Few, if any, states are satisfied with their lot, for they wish either to enlarge their territory or to recover what they have lost. Since man is a fighting animal, peace is envisaged, not as the normal experience of a community, but as a precarious interval spent in recovering from the last round and preparing for the next.

Chapter XIV

THE HISTORICAL WRITINGS

FREDERICK's political and military achievements loom so large that his place among German historians is often overlooked. He is the only modern sovereign to have written detailed accounts of all his campaigns and to have discussed with considerable candor the most controversial features of his policy. His historical writings are much more than an elaborate apologia or a colorless record of events. No one can doubt his inner truthfulness, declares Koser, the oracle of Frederician studies. Impartial he was not, for no maker of history can be impersonal and detached in dealing with his own performances; but he was franker than Cæsar or Napoleon. His books are full of factual errors, for he complained of a bad memory; he trusted too much to his bulletins from the seat of war, often written at top speed and compiled with a purpose, and to the dispatches of his diplomatists, frequently based on imperfect knowledge. Yet no student of his character would care to exchange the portraits, personal touches, and reflections for a more accurate and lifeless survey.

His first historical venture, *Mémoires pour servir à l'histoire de la Maison de Brandebourg,* published in 1751, embodies material from the archives, and the later chapters are of great interest. After the First Silesian War he compiled a narrative of the struggle, nearly all of which has disappeared. After the second he revised the work, added a long Introduction, and called the whole work *Histoire de Brandebourg.* Only the former was given to the public, "for the use of our youth," after portions had been read to the Academy of Sciences as they were completed. The voluminous *Histoire de mon temps,* written at long intervals and covering the whole reign, was not intended for publication during his life. The purpose of the history of the Hohenzollerns is explained in three preliminary dissertations. The Dedicatory Letter to his brother and heir August Wilhelm declares that he has concealed nothing. "I have shown the princes of your house as they were. The same brush that has painted the civil and military virtues of the Great Elector has indicated the failings of the first King of Prussia. I have risen above all prejudice. I have regarded princes, kings, relatives as ordinary men. Far from being led astray by my position, far from idolizing my ancestors, I have boldly censured their vices, for vice should find no refuge on the throne. I have praised virtue wherever I found it, guarding myself against the enthusiasm it inspires so that truth pure and simple may prevail." After this parade of impartiality it is curious to find an extravagant eulogy of the mediocre heir. His brother, he declares, was worthy of his rank. He had coolly exposed his life in battle and subordinated all private interest to the welfare of the state. The gentleness and humanity of his character were the pledges of the happiness of his future subjects. The Preface and the Preliminary Discourse explain that, despite the multitude of historical works on the market, the story of Brandenburg had never been told. Having discovered this vacuum, he had endeavored to fill it. He had utilized the royal archives and had tried to tell the truth. The study of history was as useful to subjects as to princes. He had dealt very briefly with the early rulers, for the story only became important with John Sigismund, in whose reign East Prussia and Cleves were added to the state. The Thirty Years' War could not be ignored by any German or Prussian, for it continued to color affairs. The design of the house of Austria to establish despotism in the Empire had failed, and the Peace of Westphalia had restored the equilibrium between the ambition of the emperors and the Electoral College.

After a few arid pages on the first two centuries of Hohenzollern rule the historian begins his detailed narrative with George William, whose reign he describes as the darkest chapter in the annals of the dynasty. "His territories were desolated during the Thirty Years' War, the deep traces of which are visible to this day. All the plagues in the world broke over this ill-fated Electorate—a prince incapable of governing, a traitor for his Minister, a war or rather a universal cataclysm, invasion by both friendly and enemy troops equally thievish and barbarous like waves driven by a tempest, and finally pestilence that completed the desolation." The sack of Magdeburg, vividly described, was merely the worst of many horrors. "Though George William cannot be held responsible for all the misfortunes which befell his territories, his mistakes were numerous and costly. He trusted

Schwartzenberg, who betrayed him. An army of 20,000 men, which he could well afford, might have defended the country against violations of its neutrality. It would have secured him consideration from the Emperor, and he could have chosen whether to become the ally or the enemy of the Swedes instead of being the slave of the first comer. His weakness only left him a choice of errors. He had to choose between the imperialists and the Swedes, and his allies were always his masters. Sometimes, outraged by the harshness of Ferdinand II, he threw himself in despair into the arms of Gustavus Adolphus; at other times, exasperated by the projects of Oxenstierna, he sought aid from the court of Vienna. Powerless and in continual uncertainty, he always changed over to the strongest side; but he could offer too little to his allies to secure their protection against their common enemies." The sorry plight of his great-great-grandfather, faithfully described except in the presentation of Schwartzenberg as a traitor, confirmed the author's conviction that his country must be strong if it was not once again to be trampled underfoot.

Frederick William I, deservedly known as the Great Elector, is acclaimed in terms of rapturous enthusiasm. "Heaven had fashioned him expressly to establish order in a state that the misrule of the preceding reign had thrown into total confusion, to be the defender and restorer of his country, the honor and glory of his nation. The merit of a great King was mated to the humble fortune of an Elector. Rising above his rank, he displayed the virtues of a steadfast soul and a superior genius, sometimes tempering his heroism with prudence, sometimes giving rein to that noble enthusiasm which compels admiration. He restored his old possessions by his wisdom and secured new ones by his policy. He formed his projects and carried them out himself. His good faith enabled him to aid his allies, his valor to defend his peoples. He confronted unexpected emergencies with improvised resources. In little things and important affairs he always appeared equally great. The rout of the Swedes at Fehrbellin was the crowning triumph of the reign. He was praised by his enemies and blessed by his subjects, and his posterity dates the rise of the house of Brandenburg from this memorable day."

The defender of his peoples in time of war was inspired by the noble ambition to be their father in the years of peace. "He succored the families ruined by the enemy; he rebuilt the ruined villages; deserts were transformed into cultivated fields; forests gave place to villages; settlers pastured their flocks in places that the ravages of war had made the lair of wild beasts; agriculture was encouraged; every day witnessed fresh initiatives. He was even greater in his goodness and devotion to the public weal than in his military prowess. His skillful policy led him to do everything at the right moment and in the way essential to success. Valor makes great heroes, humanity good princes." The virtues of "the oracle of Germany" were recognized far and wide. "His fine qualities earned the confidence of his neighbors. His sense of equity made him a sort of supreme tribunal beyond his frontiers, whence he judged or reconciled sovereigns and kings." His welcome to twenty thousand industrious Huguenots was among the wisest of his acts; religious toleration became one of the principles of the state.

The chapter closes with a burst of trumpets. "He had all the qualities that make great men, and providence furnished him with occasions to display them. He was prudent when youth is usually sowing its wild oats. He fought only to defend his country and to succor his allies. He was cautious and wise, which made him a great statesman; laborious and humane, which made him a good prince. Insensible to the seductions of love, his only weakness was for his wife. If he loved wine and company, he set limits to his indulgence. His warm temper sometimes led to a loss of self-control; but if he failed to repress the first emotion, he always mastered the second, and his heart fully repaired the mistakes of his hot blood. Prosperity could not intoxicate him nor misfortune break his spirit. Magnanimous, polite, generous, humane, he never belied his character. He became the restorer and defender of his country, the founder of the power of Brandenburg, the arbiter of his equals, the honor of his nation. In a word, his life is his eulogy." He surpassed Louis XIV, not in power or splendor, but in merit, for he had no Richelieu to smooth his path, no Condé to win him victories, no Colbert or Louvois to aid his efforts. Thus, while the greatness of the one was the work of his ministers and generals, the heroism of the other was entirely his own. His supreme merit was that he never despaired of his country. Both broke treaties, the one from ambition, the other by necessity. "Powerful princes escape from bondage to their word by their own free will; weak ones fail in their engagements because they are often overpowered by circumstances. Both met death stoically, ruling till the end, directing their last thoughts to their people, whom they confided to their successors with paternal tenderness." Here is something more than a chapter in the history of the author's country: it is his ideal of statecraft. In these glowing pages we sense his desire that history would offer a similar tribute to himself.

Everything, we are expected to realize, depends on the character and capacity of the ruler. The chronicler finds little to admire in Frederick, the first King, least of all his subservience to the house of Austria. His Francophobia was nourished by Vienna with the legend of universal monarchy in which half of Europe was persuaded to believe. "Germany was often impressed by this puerile trick and plunged into wars that did not concern her. Yet, as the best blades become blunt, these arguments insensibly lost their hold, and the German princes realized that, if despotism threatened, it was not that of Louis XIV. Caring more for show than for realities, more for ceremonial than for business, more for flattery than for truth, he coveted the royal title won by the Elector of Saxony in Poland and the Prince of Orange in England. Yet the crown, desired for reasons of vanity, turned out to be a political master-stroke, which rescued the house of Brandenburg from the yoke imposed by Austria on all the German princes. I have acquired a title, he seemed to say to his successors; show yourselves worthy of it. I have laid the foundations of your greatness; it is for you to complete the work." To secure the prize he employed every kind of intrigue and was prepared for almost any sacrifice. The support of the Emperor, which was essential, was bought by the return of the Circle of Schwiebus and by the provision of troops in the conflict with France. His promotion found many critics within and beyond his frontiers, and cost the lives of thirty thousand soldiers. "He desired the dignity so eagerly merely to satisfy his taste for ceremonial as an excuse for his extravagance. The crowd applauds the magnificence of princes, but a sovereign should remember that he is the first servant and the first magistrate of the state. He trampled on the poor in order to pander to the rich. His favorites received large pensions while his people were in misery. His stables were of Asiatic magnificence. He was great in little things and small in great issues." The only virtues allowed him by his contemptuous grandson were a good heart and fidelity to his wives. Voltaire, whose task it was to revise the work before publication, suggested that the attack was pressed too far, but his protests were in vain.

The closing chapter was the most difficult to write, for the torments of his youth were fresh in the author's memory, but he skates over thin ice with skill and writes with filial piety. "Frederick William I combined an instinct for work with a robust body. No man ever had such capacity for details. He busied himself with the smallest affairs because he felt that they add up to great totals. He related every aspect of his work to his general policy so that the perfection.of each part should produce the rounded whole. His example of austerity and frugality were worthy of the early days of the Roman Republic." The object of his domestic reforms and economies was to render himself formidable to his neighbors by the possession of a large army. The fate of George William had taught him the peril of a prince unable to defend himself, and the traces of his wisdom would remain as long as Prussia was a nation.

The most striking feature of the chapter on his father is the author's detestation of Austria. The evil genius of the reign was her agent Seckendorf, of whom he speaks with anger and contempt. Lying was so ingrained in him that he had lost the habit of truth. The soul of a usurer was embodied sometimes in the soldier, sometimes in the diplomatist. He argued that the Emperor was a better ally than the King of England, and promised support for the succession of Berg. He gained possession of the King's mind so skillfully that he persuaded him to sign the Treaty of Wusterhausen, and it was his ambition to govern the whole court. The King, who was as honorable in politics as in his private life, was no match for this unscrupulous intriguer. "His example showed that good faith and virtue, being alien to the corruption of the century, cannot prosper." The scales fell from his eyes when the promises concerning Berg were unfulfilled. A visit to the Emperor at Prague ended the friendship of the two courts, for the King was incensed by the bad faith and the arrogance that he met. Despite this disillusion he married his eldest son to a niece of the Empress out of complaisance for Vienna. He kept out of war, and his grave illness in 1734 increased his dislike of risks. In his last years he was only kept alive by the care

of his doctors; and he met death with the firmness of a philosopher and the resignation of a Christian. "His policy was rooted
in justice. Armed always for defense, never for the detriment of
Europe, he preferred the useful to the agreeable. Building lav-
ishly for his subjects and only spending the minimum for his
own accommodation, cautious in his engagements, faithful to his
promises, austere in his habits and rigorous in regard to others,
insistent on military discipline, governing his state on the same
principles as his army, he thought so well of humanity that he
assumed his subjects were stoics like himself. He left an army
of 66,000 men, his finances improved, the treasury full, and mar-
velous order in all his affairs. The whole world will agree that
the laborious life and wise measures of this prince embody the
principles of prosperity that his house has enjoyed since his
death." The dark shadows of the reign are indicated in a single
tactful sentence. "We have passed over in silence the domestic
vexations of this great prince; one should have some indulgence
for children's faults in favor of the virtues of such a father."

Frederick's largest and most important historical work,
Histoire de mon temps, which opens with his accession, was begun after the close of the First Silesian War; revised and continued after the second, again revised and continued in the
evening of his life. "My works are scarcely worth reading," he
wrote to his brother in 1746. "I write partly for my amusement,
partly to show posterity my actions and motives. I ask neither
praise nor blame. I only desire to escape self-reproach. We all
know that it is impossible to satisfy everyone." Like Cæsar, he
writes throughout in the third person. The Preface of 1746 denounces the performances of others and makes high claim for his
own impartiality. Many have written history, he declares, but
very few have told the truth. Some have reported anecdotes at
second hand or invented them; others have merely collected
materials, rumors, and popular superstitions; still others have
published insipid and diffuse journals of campaigns. In these
romances the principal facts are scarcely to be recognized. The
heroes think, speak, and act as the author directs. We are offered
his dreams, not their actions. Such books are unworthy to survive, yet Europe is swamped with them, and people are foolish
enough to believe what they tell. Except for the sage de Thou,
Rapin, and a few others, we have only feeble historians, who must

be read with particularly critical eyes. Truth of fact is important, but it is not enough. The historian must be objective, must write with discernment, and above all must consider things with a philosophic eye.

Frederick's object is to record the experiences and reflections of an actor in the scenes he describes. "It is to you, posterity, that I dedicate this work, in which I try to sketch the affairs of other powers and less briefly those of Prussia directly concerning my house, which may regard the acquisition of Silesia as the beginning of its growth." The fragment of history he proposed to write was particularly attractive since it was filled with outstanding events. "Indeed, I venture to suggest that since the fall of the Roman Empire there has been no epoch more deserving of study than that of the death of the Emperor Charles VI, the last male of the Hapsburg line, which led to that famous league or rather conspiracy of so many kings pledged to the ruin of the house of Austria." Nothing would be stated without proofs from the archives and the testimony of reliable witnesses; the account of the campaigns would record the immortal glory of the officers and would serve as an expression of the author's gratitude. He would try to compare the present with the past, to survey Europe as a whole, to include the little details that led to the greatest events. Writing only for posterity, he would be fettered by no thought of the public response. "I shall say out loud what many persons think secretly, painting princes as they are, without prejudice against my enemies or predilection for my allies. I shall only speak of myself when I must; no one is worthy of the attention of future centuries. During his lifetime a king is the idol of his court; the great burn incense, the poets sing his praises, the people fear him or love him tepidly. When he is dead the truth appears, often revenging itself to excess for insipid flattery. Posterity will judge us after our death and we must judge ourselves during our life. When our intentions are pure, when we love virtue, when our heart is not the accomplice of the errors of our mind, when we feel we have done our peoples all the good we can, that should be enough for us."

Frederick proceeds to explain the most controversial incident in his career. "Here you will find treaties made and broken. I must point out that we are conditioned by our resources and capacities, and when our interests change we must change with them. Our task is to watch over the happiness of our peoples. When we find they are endangered by an alliance, it is our duty to break it, the sovereign thereby sacrificing himself for their welfare. History is full of such examples and indeed there is no alternative. The stern critics who condemn this conduct are people who regard a pledge as something sacred. They are right and as a private person I agree, for honor is above interest. But a prince who makes engagements exposes his state to a thousand mishaps; thus it is better that the sovereign should break his word than that the people should perish. What should we say of a ridiculously scrupulous surgeon who declined to cut off a gangrened arm in order to save life? Acts should be judged good or bad according to circumstances and results. Yet how few judge from knowledge of causes! Human beings are like sheep following their shepherd. What a clever man says a thousand fools repeat."

The discursive Preface closes with reflections inspired by the events described. Princes who fight too far beyond their frontiers are always unfortunate, since they cannot supply or rescue the exposed troops. Nations are more courageous when they fight for their homes than when they attack their neighbors. "The war that started in Silesia is becoming epidemic and grows in malignity as it spreads. Fortune is inconstant. No power enjoys uninterrupted success. The worst feature is the horrible effusion of blood. Europe is like a slaughter-house, bloody battles everywhere. One would think the kings had resolved to depopulate the world. The complexity of events has changed the causes of wars. The effects continue when the motive changes. I seem to behold gamblers who, in the heat of the game, keep on till they have lost everything or ruined their adversaries. The history of cupidity is the school of virtue." The Preface of 1775 reiterates and expands the arguments and reflections of 1746 without adding anything of interest.

The long Introduction contains a vivid and valuable survey of the resources, rulers, and culture of the chief European states when the author ascended the throne. In Prussia the chief weakness was the lack of industries. The prestige of Austria had waxed with the victories of Prince Eugene and waned on his death, for the Emperor Charles VI was a well-meaning mediocrity—a good

linguist, a good father, a good husband, but bigoted and superstitious like all the princes of his house. Under the wise, thrifty,
and pacific guidance of Cardinal Fleury, France had largely
recovered from the disasters of the closing years of Louis XIV.
Yet "the arbiter of Europe" suffered from serious weaknesses. The
people were poor, though the luxury of Paris recalled the Rome
of Lucullus. The moral standard was low, and the French, above
all the Parisians, were enervated by their pleasures. Spain, with
a moody King and an ambitious Queen, was on the down grade.
Her population was too small to cultivate the soil, and superstition ranged her with half-barbarian nations. The portrait of
George II, the author's uncle, is painted in a few vigorous strokes
of the brush. He had virtues and talent, but his passions were
too strong. "Firm in his resolutions, avaricious rather than eco-
nomical, capable of work but not of patience, violent, brave, governing England in the interests of Hanover, he was too little
master of himself to direct a nation idolizing its liberty." Peter
the Great had made Russia the arbiter of the north; the failure of
Charles XII had proved that nothing was to be gained and everything might be lost by attacking such a colossus.

The verdict on Poland is particularly severe. "This kingdom is
in a state of perpetual anarchy. The great families are at loggerheads. They prefer their interests to the public welfare, and agree
only in their harshness towards their dependents, whom they
treat less as human beings than as beasts of burden. The Poles
are vain, arrogant in good fortune, broken in adversity; capable
of the greatest infamies in amassing money, which they hasten
to waste; frivolous, without judgment, capable of forming and
abandoning plans without cause and of ruining themselves by
their inconsequence. Laws exist, but for lack of sanctions they
are ignored. The King sells posts. A single member of the Diet
can veto its decisions. The women intrigue and decide everything, while their husbands get drunk." Saxony, a country with
a richer soil, was ruled by Brühl, the extravagant and contemptible favorite. "He understood nothing but the finesses and ruses
that constitute the policy of princelets; he was double-dealing,
false, and capable of the basest actions to keep his power. No
man of his century had so many clothes, watches, belts, shoes,
and slippers or so much lace. Only with a prince like Augustus

III could a man of this type play the part of Prime Minister." Bavaria, the most fertile part of Germany, had the smallest brains —an earthly paradise inhabited by animals.

The description of the Empire is unflattering but not unjust. Judged by the number of kings, electors, and princes, it was powerful; owing to the clash of interests it was weak. The Diet at Regensburg was a ghost, a gathering of publicists caring more for forms than realities. If a question of war arose, the Imperial court cleverly identified its quarrel with the interests of the Empire in order to use German strength for its own ambitions. The different Churches continued to exist, but their zeal had diminished. Many politicians were surprised that such a singular system could survive so long, and they attributed it to the national indifference. That was not the reason. The emperors were elective, and since the extinction of the Carolingians different families had been raised to the throne. Quarrels with their neighbors and the popes prevented the establishment of despotism in the Empire. The electors, certain princes and bishops were strong enough if united to oppose the ambition of the emperors, but not to change the form of government. Since the Imperial crown had been worn by the house of Austria the danger of despotism became more apparent. Charles V could have made himself sovereign after the Battle of Mühlberg, but he missed his chance. When Ferdinand II and III attempted the enterprise, the jealousy of the French and Swedes frustrated their plan. The princes, for their part, were kept from aggrandizement by mutual jealousies.

After all this acid criticism of the states and statesmen of Europe it is refreshing to find a little praise. Since the time of Cæsar, Switzerland had preserved her liberty except for a short period when she was subdued by the Hapsburgs; subsequent attempts to reimpose their yoke failed. "The love of liberty and the mountains were their bulwarks against the ambition of their neighbors." Despite the differences of race, language, and religion, the people had never swerved from the principles of moderation and had reaped their reward. The barbarous custom of selling their sons as mercenaries was their only fault. A contemptuous reference to the Papacy concludes the panorama of the European stage. By 1740 the Pope was merely the first bishop of Christendom. The sphere of faith was left to him, but his political influence had waned. The Renaissance and the Reformation had

322

struck a mortal blow at superstition. A saint was canonized from time to time so as to keep up the tradition, but a pope who tried to preach a crusade in the eighteenth century would not have collected a score of rascals. He was reduced to exercising his priestly functions and to making the fortunes of his nephews.

The author turns with relief from "the imbeciles and charlatans" on the political stage to the solid triumphs of the human spirit in science and philosophy, literature and the arts. Writing as a grateful child of the *Aufklärung,* he salutes the English sage who made experience his only guide. Locke tore away the bandage of error that the skeptic Bayle, his precursor, had partially detached. Fontenelle and Voltaire appeared in France, Thomasius in Germany, Hobbes, Collins, Shaftesbury, and Bolingbroke in England. "These great men and their disciples struck a mortal blow at religion. Men began to examine what they had stupidly adored; reason overthrew superstition; people became disgusted with the fables they had believed and turned away in horror from the blasphemies they had piously accepted. Deism, the simple cult of the Supreme Being, gained many followers. With this sensible religion, toleration came in and ideological differences no longer bred hostility. Epicureanism destroyed pagan idolatry, and deism was not less fatal to the Judaic visions adopted by our ancestors."

If England, where liberty of opinion prevailed, had led the way in philosophy, France, with her instinct for method and taste, was supreme in literature. A man of judgment would prefer the *Henriade* to Homer, for Henri IV and Gabrielle d'Estrées were real persons. Boileau was comparable with Juvenal and Horace; Racine surpassed all his rivals in antiquity; Bossuet approached Demosthenes in eloquence; Montesquieu's *Lettres Persanes* and *Décadence de l'Empire Romain* were masterpieces. Why did German culture lag so far behind? Firstly because of the wars: the peoples were miserable, the princes poor. The urgent task was to grow food. There was no capital like Rome and Florence, Paris and London. There were universities with learned pedants, but students were few. Only Leibnitz and Thomasius were an honor to the nation. While German scholars were mostly artisans, French scholars were artists. For this reason French works circulated everywhere and French superseded Latin. The use of this foreign tongue injured the native idiom, which, being employed by the common people, lacked the polish only attainable in good society. German was too verbose; it needed tightening up and the softening of words difficult to pronounce. "Our sterility drove us to the abundance of the French, and in most courts French companies played the master-pieces of Molière and Racine." German architecture, on the other hand, had made strides. The best edifices, such as the Palace in Berlin, though inferior to those of Rome and Athens, surpassed the Gothic of the Middle Ages.

At the close of his encyclopedic survey of the mind and face of Europe the author returns to his starting-point in Prussia. Frederick William I had left savings that, though inconsiderable, would suffice for a favorable opportunity; but prudence was needed, and if wars were undertaken they would need to be short. Prussia's chief disadvantage was her irregular shape, for small and disconnected provinces were scattered from Kurland to Brabant, which increased the number of her neighbors and potential enemies. She could act only if she leaned on France or England. France was bent on abasing the house of Austria, and England's subsidies were only forthcoming in pursuit of her own interests. All Europe was concerned in the Austrian succession when the Emperor should die. Frederick William I had guaranteed the Pragmatic Sanction on condition that the court of Vienna assured him the reversion of Jülich and Berg. The Emperor broke his promise and thereby canceled the obligation. Believing his end to be near, Frederick William I made no alliances, leaving his successor at liberty to seek contacts as time and circumstances dictated. The new monarch found that no one cared whether he or some other prince obtained the Duchy of Berg. France consented to his having a strip, but this was too little to content an ambitious young King who desired all or nothing. The Emperor had promised the duchy not only to Prussia but to the Elector of Saxony and to the Prince of Sulzbach, the heir of the Elector Palatine. "Was one to sacrifice oneself to the perfidy of the court of Vienna, to content oneself with this strip of the Duchy of Berg, or should one secure one's rights by force of arms? In this crisis the King decided to use all his resources to strengthen his position. By economizing he raised fifteen new battalions and awaited developments in order to secure the justice that others denied him."

The second chapter develops the argument that the seizure of Silesia was fully justified. He had only 60,000 troops and the treasure bequeathed by his father. To conquer the Duchy of Berg he would have had to employ the whole of his army, since it would have entailed war with France. Other objections to this plan were the rival claim of Saxony and the jealousy of Hanover, who in case of war would have invaded the central portions of his dominions while his entire army was in the west. "If these considerations moderated the desire for glory that animated the King, motives no less powerful urged him to inaugurate his reign by signs of vigor and resolution in order to win respect for his nation in Europe. Good citizens were exasperated by the lack of consideration shown to the late King, particularly in his closing years, and by the general contempt for the Prussian name." His known moderation led his neighbors to conclude that they could insult him with impunity. His broken health was another factor making for peace, for he would never have entrusted the command of his troops to other hands.

These experiences taught the new King that a prince must secure respect for himself and still more for his nation, that moderation is a virtue that statesmen cannot always practice owing to the corruption of the time, and that the change of ruler should be marked by firmness rather than gentleness. Moreover Frederick I, in making Prussia into a monarchy, had unwittingly planted a germ of ambition in his descendants which was bound sooner or later to bear fruit. "He bequeathed a sort of hermaphrodite, more of an electorate than a kingdom. There was glory in removing the anomaly, and this sentiment strengthened the King in the great enterprise to which he was impelled by so many motives." Even had the acquisition of the Duchy of Berg been practicable, it would have added little to the territory of the house of Brandenburg. The King therefore turned his eyes to the house of Austria, where a larger prize might be obtained.

The news of the Emperor's death reached Rheinsberg on October 26, 1740. The King was in bed with fever, but he took strong medicine despite the advice of the doctors, for he had other things to think of than his health. "He promptly resolved to demand the Silesian principalities to which his house had incontestable rights, and prepared to sustain them in case of need by force of arms. This project dominated his policy; it was a means of acquiring reputation, increasing the power of the state, and of terminating the dispute about the succession to Berg. Yet, before finally deciding, he balanced the risks of a war against the advantages for which he hoped." On the one hand there was the powerful house of Austria, with the resources of its vast provinces, an Emperor's daughter attacked who would find allies in England, Holland, and most of the princes of the Empire who had guaranteed the Pragmatic Sanction. The Duke of Kurland, who controlled Russia, was in the pay of Vienna, and the young Queen of Hungary could secure Saxony by ceding parts of Bavaria. Moreover, the bad harvest of 1740 complicated the provisioning of the troops. The risks were great, the appeal to arms uncertain; a lost battle might be decisive. The King had no allies and he could only oppose untried troops to veteran campaigners. On the other hand, there were many grounds for hope. The situation of the Austrian court was deplorable; the finances were in confusion, the army neglected and discouraged by its failures against the Turks, the Ministry disunited, an inexperienced Princess having to defend a contested succession. Moreover, the King could be sure of allies. The rivalry between France and England ensured the support of one or the other, and the interests of the pretenders to the succession of the house of Austria would coincide with those of Prussia. The final decision was due to the death of Anne, Empress of Russia, shortly after that of the Emperor, which gave the crown to the King's young brother-in-law. "Add to these reasons an army prepared for action, ready money, and perhaps the desire to make his name. Such were the causes of the war."

The audacious Silesian project aroused a ferment. Timid souls foretold the collapse of the state, and others believed that the ruler was gambling on the model of Charles XII; but the officers hoped for good luck and promotion. Prince Leopold of Anhalt (the Old Dessauer) was furious that he had not thought of the plan and was not the chief agent in its execution; like Jonah, he prophesied disasters, which happened neither to Nineveh nor to Prussia. He regarded the Imperial army as his cradle, and he feared that the growing prestige of the King would reduce his stature. He sowed mistrust and fear and would have intimidated the King had it been possible. However, to counterwork any evil influence he might possess, the King addressed the officers of the Berlin garrison on the eve of his departure. "Gentlemen, I am embarking on a war in which my only allies are your valor and good will. My cause is just and I trust in my luck. Remember the glory won by your ancestors. Your fate is in your hands; distinctions and rewards are waiting for you to earn them. But I need not excite you to glory; it is always before you, the only object of your labors. We shall confront troops who under Prince Eugene won great renown. It will be all the more honor to vanquish brave soldiers. Adieu! I shall follow you without delay to the rendezvous of the glory that awaits you!" The occupation of Silesia was facilitated by the fact that two thirds of the population were Protestants, who, long oppressed by Austrian fanaticism, regarded the King as a heaven-sent savior. The Battle of Mollwitz is declared to be one of the most memorable days of the century, because two little armies decided the fate of Silesia and Prussian troops won a reputation which neither time nor envy could dim. The Empire was amazed to learn that the old Austrian forces had been defeated by soldiers with little experience, and France, seeing a chance of destroying the house of Austria, offered an alliance. The author's flight from the battlefield when defeat seemed inevitable is discreetly omitted.

The conquest and retention of Silesia required political as well as military skill, and he proceeds to justify the secret truce of Kleinschnellendorf in the autumn of 1741. France and Bavaria, it is true, were his allies, but their purposes were very different from his own. France believed that Austria's day was over and desired to erect on the ruins four sovereignties in regard to which she would play the part of arbiter since they would never agree. Maria Theresa would keep Hungary and the core of the Hapsburg possessions; Bavaria would obtain Bohemia and Tyrol; Prussia would gain Lower Silesia, while Saxony would annex Upper Silesia and Moravia. This prospective partition was not at all to the taste of the King, who strove for the elevation of his house and had no intention of sacrificing his troops to strengthen his rivals. Had he become the tool of French policy he would have played France's game, and Louis XV might have achieved the universal monarchy of which Charles V was believed to dream. Moreover, had he supported the French troops with excessive zeal, their success would have turned an ally into a vassal, driven him farther than he desired to go, and compelled him to accept all the wishes of France, since he could neither resist nor find allies who might help his escape from such slavery. Prudence demanded a cautious policy by which he would hold the balance between the Hapsburgs and the Bourbons. The Queen of Hungary was on the brink of a precipice. A truce would give her a breathing-space, and the King could end it when he chose. Moreover he had discovered secret dealings between Fleury and Vienna indicating his readiness to sacrifice Prussia in return for Luxemburg and part of Brabant. The chief advantage of the truce with Austria was that the Prussian army could be strengthened with the aid of the Silesian revenues.

Frederick concludes his account of his first war and of the Treaty of Breslau, which ended it, on a note of unalloyed satisfaction. "Thus Silesia was added to the Prussian state. Two years of war—he might have said two battles—sufficed for the conquest of this important province. The treasure bequeathed by the late King was almost spent, but to obtain the province for seven or eight million crowns was a good bargain. Circumstances favored the enterprise. It was necessary that France should come in, that Russia should be attacked by Sweden, that the timidity of the Hanoverians and Saxons should keep them inactive, that there should be no reverses, and that the King of England, an enemy of the Prussians, should become the instrument of their aggrandizement. The chief factors in the conquest were an army formed during twenty-two years by an admirable discipline and superior to any troops in Europe, generals who were good citizens, wise and incorruptible ministers, and finally a certain luck, which often accompanies youth and is denied to old age. If this great enterprise had failed, the King would have passed for an obscure prince who had undertaken a task beyond his strength. Success made people regard him as a happy man. In reality fortune alone decides on reputations. The lucky are applauded, the unlucky condemned."

Frederick justifies his much criticized retirement from the fray in 1742 by the failure of France to play her part. "The course of the war," he wrote in announcing his decision to Fleury, "is only a tissue of marks of goodwill that I have given to my allies." France, on the other hand, had not taken her expected share in the conflict, and he had to think of the defense of his country against Austrian and possibly even Saxon troops. "The future is dark; in such a critical situation I find myself compelled to avert the shipwreck. If untoward events have obliged me to take a course justified by necessity, you will always find me ready to fulfill engagements the execution of which depends solely on myself." "Such," concludes the author, "was the end of the alliance, where each of its members played for his own hand, where the troops disobeyed their commanders, where the camps were in a condition of anarchy, where all the plans of the generals were submitted to the revision of an old priest who knew nothing either of war or of the terrain." It was a miracle that saved the house of Austria, for a wiser course would have ensured her destruction. He was glad to be out of it. The longer the conflict lasted, the more her resources were used up, while the longer Prussia remained at peace, the stronger she became. The most difficult problem was to hold the balance between the belligerents so that neither side should become too powerful. To save the Emperor was clearly impossible. The French generals had lost their heads, and the princes of the Empire were terrified by Austrian threats. Prussia used the breathing-space to restore her finances, strengthen the Silesian fortresses, increase the army, construct canals, and foster the silk industry. "Thus, far from profiting by this tranquillity to grow soft, peace became a school of war for the Prussian troops."

If it is a capital error to trust to a reconciled enemy, declares Frederick, it is even worse for a weak power to wage a long war against a powerful monarchy possessing superior resources. "This must be borne in mind by critics of the King's conduct. Was it necessary, they ask, to put himself at the head of a league to crush the new house of Austria and then allow it to regain the upper hand and to evict the French and Bavarians? But what was his object? To conquer Silesia. How could he have attained it if the war had continued, seeing that his finances could not face a long strain? Peace gave him time to breathe and to prepare for war. Moreover the animosity between France and Austria was so strong and their interests so antagonistic that reconciliation seemed very distant. To foresee everything is impossible." The successes of the Austrian armies influenced their ambition and they wished to dethrone the Emperor. The feebleness of Charles VII and the enormous pretensions of the Queen of Hungary warned the princes that they would not long remain spectators of a conflict in which their interest and their glory counseled them to resist the old enemies of German liberty. These considerations were particularly cogent for the King of Prussia. Neither the Queen of Hungary nor the King of England concealed their hostility. "Since he was always mistrusted by the enemies with whom he had made peace, he had to be ready for any event. The damage of the late war was partially made good and sufficient money for two campaigns was put aside. True, the fortresses were rather planned than completed, but the army was increased, munitions and food were collected sufficient for a single campaign. In a word, the acquisition of Silesia having given new strength to the state, Prussia could vigorously execute the designs of her rulers." It remained to take measures to avert danger from his neighbors. Of these the Russian Empire deserved chief attention because it was the most dangerous. "All future rulers of Prussia must cultivate the friendship of these barbarians." He particularly feared the swarms of savage Cossacks and Tartars, who ruin the country they invade. Retaliation for damage inflicted was possible with other countries, but not with Russia unless a fleet were available to cover operations against St. Petersburg.

Having sensed that Austria would become strong enough to threaten the retention of Silesia unless she were speedily checked, Frederick decided to re-enter the war and signed a new treaty with France in June 1744. He had little faith in his old ally, with the court governed by intrigues and its armies led by faint-hearted generals. France, he declared, was more successful in sieges than in battles, for her engineers were the best in Europe. Prague was quickly taken but could not be held. The great nobility and the clergy of Bohemia were deeply attached to the house of Austria, while the peasants, all of whom were serfs, had been ordered to bury their corn and hide in the woods. The Prussian army, finding empty villages and little food, was forced to retreat. Nowhere was it so difficult to fight as in Bohemia with its mountain barrier, where communications are easily cut. No general committed more mistakes than himself in the campaign of 1744, writes the author with commendable frankness. The first was the neglect to provide sufficient supplies for at least six months in Bohemia, since an army depends on its stomach. Moreover his strategy was faulty, whereas that of Daun, the Austrian com-

330

mander, was a model. "The King admits that he regarded this campaign as his schooling and Daun as his teacher. Good fortune is often more disastrous for princes than adversity. While the former intoxicates, the latter makes them careful and modest."

The disappointments of 1745 turned Frederick's thoughts once more to peace. France had promised vigorous assistance, of which he reminded Louis XV; but his reply was chilly, though war in Bohemia had been undertaken only to save Alsace. The death of the Emperor early in 1745 had increased the desire to withdraw from the struggle. His name had covered the association of the princes who had undertaken his defense, and all their steps had been in conformity to the laws of the Empire; now he was gone, the object of the partners disappeared, and the princes of the Empire had no longer a common purpose. It was clear that the new house of Austria would do its utmost to regain the Imperial crown. The French secretly welcomed his death as a means of escape from their embarrassments. They were tired of paying large subsidies and believed they could secure a good peace at the price of the Imperial crown. Besides, what candidate could be set up against the Grand Duke of Tuscany, supported as he was by the armies of the Queen of Hungary, English money, and the intrigues of the clergy? The only hopeful sign was that England began to turn towards Berlin. The outlook for Prussia at the opening of 1745 was dark, for her finances were almost exhausted. The King explained to his French ally that he could not long carry on the war, the whole burden of which rested on his shoulders. Louis XV was urged either to pay subsidies or to make an effective diversion. The appeal was in vain, but Frederick retrieved his fortunes by victories at Hohenfriedberg and Soor. At last he felt not only that he should but that he could make peace.

Posterity, writes the King in surveying the campaign of 1745, would doubtless ask why his army withdrew from Bohemia after two victories. The reasons were to be found in the ring of mountains, in the gorges separating Bohemia from Silesia, in the difficulty of feeding the troops, in the enemy's superiority in light troops, and finally in the weakening of the army. The most pressing anxiety was the lack of money, and the harvest was bad. Nothing more could be expected from France, and there was a danger of Russian intervention. "Peace was the only remedy for

all these evils. It may seem surprising that the King should propose such moderate conditions, but remember that his situation
compelled him to avoid risks. To exact concessions from the
King of Poland would have driven him into the arms of Austria.
Moreover Europe was jealous of the acquisition of Silesia, and it
was necessary to efface instead of renewing suspicion. Thus the
easiest road to peace was the restoration of the territorial *status
quo* before the war. Since the proposed conditions were mild,
they might secure a stable peace. These principles guided the
King, and despite the success of his enterprises he never departed
from them." To will peace, however, was not to achieve it, for
Brühl, boasting of Russian support and of the ample resources of
Saxony, held out for terms that Frederick was unable to accept.
"He realized that henceforth it would be necessary to negotiate
only by victories." When the Saxons were defeated at Kesselsdorf the last obstacle was removed. By the end of 1745 Prussia
was once more at peace.

"Thus finished this second war, which lasted sixteen months
and was fought with extreme fierceness; in which the Saxons
displayed all their fury against the Prussians and their jealousy of
their neighbor's aggrandizement; in which the Austrians fought
for the Empire and for hegemony; in which the Russians desired
to intervene in order to have a finger in the German pie; in
which France should have taken interest but failed to do so; in
which Prussia was exposed to imminent danger but triumphed
owing to the discipline and heroism of her troops. The unexpected death of Charles VII destroyed the plan of permanently
severing the Imperial dignity from the house of Austria. Thus we
must admit that in some aspects this war caused a most useless
shedding of blood, and that a series of victories merely seemed
to confirm Prussia in possession of Silesia. It cost her eight million
crowns, and at the end only fifteen thousand were left." Upper
Silesia suffered most, even more than Bohemia and Saxony. The
King's first care was the renovation of his army, in large part from
Austrian and Saxon prisoners; only seven thousand Prussians
were required to fill the gap left by so many bloody battles. Yet
the balance-sheet aroused no enthusiasm. "Since the establishment of a certain equilibrium between sovereigns the largest
enterprises rarely produce the expected results. As a result of
the equality of forces and the alternation of losses and gains the

antagonists find themselves at the close of a most desperate war much where they were before it began. Finally, financial exhaustion produces peace, which ought to be the result of humanity, not of necessity. In a word, if reputation in arms is worth an effort, Prussia in gaining it was recompensed in the second war she undertook; but that is all she got, and it aroused envy."

The *History of the Seven Years' War,* like that of the first two Silesian conflicts, fills two volumes. It was compiled during the first year of peace, and the Preface is dated 1764. That it was so speedily completed was due to the fact that the author utilized the elaborate reports that he had drawn up at the close of each campaign. "I had two principal objects in view. The first was to prove that it was not in my power to avert the war, and that the honor and welfare of the state prevented me from making peace except on the conditions finally obtained. The second was to narrate the military operations with the utmost clarity and precision. I have made it a rule to keep scrupulously to the truth and to be impartial. Animosity and hatred instruct nobody, and there is weakness and even cowardice in speaking evil of one's enemies and in refusing them the justice they deserve." The claim to truthfulness and impartiality is better founded in the military than in the political sphere, yet in vindicating his policy he never forgets how many factors go to the making of history. "These memoirs," he wrote to the elder Keith, "convince me more than ever that to write history is to compile the follies of men and the strokes of fortune. Everything turns on these two articles, and it has always been like that. We are a poor species while we vegetate on this little atom of mud which we call the world. I am forced to revolve like a mill-wheel, for one is carried forward by one's destiny."

The drama opens with a prologue on the decade of peace between the Second and Third Silesian Wars. The author briefly but proudly describes his reforms of the army, the police, finance, agriculture, industry. Justice, he declares, which had been badly administered in the previous reign, required particular attention. "It was enough to be rich to win one's case and to be poor to lose it." The task was entrusted to Cocceji, a magistrate worthy of the best days of the Roman Republic. The whole domestic program was a race against time. Prussia, with her scattered provinces, had always to be ready for emergencies, and now she was faced by an ambitious and revengeful enemy in the person of the Empress, all the more dangerous because of her sex, obstinate and implacable. "This proud woman, devoured by ambition, wished to reach the goal of glory by every path." She introduced order into the finances of the state unknown to her ancestors, not only repairing what she had lost by provinces ceded to the Kings of Prussia and Sardinia, but considerably increasing her revenues. "Thus the two powers in time of peace prepared for war, like athletes who sharpen their weapons and burn with impatience to use them." The Peace of Dresden had the same fortune as most treaties: it suspended hostilities without eradicating the germs of discord. Whatever dissimulation the court of Vienna employed, it felt too deeply injured by the loss of Silesia to hide its resentment. Intrigue, ruse, fraud, artifice were its weapons to stir up enmity against Prussia in all the courts of Europe. The chief colleague and instrument of the Empress was Kaunitz, "so frivolous in his tastes, so profound in his decisions."

In the chapter on the outbreak of war in 1756 Frederick reveals two sources of information about the plans of his enemies— a secretary of the Austrian Ambassador in Berlin and a clerk in the Saxon Foreign Office at Dresden. Despite these subterranean reporters he is incorrect in stating that Russia desired to postpone the attack till 1757: she was ready in 1756 and it was Austria who requested delay. The King had to decide whether it was more advantageous to anticipate the blow or to wait till his enemies had completed their preparations. In any case war was inevitable. An important consideration was that the little Saxon army, at the moment only 17,000 strong, was to be raised to 40,000 during the winter. Moreover, to delay was to invite invasion instead of fighting beyond the frontiers. Under these circumstances delicacy would have been misplaced. "As for that terrible name of aggressor it was only a scarecrow, which could merely impose on timid folk and which deserved no attention in a situation where the safety of the fatherland was at stake, since the real aggressor is obviously he who compels the other to arm, and of two evils one must choose the least."

The history of the campaigns is too detailed to be of much interest to the general reader. Frederick praises his best generals, Ferdinand of Brunswick and Prince Henry, and there is no self-glorification even in describing his most sensational triumphs.

Rossbach, for instance, the cheapest of his victories, where the fighting was over in an hour and a half, "only brought to the King of Prussia liberty to go and seek fresh dangers in Silesia." The campaign of 1759 was the worst of all, and it would have been all up with Prussia if her enemies had known how to exploit their victories. After Kunersdorf—"a Russian victory, though it cost them dear"—the situation was desperate, though he suppresses the fact that he had thoughts of suicide. For the moment things turned out better than he dared to expect, but the war became more difficult to sustain and the hazards greater from day to day. The campaign of 1760 was expected to be even worse than 1759, but he was saved once again by the dearly bought victory at Torgau. Yet no success could compel peace. At the end of 1761 the outlook was once more dark indeed. Nothing prevented the Russians from besieging Stettin in the coming spring or seizing Berlin and the whole Electorate of Brandenburg. The King had only 30,000 troops in Silesia; Prince Henry had no more, and of the forces who had served in Pomerania against the Russians scarcely half were left. Most of the provinces were invaded or devastated. He no longer knew where to find recruits, horses, supplies, food, or how to bring munitions to the army.

Private grief was added to public calamity. The King's mother died at the age of seventy in 1757. "He received the fatal news after the Battle of Kolin, at a moment when fortune had strongly declared against the Prussians. He was deeply touched. He had revered and adored this princess as a tender mother, whose virtues and great qualities aroused the admiration of those who had the happiness to know her. The great missed her easy and gracious manner, the small her kindliness, the poor their refuge, men of letters their protectress; members of her family closest to her felt they had lost a part of themselves." Perhaps for once Frederick said a little more than he meant. On the other hand, the tribute to Wilhelmina, who died a year later, rings true, for they were devoted friends. "She was a princess of rare merit; she had a cultivated and richly stored mind, all-round ability, and a remarkable talent for the arts. Yet these happy gifts of nature were the least part of her merit. The goodness of her heart, her generous instincts, the nobility and loftiness of her soul, the sweetness of her character, were united to brilliant intellectual gifts and solid virtue. She often experienced the ingrati-

335

tude of those whom she had loaded with favors, yet she never let anyone down. The most tender, the most constant friendship united the King and this worthy sister. These ties were formed in their earliest childhood, strengthened by the same education and the same sentiments, and rendered indissoluble by unchanging fidelity on both sides. This delicate princess took the dangers threatening her family so much to heart that her health gave way." It is perhaps the only passage in a rather colorless work that is written from the heart. The death of his brother and heir in the same year is recorded in a single perfunctory sentence. "He was regretted for his good heart and his range of knowledge, which gave hope of a mild and happy reign." That the Prince of Prussia died in deep disgrace and, as some people believed, of a broken heart is omitted by the Generalissimo who had angrily deprived him of his command for a military blunder.

With the carnage of Torgau the worst of the fighting was over, and in the later chapters the main interest passes from the battlefield to courts and cabinets. British subsidies had been of more use to Frederick than British arms, which were largely occupied in the far places of the earth. He complains that his requests for a squadron to defend his ports in the Baltic, threatened by the Russian and Swedish fleets, had been ignored. "This proud and happy nation, thinking only of its commercial advantages, despised its allies, whom it regarded as pensioners. Thus the war in Germany and the interests of the King were never really considered by Parliament or the people, which despises everything that is not English." They were indeed such bad allies that they thwarted his efforts to mobilize the Turks against Austria. From this indictment he expressly excepts Pitt, "a lofty soul, a spirit capable of great projects and of firmness in their execution, an inflexible attachment to his opinions, because he believed them to be advantageous to his beloved country." Bute, on the other hand, who discontinued the subsidy, is scourged with a passion displayed nowhere else in the book. Possessing more ambition than ability, he wished to rule under the shadow of the King's authority. He believed that the raiment of honor for every statesman must be of coarse texture. "This Englishman believed that money does everything and that money was only to be found in England." He thought that by purchasing peace at any price for his nation he would become its idol, instead of which he became an object of execration. "To desert one's ally, to engineer plots against him which his enemies would hardly undertake, to work with ardor for his destruction, to betray him, sell him, assassinate him: such attacks, such abominable actions, ought to be recorded in all their atrocity so that the judgment of posterity may frighten away all who might be capable of imitating them."

The defection of England was far more than outweighed by the sudden death of the Tsarina Elizabeth on January 5, 1762. The state, which seemed to be lost, comments Frederick, was saved by a happy event that repaired all its losses—another proof that appearances are deceptive and that only by perserverance can we surmount the perils that surround us. The new Tsar, Peter III, is the only sovereign who is praised above his deserts. Readers of the *Memoirs* of Catherine the Great will smile at the verdict that her drunken, boring, and half-crazy husband had an excellent heart and nobler sentiments than are usually found on a throne. The explanation of the compliment is to be found in the next sentence. "He accepted all the King's desires and went even farther than could be expected." He recalled the Russian troops, hastened the conclusion of peace, demanded no territory, merely asking the friendship and alliance of the King. "Conduct so noble, so generous, so uncommon, should not only be recorded for posterity but should be engraved in letters of gold in the cabinet of every king." Unfortunately his mistakes and impatience created enemies, and his life was soon in danger from his exasperated subjects. The King warned him of the peril, but in vain, and when the news of his assassination arrived, it was like a stroke of lightning. The acute anxiety passed, for Catherine, the new ruler of Russia, had no intention of re-entering the fray as an enemy of Berlin, and by this time even Maria Theresa had had enough of the unprofitable strife. Rescued from utter destruction at the eleventh hour, the King was only too glad to get out of the war on what he calls modest and moderate terms. He could only have secured compensation by fresh victories, which the army was in too ruinous a condition to win. Good generals were becoming rare; the old officers had perished on the battlefield; the young officers were too raw to count. Of the rank and file many were deserters or under eighteen. Prussia had no allies. Pestilence threatened the hunger-stricken people. Sixteen pitched battles had been fought and 180,000 men had been lost, without counting civilian casualties.

Frederick concludes his record of the Seven Years' War with some general reflections. Is it not clear that fortune plays with the projects of mankind? Who could imagine that Prussia, attacked by the forces of Austria, Russia, France, Sweden, and the whole of the Empire, would resist this formidable league and emerge without loss of any of her possessions? Who could believe that France, with all her resources and alliances, would lose her principal possessions overseas? Prussia was rescued by the political disunion of her enemies; by the lack of military coordination between the Austrian and Russian Generals, who, if they had acted with vigor, could have crushed her; and by the death of the Tsarina Elizabeth. "Time, which heals and effaces all evils, will doubtless soon restore to the Prussians their abundance, their prosperity, and their earlier splendor. The other powers will also recover. Then other ambitious persons will start new wars and cause new disasters. For it is the nature of man that no one learns by experience. The follies of the fathers are lost on their children. Each generation has to commit its own." Such a philosophy, in the writer's view, was not cynicism but the plain teaching of history.

The account of the second half of the reign is naturally much less dramatic, and the two parts that compose it fill only a single volume. In the Preface to the section covering the years 1763–74 the King explains that he had not at first intended to continue his narrative beyond the close of the Seven Years' War. "So many laborious campaigns had tired me, while advancing age and infirmities made me expect an early close to my career. The only service I could render to the state, I felt, would be to heal the infinite evils of war by wise and vigorous administration." Prussia was like a man covered with wounds, weakened by loss of blood, ready to succumb under the burden of his sufferings, needing tonics to restore his strength and balm for his sores. The duty of the government was to act like a wise doctor who, with the aid of time and gentle remedies, revives his strength. "These considerations were so powerful that the internal administration of the state absorbed my whole attention. The nobility were exhausted, the little people ruined, many towns and villages burned or destroyed by sieges; disorder was rife among the police and in the administration; the finances were in utter confusion; in a word, there was general desolation. Many of the old officials had died during the war. The army needed renovation from top to bottom. The political outlook was equally unfavorable, for England's desertion left Prussia without a friend." The Preface concludes with the customary claim to accuracy and clarity without exaggerating or falsifying the smallest circumstances. "I have never deceived anyone during my life. Still less will I deceive posterity."

The author begins his survey of European politics after the return of peace, composed in 1775, by emphasizing the financial exhaustion of France and Austria. The King of Prussia alone possessed some cash, for he always kept a year's supply in his coffers. With the fall of Choiseul, his *bête noire,* France fades out of the picture, and the story revolves round the relations of Prussia to the empires of eastern Europe. The diplomatic tension was relieved by the treaty concluded with Catherine in 1764, which removed the danger of a fresh Austrian attempt to reconquer Silesia; yet the growing strength of Russia as manifested in her victories over the Turks was not without its dangers. Why should not the old antagonists, Austria and Prussia, draw together in case the Slav colossus might be tempted to abuse its power? Frederick proposed a meeting with Joseph shortly after he succeeded his father as Emperor in 1765, but, to his annoyance, the project was vetoed by Maria Theresa and Kaunitz. Four years later, in 1769, the two Philosophic Despots met at Neisse. "This young prince," writes the King, "affected a frankness that appeared natural to him; his amiable character displayed gaiety and great vivacity. He was anxious to learn but lacked patience to instruct himself; his great position made him superficial. What revealed his real nature more than anything else were the unpremeditated expressions of the unmeasured ambition by which he was consumed. Despite all this the two monarchs entertained feelings of friendship and esteem for each other. The King observed that he regarded the day as the happiest of his life, since it reconciled the two houses, which had too long been enemies and whose mutual interest it was to aid and not to destroy each other. The Emperor replied that for Austria there was no longer a Silesian question, though he added that during the lifetime of his mother he was not in sole command." At a second meeting in the following year, at Neustadt in Moravia, Kaunitz was present. "To interrupt him while he was speaking was an insult; instead of conversing he lectured, preferring to hear himself talk than to listen to replies." Russia, he argued, was now the danger, and only the union of Prussia and Austria could arrest the torrent that threatened to inundate all Europe. The King poured water into his wine by reminding him of the alliance between Prussia and Russia, though he would do his best to reconcile the two Empires and to prevent the extension of the Russo-Turkish War.

The Prusso-Russian entente took practical shape in the First Partition of Poland. Frederick minimizes his share in the transaction, the origin of which he traces to Austria's seizure of the County of Zips. Not that he is in any way ashamed of a policy that added a valuable province to his country, averted an otherwise inevitable war between the neighbors of the victim, and by the fair distribution of territory maintained the balance of power. "It was the first example in history of a partition peacefully arranged and terminated by three powers." He sheds no tears over the fate of the Poles, "the most superficial and frivolous nation in Europe." Whether it was right to carve up a living nation because it was weak is a question that does not concern him, since, like his partners, he was guided solely by *raison d'état*. Though an awkward corner had been turned, he entertained no illusions about the coming years. Writing in 1775, shortly after the partition, he laments that Europe was not in a stable condition: everywhere the flames smoldered under the cinders. The greatest danger threatened from the unbridled ambition of the young Emperor, seconded by the intrigues and perfidies of a Minister (Kaunitz) who made it a point of honor to trick those with whom he dealt. All these considerations compelled prudent sovereigns to remain on guard, to keep up their forces, never to turn their eyes from matters that might cause an explosion when it was least expected. "History teaches that vicissitudes and revolutions are among the permanent laws of nature."

The attack on the Emperor Joseph is continued in a sketch of the years 1774–8, written in 1779, which forms the final portion of the record of the reign. Vienna is described as the hotbed of European intrigues, though Maria Theresa is now presented as the powerless advocate of peace. "This arrogant court looked round in all direction, with a desire to extend its possessions and engulf its neighbors. The Emperor was too immature to know how to conceal his vast designs. His vivacity often betrayed him, and he was unaware to what extent dissimulation is necessary in the handling of political affairs." For instance, when Frederick had some sharp attacks of gout in 1775, and the Austrian Ambassador at Berlin reported that his death was expected, the Emperor set his troops in motion, impatiently awaiting the joyful tidings to push forward into Saxony, whence he would offer the new King of Prussia the choice of restoring Silesia or being crushed. The King quickly recovered, but the young Emperor, devoured by ambition, thirsting for glory, and only awaiting an opportunity to disturb the peace of Europe, also cast covetous eyes on Bavaria. His army was better than ever, and Austria had become more formidable than under any preceding Emperor, not excluding Charles V. The death of the Elector of Bavaria in 1777 without legitimate children gave him his chance, and the War of the Bavarian Succession broke out. Frederick speaks of Joseph with the severity employed by an earlier generation towards himself. "This enthusiasm of the young Cæsar for war arose from his false notions of glory. He believed that it sufficed to make a noise in the world, to invade provinces, to extend his Empire, and to command armies in order to acquire reputation, and he was oblivious of justice, equity, and wisdom. His ideas about military matters were equally false. He thought that the mere presence of an Emperor with his army was enough to reap a rich harvest of laurels. Experience had not taught him how much labor and care are needed to gather even a small branch." The whole Bavarian enterprise revealed him as a bungling amateur. His first move should have been to reach an arrangement with France or Russia. Thus, when France stood aloof and Prussia championed the cause of Bavarian independence, Austria found herself alone and had to draw back, despite the failure of the Prussian generals, himself included, to take full advantage of their military opportunities.

Writing at Potsdam in the summer of 1779, on the termination of the last of his wars by the Peace of Teschen, the veteran concludes the record of his stormy life on a note of resignation. "Imperfection is our destiny. Man has to content himself with approximations. What is the upshot of this war which threatened to set all Europe in motion? For the time Germany has been saved from the despotism of the Empire, and the Emperor has suffered a rebuff in having to restore what he had usurped. But what of its ulterior effects? Will he become more prudent? Will everyone be able to cultivate his fields in tranquillity? Will peace be more secure? We can only guess. Anything is possible. Our eyes cannot pierce the future. We can merely trust to providence or rather to fate, which will shape the future as they have shaped the whole history of mankind."

Chapter XV

THROUGH GERMAN EYES

LORD ROSEBERY's description of Frederick II as the Patron Saint of Germany was not intended as a compliment either to the King or to his people. In 1916, when the phrase was coined, the greatest of the Hohenzollerns was generally regarded as the father of the aggressive militarism from which Europe had suffered ever since. Prussia, he added, had been like a pike in a pond, armed with sharp teeth and endless voracity, poised for a dart when proper prey should appear. Most of his countrymen, on the other hand, would probably accept the title while giving it a very different interpretation. Friedrich der Einzige (Frederick the Unique), they would say, was not merely the Patron Saint of Germany but the greatest monarch in modern history, with an honored place in the German Valhalla beside Luther and Goethe, Kant, Beethoven, and Bismarck. As knowledge of his labors and their results increased, his fame has steadily grown. The masterpiece of Schinkel and Rauch, which holds the place of honor in Unter den Linden, was decorated with laurels and flowers when the news arrived of Königgrätz and Sedan. Menzel's spirited illustrations to Kugler's popular biography made Old Fritz and his circle familiar to the multitude. The Third Reich was inaugurated in the Garnisonkirche at Potsdam in 1933 by Hitler and Hindenburg. Plays and poems, histories and biographies, monographs and novels have poured forth in a never ending stream. *"Toujours lui, lui partout!"* exclaimed Victor Hugo as he gazed at the towering figure of Napoleon. What a great people thinks of its celebrities, which of them it selects for special admiration, which qualities are stressed as particularly worthy of esteem, are matters of international concern. What Germans—above all, German historians—have thought of Frederick II is of peculiar significance in view of their craving for leadership, their political romanticism, their worship of efficiency, their intellectual glorification of war. From the broad standpoint of European history his incomparable prestige is not the least important aspect of his work.

343

The systematic study of the man and the reign begins with the official publication of his writings in the middle of the nineteenth century.[1] Of the thirty volumes of the *Œuvres* that appeared between 1846 and 1857, seven were devoted to the histories, six to the poems, two to the philosophical works, three to the military treatises, twelve to the correspondence. *The Memoirs of the House of Brandenburg, L'Antimachiavel,* and a few youthful essays and poems had appeared during his life. A mass of new material and correspondence was contained in the *Œuvres Posthumes* published shortly after his death by order of his nephew and successor, Frederick William II; but so execrable was the editing, so numerous the mutilations and omissions, that the necessity for an edition worthy of his fame was recognized on all hands. The decision to publish his historical writings was taken by his great-nephew Frederick William III, and when the studious Frederick William IV ascended to the throne in 1840, the centenary year, the scheme was widened to include his other works. The task was entrusted to the Prussian Academy, funds were provided, and Preuss, the Historiographer of the house of Brandenburg, was appointed editor. He was the obvious man for the task, for he had compiled the first documentary record of the reign in the four volumes published in 1832–4, and his admiration for the hero knew no bounds. Everything was of importance, he declared, that related to the character of a ruler so full of wisdom, gaiety, and heart. It was not his fault that the two massive Political Testaments of 1752 and 1768 were withheld from publication. Two editions of the *Œuvres de Frédéric le Grand* were issued, one of them a richly illustrated quarto limited to two hundred copies to be distributed at the discretion of the King. The *Political Correspondence,* which reveals the secrets of his diplomacy, had to wait for a later generation and is still in progress.

The first competent German scholar to deal with Frederick was the man who has been justly described as the Goethe of German historians. After winning world-wide fame by his *History of the Popes* and his *German History in the Reformation Era,* Ranke published his *Nine Books of Prussian History* in 1847–8, bringing the story to the outbreak of the Seven Years'

[1] A brief sketch of Frederician studies entitled *Some Interpretations of Frederick the Great* is given by Veit Valentin in *History,* September 1934.

344

War. It was carefully revised and considerably enlarged into *Twelve Books* for insertion in the *Collected Works* in 1874, and it may now be studied in the annotated Academy edition, published in 1930. Though less popular than his earlier masterpieces, it was no less a landmark in historical studies, for he was the first to be allowed the run of the state papers. Ranke was never tempted by biography. Though there are some striking pictures in his immense portrait gallery, he was more interested in states than in individuals. His first plan was a history of Frederick's reign, suggested by his study of the dispatches of the French Ambassador in the Paris Archives in 1843. What he calls the surprising picture of the King there painted suggested the need for further research, and he crossed the Channel in order to obtain another angle of vision. Diplomacy, however, was not enough, for he felt that he must understand the structure and functions of the Prussian state: the achievement of Frederick II could only be explained in the light of his father's heroic labors. For a time he contemplated a study of the Silesian wars with a long Introduction. The Introduction, which grew into a comprehensive survey of the making of the Prussian state, presented a new and juster conception of Frederick William I and set him in the place of honor that he was henceforth to hold in Prussian hearts. The dazzling figure of the Great Elector had never needed a pedestal, but his grandson, the founder of the military-bureaucratic system, required and at last received the attention that was his due.

Half of the three stout volumes of the *Prussian History* in its final form is devoted to the first sixteen years of the reign of Frederick II. Though a Saxon by birth and with a kindly feeling for Austria, which never left him, Ranke's admiration of the King is unconcealed. The seizure of Silesia is justified on the ground that Austria had not played the game. "No one will maintain that a power is tied to a treaty when the other party for any reason abandons it." Frederick William I had accepted the Pragmatic Sanction on the understanding that Vienna would help him to the Duchy of Berg, a condition that was not fulfilled. "There was no trace of hatred or personal revenge, but father and son were full of ambition and determined not to be ignored or despised. Since the old friendship had ceased, there was nothing to prevent the revival of ancient claims. The house of Bran-

345

denburg acted in good faith and had a good case. Convinced that a large part of Silesia ought to be his, Frederick felt it an obligation of honor to assert his rights. Picture the prince, a young man thirsting for action, resentful of recent errors, and with latent but all the stronger consciousness of ancient rights of which his house was deprived, and the feeling that the enterprise would make him a really powerful king." Even had there been no Prussia and no Frederick, the end of the male Hapsburg line would have caused a war of succession. France would have resumed the old struggle, and the Wittelsbachs would have presented their claims. "It was fortunate that there was at any rate one state that fought for its own cause and acted without seeking foreign counsel. Prussia desired neither the Imperial title nor separation from the Reich; but she did not wish to see the supreme authority in hostile hands, and for this reason she supported the candidature of the Elector of Bavaria as Emperor." The twelfth and last book of the *Prussian History,* entitled "Years of Peace," depicts Frederick as a ruler no less eminent and praiseworthy in peace than in war. It is unjust, declares Ranke, to compare him with Charles XII, who confessed that in deciding to make peace he was thinking of the next war since he could not live quietly at home. Frederick, on the contrary, made a conquest that he believed to be necessary for the safety and dignity of Prussia: henceforth he drew the sword only to preserve it.

The story of the reign was summarized and the main verdicts reiterated in the comprehensive article contributed by the octogenarian Ranke to the *Dictionary of German Biography.* "A heroic life, inspired by great ideas, filled with feats of arms, exertions, and fateful events, immortalized by the raising of the Prussian state to the rank of a power, inestimable in its legacy to the German nation and the world." There is not a word of blame for the seizure of Silesia. "Imagine a young Prince, able and ambitious, coming into the rights that his ancestors were unable to vindicate and also into the power to do so. Was it not inevitable that he should desire to act? He did not challenge the succession of Maria Theresa, but he thought the Silesian principalities had never been her father's property. He vindicated for his house an inalienable right to them, which the time had come to assert. Never was any acquisition more opportune and important for a state. No one can doubt that the enterprise could be undertaken with a good conscience. Resistance was inevitable: both attack and defense were legitimate. Prussia had accepted the Pragmatic Sanction, but Austria had broken the conditions of the recognition of Maria Theresa's claims. It was not hatred, but the house of Brandenburg felt itself freed from its obligations, and in the general confusion Frederick consulted his own interest." Among the later works of the Nestor of German historians was an elaborate study of the *Fürstenbund,* the last and not the least of Frederick's efforts to checkmate the house of Hapsburg.

Despite these sincere and impressive eulogies Ranke was regarded as too academic and too friendly to Austria by the founder of the Prussian school who harnessed history to patriotism and proclaimed that to work for Prussia was to work for Germany. Droysen had won his spurs by solid studies of the Hellenistic era; but in middle life he transferred his attention to modern history, writing and lecturing with patriotic fervor on the War of Liberation. In the gloomy years following the fiasco of the Frankfurt Parliament, when the hand of Schwarzenberg lay heavy on the German Bund and the hegemony of Austria was tamely accepted by Frederick William IV, he emerged as the most eloquent champion of Prussia's right and duty to make a nation state. The battle between the *Grossdeutsch* and *Kleindeutsch* parties (a Reich with or without Austria) was joined in the lecture-rooms of the universities as well as in the Diet at Frankfurt and finally on the stricken field of Sadowa. It was Droysen's ambition to prove that Prussia's whole record prepared her for the gravest tasks of the new era owing to her Protestantism and to her instinct for the interests of Germany as a whole.

His thesis of Prussia's mission, expounded in the fourteen closely packed volumes of the *History of Prussian Policy,* failed to convert even friendly experts such as Sybel and Koser; but the power and erudition of this colossal documented apologia rendered it one of the outstanding achievements of modern German scholarship, even though he never worked in foreign archives. Prussia, he reminds us, had no natural frontiers; yet her history revealed a steadiness of growth and a clearness of purpose that only the most dynamic state structures possess—advantages of which the luck and the skill of her rulers were the expression rather than the cause. "What has founded, sustained, and guided this state is, if I may use the phrase, a historical necessity. To its essence belongs the call of the whole, in which it has found its justification and its strength; it would become superfluous were it to forget. Whenever it failed to remember, it was weak, decadent, more than once near collapse." That Prussia was not generally beloved is immaterial, for a lofty purpose was being fulfilled. The Great Elector is hailed as the second founder of the state, "which henceforth, despite emperor and pope, despite all foreign and un-German frowns, has grown deeper and deeper into Germany and gathered the awakening and creative life of the nation around and in itself." The author had sat at the feet of Hegel in Berlin, and his conception of the national idea working itself out through the centuries over the heads of men was thoroughly Hegelian.

With such a reading of Prussia's historic role it is not surprising that the four massive volumes on the reign of Frederick down to the eve of the Seven Years' War, published between 1874 and 1886, are a full-throated hymn of praise. That his great-grandfather and his father had prepared the ground is gratefully recognized. After the close of the Middle Ages, we are reminded, men craved for strong states, for the overcoming of the forces —feudalism, the privileged classes, the Church, and the estates —that obstructed their creation. The poor, possessing no champions, had no defense. The Treaty of Westphalia seemed to stereotype the fragmentation and therefore the impotence of Germany, a living corpse in the heart of Europe. Was there then no hope? The Great Elector proved that there was. By destroying the power of the estates, by substituting long-service soldiers for mercenaries, by complete religious toleration, he emphasized the principle of the general good and repudiated the prevailing notion that the country was the private property of the ruler.

Frederick William I, a still greater administrator, was surrounded by neighbors eager to squeeze him to the wall and to withhold what was his due. "Not openly, sword in hand—for then he would have hit back—but with diplomatic stratagems, secret treaties, conference decrees, he was driven from pillar to post and checkmated. This Prussia, which amidst the misrule and somnolence of the other states was full of sap and enterprise, militarily and financially prepared, seemed to be slowly undermined by the abscesses hiding behind such phrases as "international law," "balance of power," "European interests," which were presented as the salvation of mankind, whereas Austrian policy was always the first consideration. His great services and honorable devotion were rewarded by the ingenious tactics of the Empire to misuse him." With a ruler at once so loyal and so pacific, no longer feared by the small and despised by the great, the prestige of Prussia steadily declined. That the Prussians did not count was the opinion of the world.

Under these circumstances it is not surprising that Frederick's accession is greeted by Droysen with lyrical enthusiasm. The tragedy of Küstrin had banished frivolity and taught him the need of self-discipline and hard work. "There was a feeling of spring in the air—not merely the dutiful obedience of the late reign but the joy of service, a competition in honor, a quickening of pulse. The change is felt in the distant garrisons, the remotest villages. The neighboring lands give ear. The oppressed Protestants in Silesia recalled ancient prophecies of help in their extremity. He possessed the industry, the knowledge, the intellectual stature to embrace and to direct all the functions of state." Wilhelmina's criticisms of her brother are angrily dismissed as a malicious caricature. Henceforth, wrote the new monarch, his people, whom he loved, was the only God he served. "My duty is my supreme God."

His first duty was to win for Prussia the place that was her due. His debut was a great political act that, in Droysen's eyes, calls for gratitude, not apology. The hero had a good case, but he acted "certainly not without proudly coveting victory and fame, certainly not exclusively for his rights. Scarcely on the throne he sought and found the opportunity to draw the sword. Never did a prince defend himself with better justification. It was high time to act if the Prussian state was not to run down internally and suffocate under external pressure." Offensive war was authorized in *L'Antimachiavel* in order to anticipate a threatened attack, and throughout his reign he believed in taking the initiative. He saw in the circumstances of other states, in the insincere groupings of the powers, in the approaching crisis of the European system, the possibility of establishing the real importance of Prussia. "In the five months since the change of ruler the political scene had undergone an extraordinary transformation, and there could be no doubt as to its cause. This Prussia, so long cowed and timid, lonely and ignored, stood erect, stretched her limbs, and began to arouse anxiety by her internal strength and her taut muscles."

As Crown Prince, Frederick had decided to fight for Jülich and Berg when his time should come, but the death of Charles VI offered a far more tempting prize. In the secret treaty of 1728 the Emperor had guaranteed the Jülich-Berg succession to Prussia, but in 1739 he recognized the claim of Pfalz-Sulzbach. After this breach of faith the Austrian succession was an open question for Prussia. During the negotiations for the recognition of the Pragmatic Sanction Austria promised compensation in Silesia if she could not secure Berg. Yet was Austria likely to keep her promise? Silesia was a corridor to the Mark, a bastion on the north, and Vienna hated the idea of Silesia in Protestant hands. How could Frederick hesitate? He saw the old system rocking on its foundations, a new order in process of birth, in which Prussia was bound to take her stand. Austria had the choice either to accept her hand and to pay her price or to throw herself into the arms of France or England. In that case the one not chosen would seek to make Prussia an ally. Prussia had the best right to Silesia as compensation for unparalleled deceit. In 1686 the Great Elector had ceded his rights in Silesia for the return of the Schwiebus Circle to Prussia. "Without this initiative Prussia (who between England, Hanover, and Saxony-Poland with Austria's active co-operation had been squeezed out of her military and political positions) was in danger of becoming a cipher. With the gathering of the European crisis the last moment had arrived to rescue her from sinking. Without this initiative Germans would have either been cast into the furnace for the naval supremacy of England or become wholly dependent on France. If a German nation had existed at that time, it would have realized that Frederick was doing its business. On November 17, 1740 he wrote: 'I should never have believed I was such a good German.' "

Frederick did not envisage a reform of the Empire: for the time a strong Prussia sufficed. Nor did he aim at the disintegration of the house of Austria. But he would have failed in duty to his state had he rendered service to this declining house (which had so often and so grievously sinned against Prussia) without compensation. For Silesia he was ready to transfer his claim on Jülich and Berg to Austria. "Prussia's right to Silesia was not the ground and the leading idea of this combination, but this right provided the opportunity to inaugurate the discussion which her policy demanded. She had rights to Jägerndorf, Liegnitz, Brieg, and Wohlau, but had ceded them to Austria because she was then too weak to resist pressure. Now Austria was weak, and her weakness was a danger for Germany and Europe. If she accepted Prussia's offer, Germany would be safer and worthier than for centuries. If she refused, the treaties were tainted with guilt. Frederick felt himself morally justified in demanding atonement and in enforcing it by arms. In one point alone was he inconsistent. In his first letter to Maria Theresa he called her Queen of Hungary and Bohemia, a title that in a certain sense included her right to Silesia. Perhaps he hoped that she would be more inclined to agree. He was mistaken. Her refusal led him to actions that contradicted his recognition, compelled him to abandon the connections he hoped to establish and to make connections that he hoped to avoid. This gave his further actions an appearance of ambiguity and untruthfulness, which weakened the popular effect of his intervention and presented his opponents with the occasion for moral indignation. It was the interest of Prussia and Germany not to be taken in tow by France and England or any other alien policy, but to go their own way. This approach to Vienna was wise. Now he could say with truth that his case had nothing to do with the question of the Pragmatic Sanction, that he asked nothing of the Queen of Hungary except compensation for ancient injury and suitable payment for the services expected of him."

On reaching the end of the First Silesian War, Droysen utters a cry of delight. Thanks to the army, Prussia was prouder than ever, strong enough to make war or conclude peace according to her own interest, like the great powers, of which she was now one. It was a satisfaction to have triumphed over the old domineering Austria. "The significance of Prussia was that, raising herself out of the ruins of the Thirty Years' War, she had grown into an organized state, a German state within the empty shell of the Empire, not dynastic but monarchical, not estate-ridden but military, not confessional but based on equal confessional rights. That such a state arose on German soil showed what vital and deep-seated forces were at work in her. That she now began the struggle for Silesia, that Frederick's victories diminished the power of the Imperial house by the loss of a rich province, that thereby the foundations of the old state system were destroyed, seemed to break the spell that lay over Germany and to open a prospect for the nation. Though Maria Theresa had a Brunswick mother, Austria was largely non-German." That was her fatal disability and that was the core of Prussia's case.

Frederick, according to Droysen, had no thought of reforming the Reich when he marched into Silesia. If Vienna yielded he was ready to support the Pragmatic Sanction and the election of Francis as Emperor; repulsed, he hesitated long before deciding which candidate for the Imperial title to favor. His choice fell on France's nominee, the Elector of Bavaria, whereby the house of Austria lost its three-century-old position in the Reich. The German question was not solved, but the ice was broken, for Austria now opposed both Kaiser and Reich. Frederick was compelled to make peace at Breslau in 1742 by the slackness and shiftiness of his French ally, but he kept what he had won. "Now we must accustom the cabinets to see us in our new position," he wrote; "I believe that in showing moderation and patience with all our neighbors we can do it." The universal mistrust was a measure of his importance. When the Second Silesian War confirmed the verdict of the first, Droysen again shouts with delight. Silesia was the proof that Frederick was even greater as the *Landesvater* than in war. "He never envisaged the interest of his state otherwise than in connection with that of others, with the general interest. His conception, his resolution, and his acts were in the grand style. That heavy defeats did not bend him and astonishing successes did not blind him, that without caprice or passion, impersonally so to speak, he desired only what was commensurate with his resources and did only what the situation demanded, that after such victories he gave such a peace to the defeated, even his enemies had to recognize, even those who saw in it only tactics and dissimulation, even those who reluctantly confessed that he excelled them not only in energy, brains, generalship, but in moderation, wisdom, nobility of soul, princely greatness. What he did and what he was gave to the peoples a new standard, to crowned heads a mirror that did not flatter them, a spur to self-education." Maria Theresa reformed her army, her administration, her finances partially on the Prussian model in order to prepare for the next round.

To the charge that Frederick destroyed the venerable Empire, Droysen rejoins that the rise of the princes naturally diminished its power and prestige, but argues that the house of Austria deserved it since it had always subordinated that institution to its own interests. With the Reformation, Protestantism became part of the national idea, and Austria ceased to share the growing intellectual life of Germany. The opposition to the Bavarian Emperor was treachery to the Golden Bull by implicitly claiming a monopoly of the highest post. Francis as Emperor was merely the puppet of Vienna. Prussia, on the other hand, had many claims to leadership. She was Protestant and tolerant, Austria papal and intolerant; in her internal policy she was as advanced as Austria was out of date; she was monarchical and centralized, Austria only just emerging from a personal union into a state; she was German in all her territories, while Austria possessed German, Slav, Hungarian, Walloon, and Italian territories, the non-German portion being three or four times the larger. "In a word, Prussia was the positive pole of German development, Austria the negative." The growth of Prussia's power and prestige was naturally unbearable to Austrian pride, but the nation realized what this state meant to it. Soon official Germany, the territorial princes, had no protection against Austrian encroachments and ambitions except what Prussia could supply.

At the end of Frederick's life his partners in the *Fürstenbund* gratefully accepted what they despised in 1743 and 1744. "Prussia, satisfied with her position, stood firmly in the midst of the Continent, in the center of the Reich. With her as a nucleus the chaos of Germany and Europe would be cleared up; with the changed distribution of power a stable relation between large and small states could develop, a blessing to the peoples no less than to the states. Yet the great powers detested her—France because she had been deserted in the two Silesian wars, Austria on account of the loss of Silesia and the Imperial dignity for five years, England because Hanover was overshadowed, Russia because the road to the west was barred." To historians of the Prussian school such enmity was a source of satisfaction as a tribute to the importance of the state under whose banner they proudly marched. When Droysen died in 1886, at the age of seventy-eight, he had brought his narrative of Prussian foreign policy to the opening of 1756. He had lived long enough to vindicate his faith in Prussia, to pro-

353

claim his boundless devotion to the greatest of her kings, and to welcome the Hohenzollern Empire.

The Prussian school reached its culmination in Treitschke, the German Macaulay. The first volume of his famous *German History in the Nineteenth Century,* published in 1876, opens with a majestic retrospect of the decline of the Empire and the rise of Prussia. Written with a narrative power and brilliance entirely beyond the range of Ranke or Droysen, the chapter on Frederick the Great found thousands of readers for every student of the *History of Prussian Policy.* The picture of the reign was painted at a time when the author, like his countrymen, was quivering with the patriotic emotions of Sadowa and Sedan. "I write for Germans," he bluntly announced in the Preface; "the narrator of German history should feel and create in the hearts of his readers delight in the Fatherland." In the history of Prussia there was nothing to conceal; the errors and sins had long been known, and honest research revealed that even in times of weakness her policy was better than it seemed. Such a sprawling territory was compelled to round off its provinces. The Prussian state was the work of its princes. Frederick William I ranked with Napoleon and Stein as an administrator, and he was the first to proclaim that every subject was born to bear arms, though conscription was only applied in certain country districts. In the field of foreign affairs, on the other hand, he was always an amateur, only realizing the trickery of Austria at the end of his life. Foreigners used to say that he stood with his gun fully loaded but would never pull the trigger.

Frederick II is saluted by Treitschke as the greatest figure in Germany since Gustavus Adolphus. His central characteristic was his pitiless realism, his combination of an instinct for the practicable with the boldness and insight of genius. To the shadowy outlines of the Holy Roman Empire he opposed the throbbing vitality of a modern state. German history since Luther and the Schmalkaldic League had been in the main an unceasing struggle against the despotism of the house of Austria, upon which the Prussian school never ceased to pour out the vials of its wrath. To Frederick German freedom meant the formation of a great German power capable of defending the fatherland in the east and the west, which was beyond the power of the Empire. To work for Prussia was to work for Germany. It was not the habit of this hater of phrases to talk much about the fatherland, yet his soul was animated by a vigorous national pride; he felt it a dishonor that foreign nations should play the master on German soil. "Throughout life he was exposed to the accusation of faithless cunning, for no treaty and no alliance could ever make him renounce the right of free self-determination. The courts of Europe spoke angrily of "working for the King of Prussia." Accustomed from of old to dominate German life, they found it almost impossible to grasp the new situation and to understand that at last the resolute egoism of an independent German state could successfully oppose their will." Sometimes in war his fiery spirit led him beyond the bounds of prudence, but in the realm of statecraft he always preserved perfect moderation and a sense of proportion.

When the opportunity arose in 1740 to become a great power and to secure complete freedom of movement, Frederick, in Treitschke's opinion, was right to seize it. After Maria Theresa repulsed his advances he decided to separate the Imperial crown from the Hapsburgs, thus severing the last link connecting them with Germany. Instead of being the creator of dualism, he strove to end it, turning to Bavaria with the offer of the crown and a Bavarian empire under Prussian patronage. When Bavaria failed and the crown returned to the Hapsburgs, Austria regained the shadow while Prussia retained the substance. "The peaceful labor of administration gave a moral justification to the conquest of Silesia, and furnished the proof that his widely censured act of daring was a genuinely German deed. Thus was restored to the German nation this magnificent frontier-land which had been partially overwhelmed by foreign influences. The victor restored the rights of the Protestants while leaving the Catholics more rights than they enjoyed in any other Protestant state. The prosperity of Silesia under Prussian rule showed that it had found its natural master."

In 1756, unlike 1740, the King had no choice, for his foes were combining to destroy him. Only with the aid of Rome could the two ancient enemies, the two great Catholic powers of Austria and France, unite against Prussia with the object of perpetuating the impotence of Germany. By a daring onslaught he saved his crown from certain destruction. After the Seven Years' War Prussia seemed to stand once more in the same position as at the start, yet the outcome of the struggle, in appearance so fruitless, was a colossal success. The new order in Germany that had begun with the foundation of Prussian power had proved itself an irrevocable necessity. The victory was gained by German arms alone. Germany's star was once again in the ascendant. The veil was stripped from the colossal lie of the Holy Roman Empire, and the German nation loudly acclaimed the victor of Rossbach. The establishment of the German Protestant great power was the most serious reverse that the Roman See had experienced since Luther. Frederick, in truth, as the British Ambassador Mitchell phrased it, had been fighting for the freedom of the human race. In the school of struggle and suffering the people of Prussia acquired a vivid sense of nationality, so that the King was justified in speaking of his Prussian nation. To be a Prussian had at last become an honor. The conception of the state and of the fatherland arose in a million hearts, whereas a deep inner affinity united the degermanized Empire with the Papal See. "The twelve campaigns of the Frederician epoch have impressed their stamp forever upon the warlike spirit of the Prussians and the Prussian army. A happy understanding existed between the King and the people, which was moved to the depths by the contemplation of true human greatness." As Goethe said of himself and his friends, they were Fritz-possessed. The first man of his century ranked with Luther and Gustavus among the heroes of the German people. "Gradually even the masses began to feel that he was fighting for Germany. Of all his victories Rossbach most powerfully influenced our national life. The monarchy had now completely outgrown the narrow-mindedness of territorial life and attracted all the healthy energies of the Empire. Prussia was now the one really living state among the German peoples."

The partition of Poland, the greatest achievement of the latter half of the reign, is acclaimed by Treitschke as above all a checkmate to Russia. Since the Seven Years' War the Poles had been subject to the will of the Tsarina, and her absorption of the distracted state seemed only a matter of time. Accordingly Frederick conceived the idea of a partition that would limit her westward advance. It was a victory of German diplomacy over the eternal land-hunger of Russia. Moreover, the annexation of West Prussia rescued the exposed land of East Prussia, the historic home of the Teutonic Knights, from the peril of Russian aggression, though not a soul in the Reich thanked the King. A further service was the frustration of the ambitions of Joseph II, first by the War of the Bavarian Succession and later by the creation of the *Fürstenbund*. Frederick was now the acknowledged protector of Germany. Though there hardly existed even the beginning of a national party, he bequeathed a state that might one day summon Germany to a new life.

Treitschke left no successor and founded no school, but his ideology was shared by his lifelong friend Gustav Freytag, the most popular writer of the third quarter of the nineteenth century. The author of *Soll und Haben* was deeply interested in the history of his country, and his *Pictures from the German Past* (*Bilder aus der deutschen Vergangenheit*) enjoyed well-deserved popularity. His purpose was to visualize the life of the people through the ages from little-known contemporary material. "My object," he wrote in the Preface to the fourth and last volume, covering the years 1700–1840, published in 1867, "is to show how Germans were gradually transformed from private persons into political beings by the Hohenzollern state." The picture of the reign of Frederick the Great, one of the best-known portions of the whole work, is painted in glowing colors. "One had the right to admire the providential character of the Prussian state." He challenges the notion that the King had a cold heart: at bottom he had a poet's nature. He lost friends by his sharp tongue, but he was really fond of Jordan and once he kissed the hand of Voltaire. There was no favoring of the rich, for he was the friend of the small man. In his belief it was best that everyone should stay in his own class and prosper therein. The weakness of the system was that he attempted to do everything himself.

As a native of Silesia, Freytag devotes special attention to the first and most important of Frederick's acquisitions. Austrian rule was slack, and taxation, though not heavy, was unfairly distributed. With the change of master a new type of official appeared on the scene, efficient and conscientious, working hard for a modest salary. Only the once privileged classes complained. Yet life in Silesia, as elsewhere, was monotonous; there was very little relaxation or charm. The King's own circle was more like an order than a court; discipline, renunciation, and not a woman to be seen. "Something of this spirit of self-suppression passed

357

into the people. It is the secret of the greatness of the Prussian state, the best guarantee of its survival." The acquisition of West Prussia from Poland confronted him with a more formidable task. "If the claim to Silesia was doubtful, it needed all the wits of his officials to deck out the nebulous claims to West Prussia. The King took little interest in the question. The real justification and the most blessed of all his gifts to the German people was that he saved it from Russia." The province had been grossly neglected and misruled, and the Protestants had been persecuted. Conditions were incredibly poor and primitive.

"As his struggle in the Seven Years' War may be called superhuman," writes Freytag, "so now in his work there was something monstrous, seeming to contemporaries sometimes superhuman, sometimes inhuman. It was great but also terrible how the well-being of the whole was ever the decisive factor and the comfort of the individual so utterly ignored." The closing passage of the whole work illustrates the mood of pride and gratitude in which it was written. "1648–1848 witnessed the memorable ascent of the German people. After an unparalleled destruction its soul waxed in belief, in scholarship, in political enthusiasm. It is now in the middle of the strenuous effort to create the state, the highest earthly possession. It is a delight to live in such a time. A glow in the heart, the feeling of youthful power, fills hundreds of thousands. It has become a joy to be a German; before long it may be reckoned among other nations as a high honor."

Soon after Germany was unified and King William had become German Emperor, Sybel was appointed Director of the Prussian Archives. He had been one of the founders and leaders of the National Liberals in the Prussian Parliament, and no one greeted the stupendous events of 1870 with deeper thankfulness. Bismarck expressed his gratitude "for long co-operation in common work for the fatherland," suggested that he should devote his remaining years to describing the foundation of the German Empire, and allowed him access to the archives. His seven volumes, published between 1889 and 1894, are a pæan to the Iron Chancellor and to the predecessors who made his work possible. The introductory chapters emphasize the failure of the Hapsburgs to provide either unity or security. Germany, he argues, had good reason to wish that other powers might arise by the side of Austria to protect the northern and western frontiers.

The conflict with Austria, it is true, was not carried on in a national spirit nor in order to improve the Constitution. Both Prussia and Austria worked for their own ends, but the defeat of the former would have been a fatal blow to German liberty. "The splendid resistance of Frederick the Great averted this calamity, though he aimed merely at the independence and greatness of Prussia. The same was true when he formed the *Fürstenbund* against the Emperor. His object was not to make a nation but to keep the Imperial system weak; for any strengthening of it would strengthen the Imperial idea, which would hinder the free movements of Prussia and the formation of a party devoted to her interests." His immortal services to Germany were that his mighty personality inspired a patriotic pride, that he protected the north, so long defenseless, and that he set a new standard for rulers. Curiously enough, Sybel expresses neither approval nor blame for the seizure of Silesia.

Not every German accepted the slogan of the Prussian school that to work for Prussia was to work for Germany. The most violent onslaught ever directed against the greatest of her rulers was launched by Onno Klopp, a native of Oldenburg, a friend of the last King of Hanover, an angry critic of Droysen, and later a professor at Vienna. *King Frederick II and His Policy,* of which a revised and enlarged edition appeared in 1867, is a fighting book with a fighting Preface: all that has been and can be said against Prussia is to be found in the six hundred pages of this arsenal of the *Grossdeutsch* party. The first edition, published early in 1866, was sharply attacked by the school "which for the time is in the ascendant." Hostility in that hated quarter, even more than the approval of friends, convinced the author that his reading of history was correct. The first edition had ended with a plea for a close alliance between Austria and Prussia in the general interest of Germany. "We strove for a Germany in harmony with the character of the nation, on a federal basis peacefully arranged, and we hoped that Prussia might prefer these thoughts of peace and right to the Frederician tradition. We were wrong. The leaders of the state which he created stand on his shoulders and follow the principle of utility which he embraced. The patriotic hope that Prussia could ever desire anything but aggrandizement at any price was killed in 1866." Old Fritz—never referred to as Frederick the Great—was only the worst specimen of his House.

359

In the first edition Klopp had charged him with breaking the dynastic tradition of loyalty. Further study had revealed that this statement was incorrect, for his ancestors had been equally calculating. The stinging characterization by Leibnitz of the Great Elector: "I join the highest bidder," was true of them all. Frederick merely acted with less concealment and on a larger stage.

The fundamental difference between *Grossdeutsch* and *Kleindeutsch* statesmen and historians was the assumption of the former that Austria was German and of the latter that she was not. Before Klopp trains his batteries on the villain of the piece he surveys the sixteenth and seventeenth centuries from the standpoint of an ardent Austrophil. The Reformation and the Treaty of Westphalia inaugurated the era of the territorial princes and the system of *Cujus regio, ejus religio.* Yet even after 1648 the Empire still possessed unchallenged hegemony; no prince dreamed of equality with the Hapsburgs; there were still many bonds, and the possibility of closer union on a federal basis was not ruled out. Leibnitz reverenced the Empire, though he realized its fragility and the perils of particularism. Germany without Austria, he declared, was a rump without a head. The Germans enjoyed the advantage, beyond all Christian nations, of the Holy Roman Empire, and must show themselves worthy of their good fortune. The Hohenzollerns, on the other hand, stood for military absolutism. At first the two houses had helped each other. A Hohenzollern had brought the news of his election as Emperor to Rudolf of Hapsburg and was rewarded by the appointment as Burggraf of Nuremberg. Charles IV made the Hohenzollerns princes of the Empire, and Sigismund gave them Brandenburg and the Electoral title. Frederick I and his successors were energetic, thrifty, and eager for aggrandizement, and their loyal services seldom went unrewarded.

A change for the worse, according to Klopp, began in 1525, when Albert of Hohenzollern, Grand Master of the Teutonic Knights, secularized the order and took East Prussia for his family. The second milestone in the rake's progress was the creation of a standing army by the Great Elector, for henceforth Prussia's rulers possessed a ready instrument of their policy. Neither attacking nor defending the Empire, he pursued a course of particularism and opportunism, though he never dreamed of setting up Brandenburg as a rival to the Emperor. A third milestone was the grant of the royal title to his son Frederick, which stimulated the ambitions of a greedy dynasty. The misfortunes of the house of Hapsburg flowed from attributing its own honorable standards to others. A fourth was the creation of a large and highly trained army based on conscription by Frederick William I, though he had no desire to use it in war. When the French Ambassador in Berlin advised him in 1735 to seize Silesia, he replied: "I do not see why I should break with the Emperor; I have no quarrel with him." The notion of dualism never entered his head. "We must have an emperor," he remarked, "so it is better to stick to the house of Austria."

With the accession of his son and the invasion of Silesia, Klopp's voice rises to a scream. Frederick's argument that the Pragmatic Sanction was recognized by his father on condition that the Emperor should help him to get Jülich and Berg is rejected on the ground that no reference to it occurs in the declaration of acceptance. The action of the new ruler was the seed not of one war but of a long series of conflicts the end of which was not yet in sight. They differed in detail, not in essence. "This essence of the Hohenzollern state was the lust of conquest by long prepared and powerfully launched aggression in the field of foreign affairs and at home in the consequential military absolutism, both covered by falsehood and untruth." Frederick William I never made claims in Silesia. If any existed they were canceled by the secret treaty of 1728; of all Frederick's subjects only a Halle jurist was aware of their existence. Before him there was antagonism between German, French, or Russian, but not between Prussian and Austrian Germans. "He not only destroyed the Empire of a thousand years: he made peace among Germans impossible." The Reformation and the Thirty Years' War loosened the bonds of the Reich, but the forms remained that might be revitalized in happier times. "With Frederick this chance was gone. He sacrificed what was left of the Reich, he whose soul had shaken off all the holy bonds of piety in pursuing the phantom of his hollow fame. He created dualism—not as a permanent system, but as the beginning of a new era with the aggrandizement of the Hohenzollern at any price and by any means as his goal. For this it was necessary to destroy Austria, the guardian of established rights."

Klopp finds nothing to praise even in the decade of peace, for

Frederick's boasted reforms were motivated by the desire to prepare for another attack on Austria. He kept the army in being by rough discipline and by promoting the most brutal of his officers. He never dreamed of abolishing serfdom, and conscription increased the hardships of the peasantry. He encouraged agriculture as the means of providing cannon fodder, and his settlers were mostly loafers and vagabonds. Education was grossly neglected, and this Frenchified King prescribed that the papers read to the Academy should be in Latin or French. His *History of the House of Brandenburg* is dominated by hate of Austria, who is always presented as striving to tyrannize over the German princes and destroy German freedom.

The chapters on the Seven Years' War are prefaced by a glowing tribute to Austria. Aggression, declares Klopp, was not in the Hapsburg tradition. The wars of Charles V against France were defensive, and the shielding of Christendom from the Turks was a duty. Since France had consistently striven to weaken the Hapsburgs by fostering German particularism, Frederick felt sure she would approve the seizure of Silesia. Her support of Prussia in the Second Silesian War, despite having been let down in the first, turned the thoughts of Kaunitz and Maria Theresa to the idea of a French alliance as dreamed of by Prince Eugene in 1710. The unselfish and trustworthy Kaunitz was convinced that no peace was possible for Europe while Frederick was backed by France and retained Silesia. In opposing the Prussian parvenu, Austria worked in the interest of Germany and Europe, even of the Prussians themselves, who were mere cannon fodder. Klopp sorrowfully admits that Frederick's clever apologia in his *History of the Seven Years' War* has been accepted by most Germans. "Such is Fredericianism—violence and untruth."

Three years later Frederick embarked on another adventure with his usual unblushing cynicism. Sharply differentiating Prussians from other Germans, Klopp argues that the Prussianizing of the Poles was as distasteful to every real German as to the Poles themselves. Austria, alone of the three partitioning powers, left Polish culture unimpaired, and Galicia was the only province of the Hapsburg Empire held by the sword. By her very nature Austria could be neither aggressive nor centralized nor authoritarian. In contrasting Maria Theresa with her wicked enemy he becomes quite lyrical. "A princess, a woman, a mother like her the world has never seen." Had Frederick a single friend? she asked. "What a joy to be loved and still more to deserve it! That is the only reward of our endeavors." When, however, her champion declares that she had no offensive plans against Prussia in 1756, he does injustice to her dauntless spirit, for it was only after the long agony of the Seven Years' War that she sorrowfully reconciled herself to the loss of Silesia.

Klopp pursues his hated enemy with shrill vituperation to the grave. The War of the Bavarian Succession is presented as the fourth aggression against Austria. Frederick, not Joseph, we are told, started the conflict, for the heir to Bavaria was ready to accept the Austrian plan. "For thirty-seven years," cried Maria Theresa, "this man by his despotism and violence has been the misfortune of Europe." The historian agrees. "The war was unpopular in Prussia, and there were many desertions from the ranks." One man alone was responsible for all the strife and bloodshed. The *Fürstenbund* was his final blow at the house of Hapsburg which he detested and injured throughout life. His evil spirit brooded over the unborn generations. "Fredericianism means aggression abroad and military absolutism at home in order to be ready at any moment for a war of conquest. This fearful system of immorality was unredeemed by any such cultural services as were rendered by the Roman Empire." The Peace of Basel in 1795 was a desertion of Austria in her struggle for ungrateful Germany, and in 1866 Bismarck proved himself the true heir and disciple of Frederick. Once again Austria could not believe that Prussia would attack, and once again the existence of Prussia proved a misfortune for Germany and Europe.

Klopp's indictment was too passionate and too blindly Austrophil to be taken seriously in the academic world. A little book of Max Lehmann, on the other hand, entitled *Frederick the Great and the Origin of the Seven Years' War,* published in 1894, provoked a storm of academic controversy, for the biographer of Scharnhorst and Stein was too good a scholar to be ignored. After recalling Austria's attempts to secure France and Russia as partners in a war against Prussia, he proceeds to argue that Frederick's attitude in 1756 was not so purely defensive as he claimed and as the Prussian school believed; for in 1752 he had recorded his ambitions in his First Political Testament. The quotation of certain passages was vetoed by the Foreign Office, since Bismarck had written on the cover *"Dauernd zu Sekre-tieren,"* but some tasty morsels were produced. Prussia, declared the King in that year, was too small, the army good but too weak to resist its foes, the finances unequal to a major effort. Only aggrandizement could solve the problem, for Prussia was neither a small nor a great state. He agreed with Machiavelli that an unselfish state surrounded by ambitious powers was doomed to disappear. For Saxony, his chief desire, he was prepared to sur-render East Prussia and his territories in the Rhineland. A village on the frontier, he declared, was worth a principality sixty leagues away; and we must remember that Saxony was twice as large at that time as it was left by the Congress of Vienna.

With these passages in mind Lehmann declares that the ac-quisition of Saxony was Frederick's main aim in 1756 and that in consequence it was not an exclusively defensive war. Two offensives met. Maria Theresa wished to recover Silesia, Fred-erick to secure Saxony and West Prussia, hoping to indemnify the Elector, who was also King of Poland, with Bohemia. Thus it was no longer a conflict of darkness and light. Lehmann had not spared the champions of the great King, and he could hardly expect to escape the rod. One irate patriot, he relates in his auto-biography, clamored for punishment. Undeterred by the outcry, Althoff, the distinguished permanent head of the Kultusminis-terium, sent a presentation copy of the book to the Minister, and drafted a letter of thanks to the author which was signed by his chief. In the lively controversy that ensued, Delbrück took his side. But most of the experts rejected his contention and agreed that he fought neither for glory nor for territory, but in self-defense. The angry excitement aroused by this professorial bombshell illustrates the unique and almost sacrosanct place held by the Prussian hero in the national tradition.

No German scholar has devoted so much research to the study of Frederick as Koser, the greatest of Droysen's pupils, and no one has written about him with such authority. He is not only the supreme court of appeal but the author of the only full-length biography in existence. Ranke and Droysen were mainly concerned with foreign affairs, and their narratives end in 1756. Carlyle tired of his task, and his survey of the second half of the reign is a mere outline. Koser, on the other hand, traced his career from the cradle to the grave and attempted to do justice to every aspect of his activity. Though a life of Frederick, like a life of Bismarck, is inevitably a history of the time, the personality of the principal actor stands out in bold relief. The first installment, *Frederick as Crown Prince*, appeared in 1886, the volumes on the reign in 1889. The work was kept up to date, and the three stout volumes of narrative, enriched by a supplementary volume of notes, rank among the masterpieces of modern scholarship. At the close of the century an army of experts was at work on Prussia and her rulers in the eighteenth century. The vast publication, entitled *Acta Borussica*, contained material illustrating various aspects of the internal administration. A new journal, *Forschungen zur preussischen and brandenburgischen Geschichte*, was established to facilitate research. The *Hohenzollern Jahrbuch* issued a series of valuable monographs. A large-scale history of the campaigns, *Die Kriege Friedrichs des Grossen*, compiled by the General Staff at Moltke's suggestion, began to appear in 1890. Finally the *Politische Correspondenz*, the largest enterprise in the whole field of Frederician studies, started its course in 1879 under the auspices of the Prussian Academy and under the supervision of Droysen, Duncker, and Sybel. Forty-six large volumes, bringing the story down to 1782, had appeared when the Second World War broke out in 1939. All this and much other material, some of it admirably edited by himself, was utilized by Koser.

Koser is a trifle more inclined to criticize than Ranke, Droysen, or Treitschke, but his admiration is no less profound. He conveys a sense of the dynamic personality of his hero and emphasizes the permanence of most of his work. When Voltaire finished his *Siècle de Louis XIV*, Chesterfield urged him to write the history of Frederick, "a great King who is also a great man." Such is also the verdict of Koser, for he would have been an arresting figure had he never worn a crown. The essential part of his legacy, the elevation of Prussia to the status of a great power, remained, while the self-confidence bred of his victories survived the catastrophe of Jena and fostered the national revival in the Wars of Liberation. The full dimensions of his achievement only became visible in the Bismarck era. Koser admits the element of ambition in the seizure of Silesia, like Frederick himself, who in the latest revision of his *Memoirs* confessed to a desire to make his name; yet the verdict on this decisive event is none the less favorable. "It was an ambition ennobled by the fact that he warmed it at the holy fire of patriotism. For inseparable from personal ambition was the noble passion to win consideration for his people in Europe, to expunge the unfortunate impressions of the past, to place Prussia in the rank of the great powers." In a word, the end justified the means.

On the second fundamental decision, the offensive of 1756, Koser's verdict is again an acquittal. The arming of Prussia in the early summer of that year, in his opinion, was justified by what he knew and still more by what he did not. Sir Andrew Mitchell, the British Ambassador, was convinced that his wishes and interests were for peace. That he would be able to compensate himself with new territory, if completely victorious, was true enough, but this possibility was in no sense the cause of the war. "The choice was not in his hands; his action was purely defensive, even if at favourable moments old desires appeared within his grasp." Moreover, on this occasion he was defending the German cause. Though the Treaty of Hubertusburg brought him no material reward, the acquisition of West Prussia in the First Partition of Poland nine years later was the direct result of the struggle in which he had finally won recognition of his power. That his economic policy was too narrow and his whole political system too dependent on the monarch's individual capacity is admitted; yet Stein's complaint that he did everything himself is parried by the argument that in teaching his countrymen to work he prepared the way for the introduction of partnership by Stein and Hardenberg. To the charge by Arndt that he was an un-German, Koser rejoins that he formed the nucleus of the future nation state. A German Great Power was needed since Austria was merely a racial mosaic. Prussia's gains were gains for Germany, and his proud monument is the German Reich.

There is no difference in standpoint between the *magnum opus* of Koser and the more popular biography by Georg Winter, published in 1907. The biographer of Zieten had mastered the whole mass of printed material, and his work in three small volumes is still the best comparatively brief survey of the manifold activities of Frederick the Great. His admiration and enthusiasm, he declares, had grown as he worked, and the whole story glows with patriotic pride. He is particularly concerned to show that "the hero of the century" was as great in peace as in war, though he made a few mistakes in both, and the chapters on domestic administration are among the best in the book. "We all stand on his shoulders. The larger part of what is sound, vigorous, and healthy in our people and state derives from his lifework. He placed the stamp of his genius on the Prussian state for all time—the strict and indeed almost harsh performance of duty and self-sacrifice in the service of the whole community. He was a hard taskmaster, but hardest on himself, the educator as well as the ruler of his people, the embodiment of the state idea." Seen in historical perspective he is of no less significance for non-Prussian Germans than for the children of his own land. "For us Germans he is the great heroic figure who laid the foundations on which, in the fullness of time, a united, powerful, and free fatherland could be built."

Much the same radiant picture emerges in the massive volume *Die Hohenzollern und ihr Werk* by Otto Hintze, published in 1915. Designed to celebrate the fifth centenary of the appointment of Frederick of Hohenzollern as Margrave and Elector of Brandenburg, it presents the most authoritative account of the evolution of Brandenburg-Prussia that we possess. Though Hintze, as one of the editors of the *Acta Borussica,* speaks with special authority on internal affairs, he embraces every aspect of the national life. The book, he explains, is a narrative, not an apologia, for the record of the dynasty needs no defense. "The strong military-monarchical power alone enabled Prussia and Germany to lead an independent life and to win respect for the German name, situated as it is in the middle of the Continent, surrounded by strong and often unfriendly neighbors. England, in her island security, can manage with very little coercion by the state, and has therefore developed parliamentary government, which is falsely assumed to be the only form for a free modern people. We, on the other hand, in our dangerous position between the strongest powers of the Continent, required another sort of constitution, which is in the main the work of the Hohenzollerns." Yet his admiration has its limits, and he rejects Droysen's picture of the dynasty "surrounded by a halo of national idealism and selfless devotion to the Imperial idea." Frederick had no notion of German nationalism, only of Prussian interest.

Hintze presents the seizure of Silesia as the discharge of a duty to the country. Frederick William I had come to recognize his humiliating position, though he lacked the resolution to change it by force. Austria's invariable maxim, he complained to his heir on his death-bed, was to hold Prussia down, to prevent her expansion by every means. "Here is the world-historic significance of Frederick's enterprise against Silesia, that Prussia with unflinching determination challenged the Austrian policy of suppression, thereby generating an antagonism that lasted till 1866." Thus the ultimate responsibility for the long conflict is placed on Austria. Silesia was an old object of Prussian ambition, though Frederick William I did not include it in his Political Testament of 1722 among the claims of his house. "There can be no question of an unambiguous legal claim: rather one should speak of retaliation for Austria's treatment of Prussia in the question of Berg." Frederick's double desertion of his French allies is attributed to sheer inability to conduct a long campaign. He could not afford to exhaust his resources, for he knew that Maria Theresa would not swallow the loss of Silesia without a further effort. "It is a tragic feature in this heroic career that from the free decision of 1740 sprang the compulsion of his life." More detached observers might prefer the formula that he reaped what he had sown.

Neither Frederick's decision in 1756 to smash the hostile coalition before it was ready nor his contemplation of possible rewards in Saxony and West Prussia is held to contradict his assertion that it was a war of defense. "His principle was that a conflict that does not bring new territory is disadvantageous to a state, but it is incorrect to say that he had long resolved to fight for these acquisitions. He did not think the situation so favorable as he had stipulated in his Political Testament as the condition of a successful war. The primary consideration was the maintenance of the power—indeed, the existence—of his state in face of a coalition that threatened to destroy him if he did not anticipate the blow." His bold initiative was justified by the result, for the conflict left Prussia the first military power in the world.

The acquisition of West Prussia in 1772 is equally approved by Hintze. "It was old German colonial territory. Any injustice to Poland was fully compensated—at least before the judgment seat of impartial history—by the paternal care it received. Of course for Poland it was the beginning of the end, but we must remember that the idea of a national state had not emerged." The bloodless War of the Bavarian Succession resulted in frustrating the ambitions of Joseph II and of securing recognition of Prussia's reversionary claim to Anspach and Bayreuth. The formation of the *Fürstenbund* in 1785 had been conceived when Russia ceased to be a reliable ally owing to her rapprochement with Austria in the struggle against the Turks. Finding himself isolated and with waning prestige, he took the lead against Joseph II in the name of the Reich. It was the obvious course, for the acquisition of Bavaria would have made Austria supreme in Germany and threatened the position of Prussia. Thus all the major decisions of his life were right. His whole policy was based on the correct assumption that only the permanent weakening of Austria and the permanent strengthening of Prussia could bring lasting peace.

Hintze finds as much to applaud in the domestic as in the foreign sphere, and the verdict on Frederick's economic system is unusually favorable. He combined the zeal for industry of an orthodox mercantilist with a determination to preserve a vigorous peasantry. His state bank, silk industry, and porcelain factory were valuable contributions to the permanent welfare of his people. Even the rigid social stratification, which he inherited and preserved, though it could not last forever, had its good side; for by allotting to the nobility, the bourgeoisie, and the peasantry their special function and seeing that it was performed, he helped to break down provincial feeling, to foster the sentiment of the whole, to lay the foundation of the organic state. He was the first monarch to conceive the ruler as an agent of his superior, the state. In other words, autocracy was the prelude to the modern constitutional system. In addition to making Prussia a great power he gave her the strength to bear the burden of greatness and thereby to survive the catastrophe of Jena. His harsh contempt for mankind grew on him with advancing years, though he was occasionally in a gentler mood. His trade had made him what he was. "The princes of this state must have strong nerves," he wrote to Prince Henry; "otherwise they are lost."

While the professors sang in chorus, Thomas Mann, the leading figure among the younger generation of men of letters, challenged the traditional judgment in a brilliant little book entitled

Frederick and the Great Coalition, written during the first few weeks of the war of 1914. Defining it as a tract for the times, he began by admitting both the extent and the justification of foreign hostility. Maria Theresa was right to call him the wicked man, for he had a bad heart. The seizure of Silesia was robbery. The invasion of Saxony in 1756, which unleashed the Seven Years' War, aroused scarcely less horror, earning him in France the title of the barbarian and the monster of the north. That powerful enemies were leagued for his destruction is true enough, but the coalition was mainly of his own making. "If right is to be determined by convention, the verdict of the majority, the voice of mankind, it was not on his side. His right was that of a rising power, a problematical, illegitimate right that had to be fought for before it could be established. In its deepest causes this monstrous conflict was an offensive war, for a young and rising power is, psychologically speaking, always on the offensive. Yet it was also a war of defense. Prussia was hemmed in and marked down for destruction, and one against five indicates defense." This is much the same attitude as the verdict of Lehmann that two offensives met. The picture of the old warrior, broken in health, a legendary figure in his own lifetime, is drawn in dark colors. "The fires burned low; ill-tempered and lonely, he loved no one and no one loved him." His passion for work had something inhuman about it. He was like a monk in blue uniform; there was no joy in his life or his entourage, and his misogyny was a sign of emotional abnormality. Though Thomas Mann was not a historian, he had devoted a good deal of attention to Frederick and had planned to write a historical novel on the period. His onslaught was ignored by the specialists, but it was widely read and provoked angry replies from amateur apologists. No figure on the German stage since Luther has provoked so much controversy and so much heat as Prussia's superman.

The defeat of Germany and the proclamation of a republic in 1918 made no difference to the cult of Frederick the Great. Indeed, his gigantic figure seemed to grow in stature as a bewildered people looked wistfully back to the pilot who had weathered a similar storm. *Fredericus Rex,* a rather trashy historical novel by Walter von Molo, describing a single day of the Seven Years' War, proved a best seller. Of far higher literary value is Bruno Frank's *Tage des Königs* (*The Days of the King*), containing vivid reconstructions of Frederick's stormy interview with the magistrates concerned in the Miller Arnold case and of his last intimate talk with the nonagenarian Keith.

Among those who sang his praises in these dark days was the lonely exile at Doorn. After compiling his *Memoirs* William II proceeded to describe and glorify the work of his house. *My Ancestors,* published in 1929, proclaims the familiar *Kleindeutsch* thesis that, while the Hapsburgs only cared for their dynasty, the Hohenzollerns thought of their state. Starting with the assumption that the history of a people is made by its great men, he salutes all his predecessors except Frederick William II. The Great Elector created the first standing army and ended Swedish interference in Germany. Frederick I acquired the royal title and founded the officers' corps, achievements beside which his extravagance was a trifling weakness. Frederick William I, though harsh to his family, taught his people to work. Frederick II boldly and unflinchingly carried out his political plans *ad majorem Prussiæ gloriam.* There was once more a German hero, like the Great Elector, who taught Germany's hereditary enemy (France) not to insult her; and men began to feel that the King of Prussia belonged to Germany as well. The Kaiser's only criticism is that the hero allowed too much French influence, since such cultural adulteration is always bad. "Voltaire and the French spirit could not harm him personally, but it was a calamity for the sentiment, the habits, and the intellectual tendency of his people, so much so that it endangered the work of his father and himself. He could keep foreign influence within bounds during his lifetime, but later his people lacked the mental toughness needed to resist the softening process. It penetrated to the heart of the army, and Jena was the result." After lamenting and exaggerating this spot on the sun, the author resumes his hymn of praise. Frederick, we are told, was at bottom a religious man, for he was inspired by the categorical imperative of duty and could never have done his work without deep religious feeling. His versatility was displayed in his love of pictures and architecture, in his exquisite color schemes at Sans Souci, in his spirited marches for the army and his charming compositions for the flute.

The most solid contribution to Frederician studies since the fall of the dynasty is the first volume of Arnold Berney's biography, published in 1934. Since it only reaches 1756, it cannot compete with Koser, and in any case it is on a much smaller scale. The attitude of admiration is much the same, but his comments on the seizure of Silesia are unusually frank. Frederick, he declares, had a politico-moral though not a juridical right, and he confessed to his intimates that he was motived by deeper causes than any legal claims. Any argument, he realized, was a swindle. Having underestimated the political and ethical consequence of this coup, he turned to France as the only means of keeping what he had got, though he never trusted her. He hated the idea of the Hapsburgs treating the German princes as vassals, and he hated Austria, though not Maria Theresa. He despised Austrian policy too much, and he underestimated both the hostility and the strength of Russia. In a word, he had much to learn, as is indicated by the subtitle, *The Evolution of a Statesman*. In a striking analysis of his political ideology Berney depicts the King as living up to his ideal of the enlightened autocrat, recognizing the right of the people to happiness, the watchful champion of the rights of the poor, filled with a cold passion for duty and service. He never despised the people, only lazy kings, bad ministers, bigots, flatterers, corrupt officials. "He wanted a bigger and stronger Prussia, but he was no conqueror. He required the greatest effort and the hardest service from his subjects, but he was no tyrant. He cut Prussia adrift from the dying Empire."

In Berney's extensive bibliography we look in vain for a popular work which sharply challenged the traditional estimate of the national hero and dismissed his academic admirers with contempt. *Frederick the Great*, by Werner Hegemann, published in 1924 and enlarged in 1925, is the work of a clever amateur. Rejecting the temptation to compile a new biography, he presents his conclusions in a series of dialogues. The polemical purpose of what he describes as a tract for the German public is announced in the Foreword to the slightly abridged English edition published in 1929. "Whether Frederick II. was a great king, worthy of international admiration, as Carlyle and many non-Germans claim, or whether he was one of the most obnoxious figures in the history of the world, as the present volume claims, does not affect German politics alone. It is a question of international and of high moral significance. . . . The fact that he could be held up as the model for kings, seems to me a world tragedy." Kingship would survive among the German people, openly or secretly, so long as they retained their belief in "the great King," clear-sighted, swift and sure in his judgments, prompt and unerring in his deeds, an inspired man of action and a philosopher King.

The conversations are assumed to have taken place in the luxurious Neapolitan villa of Manfred Ellis, an American citizen with an Austrian mother, who admires Goethe as profoundly as he despises Frederick. Thomas Mann, Georg Brandes, and other celebrities take part in the imaginary symposium. The idolatry of Frederick is presented as a source of weakness, not of strength. "Today the fatherland threatens to collapse. Our ship is in danger. The crew is as if paralyzed by its blind confidence in the pretended power of its lost captain, without whom it has no faith in its power to live or act." On closer acquaintance, according to Ellis, the national hero turns out to be a fraud. In social intercourse he was a bully, in conversation a bore, in war a blunderer, in administration a bad economist. Not even a hard worker, he sat long at table and spent many hours at his poems, his histories, and his flute. He wasted money on the Neues Palais, and gave arbitrary decisions on trifling personal matters. In diplomacy he was outmatched by Kaunitz. He broke up the Empire beyond the possibility of reconstruction and had nothing to put in its place, for he had no large national aims. Hegemann's lively volume found many readers, but his judgments were much too sweeping and his tone far too shrill. If the pundits were too inclined to adulation, the amateur iconoclast, forgetful of Renan's maxim *"La vérité est dans les nuances,"* produced a caricature.

The traditional view was eloquently and unblushingly restated by Gerhard Ritter in *Friedrich der Grosse: ein historisches Profil,* based on his university lectures and published in 1936. As a combatant in the First World War, a biographer of Stein, and editor of Bismarck's *Reflections and Recollections,* the Freiburg professor naturally sounds the patriotic note. All the major decisions of his hero's life are approved, though no attempt is made to square them with the precepts of strict morality. "For the first time in modern history cold and hard *raison d'état* took human form among us Germans." The seizure of Silesia is described as an improvisation of genius, partly motivated by the conviction that other powers were about to swoop down on the prey. "He laid the foundations of Prussia's greatness, and thus his action is justified by history—an action *sui generis,* the bold but inescapable attempt of a state to break out of the narrowness and obscurity of humble station towards a leading position on the world's stage." The invasion of neutral Saxony in 1756 is compared to the invasion of neutral Belgium in 1914. "The threatened situation of a state which sees itself surrounded by hostile coalitions forbids long hesitation and demands quick and vigorous decisions. Even if it were wiser to await the attack, what responsible person will not be inclined to seek salvation in rapid action instead of sitting still and anxiously asking: What will the others do? Will tomorrow be too late? We violated Belgian neutrality because there was literally no other way to the decisive battle in France, and because we were lost if the western enemy marched into the industrial region of the lower Rhine. Frederick overran Saxony because Saxony's northern frontier was only seven [German] miles from Berlin and because, after the experiences of the Second Silesian War, a real offensive against Austria was impossible with a hostile Saxon army on his flank."

The First Partition of Poland is judged in the same crudely realistic spirit. "Not antiquarian claims but vital rights had to be asserted by Germany: the right of a nation at length awakening from a long faint to recover frontier territories torn from it by neighbors in times of weakness. How much was knocked off the body of the old Reich since the great days of the Middle Ages! How much is lost forever, including lands of the oldest and richest German *Kultur!* Here in West Prussia it was not a question of some forgotten fragment of old German soil with which the German state could dispense in its political existence. The acquisition of this province was a political necessity in regard to which political reasoning was beyond doubt. That this claim clashed with the political needs and wishes of the Polish people is one of those tragic complications in which Europe, with its mixed populations, is particularly rich. If a historical claim can be established by practical constructive work, the moral justification of this acquisition is unchallengeable. The restoration of West Prussia, the termination of barbaric conditions by the intro-

duction of state discipline, established law, and economic order
—despite the harshness of method—ranks among the triumphs
of Frederician administration." The hymn of praise concludes
with a testimony that would have warmed the heart of the warrior King. "We front-line soldiers [in the First World War] felt
the spirit of Frederick the Great still alive within us."

The problem of Frederick's place in European history was approached from an unfamiliar angle in Ritter von Srbik's masterpiece, *Deutsche Einheit*, of which the first volume was published
in 1936. The academic world, hitherto sharply divided between
the *Grossdeutsch* and *Kleindeutsch* camps, was invited by Austria's leading historian to accept the formula of reconciliation
enshrined in his title. There is no need, he argues, for scholars
to be *Grossdeutsch* or *Kleindeutsch,* Austrian or Prussian: all
should be *Gesammtdeutsch,* adopting and proclaiming the idea
of the integrated national state. Srbik, who had won fame by his
monumental eulogy of Metternich, proclaims his love of the
whole German people and his conviction of the inescapable connection of Austria with the fortunes of Germany. He was unable to regard the Hohenzollern Empire as the last word of destiny, for the people, not the state, was the real subject of German
history. The Bismarckian structure, though a notable milestone,
was not the solution of the eternal German problem. The cultural unity of the people had grown even in times of military
conflict and political decline, and geography also suggested a
Mitteleuropa. "The Austrian idea always seemed to me essentially a German idea, for Austria's historical mission is inseparable from the whole nation." The universalism of the Holy Roman Empire lived on in the Austrian Empire. Defining his task
as a study of ideas and institutions, he surveys the past from his
lofty watchtower without passion or prejudice. Though the
majesty of the old Reich is fully recognized, he realizes that
changes were inevitable and declares that the Reformation gave
precious values to the German people. Immense prestige continued to attach to the Imperial title, and Austria alone could
defend the German people against the Turks. When the Treaty
of Westphalia ended the Wars of Religion, it was natural that
the Hapsburg emperors should dislike and fear the growth of
Prussia, both as the leader of German Protestantism and as a rival
to their authority in the Reich. Yet Srbik speaks of the new power

with a tolerant understanding unexampled among Austrian scholars.

Frederick is described as the first of his house to think of Austria as a power like the rest: the Reich, in his eyes, was merely an instrument of her policy. As an impecunious Crown Prince he had accepted a pension from Vienna, but he felt neither gratitude nor obligation, and he was completely estranged by the failure to help in securing the Duchy of Berg. In seizing Silesia he was not interested in the question of legal right: the King of Prussia, it appeared to him, must be the equal of the Emperor. He never dreamed of destroying Austria, yet the loss of Silesia broke her leadership in the Reich and her power to defend it against France. Srbik recognizes that admiration for his deeds strengthened German self-consciousness, though this gain was purchased at a high price. Moreover, he inherited a tradition of considerable independence. The Hapsburgs had never exercised the same influence in the north as elsewhere, and Protestantism widened the gulf. "However much he was of an initiator, he also embodied the century-old tendency towards the detachment of the north from the other parts of the Reich. Moreover, his triumphs, his personal example, his discipline, his doctrine of the state 'always on guard,' left profound traces in the German character." No one has written more justly of the great King than Srbik, avoiding the excesses of praise or blame. Germans and non-Germans, admirers and critics, experts and amateurs agree at any rate that the history of Europe for the last two centuries is barely intelligible without some knowledge of the character, methods, and achievements of the superman who set Prussia on the blood-stained road that led to the brief and perilous hegemony of continental Europe.

INDEX

A NOTE ON THE TYPE USED IN THIS BOOK

This book was set on the Linotype in GRANJON, *a type named in compliment to Robert Granjon, type-cutter and printer—1523 to 1590, Antwerp, Lyons, Rome, Paris. Granjon, the boldest and most original designer of his time, was one of the first to practice the trade of type-founder apart from that of printer.*

Linotype GRANJON *was designed by George W. Jones, who based his drawings upon a face used by Claude Garamond (1510–1561) in his beautiful French books.* GRANJON *more closely resembles Garamond's own type than do any of the various modern faces that bear his name.*